Lecture Notes in Computer Science 4710

Commenced Publication in 1973
Founding and Former Series Editors:
Gerhard Goos, Juris Hartmanis, and Jan van Leeuwen

T0223138

Chris W. George   Zhiming Liu
Jim Woodcock (Eds.)

Domain Modeling and the Duration Calculus

International Training School
Shanghai, China, September 17-21, 2007
Advanced Lectures

 Springer

Volume Editors

Chris W. George
Zhiming Liu
United Nations University
International Institute for Software Technology
P.O.Box 3058, Macau SAR, China
E-mail:{cwg, z.liu}@iist.unu.edu

Jim Woodcock
University of York
Department of Computer Science
Heslington, York YO10 5DD, UK
E-mail: jim@cs.york.ac.uk

Library of Congress Control Number: Applied for

CR Subject Classification (1998): F.3, D.2.11, D.2.4, D.2.2, F.2.2

LNCS Sublibrary: SL 1 – Theoretical Computer Science and General Issues

ISSN   0302-9743
ISBN-10   3-540-74963-2 Springer Berlin Heidelberg New York
ISBN-13   978-3-540-74963-9 Springer Berlin Heidelberg New York

Springer is a part of Springer Science+Business Media

springer.com

© Springer-Verlag Berlin Heidelberg 2007
Printed in Germany

Typesetting: Camera-ready by author, data conversion by Scientific Publishing Services, Chennai, India
Printed on acid-free paper   SPIN: 12124022   06/3180   5 4 3 2 1 0

Preface

This volume contains a record of the lectures given at the *ICTAC Training School on Domain Modelling and Duration Calculus*, held during the 17th–21st September 2007 in Shanghai. The *School* was organised by East China Normal University, UNU-IIST, and the University of York as part of the celebrations of the 70th birthdays of Dines Bjørner and Zhou Chaochen. There were two associated events:

- *Essays in Honour of Dines Bjørner and Zhou Chaochen on the Occasion of their 70th Birthdays.* Papers presented at a Symposium held in Macao on 24th & 25th September 2007. LNCS volume 4700. Springer 2007.
- *Proceedings of the International Colloquium on Theoretical Aspects of Computing.* Held in Macao during 26th–28th September 2007. LNCS volume 4711. Springer 2007.

The *school* is aimed at postgraduate students, researchers, academics, and industrial software engineers who are interested in the state of the art in these topics. No previous knowledge of the topics involved is assumed. Two of the courses are in the area of domain engineering (and in formal, abstract modelling in general) and two are in the area of duration calculus; the fifth links the two areas. The five courses are taught by experts in these fields from Europe and Asia.

We are happy to acknowledge sponsorship from the following organisations:

- China International Talent Exchange Foundation
- East China Normal University
- United Nations University International Institute for Software Technology
- University of York

The proceedings were managed and assembled using the EASYCHAIR conference management system.

Contributors

ALAN BURNS is a professor of computer science at the University of York. His research interests are in real-time systems, including the assessment of real-time programming languages, distributed operating systems, the formal specification of scheduling algorithms and implementation strategies, and the design of dependable user interfaces to real-time applications.

DANG VAN HUNG is a research fellow of UNU-IIST. He received a doctoral-level degree in computer science in 1988 from the Computer and Automation Research

Institute, Hungarian Academy of Sciences. His research interests include formal techniques of programming, concurrent and distributed computing, and design techniques for real-time systems.

CHRIS GEORGE is the Associate Director of the United Nations International Institute for Software Technology (UNU-IIST) in Macao. He is one of the main contributors to RAISE, particularly the RAISE method, and that remains his main research interest. Before coming to UNU-IIST he worked for companies in the UK and Denmark.

MICHAEL REICHHARDT HANSEN is an associate professor at the Technical University of Denmark. His research interests include duration calculus, interval logic, and formal methods. He is one of the authors of the book *Duration Calculus* with Zhou Chaochen.

CLIFF JONES was a professor at the University of Manchester, worked in industry at Harlequin for a period, and is now a professor of computing science at Newcastle University. He is Editor-in-Chief of the *Formal Aspects of Computing Journal*. He undertook the DPhil at Oxford University Computing Laboratory under Prof. Sir Tony Hoare FRS, awarded in 1981. He worked with Dines Bjørner and others on the Vienna Development Method (VDM) at IBM in Vienna. He is a Fellow of the Royal Academy of Engineering.

Lecture Courses

Course 1: Delivering Real-Time Behaviour. This series of lectures is given by Alan Burns, and it focuses on how to engineer systems so that they can meet their timing requirements. Four separate, but related, issues are addressed.

1. A time band model that caters for the broad set of granularities found in a typical complex system.
2. The delay and deadline statements that allow timing requirements to be specified.
3. Scheduling analysis that enables a set of concurrent deadlines to be verified.
4. Timing analysis that enables sequential code to be inspected to determine its worst case behaviour.

These four topics—together with a number of other techniques and tools described in the course—allow real-time behaviour to be delivered.

Course 2: Applicative Modelling with RAISE. This course—given by Chris George—provides an introduction to the RAISE Specification Language and to the RAISE method. The course concentrates on the applicative style of RAISE, the style most commonly used initially in development. It also describes two examples. The first is a simple communication system that allows the transmission of messages with the possibility of higher priority messages overtaking others. The example illustrates the use of abstract initial specification to capture vital properties, and of more detailed concrete specification to describe a model having those properties. The second example is a control system of a lift and illustrates the use of model checking to gain confidence in a RAISE model.

Course 3: A Theory of Duration Calculus with Application. This course is given jointly by Dang Van Hung and Michael Hansen. It presents selected central elements in the theory of the *duration calculus* and gives examples of applications. The lectures cover syntax, semantics, and a proof system for the basic logic. Results on decidability, undecidability, and model-checking are also presented. Some extensions of the basic calculus are described; in particular, hybrid duration calculus and duration calculus with iterations. The concepts are illustrated by a case study: the bi-phase mark protocol. References are provided for further study.

Course 4: Understanding Programming Language Concepts via Operational Semantics. Cliff Jones's lectures cover five topics.

1. **History of Verification.** This is based on his *Annals of the History of Computing* paper [Jon03]; this lecture adds more on semantics.
2. **Rely/Guarantee Method.** The most accessible reference for this is [Jon96] but the origins lie a long way back [Jon81,Jon83a,Jon83b] (see the extensive list of publications on various forms of rely/guarantee conditions at homepages.cs.ncl.ac.uk/cliff.jones/home.formal).
3. **Deriving Specifications.** This lecture is described in the accompanying *Festschrift* volume [JHJ07]; there is an earlier conference paper [HJJ03]).
4. **Semantics of Programming Languages.** This lecture is published in this volume. Chris George covers the idea of abstract modelling in general; Cliff Jones focuses on the application of this idea to programming languages.
5. **Soundness of Rely/Guarantee Proof Rules.** This final lecture justifies a set of proof rules like those introduced in Lecture 2 based on a semantics like that in Lecture 4. The proof is published in [CJ07]. This material links to "Refining Atomicity" [JLRW05,BJ05,Jon05,Jon07].

July 2007   J. C. P. W.

References

[BJ05]   Burton, J.I., Jones, C.B.: Investigating atomicity and observability. Jour-
            nal of Universal Computer Science 11(5), 661–686 (2005)
[CJ07]   Coleman, J.W., Jones, C.B.: Guaranteeing the soundness of
            rely/guarantee rules (revised). Journal of Logic and Computation
            (in press, 2007)
[HJJ03]   Hayes, I., Jackson, M., Jones, C.: Determining the specification of a control
            system from that of its environment. In: Araki, K., Gnesi, S., Mandrioli,
            D. (eds.) FME 2003. LNCS, vol. 2805, pp. 154–169. Springer, Heidelberg
            (2003)
[Jon81]   Jones, C.B.: Development Methods for Computer Programs including a
            Notion of Interference. PhD thesis, Oxford University, June 1981 Printed
            as: Programming Research Group, Technical Monograph 25 (1981)
[Jon83a]   Jones, C.B.: Specification and design of (parallel) programs. In: Proceed-
            ings of IFIP 1983, pp. 321–332. North-Holland, Amsterdam (1983)
[Jon83b]   Jones, C.B.: Tentative steps toward a development method for interfer-
            ing programs. ACM Transactions on Programming Languages and Sys-
            tems 5(4), 596–619 (1983)
[Jon96]   Jones, C.B.: Accommodating interference in the formal design of con-
            current object-based programs. Formal Methods in System Design 8(2),
            105–122 (1996)
[Jon01]   Jones, C.B.: On the search for tractable ways of reasoning about programs.
            Technical Report CS-TR-740, Newcastle University, Superceded by (2001)
[Jon03]   Jones, C.B.: The early search for tractable ways of reasoning about pro-
            grams. IEEE, Annals of the History of Computing 25(2), 26–49 (2003)
[Jon05]   Jones, C.B.: An approach to splitting atoms safely. In: Electronic Notes
            in Theoretical Computer Science, MFPS XXI, 21st Annual Conference of
            Mathematical Foundations of Programming Semantics, pp. 35–52 (2005)
[Jon07]   Jones, C.B.: Splitting atoms safely. Theoretical Computer Science 357,
            109–119 (2007)
[JHJ07]   Jones, C., Hayes, I., Jackson, M.A.: Specifying systems that connect to the
            physical world. In: Essays in Honour of Dines Bjørner and Zhou Chaochen
            on the Occasion of the 70th Birthdays. Papers presented at a Symposium
            held in Macao on 24th & 25th September 2007. LNCS, vol. 4700, Springer,
            Heidelberg (2007)
[JLRW05]   Jones, C.B., Lomet, D., Romanovsky, A., Weikum, G.: The atomicity
            manifesto (2005)

Coordinating Committee

Chris George	UNU-IIST
He Jifeng	East China Normal University
Zhiming Liu	UNU-IIST
Geguang Pu	East China Normal University
Jim Woodcock	University of York
Yong Zhou	East China Normal University

Table of Contents

Delivering Real-Time Behaviour

Alan Burns and Andy Wellings

Real-Time Systems Research Group
Department of Computer Science
University of York, UK
{burns,andy}@cs.york.ac.uk

Abstract. This paper focuses on how we can engineer systems so that they can meet their timing requirements. Four separate, but related, issues are addressed: a time band model that caters for the broad set of granularities found in a typical complex system, the delay and deadline statements that allow timing requirements to be specified, scheduling analysis that enables a set of concurrent deadlines to be verified and timing analysis that enables sequential code to be inspected to determine its worst case behaviour. These four topics together with a number of other techniques and tool described in the paper allow real-time behaviour to be delivered.

1   Introduction

In the construction of real-time systems it is vital to ensure that timing requirements are satisfied by the system under development. To do this requires a number of different techniques that must be integrated into an engineering process[13]. In this paper we support the rigorous verification of timing requirements by proposing an engineering process and populating it with existing/modified methods such as model checking, schedulability analysis and timing analysis. The development of large computer-based systems, with embedded components, imposes a number of significant challenges, both technical and organisational. Their complexity makes all stages of their development (requirements analysis, specification, design, implementation, deployment and maintenance/evolution) subject to failure and costly re-working. Even the production of an unambiguous behavioural description of an existing system is far from straightforward.

The process discussed here by which real-time behaviour is delivered comes from the synergy of many existing methods and proposals. It is not entirely formal but is strongly influenced by the need to engineer real systems with industrial strength tools and methods. The key dimensions of the process are:

1. Time bands – to situate the proposed system in a finite set of distinct time scales.
2. Delay and Deadline Primitives – to capture timing requirements in each band.
3. Scheduling analysis – to manage the resources needed at each band to ensure the system makes appropriate progress (i.e. meets its deadlines).
4. Timing analysis – to ensure activities defined within a single band have a bounded resource requirement.

These four dimensions are supported by

C. George, Z. Liu, and J. Woodcock (Eds.): Domain Modeling, LNCS 4710, pp. 1–50, 2007.

– A modelling and verification formalism based on a restricted use of Timed Automata in which timing requirements within an automaton are represented by *delay* and *deadline* conditions.
– A program model that utilises common pattern to implement the require behaviour – typical patterns being periodic and sporadic processes, consumer/ producer relations and shared objects. The program model can be realised in languages such as Spark [26].

One characteristic of computer-based systems is that they are required to function at many different time scales (from microseconds or less to hours or more). Time is clearly a crucial notion in the specification (or behavioural description) of computer-based systems, but it is usually represented, in modeling schemes for example, as a single flat physical phenomenon. Such an abstraction fails to support the structural properties of the system, forces different temporal notions on to the same flat description, and fails to support the separation of concerns that the different time scales of the system facilitate. Just as the functional properties of a system can be modeled at different levels of abstraction or detail, so too should its temporal properties be representable in different, but provably consistent, time scales.

To make better use of 'time', with the aim of producing more dependable embedded systems, we propose a framework that explicitly identifies a number of distinct *time bands* in which the system under study is situated [11,10]. Within each time band, timing requirements are represented by delay and deadline primitives. Delay ensures the technical system does not 'get ahead' of its environment; deadlines ensure the system does not get too far behind. The key role of the implementation (as well as obvious functional correctness) is to satisfy the deadline constraints. To examine these constraints, the sequential code must be amenable to timing analysis and the concurrent system amenable to scheduling analysis.

The four dimensions identified above are addresses in the four main sections of this paper. First, time bands are motivated and then described. Next timing requirements within each bands are considered using delays and deadlines. Then schediling analysis is outlined and finally a brief review of timing analysis is given. Conclusions are provided in section 6.

2   Time Bands

The aim of this section of the paper is to motivate a modeling framework in which a multi-banded representation of time is advocated. Much of this material is necessarily focused on an informal description of the framework. A brief discussion on the formalisation of the framework in provided in a later section (2.8).

The framework enables the temporal properties of existing systems to be described and the requirements for new or modified systems to be specified. The concept of time band comes from the work of Newell [43] in his attempts to describe human cognition. Newell focuses on hierarchical structures within the brain and notes that different time scales are relevant to the different layers of his hierarchy. By contrast, we put the notion of a time band at the centre of our framework. It can then be used within any organisational scheme or architectural form — for they all lead to systems that exhibit a wide variety of dynamic behaviours.

2.1 Informal Description of the Framework

The domain of any large computer-based system exhibits dynamic behaviour on many different levels. The computational components have circuits that have nanosecond speeds, faster electronic subcomponents and slower functional units. Communication on a fast bus is at the microsecond level but may be tens of milliseconds on slow or wide-area media. Human time scales as described above move from the 1ms neuron firing time to simple cognitive actions that range from 100ms to 10 seconds or more. Higher rational actions take minutes and even hours. At the organisational and social level, time scales range from a few minutes, through days, months and even years. Perhaps for some environmentally sensitive systems, consequences of failure may endure for centuries. To move from nanoseconds to centuries requires a framework with considerable descriptive and analytical power.

Most formulations that attempt to identify time granularity do so by mapping all activities to the finest granularity in the system. This results in cumbersome formulae, and fails to recognise the distinct role time is taking in the structuring of the system. An exception is the work of Corsetti *et al*[21,16]; they identify *"a finite set of disjoint and differently grained temporal domains"*. Their framework is not as extensive as the one developed here, but they do show how the notion of temporal domains can be embedded into a logical specification language. We are not aware of any other work that uses the existence of distinct time scales as the basis of system modeling.

2.2 Definition of a Band

A band is represented by a granularity (expressed as a unit of time that has meaning within the band) and a precision that is a measure of the accuracy of the time frame defined by the band. The precision of a band defines the tolerance over the requirements for two or more events to occur simultaneously. System activities are placed in some band B if they engage in significant events at the time scale represented by B. They have dynamics that give rise to changes that are observable or meaningful in band B's granularity. So, for example, at the nanosecond band, gates are firing; at the 10 millisecond band, human neural circuits are firing, significant computational functions are completing and an amount of data communication will occur. At the five minute band, work shifts are changing, meetings are starting, etc. For any system there will be a highest and lowest band that gives a temporal system boundary — although there will always be the potential for larger and smaller bands. Note that at higher bands the physical system boundary may well be extended to include wider (and slower) entities such as legislative constraints or supply chain changes.

Time has both discrete and continuous characteristics within the framework. Both are needed to capture the essential properties of complex systems; the term *hybrid system* is often used to indicate this dual need. A time band defines a temporal frame of reference (e.g., a clock that *ticks* at the granularity of the band) into which discrete actions can easily be placed. But continuous entities can also be placed in this band if they exhibit significant observable events on this time scale. For these entities, time is continuous but significant events occur at a frequency of no more than (but close to) once per 'tick' of the band's abstract clock.

By definition, all activities within band B have similar dynamics. Within any modeling framework there is considerable advantage in assuming that actions are instantaneous. They represent behaviours that are atomic; the combined behaviour of a number of concurrent yet atomic actions is easy to assert as there is no interference between behaviours. However in real-time embedded systems it is also necessary to consider the real duration of actions. Within a band, *activities* have duration whilst *events* are instantaneous — "take no time in the band of interest". Many activities will have a repetitive cyclic behaviour with either a fixed periodicity or a varying pace. Other activities will be event-triggered. Activities are performed by agents (human or technical). In some bands all agents will be artificial, at others all human, and at others both will be evident. The relationship between the human agent and the time band will obviously depend on the band and will bring in studies from areas such as the psychology of time [27,28,47] and the sociology of time [39]. Embedded software will populate a number of bands, the execution time of a single instruction will denote one band, the completion of distinct unit funtions are best described at another band, and complete schedulable tasks will typically be mapped to yet another band.

In the specification of a system, an event may cause a response 'immediately' – meaning that at this band the response is within the granularity of the band. This helps eliminate the problem of over specifying requirements that is known to lead to implementation difficulties [33]. For example, the requirement 'when the fridge door opens the light must come on immediately' apparently give no scope for an implementation to incorporate the necessary delays of switches, circuitry and the light's own latency. By making the term 'immediate' band specific, it enables a finer granularity band to include the necessary delays, latencies and processing time that are needed to support the immediate behaviour at the higher band.

Events that are instantaneous at band B map to activities that have duration at some lower band with a finer granularity – we will denote this lower band as C. A key property of a band is the precision it defines for its time scale. This allows two events to be simultaneous ("at the same time") in band B even if they are separated in time in band C. This definition of precision enables the framework to be used effectively for requirements specification. A temporal requirement such as a deadline is band-specific; similarly the definition of a timing failure. For example, being one second late may be a crucial failure in a computing device, whereas on a human scale being one second late for a meeting is meaningless. The duration of an activity is also 'imprecise' (within the band). Stating that a job will take three months is assumed to mean plus or minus a couple of days. Of course the precision of band B can only be explored in a lower band.

From a focus on band B, two adjacent bands are identified. The slower (broader) band (A) can be taken to be unchanging (constant) for most issues of concern to B (or at least any activity in band A will only exhibit a single state change during any activity within band B). At the other extreme, behaviours in (the finer) band C are assumed to be instantaneous. The actual differences in granularity between A, B and C are not precisely defined (and indeed may depend on the bands themselves) but will typically be in the range 1/10th to 1/100th. When bands map on to hierarchies (structural or control) then activities in band A can be seen to constrain the dynamics of band B, whereas those at C enable B to proceed in a timely fashion. The ability to relate behaviour at different time bands is one of the main properties of the framework. For example, when focusing on the behaviour of an embedded system task, the computation time of each instruction can be assumed to be zero. This is not to say that a significant series of instructions will not take time to execute, but that the duration of a single instruction can be ignored when evaluating the temporal behaviour of the software at the task level.

As well as the system itself manifesting behaviour at many different time bands, the environment will exhibit dynamic behaviour at many different granularities. The bands are therefore linked to the environment at the level determined by these dynamics. In many system abstractions it is useful to assume the environment is in some form of steady state. But this assumption is clearly false as environments evolve, perhaps as a result of the deployment of the embedded system under development. By mapping the rate of this evolutionary change to an appropriate (relatively slow) time band one can gain the advantage of the steady state abstraction whilst not ignoring slower dynamics.

2.3   Behaviour Within a Band

Most of the detailed behaviour of the system will be specified or described within bands. Issues of concurrency, resource usage, scheduling and planning, response time (duration) prediction, temporal validity of data, control and knowledge validity (agreement) may be relevant at any band.

We do note however that with human agents (and potentially with artificial learning agents) time itself within a band will play a central role. Time is not just a parameter of a band but a resource to be used/abused within the band. Users will interpret system behaviour from temporal triggers. In particular the duration of an activity will be a source of knowledge and possibly misconceptions; and may be used to give validity (or not) to information, or to infer failure. This use of temporal information to infer knowledge is termed *temporal affordance* [19]. For some bands, agreement (distributed consensus) may depend heavily on such affordances. Plans, schedules or even just routines may give rise to these affordances. Affordances provide robustness; they may be defined into the system but are often developed informally over time by the users of the system. They may be extremely subtle and difficult to identify. Nevertheless the movement of an activity from one band to another (usually a quicker one) may undermine existing affordances and be a source of significant decreased dependability.

Within a band, a coherent set of activities and events will be observed or planned, usually with insufficient agents and other resources. Robustness and other forms of fault tolerance will also play a crucial role in the description/specification of the behaviour within a band. The specification of some behaviours will require a functional view of time that places 'time' at the centre of the design process. To support this process a range of visualisation, modeling and analysis techniques are available including, timed sequence charts, control theory, scheduling analysis, constraint satisfaction, queueing theory, simulation, temporal and real-time logics, timed automata, timed Petri nets, hybrid automata, model checking and FMEA (failure modes and effects analysis).

In all bands, a common set of temporal phenomena and patterns of behaviour are likely to be exhibited by the system itself or its environment. For example, periodic (or regular or cyclic) activities, event handling (responding to an event by a deadline), temporal reasoning (planning and scheduling), interleaving and multi-tasking (and other aspects of concurrency), pausing (or delaying), analysis of response (or completion) time, deadline driven activities, and various aspect of dynamic behaviour such as rates of change. Whilst evident in all bands, these phenomena are not identified using the same terminology in the various time bands of interest (i.e., in the technical, psychological and sociological literature).

2.4 Behaviour Between Bands

To check the coherence of a description, or the consistency of a specification, for a complex embedded system, requires behaviours between bands to be examined. This involves two issues:

1. the relationship between the bands themselves, and
2. the mapping of activities and events between bands.

The link between any two bands is expressed in terms of each band's granularity and precision. Usually the finer of the two bands can be used to express these two measures for the broader band. Where physical time units are used for both bands these relations are straightforward. For example a band that is defined to have a granularity of an hour with a precision of 5 minutes is easily linked to a band with a granularity of 10 seconds and precision of half a second. The granularity relation is a link from one time unit (1 hour) in the higher band to 360 units in the lower band. The precision of 5 minutes means that a time reference at the higher band (e.g., 3 o'clock) will map down to the lower band to imply a time reference (interval) between 2.55 and 3.05.

Granularity can however give rise to a more complex link. In particular, the duration of activities in the lower band may not be the same for all corresponding activities in the higher one. For example, a band with a granularity of 'one month' when linked to a band with a granularity of 'one day' can give rise to a granularity of 28, 29, 30 or 31 days. Here precision is exact, both bands may have the same notion of accuracy about the time reference.

The mapping of actions between high and low bands is restricted to: event to event, or, event to activity relations. So an event in some band can be identified as being coupled to (implemented by) an event or activity in some lower band. A specific named activity exists in one, and only one, band. But for all activities there are events within the same band that are defined to denote the start and end of an activity – these events can be mapped to finer bands. Moreover the whole activity may be seen as an event in a broader band. Figure 1 illustrates three bands (A, B and C) with an event E in band A being mapped to activity X in band B. The start and end events of this activity can then associated with activities in band C.

To exercise these concepts, consider the planning of a university curriculum. When planning courses on a term-by-term basis, a lecture is an event. When planning room allocations, a lecture becomes an activity of duration one or two hours (with precision 5 minutes). When planning a lecture, each slide is an event (with an implicit order). When giving a lecture each slide is an activity with duration. This description could be given in terms of a number of bands and mappings of events to activities in finer bands. Note

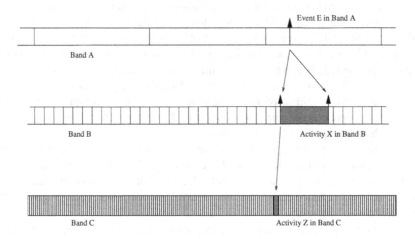

Fig. 1. Time Band Example

when focusing on the band in which slides have duration it is not possible or appropriate to consider the activities in higher bands that represent whole courses or semesters. The time bands therefore correctly help separate concerns. Students may learn that the time spent on a slide implies importance (at least in terms of the likelihood of the topic turning up in an exam). This is an example of a temporal affordance. Also illustrated by this situation is the difference between planned behaviour (as one moves down the time bands) and emergent properties that enable students to structure the knowledge and understanding they have obtained in many different ways during their progression through their degree course.

The mapping of an event in one band to an activity within another (lower) band has many of the properties of refinement, in the sense that the activity 'implements' the event. But the event still exists (e.g. the lecture as an event in the planning of a semester), it is not just an abstraction used to guide implementation. Moreover the activity may have additional properties (e.g. emergent properties or failure modes) that cannot easily be seen as a refinement of the event.

To return to the crucial issue of coherence and consistency between bands, the proposed framework facilitates this by making explicit the vertical temporal relationships between bands. Specifically, it becomes possible to check that the temporal mapping between event E in band A with activity X in band B is consistent with the bounds on the relationship identified between bands A and B. Moreover this consistency check can be extended to ordered events and causality (see next section).

2.5   Precedence Relations, Temporal Order and Causality

For the time bands associated with computational activity there is usually a strong notion of time and (adequately accurate) physical clocks that will aid scheduling and co-ordination. This is also increasingly the case with the bands of human experience as external sources of time and temporal triggers abound. But there are contexts in which *order* is a more natural way of describing behaviour [1,32] (X was before Y, e.g., "before the end of the shift", "after the plane took off", "before the flood", "after the thread has completed", "before the gate has fired"). The framework must therefore represent both precedence relations and temporal frames of reference. A frame of reference defines an abstract clock that counts *ticks* of the band's granularity and can be used to give a time stamp to events and activities. A band may have more than one such abstract clock but they progress at the same rate. For example the day band will have a different clock in each distinct geographical time zone.

There is of course a strong link between temporal order (i.e., time stamped events and activities) and precedence relations. However, in this framework, we do not impose an equivalence between time and precedence. Due to issues of precision, time cannot be used to infer precedence unless the time interval between two events is sufficiently large in the band of interest.

We develop a consistent model of time by representing certain moments in the dynamics of a band as "clock tick" events, which are modeled just like any other event. When necessary, an event can be situated in absolute time (within the context of a defined band and clock) by stating a precedence relationship between the event and one or more clock ticks.

Precedence gives rise to potential causality. If P is before Q then information could flow between them, indeed P may be the cause of Q. In the use of the framework for specification we will need to use the stronger notion of precedence to imply causality. For example, "when the fridge door opens the light must come on". As noted earlier within the band of human experience this can be taken to be 'immediate' and modeled as an event. At a lower band a number of electromechanical activities will be needed to be described that will sense when the door is open and enable power to flow to the light. Importantly, no causality relationship can be inferred (without explicit precedence) for two events occurring at the same time within their particular band. In effect they are logically concurrent and may occur in sequence or overlapped in time when mapped to a lower band.

With instantaneous events it is straightforward to specify precedence i.e. $e1 \rightarrow e2$ (in same band B). However when one maps $e1$ and $e2$ to a lower band and activates $a1$ and $a2$, what is the relationship between $a1$ and $a2$? It is too strong to require all of $a2$ to occur after all of $a1$. Indeed it is potentially restrictive to assume all of $a2$ occurred after the start of $a1$. We require, in terms of a framework definition, the weakest coherent property:

$$e1 \rightarrow e2 \Rightarrow \exists f1, f2 \bullet f1 \in a1 \land f2 \in a2 \land f1 \rightarrow f2$$

That is, some event in $a1$ is before some event in $a2$. The mapping of $f1$ and $f2$ to yet another lower band will again preserve this level of precedence.

Where bands are, at least partially, ordered by granularity, then order and hence potential causality is preserved as one moves from the finer to the coarser bands. However, as noted above, order and causality are not necessarily maintained as one moves down through the bands. This is a key property of the framework, and implies that where order is important then proof must be obtained by examining the inter-band relationship (as discussed above).

2.6   Hierarchical Resource Management

One of the challenges emerging from the next generation of embedded systems is the management of the diverse resources available on such platforms. These include various processing cores, areas of FPGA, buses of various speeds and capacities, networks both on chip (NoC) and external, specialised accelerators and different I/O devices. The management of these resources needs to deliver coordinated access, near optimal performance and adaptable allocation. Verification of these platforms is usually performed by stimulation. But it is clear that the types of simulation used to verify circuits will not scale to multi-core chips, multi-chip systems and systems of systems.

One means of controlling and verifying resource usage is to map the usage pattern of the resources on to distinct time bands and to use a combination of modeling and simulation to build up a hierarchical model of resource usage. Simulation at one time band uses a model of events from a lower band. The simulations then validate a model that can be used at the next higher band. This gives a clear framework to the hierarchial approaches advocated by some researcher [44,29].

The integrated scheduling of such resources can also be delivered by hierarchical scheduling approaches – a number of which have been described in the literature recently, see for example [22]. Again, using a clear time band separation between the levels of the scheduling hierarchy will facilitate the composability of these approaches. The general topic of scheduling, as it applies to a single band, is discussed in Section 4.

2.7   Hierarchical (Cascade) Control

Many embedded systems have a control function, and most of these use some form of feedback control. The time constraints for these control loops are determined by the dynamics of the controlled object and are naturally partitioned using the time band framework. Moreover, in more complex situations control loops form a cascade. The inner loop drives some environmental value towards a defined constant. The outer loop, on a much longer time scale is modifying this 'constant'. This structure can be repeated a number of times. Each control loop is positioned in a time band that can assume the parameters set by an upper time band are unchanging. But these parameters are themselves subject to change which is managed by feedback control within that band.

The positioning of hierarchical loops within distinct time bands can propagate out of the purely technical sphere. Human operators may use their observations of the system to modify control objectives within the minute or hour time bands, and the organisation may modify overall system objectives at high time bands such as those at the month or year level. Longer time scale still influence the objectives of the owner organisation. For example, in the electricity power generation field[2] one can identify the following time bands - all of which contain activities that aim to control the behaviour at lower levels – microseconds (wave effects and surges), milliseconds (switching), 100 milliseconds (fault protection, electromagnetic effects), seconds (stability augmentation), 10 seconds (frequency control), minutes (frequency control and load dispatching), hour (load management), day (load forecasting), month (maintenance scheduling), year (expansion planning) and 10 year (power plant site selection etc).

2.8   Time Band Model

In this section we provide a more precise definition of some of the concepts introduced above. This model forms the basis of later work to define a complete logic for the time bands which can then lead to the production of tools to support the use of banded time. There are eight central notions in the model:

- Bands
- Activities
- Events
- State
- Precedence Relations
- Clocks
- Mappings
- Behaviours

Bands. A band is defined by its granularity. This establishes a unit of time for the band. Bands are related to one another by the relationship between their granularities; this relates the 'unit' in one (the higher) band to an integer number of 'units' in the lower band. A system is assumed to consist of a partially ordered finite set of bands. If two or more events are defined to be at the same time within some band then they must be mapped to activities that contain events that occur within the *precision* of the original band.

Activities. An activity is an item of work undertaken by some agent. All state changes and effects on the system environment occur within activities. Each activity is bound to one band and has duration in that band.

Events. An event is an activity with zero duration. The start and end of any activity is denoted by an event.

State. State predicates may exist within any band. A state transition is an event within that band.

Precedence Relations. Two events from the same band have a precedence relation if one is defined to occur before the other.

Clocks. A band may have one or more abstract clocks that define temporal frames of reference within the band. Each such clock counts in *ticks* and measures the passing of time in the units of time of the band.

Mappings. A mapping is the means of relating behaviours in one band to those in another. Specifically a mapping associates an event in one band to an activity in a lower band. The mapping of a clock tick's start event in one band to an activity with duration in another band leads to the definition of the band's *precision*. It is precisely the duration of the associated activity (hence precision is a property of the relationship between two bands).

Behaviours. A behaviour is a set of activities and events (within the same band), partially ordered by precedence, giving rise to concurrent and sequential composition of behaviours.

A large number of relevant formalisms exist that could be used (directly or with extensions) to define the time band model. Timed process algebras (e.g. Timed CSP), temporal logics and Durations Calculus all have useful properties. Current work involves the evaluation of these approaches, in particular the combined use of Duration Calculus and CSP.

2.9 Summary

Rather than have a single notion of time, the proposed framework allows a number of distinct time bands to be used in the specification or behavioural description of a system. System activities are always relative to (defined within) a band. A (non-event) activity has duration of one or more ticks of the band's granularity. Events in a band take no time in that band, but will have a correspondence with activities within a lower band. It follows that a number of events can take place "at the same time" within the context of a specified band. Similarly responses can be "immediate" within a band.

Precedence relations between activities and events are an important part of the framework and allow causal relations to be defined without recourse to explicit references to time. Moreover they can be used to define clock tick events within a band, and hence link other events to the absolute time of the band.

We require all time bands to be related but do not require a strict perfect mapping. Each band, other than the lowest, will have a precision that defines (in a lower band) the tolerance of the band. However within these constraints we do need to be able to show that system descriptions at different bands are consistent. For this to be possible a formal description is required.

In this section we have argued that complex embedded systems exhibit behaviour at many different time levels and that a useful aid in describing and specifying such behaviour is to use time bands. Viewing a system as a collection of activities within a finite set of bands is an effective means of separating concerns and identifying inconsistencies between different 'layers' of the system. Time bands are not mapped on to a single notion of physical time. Within a system there will always be a relation between bands but the bands need not be tightly synchronised. There is always some level of imprecision between any two adjacent bands. Indeed the imprecision may be large in social systems and be a source of dependability (robustness).

Within each time bands there will be the need to specify and deliver timely behaviour. Deadlines exist at all levels, although the notion of missing a deadline is relative to the precision of the band. Being 10ms late for a meeting is meaningless, however being 10 minutes late may be significant, and being 10ms late to deliver a signal in an unstable aircraft may be more than enough to induce failure. Timing constraints are also linked to patterns of behaviour that can again be seen in all bands. Regular repeated activities, time triggered activities and event and exception handling are all likely to occur at all levels. In the next section we introduce the primitives necessary for these temporal concerns to be addressed.

3 Temporal Scopes – Delays and Deadlines

To facilitate the specification of the various timing constraints found in real-time applications, it is useful to introduce the notion of **temporal scopes**. Each band will contain such scopes with timing values reflecting the granularity and precision of each band.

Temporal scopes identify a collection of actions with an associated timing constraint. The possible attributes of a temporal scope (TS) for a single computational band are illustrated in Figure 2, and include

1. deadline – the time by which the execution of a TS must be finished;
2. minimum delay – the minimum amount of time that must elapse before the start of execution of a TS;
3. maximum delay – the maximum amount of time that can elapse before the start of execution of a TS;
4. maximum execution time – of a TS;
5. maximum elapse time – of a TS.

Temporal scopes with combinations of these attributes are also possible.

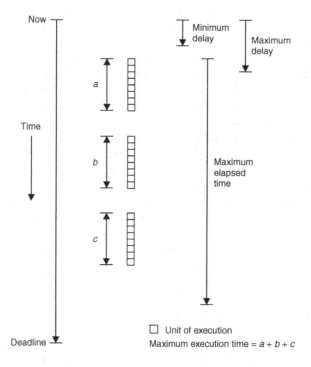

Fig. 2. Temporal Scopes

Temporal scopes can themselves be described as being either periodic or aperiodic. Typically, periodic temporal scopes sample data or execute a control loop and have explicit deadlines that must be met. Aperiodic, or sporadic, temporal scopes usually arise from asynchronous events. These scopes have specified response times associated with them.

In general, aperiodic temporal scopes are viewed as being activated randomly, following, for example, a Poisson distribution. Such a distribution allows for bursts of arrivals of external events, but does not preclude any possible concentration of aperiodic activity. It is therefore not possible to do worst-case analysis (there is a non-zero probability of any number of aperiodic events occurring within a given time). To allow worst-case calculations to be made, a minimum period between any two aperiodic events (from the same source) is often defined. If this is the case, the process involved is said to be **sporadic**.

In many real-time languages, temporal scopes are, in effect, associated with the processes that embody them. Processes can be described as either periodic, aperiodic or sporadic depending on the properties of their internal temporal scope. Most of the timing attributes given in the above list can thus be satisfied by:

1. running periodic processes at the correct rate;
2. completing all processes by their deadline.

To ensure that the correct rate is observed it is necessary to delay the activity until 'real-time' has caught up with the activity. Periodic activities typically have a common pattern. The use of *delay* to 'slow an activity down' and *deadline* 'to make sure the activity goes fast enough' together allow most (if not all) timing requirements to be specified. For example the following code pattern illustrates a periodic activity which has a period of 100ms and a deadline of 30ms.

```
period := 100ms
deadline_value := 30ms
T := clock
loop
   -- code of the activity
   deadline(T + deadline_value)
   T := T + period
   delay(T)
end loop
```

We now consider these the delay and dealdine primitives in more detail.

3.1 Deadline and Delay Primitives

Fidge et al. [25] introduce the deadline primitive to express explicitly deadlines in programming languages that lack this primitive (e.g. Ada and Java). They argue that the use of delay and deadline together allow a wide range of timing properties to be expressed. They define the two primitives using a function *Clock* that reads the current absolute time within the current band and a variable *now* that has the property $Clock \leq now$. The delay statement (using Ada/SPARK syntax):

delay until t + 10;

is formally defined as making the following true:

$$t + 10 \leq now$$

Similarly the deadline statement (which is not available in Ada):

deadline t + 13;

is formally defined as making the following true:

$$now \leq t + 13$$

Here we use these primitives within the modeling framework provided by UPPAAL. For example, a template automaton in UPPAAL for a simple periodic task which cycles every 100ms and completes all its activities within 30ms is as follows:

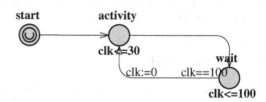

Variable clk represents a clock, which can be either global or local. As the names suggest, a global clock is available for all automata in a model, whereas a local clock is only available for the automaton which declares/introduces it. Although more than one clock can be declared, they progress at the same rate.

A state, for example activity and wait in the above example, may have a clock invariant which must remain true; similarly a transition may have a temporal guard which must be true for the transition to be taken, So in the above, the automaton must leave state wait when clk is exactly 100. As the transition is taken clk is reset to zero. The clock invariants represent system deadlines and are the only means of forcing progress.

State activity represents the work of the automaton, where the activity has further temporal properties the automaton is expanded. If any automaton has conflicting invariants and guards then model checking will detect a deadlock in the model.

The location with the symbol "∪" is an *urgent* location. Urgent locations do not allow the model to stop at these locations – the execution can stay at an urgent location as long as the clock does not progress. As expected, at least one output transaction from an urgent location must be enabled/possible, otherwise the model will deadlock. The form of TA used here makes little use of these locations. They are only employed in initial states and to model choice.

3.2 Rely and Guarantee Primitives

In a concurrent system, tasks usually cooperate to define the behaviour of the system. As such, the dependence relation among tasks should be made explicit. For example, in a producer-consumer system, tasks can be used to implement the producer and the consumer, and a shared object can be used to encapsulate the shared data and ensure that it is only accessed under mutual exclusion.

The producer task might or might not require the presence of a consumer task, and the consumer task might require the presence of a particular producer task. A task might use some subprograms of a shared object (or monitor) while requiring some other task to use other subprograms of the same shared object.

While some relations might sound obvious, clearly a cooperative/distributed system that models a producer-consumer system is wrong if, for example, a producer task is missing. Unless there is some way to make it explicit that a consumer task depends on the existence of a producer task, such properties cannot be statically verified.

In this work [13] we propose annotations to specify temporal rely and guarantee conditions [34] following Whysall's [51] use of these conditions on shared objects in his ZERO system. The rely/guarantee conditions express the allowable interference between tasks that use the same object.

As a simple example, assume that there is a periodic task `Producer` that is required to produce an item and store it in a shared object `Buffer` every 150ms. An item can be produced earlier in relation to the previous item, but no latter than 150ms after the previous item. We are free to choose both deadline and period for `Producer`[1]. An obvious choice is the one in which deadline+period is equal to 150ms, hence, we assume that the deadline is 70ms and the period is 80ms. The simple TA model is presented in Figure 3.

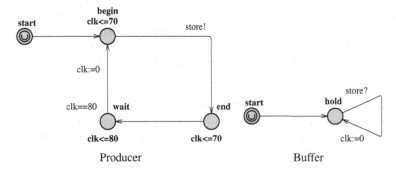

Fig. 3. Timed guarantee condition

This model has two automaton (`Producer` and `Buffer`) each with its own clock (`clk`). Identifier `store` is a standard channel and is used to model a subprogram call to place an item in `Buffer`. The clock `clk` of `Buffer` is reset to 0 every time a synchronization is performed through the channel `store`.

To verify compliance to the timing requirement, the following properties must be proved to hold:

```
A[] not deadlock
A[] Buffer.clk <= 150
```

These properties are found to be true using the UPPAAL model checker. The first property verifies that the model is deadlock free, whereas the second property verifies that

---

[1] In general a design has a number of degrees of freedom in terms of how it satisfies the system timing requirements. There is no formulaic way of fixing the free parameters – although they must of course meet any constraints imposed by the requirements. Subsequent schedulability analysis (see Section 4) may well be sensitive to these parameters, hence the need to support some form of iteration through the process, but during the modeling phase the key need is to support exploration of these free parameters.

the clock `clk` of `Buffer` is always less than or equal to 150. The symbol `A[]` implies "for all possible executions".

Obviously simple models do not need the full power of model checking to verify behaviour. A more complex example that illustrates the use of, and verification of compliance to, a timed guarantee condition is presented in Section 3.3.

By adding new components to the model it is possible to verify all end-to-end properties required of the system in the particular time band under inspection. For example in the milliseconds band, if an output must always be produced within 30ms of some input then an automaton is added whose clock is zeroed by the arrival of the input and reset by the output operations. This clock is then checked to make sure it never reaches 30.

3.3 An Example of the Use of Model Checking

The use of model checking to verify that a set of delay and deadline conditions are adequate for the model to meet its timing requirements is illustrated by the following case example. Consider a relatively simple (but not obvious) problem (in the milliseconds band):[2] a task, `Producer`, reads data from the environment via either of two devices it has access to. A primary requirement is that it generates data, which it places in shared object `input_data`, with a freshness of 300ms. The two devices have different temporal properties:

– device A is "smart", it provides a reading 30ms after it is enabled;
– device B is "simple", it must be read 10 times to gain a single reliable value – each reading must be taken between 2ms and 4ms after it is enabled and subsequent readings must be at least 10ms apart.

This specification thus has two free variables: the overall period P of `Producer`; and the enforced delay p of the inner loop for device B (which must be greater than 10ms). There is also the freedom to place extra deadline and delay statements in the code. From a schedulability point of view P and p should be as large as possible. We assume at this level of description that `Producer` makes a non-deterministic choice between the two devices. We also assume overall period equal to deadline for the periodic producer task.

Parameterizations (and subsequent verification of the timing requirement, e.g deadline and data freshness constraints) could now be undertaken in a number of ways. If there were only free variables then an algebraic formulation is possible. If there are trade offs to be made (e.g. between P and p) then it may be possible to set up a linear programming problem. However the solution may not always be found in a systematic way. The freedom to place extra delay and deadline statements/annotations in the model and code means there is considerable design freedom still available. We contend here that the use of a TA model (and model checking) allows that freedom to be explored and verification undertaken.

We will develop the automaton in stages to illustrate the procedure. A key driver here is to include only the relevant features that refer to the temporal behaviour of the code. First consider only the "smart" branch. Note that how the smart device is enabled

---

[2] From [12].

and read is not specified in the informal description. In this model, two local clocks are necessary. One to keep track of the deadline and period of the task (clk1), and another to ensure that the data is only retrieved 30ms after the smart device is enabled. The location delay models this delay. The composition and storage of the data is represented by the location compose_data and synchronization over the channel write, respectively. The period of the automaton is set to 150ms.

We will add the details of read_device_and_write shortly, but first we must ensure that the automaton makes progress. To do this we use the technique discussed earlier to bring the driving deadline back to all previous states. However, the forced delay in state delay means that start must be left after 120 (a value of 121, for example, leads to deadlock). Figure 4 illustrates the result.

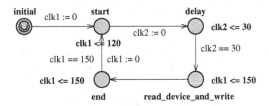

Fig. 4. Smart device

Fig. 5. Input data

The shared object, Input_Data, is represented by the automaton in Figure 5. Communication with the Producer automaton is via a channel named call. The transition from read_device_and_write to end must be changed to incorporate a synchronization on the channel call. The freshness constraint on Input_Data can now be checked via model checking by proving that idclk never takes a value greater than 300.

Now consider, again in isolation, the other branch (the simple sensor) as illustrated in Figure 6 (with period of the inner loop set to 15ms).

The locations test1 and test2 are declared as urgent because they corresponds to a logical branch.

Verification of the above model fails due to deadlock as "A[] not deadlock" is found to be false because it is possible for location write to be entered with a value of clk1 greater than 150 – this causes the automaton to deadlock. Changing the period and deadline to 200 solves this problem as long as the start location is given the constraint clk1 <= 25. Unfortunately the first path now fails; it must have a tighter deadline of 130 imposed on its cycle (see Figure 7).

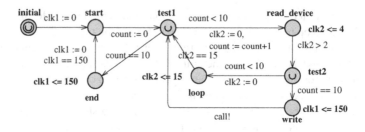

Fig. 6. Simple sensor

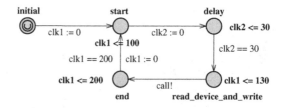

Fig. 7. Smart device (revisited again)

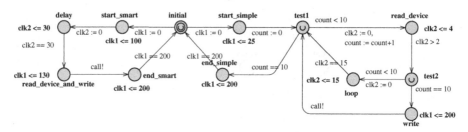

Fig. 8. Simple and smart devices

The final step is to combine the two paths. This is illustrated by the automaton in Figure 8. Although both paths on their own are correct (in their temporal properties) the combination is not. An initial execution using the smart sensor (finishing as early as possible) followed at the next iteration by the simple sensor route (finishing as late as allowed by the deadline statements) breaks the freshness constraint.

There are a number of ways this could be fixed. One is to add an extra delay of 70ms to the beginning of the smart loop, as illustrated in Figure 9. Note that the location delay_start could be removed as long the guard clk1 ≥ 70 is used in the transition from start_smart to delay. This guard would ensure a delay of at least 70 milliseconds.

Verification is now achieved:

```
A[] not deadlock
A[] Input_Data.idclk <= 300
```

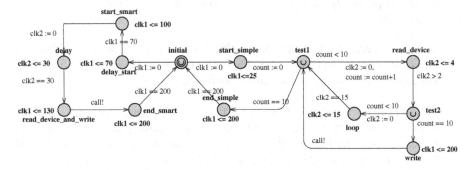

Fig. 9. Simple and smart devices (revisited)

These properties are found to be true. It is difficult to argue that these properties could be confidently verified without the support of model checking. However it is not true that model checking is needed for all application requirements – many systems have much simpler structures that can be checked by inspection.

3.4 Summary

In this section we have introduced the two main primitives that allow timing requirements to be specified. First, there is the delay statement that prevents an activity getting too far ahead of its environment. If an action must take place every hour then once completed the agent responsible must wait until the next hour is imminent. The second primitives is the deadline statement that insures an activity occurs soon enough. If the action that takes place hourly must be completed by five past the hour then there is a five minute deadline on the action. Delays and deadlines combined can therefore express a wide range of requirements.

In terms of the relationship of these primitives to time bands then they can be applied in all bands. Obviously the values used in any delay or deadline statement must relate to the granularity of the band being specified. Also the interpretation of the accuracy of the statements is that the behaviour obtained is within the precision of the band.

A system makes progress (towards its deadlines) by its use of resources e.g. people, CPUs, networks etc. The methods used to allocate these resources has a major impact on whether progress will be sufficient for deadlines to be met. The next section deals with the topic of resource management - or *scheduling* as it is usually called.

4 Scheduling

Scheduling is concerned with the allocation of resources to system activities. Here we concentrate on a technical time band and consider the allocation of the CPU to system processes. Scheduling theory usually encompasses two topics:

1. a means of allocating resources that takes into account the timing requirements of the processes, and

2. a means of predicting the worst-case behaviour of the application when this scheme is employed.

There are, in general, a large number of different scheduling approaches. A number of books exist on the topic[42,15]; the following is taken from Burns and Wellings [14]. We will consider here the two most popular approaches.

– Fixed-Priority Scheduling (FPS) – this is the most widely used approach and is the main focus of this paper. Each process has a fixed, **static**, priority which is computed pre-run-time. The runnable processes are executed in the order determined by their priority. *In real-time systems, the 'priority' of a process is derived from its temporal requirements, not its importance to the correct functioning of the system or its integrity.*
– Earliest Deadline First (EDF) Scheduling. Here the runnable processes are executed in the order determined by the absolute deadlines of the processes; the next process to run being the one with the shortest (nearest) deadline. Although it is usual to know the relative deadlines of each process (e.g. 25 ms after release), the absolute deadlines are computed at run-time, and hence the scheme is described as **dynamic**.

The bulk of this section is concerned with FPS as it is supported by various real-time languages and operating system standards. The use of EDF is also important and some consideration of its analytical basis is given in the following discussions.

In the following subsections a number of elements of a scheduling approach are outlined. The issues covered are:

– a simple process model,
– rate monotonic priority assignment,
– utilization-based tests of schedulability for fixed priority systems,
– utilization-based tests of schedulability for EDF systems,
– response time analysis for fixed priority systems,
– response time analysis for EDF systems,
– including sporadic and aperiodic processes,
– hard and soft components,
– aperiodic processes and fixed priority servers,
– aperiodic processes and EDF servers,
– processes with deadline less than period,
– proof of the optimality of deadline monotonic priority assignment,
– process interaction and blocking,
– response time and analysis and blocking,
– priority ceiling protocols,
– systems and processes with release jitter,
– processes with deadlines greater than period (arbitrary deadlines),
– fault tolerance, and
– general priority assignment.

Table 1. Standard notation

Notation	Description
B	Worst-case blocking time for the process (if applicable)
C	Worst-case computation time (WCET) of the process
D	Deadline of the process
I	The interference time of the process
J	Release jitter of the process
N	Number of processes in the system
P	Priority assigned to the process (if applicable)
R	Worst-case response time of the process
T	Minimum time between process releases (process period)
U	The utilization of each process (equal to C/T)
$a - z$	The name of a process

4.1 Simple Process Model

An arbitrarily complex concurrent program cannot easily be analyzed to predict its worst-case behaviour. Hence it is necessary to impose some restrictions on the structure of real-time concurrent programs. This section will present a very simple model in order to describe some standard scheduling schemes. The model is generalized in later sections. The basic model has the following characteristics:

- The application is assumed to consist of a fixed set of processes.
- All processes are periodic, with known periods.
- The processes are completely independent of each other.
- All system's overheads, context-switching times and so on are ignored (that is, assumed to have zero cost).
- All processes have deadlines equal to their periods (that is, each process must complete before it is next released).
- All processes have fixed worst-case execution times.

One consequence of the process's independence is that it can be assumed that at some point in time all processes will be released together. This represents the maximum load on the processor and is known as a **critical instant**.

Table 1 gives a standard set of notations for process characteristics.

4.2 FPS and Rate Monotonic Priority Assignment

With the straightforward model outlined above, there exists a simple optimal priority assignment scheme known as **rate monotonic** priority assignment. Each process is assigned a (unique) priority based on its period: the shorter the period, the higher the priority (that is, for two processes i and j, $T_i < T_j \Rightarrow P_i > P_j$). This assignment is optimal in the sense that if any process set can be scheduled (using preemptive priority-based scheduling) with a fixed-priority assignment scheme, then the given process set can also be scheduled with a rate monotonic assignment scheme. Table 2 illustrates a five process set and shows what the relative priorities must be for optimal temporal behaviour. Note that priorities are represented by integers, and that the higher the integer,

Table 2. Example of priority assignment

Process	Period, T	Priority, P
a	25	5
b	60	3
c	42	4
d	105	1
e	75	2

Table 3. Utilization bounds

N	Utilization bound
1	100.0%
2	82.8%
3	78.0%
4	75.7%
5	74.3%
10	71.8%

the greater the priority. Care must be taken when reading other books and papers on priority-based scheduling, as often priorities are ordered the other way; that is, priority 1 is the highest. In this paper, *priority 1 is the lowest*, as this is the normal usage in most programming languages and operating systems.

4.3 Utilization-Based Schedulability Tests

This section describes a very simple schedulability test for FPS which, although not exact, is attractive because of its simplicity.

Liu and Layland [40] showed that by considering only the utilization of the process set, a test for schedulability can be obtained (when the rate monotonic priority ordering is used). If the following condition is true then all N processes will meet their deadlines (note that the summation calculates the total utilization of the process set):

$$\sum_{i=1}^{N} \left(\frac{C_i}{T_i} \right) \leq N(2^{1/N} - 1) \tag{1}$$

Table 3 shows the utilization bound (as a percentage) for small values of N. For large N, the bound asymptotically approaches 69.3%. Hence any process set with a combined utilization of less than 69.3% will always be schedulable by a preemptive priority-based scheduling scheme, with priorities assigned by the rate monotonic algorithm.

Three simple examples will now be given to illustrate the use of this test. In these examples, the units (absolute magnitudes) of the time values are not defined. As long as all the values (Ts, Cs and so on) are in the same units from the same time band, the tests can be applied. So in these (and later examples), the unit of time is just considered to be a *tick* of some notional time base.

Table 4 contains three processes that have been allocated priorities via the rate monotonic algorithm (hence process c has the highest priority and process a the

Table 4. Process set A

Process	Period, T	Computation time, C	Priority, P	Utilization, U
a	50	12	1	0.24
b	40	10	2	0.25
c	30	10	3	0.33

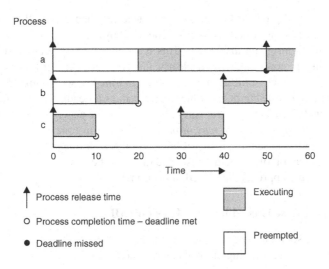

Fig. 10. Time-line for process set A

lowest). Their combined utilization is 0.82 (or 82%). This is above the threshold for three processes (0.78), and hence this process set fails the utilization test.

The actual behaviour of this process set can be illustrated by drawing out a **time-line**. Figure 10 shows how the three processes would execute if they all started their executions at time 0. Note that, at time 50, process a has consumed only 10 ticks of execution, whereas it needed 12, and hence it has missed its first deadline.

The second example is contained in Table 5. Now the combined utilization is 0.775, which is below the bound, and hence this process set is guaranteed to meet all its deadlines. If a time-line for this set is drawn, all deadlines would be satisfied.

Although cumbersome, time-lines can actually be used to test for schedulability. But how far must the line be drawn before one can conclude that the future holds no surprises? For process sets that share a common release time (that is, they share a *critical instant*), it can be shown that a time-line equal to the size of the longest period is suf-

Table 5. Process set B

Process	Period, T	Computation time, C	Priority, P	Utilization, U
a	80	32	1	0.400
b	40	5	2	0.125
c	16	4	3	0.250

Table 6. Process set C

Process	Period, T	Computation time, C	Priority, P	Utilization, U
a	80	40	1	0.50
b	40	10	2	0.25
c	20	5	3	0.25

ficient [40]. So if all processes meet their first deadline then they will meet all future ones. This property is not true for systems scheduled by EDF.

A final example in given in Table 6. This is again a three-process system, but the combined utility is now 100%, so it clearly fails the test. At run-time however, the behaviour seems correct, all deadlines are met up to time 80 (see Figure 11). Hence the process set fails the test, but at run-time does not miss a deadline. Therefore, the test is said to be **sufficient** but not **necessary**. If a process set passes the test, it *will* meet all deadlines; if it fails the test, it *may* or *may not* fail at run-time. A final point to note about this utilization-based test is that it only supplies a simple yes/no answer. It does not give any indication of the actual response times of the processes. This is remedied in the response time approach described in Section 4.5.

4.4   Utilization-Based Schedulability Tests for EDF

Not only did the seminal paper of Liu and Layland [40] introduce a utilization-based test for fixed priority scheduling but it also gave one for EDF:

$$\sum_{i=1}^{N} \left(\frac{C_i}{T_i} \right) \leq 1 \tag{2}$$

Clearly this is a much simpler test. As long as the utilization of the process set is less than the total capacity of the processor then all deadlines will be met (for the simple process model). In this sense EDF is superior to FPS; it can always schedule any process set that FPS can, but not all process sets that are passed by the EDF test can be scheduled using fixed priorities. Given this advantage it is reasonable to ask why EDF is not the preferred process-based scheduling method? The reason is that FPS has a number of advantages over EDF:

- FPS is easier to implement, as the scheduling attribute (*priority*) is static; EDF is dynamic and hence requires a more complex run-time system which will have higher overhead.
- It is easier to incorporate processes without deadlines into FPS (by merely assigning them a priority); giving a process an arbitrary deadline is more artificial.
- The deadline attribute is not the only parameter of importance; again it is easier to incorporate other factors into the notion of priority than it is into the notion of deadline.
- During overload situations (which may be a fault condition) the behaviour of FPS is more predictable (the lower priority processes are those that will miss their deadlines first); EDF is unpredictable under overload and can experience a domino effect in which a large number of processes miss deadlines.

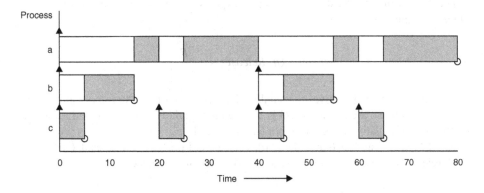

Fig. 11. Time-line for process set C

- The utilization-based test, for the simple model, is misleading as it is necessary and sufficient for EDF but only sufficient for FPS. Hence higher utilizations can, in general, be achieved for FPS.

Notwithstanding this final point, EDF does have an advantage over FPS because of its higher utilization, and hence it continues to be studied and used in some experimental systems.

4.5   Response Time Analysis for FPS

The utilization-based tests for FPS have two significant drawbacks: they are not exact, and they are not really applicable to a more general process model. This section provides a different form of test. The test is in two stages. First, an analytical approach is used to predict the worst-case response time of each process. These values are then compared, trivially, with the process deadlines. This requires each process to be analyzed individually.

For the highest-priority process, its worst-case response time will equal its own computation time (that is, $R = C$). Other processes will suffer **interference** from higher-priority processes; this is the time spent executing higher-priority processes when a low-priority process is runnable. So for a general process i:

$$R_i = C_i + I_i \tag{3}$$

where I_i is the maximum interference that process i can experience in any time interval $[t, t + R_i)$.[3] The maximum interference obviously occurs when all higher-priority processes are released at the same time as process i (that is, at a critical instant). Without loss of generality, it can be assumed that all processes are released at time 0. Consider one process (j) of higher priority than i. Within the interval $[0, R_i)$, it will be released

---

[3] Note that as a discrete time model is used in this analysis, all time intervals must be closed at the beginning (denoted by '[') and open at the end (denoted by a ')'). Thus a process can complete executing on the same tick as a higher-priority process is released.

a number of times (at least one). A simple expression for this number of releases is obtained using a ceiling function:

$$Number\_Of\_Releases = \left\lceil \frac{R_i}{T_j} \right\rceil$$

The ceiling function ($\lceil \ \rceil$) gives the smallest integer greater than the fractional number on which it acts. So the ceiling of 1/3 is 1, of 6/5 is 2, and of 6/3 is 2. The definitions of the ceilings of negative values need not be considered.

So, if R_i is 15 and T_j is 6 then there are 3 releases of process j (at times 0, 6 and 12). Each release of process j will impose an interference of C_j. Hence

$$Maximum\_Interference = \left\lceil \frac{R_i}{T_j} \right\rceil C_j$$

If $C_j = 2$ then in the interval [0, 15) there are 6 units of interference. Each process of higher priority is interfering with process i, and hence:

$$I_i = \sum_{j \in hp(i)} \left\lceil \frac{R_i}{T_j} \right\rceil C_j$$

where $hp(i)$ is the set of higher-priority processes (than i). Substituting this value back into Equation (3) gives [35]:

$$R_i = C_i + \sum_{j \in hp(i)} \left\lceil \frac{R_i}{T_j} \right\rceil C_j \qquad (4)$$

Although the formulation of the interference equation is exact, the actual amounts of interference is unknown as R_i is unknown (it is the value being calculated). Equation (4) has R_i on both sides, but is difficult to solve due to the ceiling functions. It is actually an example of a fixed-point equation. In general, there will be many values of R_i that form solutions to Equation (4). The smallest such value of R_i represents the worst-case response time for the process. The simplest way of solving Equation (4) is to form a recurrence relationship [4]:

$$w_i^{n+1} = C_i + \sum_{j \in hp(i)} \left\lceil \frac{w_i^n}{T_j} \right\rceil C_j \qquad (5)$$

The set of values $\{w_i^0, w_i^1, w_i^2, ..., w_i^n, ...\}$ is, clearly, monotonically non-decreasing. When $w_i^n = w_i^{n+1}$, the solution to the equation has been found. If $w_i^0 < R_i$ then w_i^n is the smallest solution and hence is the value required. If the equation does not have a solution then the w values will continue to rise (this will occur for a low-priority process if the full set has a utilization greater than 100%). Once they get bigger than the process's period, T, it can be assumed that the process will not meet its deadline. The above analysis gives rise to the following algorithm for calculation response times:

```
for i in 1..N loop -- for each process in turn
   n := 0
   wⁿᵢ := Cᵢ
   loop
      calculate new wⁿ⁺¹ᵢ from Equation (5)
      if wⁿ⁺¹ᵢ = wⁿᵢ then
         Rᵢ := wⁿᵢ
         exit {value found}
      end if
      if wⁿ⁺¹ᵢ > Tᵢ then
         exit {value not found}
      end if
      n := n + 1
   end loop
end loop
```

By implication, if a response time is found it will be less than T_i, and hence less than D_i, its deadline (remember with the simple process model $D_i = T_i$).

In the above discussion, w_i has been used merely as a mathematical entity for solving a fixed-point equation. It is, however, possible to get an intuition for w_i from the problem domain. Consider the point of release of process i. From that point, until the process completes, the processor will be executing processes with priority P_i or higher. The processor is said to be executing a P_i-**busy period**. Consider w_i to be a time window that is moving down the busy period. At time 0 (the notional release time of process i), all higher priority processes are assumed to have also been released, and hence

$$w_i^1 = C_i + \sum_{j \in hp(i)} C_j$$

This will be the end of the busy period unless some higher-priority process is released a second time. If it is, then the window will need to be pushed out further. This continues with the window expanding and, as a result, more computation time falling into the window. If this continues indefinitely then the busy period is unbounded (that is, there is no solution). However, if at any point, an expanding window does not suffer an extra 'hit' from a higher-priority process then the busy period has been completed, and the size of the busy period is the response time of the process.

To illustrate how the response time analysis is used, consider process set D given in Table 7.

The highest-priority process, a, will have a response time equal to its computation time (for example, $R_a = 3$). The next process will need to have its response time calculated. Let w_b^0 equal the computation time of process a, which is 3. Equation (5) is used to derive the next value of w:

$$w_b^1 = 3 + \left\lceil \frac{3}{7} \right\rceil 3$$

that is, $w_b^1 = 6$. This value now balances the Equation ($w_b^2 = w_b^1 = 6$) and the response time of process b has been found (that is, $R_b = 6$).

The final process will give rise to the following calculations:

$$w_c^0 = 5$$

$$w_c^1 = 5 + \lceil \tfrac{5}{7} \rceil 3 + \lceil \tfrac{5}{12} \rceil 3 = 11$$

$$w_c^2 = 5 + \lceil \tfrac{11}{7} \rceil 3 + \lceil \tfrac{11}{12} \rceil 3 = 14$$

$$w_c^3 = 5 + \lceil \tfrac{14}{7} \rceil 3 + \lceil \tfrac{14}{12} \rceil 3 = 17$$

$$w_c^4 = 5 + \lceil \tfrac{17}{7} \rceil 3 + \lceil \tfrac{17}{12} \rceil 3 = 20$$

$$w_c^5 = 5 + \lceil \tfrac{20}{7} \rceil 3 + \lceil \tfrac{20}{12} \rceil 3 = 20$$

Hence R_c has a worst-case response time of 20, which means that it will just meet its deadline.

Consider again the process set C. This set failed the utilization-based test but was observed to meet all its deadlines up to time 80. Table 8 shows the response times calculated by the above method for this collection. Note that all processes are now predicted to complete before their deadlines.

The response time calculations have the advantage that they are sufficient and necessary – if the process set passes the test they will meet all their deadlines; if they fail the test, then, at run-time, a process will miss its deadline (unless the computation time estimations, C, themselves turn out to be pessimistic). As these tests are superior to the utilization-based ones, this paper will concentrate on extending the applicability of the response time method.

4.6 Response Time Analysis for EDF

One of the disadvantages of the EDF scheme is that the worst-case response time for each process does not occur when all processes are released at a critical instant. In that situation only processes with a shorter relative deadline will interfere. But later there may exist a position in which all (or at least more) processes have a shorter absolute deadline. For example, consider a three process system as depicted in Table 9. The behaviour of process b illustrates the problem. At time 0, a critical instant, b only gets interference from process a (once) and has a response time of 4. But at its next release (at time 12) process

Table 7. Process set D

Process	Period, T	Computation time, C	Priority, P
a	7	3	3
b	12	3	2
c	20	5	1

Table 8. Response time for process set C

Process	Period, T	Computation time, C	Priority, P	Response time, R
a	80	40	1	80
b	40	10	2	15
c	20	5	3	5

Table 9. A process set for EDF

Process	T(=D)	C
a	4	1
b	12	3
c	16	8

c is still active and has a shorted deadline (16 versus 24) and hence c takes precedence; the response time for this second release of b is 8, twice the value obtained at the critical instant. Later releases may give an even larger value, although it is bounded at 12 as the system is schedulable by EDF (utilization is 1). Hence to find the worst case is much more complex. It is necessary to consider all process releases to see which one suffers the maximum interference from other processes with shorter deadlines.

In the simple model with all periodic processes, the full process set will repeat its execution every *hyper-period*; that is, the least common multiple (LCM) of the process periods. For example, in a small system with only four processes but periods of 24, 50, 73 and 101 time units, the LCM is 4 423 800. To find the worst-case response time for EDF may require each release within 4 423 800 to be considered – remember with FPS only the first release needs be analyzed (that is, the maximum time to consider is 101 time units).

Although more releases must be considered it is possible to derive a formula for computing each response time in a manner similar to that given above for FPS [49].

4.7   Sporadic and Aperiodic Processes

To expand the simple model of subsection 4.1 to include sporadic (and aperiodic) process requirements, the value T is interpreted as the minimum (or average) inter-arrival interval [4]. A sporadic process with a T value of 20 ms is guaranteed not to arrive more than once in any 20 ms interval. In reality, it may arrive much less frequently than once every 20 ms, but the response time test will ensure that the maximum rate can be sustained (if the test is passed!).

The other requirement that the inclusion of sporadic processes demands concerns the definition of the deadline. The simple model assumes that $D = T$. For sporadic processes, this is unreasonable. Often a sporadic is used to encapsulate an error-handling routine or to respond to a warning signal. The fault model of the system may state that the error routine will be invoked very infrequently – but when it is, it is urgent and hence it has a short deadline. Our model must therefore distinguish between D and T, and allow $D < T$. Indeed, for many periodic processes, it will be useful to allow the application to define deadline values less than period.

An inspection of the response time algorithm for fixed priority scheduling, described in Section 4.5 reveals that:

- it works perfectly for values of D less than T as long as the stopping criterion becomes $w_i^{n+1} > D_i$,
- it works perfectly well with any priority ordering – $hp(i)$ always gives the set of higher-priority processes.

Although some priority orderings are better than others, the test will provide the worst-case response times for the given priority ordering.

In the Section 4.11, an optimal priority ordering for $D < T$ is defined (and proved). A later section will consider an extended algorithm and optimal priority ordering for the general case of $D < T, D = T$ or $D > T$.

4.8 Hard and Soft Processes

For sporadic processes, average and maximum arrival rates may be defined. Unfortunately, in many situations the worst-case figure is considerably higher than the average. Interrupts often arrive in bursts and an abnormal sensor reading may lead to significant additional computation. It follows that measuring schedulability with worst-case figures may lead to very low processor utilizations being observed in the actual running system. As a guideline for the minimum requirement, the following two rules should always be complied with:

- Rule 1 – all processes should be schedulable using average execution times and average arrival rates.
- Rule 2 – all hard real-time processes should be schedulable using worst-case execution times and worst-case arrival rates of all processes (including soft).

A consequent of Rule 1 is that there may be situations in which it is not possible to meet all current deadlines. This condition is known as a **transient overload**; Rule 2, however, ensures that no hard real-time process will miss its deadline. If Rule 2 gives rise to unacceptably low utilizations for 'normal execution', direct action should be taken to try and reduce the worst-case execution times (or arrival rates).

4.9 Aperiodic Processes and Fixed Priority Servers

One simple way of scheduling aperiodic processes, within a priority-based scheme, is to run such processes at a priority below the priorities assigned to hard processes. In effect, the aperiodic processes run as background activities, and therefore cannot steal, in a preemptive system, resources from the hard processes. Although a safe scheme, this does not provide adequate support to soft processes which will often miss their deadlines if they only run as background activities. To improve the situation for soft processes, a **server** can be employed. Servers protect the processing resources needed by hard processes, but otherwise allow soft processes to run as soon as possible.

Since they were first introduced in 1987, a number of server methods have been defined. Here only two will be considered: the Deferrable Server (DS) and the Sporadic Server (SS) [37].

With the DS, an analysis is undertaken (using, for example, the response time approach) that enables a new process to be introduced at the highest priority.[4] This process, the server, thus has a period, T_s and a capacity C_s. These values are chosen so that all the hard processes in the system remain schedulable even if the server executes periodically with period T_s and execution time C_s. At run-time, whenever an aperiodic process arrives, and there is capacity available, it starts executing immediately and continues until either it finishes or the capacity is exhausted. In the latter case, the aperiodic process is suspended (or transferred to a background priority). With the DS model, the capacity is replenished every T_s time units.

The operation of the SS differs from DS in its replenishment policy. With SS, if a process arrives at time t and uses c capacity then the server has this c capacity replenished T_s time units after t. In general, SS can furnish higher capacity than DS but has increased implementational overheads.

As all servers limit the capacity that is available to aperiodic soft processes, they can also be used to ensure that sporadic processes do not execute more often than expected. If a sporadic process with interarrival interval of T_i and worst-case execution time of C_i is implemented not directly as a process, but via a server with $T_s = T_i$ and $C_s = C_i$, then its impact (interference) on lower-priority processes is bounded even if the sporadic process arrives too quickly (which would be an error condition).

All servers (DS, SS and others) can be described as *bandwidth preserving* in that they attempt to

- make CPU resources available immediately to aperiodic processes (if there is a capacity);
- retain the capacity for as long as possible if there are currently no aperiodic processes (by allowing the hard processes to execute).

Another bandwidth preserving scheme, which often performs better than the server techniques is **dual-priority scheduling** [23]. Here, the range of priorities is split into three bands: high, medium and low. All aperiodic processes run in the middle band. Hard processes, when they are released, run in the low band, but they are promoted to the top band in time to meet their deadlines. Hence in the first stage of execution they will give way to aperiodic activities (but will execute if there is no such activity). In the second phase they will move to a higher priority and then have precedence over the aperiodic work. In the high band, priorities are assigned according to the deadline monotonic approach (see below). Promotion to this band occurs at time $D - R$. To implement the dual-priority scheme requires a dynamic priority provision.

4.10 Aperiodic Processes and EDF Servers

Following the development of server technology for fixed priority systems, most of the common approaches have been reinterpreted within the context of dynamic EDF systems. For example there is a Dynamic Sporadic Server [15]. Whereas the static system needs a priority to be assigned (which is done pre-run-time), the dynamic version needs

---

[4] Servers at other priorities are possible, but the description is more straightforward if the server is given a higher priority than all the hard processes.

Table 10. Example process set for DMPO

Process	Period, T	Deadline, D	Computation time, C	Priority, P	Response time, R
a	20	5	3	4	3
b	15	7	3	3	6
c	10	10	4	2	10
d	20	20	3	1	20

to compute a deadline each time it needs to execute. In essence, the run-time algorithm assigns the server the shortest current deadline if (and only if) there is an outstanding aperiodic process to serve and there is capacity outstanding. Once the capacity is exhausted, the server is suspended until it is replenished.

4.11   Process Systems with $D < T$

In the above discussion on sporadic processes is was argued that, in general, it must be possible for a process to define a deadline that is less than its inter-arrival interval (or period). It was also noted earlier that for $D = T$ the rate monotonic priority ordering was optimal for a fixed priority scheme. Liu and Layland[38] showed that for $D < T$, a similar formulation could be defined – the deadline monotonic priority ordering (DMPO). Here, the fixed priority of a process is inversely proportional to its deadline: $(D_i < D_j \Rightarrow P_i > P_j)$. Table 10 gives the appropriate priority assignments for a simple process set. It also includes the worst-case response time – as calculated by the algorithm in Section 4.5. Note that a rate monotonic priority ordering would not schedule these processes.

In the following subsection, the optimality of DMPO is proven. Given this result and the direct applicability of response time analysis to this process model, it is clear that fixed priority scheduling can adequately deal with this more general set of scheduling requirements. The same is not true for EDF scheduling. Once processes can have $D < T$ then the simple utilization test (total utilization less than one) cannot be applied. Moreover, the response time analysis, discussed in Section 4.6, is considerable more complex for EDF than it is for FPS.

Having raised this difficulty with EDF is must be remembered that EDF is the more effective scheduling scheme. Hence any process set that passes an FPS schedulability test *will* also always meet its timing requirements if executed under EDF. The necessary and sufficient tests for FPS can thus be seen as sufficient tests for EDF.

4.12   Proof That DMPO Is Optimal

Deadline monotonic priority ordering (DMPO) is optimal if any process set, Q, that is schedulable by priority scheme, W, is also schedulable by DMPO. The proof of optimality of DMPO will involve transforming the priorities of Q (as assigned by W) until the ordering is DMPO. Each step of the transformation will preserve schedulability.

Let i and j be two processes (with adjacent priorities) in Q such that under W: $P_i > P_j$ and $D_i > D_j$. Define scheme W' to be identical to W except that processes i and j are swapped. Consider the schedulability of Q under W':

- All processes with priorities greater than P_i will be unaffected by this change to lower-priority processes.
- All processes with priorities lower than P_j will be unaffected. They will all experience the same interference from i and j.
- Process j, which was schedulable under W, now has a higher priority, suffers less interference, and hence must be schedulable under W'.

All that is left is the need to show that process i, which has had its priority lowered, is still schedulable.

Under W, $R_j \leq D_j$, $D_j < D_i$ and $D_i \leq T_i$ and hence process i only interferes once during the execution of j.

Once the processes have been switched, the new response time of i becomes equal to the old response time of j. This is true because under both priority orderings $C_j + C_i$ amount of computation time has been completed with the same level of interference from higher-priority processes. Process j was released only once during R_j, and hence interferes only once during the execution of i under W'. It follows that:

$$R'_i = R_j \leq D_j < D_i$$

It can be concluded that process i is schedulable after the switch.

Priority scheme W' can now be transformed (to W'') by choosing two more processes 'that are in the wrong order for DMPO' and switching them. Each such switch preserves schedulability. Eventually there will be no more processes to switch; the ordering will be exactly that required by DMPO and the process set will still be schedulable. Hence, DMPO is optimal.

Note that for the special case of $D = T$, the above proof can be used to show that, in this circumstance, rate monotonic ordering is also optimal.

4.13 Process Interactions and Blocking

One of the simplistic assumptions embodied in the system model, described in sub-section 4.1, is the need for processes to be independent. This is clearly unreasonable, as process interaction will be needed in almost all meaningful applications. All concurrent language features for communication lead to the possibility of a process being suspended until some necessary future event has occurred (for example, waiting to gain a lock on a semaphore, or entry to a monitor, or until some other process is in a position to accept a rendezvous request). In general, synchronous communication leads to more pessimistic analysis as it is harder to define the real worst case when there are many dependencies between process executions. The following analysis is therefore more accurate when related to asynchronous communication where processes exchange data via shared resources. The majority of the material in the next two sections is concerned with fixed-priority scheduling. At the end of this discussion, the applicability of the results to EDF scheduling will be considered.

Table 11. Execution sequences

Process	Priority	Execution sequence	Release time
a	1	EQQQQE	0
b	2	EE	2
c	3	EVVE	2
d	4	EEQVE	4

If a process is suspended waiting for a lower-priority process to complete some required computation then the priority model is, in some sense, being undermined. In an ideal world, such **priority inversion** [36] (that is, a high-priority process having to wait for a lower-priority process) should not exist. However, it cannot, in general, be totally eliminated. Nevertheless, its adverse effects can be minimized. If a process is waiting for a lower-priority process, it is said to be **blocked**. In order to test for schedulability, blocking must be bounded and measurable; it should also be small.

To illustrate an extreme example of priority inversion, consider the executions of four periodic processes: a, b, c and d. Assume they have been assigned priorities according to the deadline monotonic scheme, so that the priority of process d is the highest and that of process a the lowest. Further, assume that processes d and a (and processes d and c) share a critical section (resource), denoted by the symbol Q (and V), protected by mutual exclusion. Table 11 gives the details of the four processes and their execution sequences; in this table 'E' represents a single tick of execution time and 'Q' (or 'V') represent an execution tick with access to the Q (or V) critical section. Thus process c executes for four ticks; the middle two while it has access to critical section V.

Figure 12 illustrates the execution sequence for the start times given in the table. Process a is released first, executes and locks the critical section, Q. It is then preempted by the release of process c which executes for one tick, locks V and is then preempted by the release of process d. The higher-priority process then executes until it also wishes to lock the critical section, Q; it must then be suspended (as the section is already locked by a). At this point, c will regain the processor and continue. Once it has terminated, b will commence and run for its entitlement. Only when b has completed will a be able to execute again; it will then complete its use of the Q and allow d to continue and complete. With this behaviour, d finishes at time 16, and therefore has a response time of 12; c has a value of 6, b a value of 8, and a a value of 17.

An inspection of Figure 12 shows that process d suffers considerable priority inversion. Not only is it blocked by process a but also by processes b and c. Some blocking is inevitable; if the integrity of the critical section (and hence the shared data) is to be maintained then a must run in preference to d (while it has the lock). But the blocking of d by processes c and b is unproductive and will severely affect the schedulability of the system (as the blocking on process d is excessive).

This type of priority inversion is the result of a purely fixed-priority scheme. One method of limiting this effect is to use **priority inheritance** [20]. With priority inheritance, a process's priority is no longer static; if a process p is suspended waiting for process q to undertake some computation then the priority of q becomes equal to the priority of p (if it were lower to start with). In the example just given, process a will be given the priority of process d and will, therefore, run in preference to process c and process b. This is

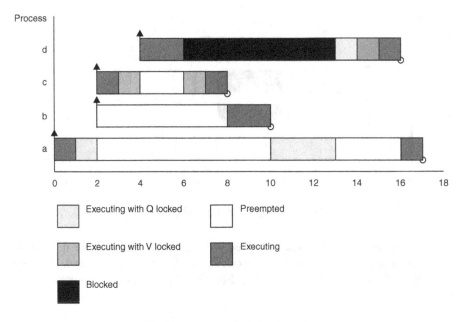

Fig. 12. Example of priority inversion

illustrated in Figure 13. Note as a consequence of this algorithm, process *b* will now suffer blocking even though it does not use a shared object. Also note that process *d* now has a second block, but its response time has been reduced to 9.

With this simple inheritance rule, the priority of a process is the maximum of its own default priority and the priorities of all the other processes that are at that time dependent upon it.

In general, inheritance of priority would not be restricted to a single step. If process *d* is waiting for process *c*, but *c* cannot deal with *d* because it is waiting for process *b* then *b* as well as *c* would be given *d*'s priority. The implication for the run-time dispatcher is that a process's priorities will often be changing and that it may be better to choose the appropriate process to run (or make runnable) at the time when the action is needed rather than try and manage a queue that is ordered by priority.

In the design of a real-time language, priority inheritance would seem to be of paramount importance. To have the most effective model, however, implies that the concurrency model should have a particular form. With standard semaphores and condition variables, there is no direct link between the act of becoming suspended and the identity of the process that will reverse this action. Inheritance is therefore not easily implemented.

Analysis of these protocols show that with a priority inheritance protocol, there is a bound on the number of times a process can be blocked by lower priority processes. If a process has *m* critical sections that can lead to it being blocked then the maximum number of times it can be blocked is *m*. That is, in the worst case, each critical section will be locked by a lower-priority process (this is what happened in Figure 13). If there are only *n* (*n* < *m*) lower-priority processes then this maximum can be further reduced (to *n*).

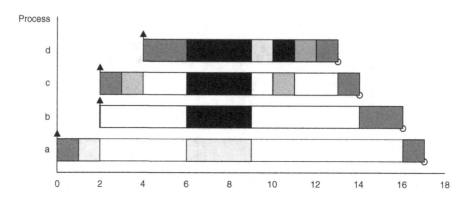

Fig. 13. Example of priority inheritance

If B_i is the maximum blocking time that process i can suffer then for this simple priority inheritance model, a formula for calculating B can easily be found. Let K be the number of critical sections (resources). Equation (6) thus provides an upper bound on B.

$$B_i = \sum_{k=1}^{K} usage(k, i) C(k) \qquad (6)$$

where *usage* is a 0/1 function: $usage(k, i) = 1$ if resource k is used by at least one process with a priority less than P_i, and at least one process with a priority greater or equal to P_i. Otherwise it gives the result 0. $C(k)$ is the worst-case execution time of the k critical section.

This algorithm is not optimal for this inheritance protocol, but serves to illustrate the factors that need to be taken into account when calculating B. In Section 4.15, better inheritance protocols will be described and an improved formulae for B will be given.

4.14   Response Time Calculations and Blocking

Given that a value for B has been obtained, the response time algorithm can be modified to take the blocking factor into account:[5]

$$R = C + B + I$$

that is,

$$R_i = C_i + B_i + \sum_{j \in hp(i)} \left\lceil \frac{R_i}{T_j} \right\rceil C_j \qquad (7)$$

which can again be solved by constructing a recurrence relationship:

---

[5] Blocking can also be incorporated into the utilization-based tests, but now each process must be considered individually.

$$w_i^{n+1} = C_i + B_i + \sum_{j \in hp(i)} \left\lceil \frac{w_i^n}{T_j} \right\rceil C_j \tag{8}$$

Note that this formulation may now be pessimistic (that is, not necessarily sufficient and necessary). Whether a process actually suffers its maximum blocking will depend upon process phasings. For example, if all processes are periodic and all have the same period then no preemption will take place and hence no priority inversion will occur. However, in general, Equation (7) represents an effective scheduling test for real-time systems containing cooperating processes.

4.15   Priority Ceiling Protocols

While the standard inheritance protocol gives an upper bound on the number of blocks a high-priority process can encounter, this bound can still lead to an unacceptably pessimistic worst-case calculation. This is compounded by the possibility of chains of blocks developing (transitive blocking), that is, process c being blocked by process b which is blocked by process a and so on. As shared data is a system resource, from a resource management point of view not only should blocking be minimized, but failure conditions such as deadlock should be eliminated. All of these issues are addressed by the ceiling priority protocols [48]; two of which will be considered in this paper: the **original ceiling priority protocol** and the **immediate ceiling priority protocol**. The original protocol (OCPP) will be described first, followed by the somewhat more straightforward immediate variant (ICPP). When either of these protocols are used on a single-processor system:

- A high-priority process can be blocked at most once during its execution by lower-priority processes.
- Deadlocks are prevented.
- Transitive blocking is prevented.
- Mutual exclusive access to resources is ensured (by the protocol itself).

The ceiling protocols can best be described in terms of resources protected by critical sections. In essence, the protocol ensures that if a resource is locked, by process a say, and could lead to the blocking of a higher-priority process (b), then no other resource that could block b is allowed to be locked by any process other that a. A process can therefore be delayed by not only attempting to lock a previously locked resource but also when the lock could lead to multiple blocking on higher-priority processes.

The original protocol takes the following form:

1. Each process has a static default priority assigned (perhaps by the deadline monotonic scheme).
2. Each resource has a static ceiling value defined, this is the maximum priority of the processes that use it.
3. A process has a dynamic priority that is the maximum of its own static priority and any it inherits due to it blocking higher-priority processes.

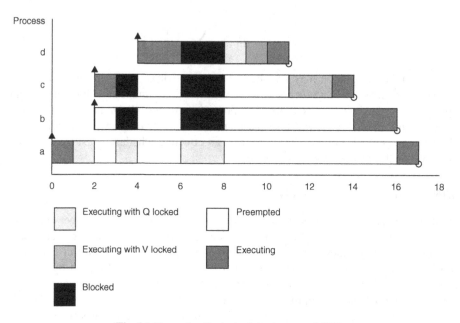

Fig. 14. Example of priority inheritance – OCPP

4. A process can only lock a resource if its dynamic priority is higher than the ceiling of any currently locked resource (excluding any that it has already locked itself).

The locking of a first system resource is allowed. The effect of the protocol is to ensure that a second resource can only be locked if there does not exist a higher-priority process that uses both resources. Consequently, the maximum amount of time a process can be blocked is equal to the execution time of the longest critical section in any of the lower-priority processes that are accessed by higher-priority processes; that is, Equation (6) becomes:

$$B_i = max_{k=1}^{K} usage(k,i)C(k) \tag{9}$$

The benefit of the ceiling protocol is that a high-priority process can only be blocked once (per activation) by any lower-priority process. The cost of this result is that more processes will experience this block.

Not all the features of the algorithm can be illustrated by a single example, but the execution sequence shown in Figure 14 does give a good indication of how the algorithm works and provides a comparison with the earlier approaches (that is, this figure illustrates the same process sequence used in Figures 13 and 12).

In Figure 14, process a again locks the first critical section, as no other resources have been locked. It is again preempted by process c, but now the attempt by c to lock the second section (V) is not successful as its priority (3) is not higher than the current ceiling (which is 4, as Q is locked and is used by process d). At time 3, a is blocking c, and hence runs with its priority at the level 3, thereby blocking b. The higher-priority process, d, preempts a at time 4, but is subsequently blocked when it attempts to access Q. Hence a will continue (with priority 4) until it releases its lock on Q and has its priority drop back to 1. Now, d can continue until it completes (with a response time of 7).

The priority ceiling protocols ensure that a process is only blocked once during each invocation. Figure 14, however, appears to show process b (and process c) suffering two blocks. What is actually happening is that a single block is being broken in two by the preemption of process d. Equation (9) determines that all processes (apart from process a) will suffer a maximum single block of 4. Figure 14 shows that for this particular execution sequence process c and process d actually suffer a block of 3 and process d a block of only 2.

Immediate Ceiling Priority Protocol. The immediate ceiling priority algorithm (ICPP) takes a more straightforward approach and raises the priority of a process as soon as it locks a resource (rather than only when it is actually blocking a higher-priority process). The protocol is thus defined as follows:

- Each process has a static default priority assigned (perhaps by the deadline monotonic scheme).
- Each resource has a static ceiling value defined, this is the maximum priority of the processes that use it.
- A process has a dynamic priority that is the maximum of its own static priority and the ceiling values of any resources it has locked.

As a consequence of this final rule, a process will only suffer a block at the very beginning of its execution. Once the process starts actually executing, all the resources it needs must be free; if they were not, then some process would have an equal or higher priority and the process's execution would be postponed.

The same process set used in earlier illustrations can now be executed under ICPP (see Figure 15).

Process a having locked Q at time 1, runs for the next 4 ticks with priority 4. Hence neither process b, process c nor process d can begin. Once a unlocks Q (and has its priority reduced), the other processes execute in priority order. Note that all blocking is before actual execution and that d's response time is now only 6. This is somewhat misleading, however, as the worst-case blocking time for the two protocols is the same (see Equation (9)).

Although the worst-case behaviour of the two ceiling schemes is identical (from a scheduling view point), there are some points of difference:

- ICCP is easier to implement than the original (OCPP) as blocking relationships need not be monitored.
- ICPP leads to less context switches as blocking is prior to first execution.
- ICPP requires more priority movements as this happens with all resource usages; OCPP changes priority only if an actual block has occurred.

Finally, note that Protocol ICPP is called Priority Protect Protocol in POSIX and Priority Ceiling Emulation in Real-Time Java.

Ceiling Protocols, Mutual Exclusion and Deadlock. Although the above algorithms for the two ceiling protocols were defined in terms of locks on resources, it must be

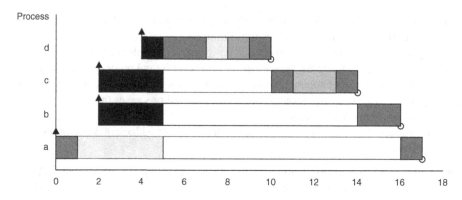

Fig. 15. Example of priority inheritance – ICPP

emphasized that the protocols themselves rather than some other synchronization primitive provided the mutual exclusion access to the resource (at least on a single processor system). Consider ICPP; if a process has access to some resource then it will be running with the ceiling value. No other process that uses that resource can have a higher priority, and hence the executing process will either execute unimpeded while using the resource, or, if it is preempted, the new process will not use this particular resource. Either way, mutual exclusion is ensured.

The other major property of the ceiling protocols (again for single-processor systems) is that they are deadlock-free. The ceiling protocols are a form of deadlock prevention. If a process holds one resource while claiming another, then the ceiling of the second resource cannot be lower than the ceiling of the first. Indeed, if two resources are used in different orders (by different processes) then their ceilings must be identical. As one process is not preempted by another with merely the same priority, it follows that once a process has gained access to a resource then all other resources will be free when needed. There is no possibility of circular waits and deadlock is prevented.

Ceiling Protocols and EDF. The approach outlined above for fixed priority systems can also be applied to EDF scheduling. Baker has derived these protocols [7,6], but they are beyond the scope of this paper.

4.16   Release Jitter

In the simple model, all processes are assumed to be periodic and to be released with perfect periodicity; that is, if process l has period T_l then it is released with exactly that frequency. Sporadic processes are incorporated into the model by assuming that their minimum inter-arrival interval is T. This is not, however, always a realistic assumption. Consider a sporadic process s being released by a periodic process l (on another processor). The period of the first process is T_l and the sporadic process will have the same rate, but it is incorrect to assume that the maximum load (interference) s exerts on low-priority processes can be represented in Equations (4) or (5) as a periodic process with period $T_s = T_l$.

To understand why this is insufficient, consider two consecutive executions of process l. Assume that the event that releases process s occurs at the very end of the periodic process's

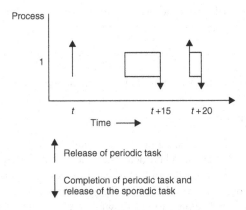

Release of periodic task

Completion of periodic task and
release of the sporadic task

Fig. 16. Releases of sporadic processes

execution. On the first execution of process l, assume that the process does not complete until its latest possible time, that is, R_l. However, on the next invocation assume there is no interference on process l so it completes within C_l. As this value could be arbitrarily small, let it equal zero. The two executions of the sporadic process are not separated by T_l but by $T_l - R_l$. Figure 16 illustrates this behaviour for T_l equal to 20, R_l equal to 15 and minimum C_l equal to 1 (that is, two releases of the sporadic process within 6 time units). Note that this phenomenon is of interest only if process l is remote. If this was not the case then the variations in the release of process s would be accounted for by the standard equations, where a critical instant can be assumed between the releaser and the released.

To capture correctly the interference sporadic processes have upon other processes, the recurrence relationship must be modified. The maximum variation in a process's release is termed its *jitter* (and is represented by J). For example, in the above, process s would have a jitter value of 15. In terms of its maximum impact on lower-priority processes, this sporadic process will be released at time 0, 5, 25, 45 and so on. That is, at times 0, $T - J$, $2T - J$, $3T - J$, and so on. Examination of the derivation of the schedulability equation implies that process i will suffer one interference from process s if R_i is between 0 and $T - J$, that is $R_i \in [0, T - J)$, two if $R_i \in [T - J, 2T - J)$, three if $R_i \in [2T - J, 3T - J)$ and so on. A slight rearrangement of these conditions shows a single hit if $R_i + J \in [0, T)$, a double hit if $R_i + J \in [T, 2T)$ and so on. This can be represented in the same form as the previous response time equations as follows [4]:

$$R_i = B_i + C_i + \sum_{j \in hp(i)} \left\lceil \frac{R_i + J_j}{T_j} \right\rceil C_j \qquad (10)$$

In general, periodic processes do not suffer release jitter. An implementation may, however, restrict the granularity of the system timer (which releases periodic processes). In this situation, a periodic process may also suffer release jitter. For example, a T value of 10 but a system granularity of 8 will imply a jitter value of 6 – at time 16 the periodic process will be released for its time '10' invocation. If response time (now denoted as

$R_i^{periodic}$) is to be measured relative to the real release time then the jitter value must be added to that previously calculated:

$$R_i^{periodic} \;=\; R_i + J_i \tag{11}$$

If this new value is greater than T_i then the following analysis must be used.

4.17   Arbitrary Deadlines

To cater for situations where D_i (and hence potentially R_i) can be greater than T_i, the analysis must again be adapted. When deadline is less than (or equal) to period, it is necessary to consider only a single release of each process. The critical instant, when all higher-priority processes are released at the same time, represents the maximum interference and hence the response time following a release at the critical instant must be the worst case. However, when deadline is greater than period, a number of releases must be considered. The following assumes that the release of a process will be delayed until any previous releases of the same process have completed.

If a process executes into the next period then both releases must be analyzed to see which gives rise to the longest response time. Moreover, if the second release is not completed before a third occurs than this new release must also be considered, and so on.

For each potentially overlapping release, a separate window $w(q)$ is defined, where q is just an integer identifying a particular window (that is, $q = 0, 1, 2, ...$). Equation (5) can be extended to have the following form (ignoring jitter) [50] :

$$w_i^{n+1}(q) \;=\; B_i + (q+1)C_i + \sum_{j \in hp(i)} \left\lceil \frac{w_i^n(q)}{T_j} \right\rceil C_j \tag{12}$$

For example, with q equal to 2, three releases of the process will occur in the window. For each value of q, a stable value of $w(q)$ can be found by iteration – as in Equation (5). The response time is then given as

$$R_i(q) \;=\; w_i^n(q) - qT_i \tag{13}$$

for example, with $q = 2$ the process started $2T_i$ into the window and hence the response time is the size of the window minus $2T_i$.

The number of releases that need to be considered is bounded by the lowest value of q for which the following relation is true:

$$R_i(q) \;\leq\; T_i \tag{14}$$

At this point, the process completes before the next release and hence subsequent windows do not overlap. The worst-case response time is then the maximum value found for each q:

$$R_i \;=\; max_{q=0,1,2,...} R_i(q) \tag{15}$$

Note that for $D \leq T$, the relation in Equation (14) is true for $q = 0$ (if the process can be guaranteed), in which case Equations (12) and (13) simplify back to the original equation. If any $R > D$, then the process is not schedulable.

When this arbitrary deadline formulation is combined with the effect of release jitter, two alterations to the above analysis must be made. First, as before, the interference factor must be increased if any higher priority processes suffers release jitter:

$$w_i^{n+1}(q) = B_i + (q+1)C_i + \sum_{j \in hp(i)} \left\lceil \frac{w_i^n(q) + J_j}{T_j} \right\rceil C_j \qquad (16)$$

The other change involves the process itself. If it can suffer release jitter then two consecutive windows could overlap if response time plus jitter is greater than period. To accommodate this, Equation (13) must be altered:

$$R_i(q) = w_i^n(q) - qT_i + J_i \qquad (17)$$

4.18 Fault Tolerance

Fault tolerance via either forward or backward error recovery always results in extra computation. This could be an exception handler or a recovery block. In a real-time fault tolerant system, deadlines should still be met even when a certain level of faults occur. This level of fault tolerance is know as the **fault model**. If C_i^f is the extra computation time that results from an error in process i, then the response time equation can easily be changed.

$$R_i = B_i + C_i + \sum_{j \in hp(i)} \left\lceil \frac{R_i}{T_j} \right\rceil C_j + max_{k \in hep(i)} \, C_k^f \qquad (18)$$

where $hep(i)$ is the set of processes with a priority equal or higher than i.

Here, the fault model defines a maximum of one fault and there is an assumption that a process will execute its recovery action at the same priority as its ordinary computation. Equation (18) is easily changed to increase the number of allowed faults (F):

$$R_i = B_i + C_i + \sum_{j \in hp(i)} \left\lceil \frac{R_i}{T_j} \right\rceil C_j + max_{k \in hep(i)} \, FC_k^f \qquad (19)$$

Indeed, a system can be analyzed for increasing values of F to see what number of faults (arriving in a burst) can be tolerated. Alternatively, the fault model may indicate a minimum arrival interval for faults, in this case the equation becomes:

$$R_i = B_i + C_i + \sum_{j \in hp(i)} \left\lceil \frac{R_i}{T_j} \right\rceil C_j + max_{k \in hep(i)} \left(\left\lceil \frac{R_i}{T_f} \right\rceil C_k^f \right) \qquad (20)$$

where T_f is the minimum inter-arrival time between faults.

In Equations (19) and (20), the assumption is made that in the worst case, the fault will always occur in the process that has the longest recovery time.

4.19 Priority Assignment

The formulation given for arbitrary deadlines has the property that no simple algorithms (such as rate or deadline monotonic) gives the optimal priority ordering. In this section, a theorem and algorithm for assigning priorities in arbitrary situations is given. The theorem considers the behaviour of the lowest priority process [5].

Theorem. *If process p is assigned the lowest priority and is feasible, then, if a feasible priority ordering exists for the complete process set, an ordering exists with process p assigned the lowest priority.*

The proof of this theorem comes from considering the schedulability equations – for example, Equation (12). If a process has the lowest priority, it suffers interference from all higher-priority processes. This interference is not dependent upon the actual ordering of these higher priorities. Hence if any process is schedulable at the bottom value it can be assigned that place, and all that is required is to assign the other $N - 1$ priorities. Fortunately, the theorem can be reapplied to the reduced process set. Hence through successive reapplication, a complete priority ordering is obtained (if one exists).

The following code in Ada implements the priority assignment algorithm; Set is an array of processes that is notionally ordered by priority; Set(N) being the highest priority, Set(1) being the lowest. The procedure Process_Test tests to see whether process K is feasible at that place in the array. The double loop works by first swapping processes into the lowest position until a feasible result is found, this process is then fixed at that position. The next priority position is then considered. If at any time the inner loop fails to find a feasible process, the whole procedure is abandoned. Note that a concise algorithm is possible if an extra swap is undertaken.

```ada
procedure Assign_Pri (Set : in out
Process_Set; N : Natural;
                      Ok : out Boolean) is
begin
  for K in 1..N loop
    for Next in K..N loop
      Swap(Set, K, Next);
      Process_Test(Set, K, Ok);
      exit when Ok;
    end loop;
    exit when not Ok;  -- failed to find a schedulable process
  end loop;
end Assign_Pri;
```

If the test of feasibility is exact (necessary and sufficient) then the priority ordering is optimal. Thus for arbitrary deadlines (without blocking), an optimal ordering is found.

4.20 Summary

There is an extensive literature on scheduling, with many techniques and theories developed and evaluated. In this section we have consider the main two approaches, fixed priority and EDF. But even for these topics we have not cover either is great detail. There is a solid body of knowledge available that allows these techniques to be used in industrial practice. For fixed priority scheduling the use of response time analysis has proved to be an effective framework for analysing a range of application characteristics and resource types. There is no single equation to apply in all circumstances, rather there is an analysis framework that allows tailored verification tools to be produced. In this section we have covered a few of the extensions that are available, many others are possible.

Scheduling and planning must take place is all time bands. For activities to make progress resources must be available and be used effectively. To guarantee that deadlines are met requires analysis that can predict the worst-case behaviour of concurrent activities on the available resources. This analysis is the topic of the final main section of the paper.

5   Timing Analysis

In all the scheduling approaches described above (that is, FPS and EDF), it is assumed that the worst-case resource usage of each activity is known. This is the maximum any activity invocation could require. In the following, we concentrate on the worst-case execution time of software activities implemented on standard CPUs.

Worst-case execution time estimation (represented by the symbol C in the scheduling analysis described earlier) can be obtained by either measurement or analysis. The problem with measurement is that it is difficult to be sure when the worst case has been observed. The drawback of analysis is that an effective model of the processor (including caches, pipelines, memory wait states and so on) must be available. The real worst-case execution of a code segment is in general not computable (it requires solving the halting problem!) but lies somewhere between the worst-case observed and the best safe estimate produced by analysis. Unfortunately the gap between these two bounds can be significant with sizeable software components running on modern hardware.

Most analysis techniques involve two distinct activities. The first takes the process and decomposes its code into a directed graph of basic blocks. These basic blocks represent straightline code. The second component of the analysis takes the machine code corresponding to a basic block and uses the processor model to estimate its worst-case execution time.

Once the times for all the basic blocks are known, the directed graph can be collapsed. For example, a simple choice construct between two basic blocks will be collapsed to a single value (that is, the largest of the two values for the alternative blocks). Loops are collapsed using knowledge about maximum bounds.

More sophisticated graph reduction techniques can be used if sufficient semantic information is available. To give just a simple example of this, consider the following code:

```
for I in 1.. 10 loop
  if Cond then
    -- basic block of cost 100
  else
```

```
        -- basic block of cost 10
    end if;
  end loop;
```

With no further information, the total 'cost' of this construct would be $10 \times 100 +$ the cost of the loop construct itself, giving a total of, say, 1005 time units. It may, however, be possible to deduce (via static analysis of the code) that the condition Cond can only be true on at most three occasions. Hence a less pessimistic cost value would be 375 time units.

Other relationships within the code may reduce the number of feasible paths by eliminating those that cannot possibly occur; for instance, when the 'if' branch in one conditional statement precludes a later 'else' branch. Techniques that undertake this sort of semantic or control flow analysis usually require annotations to be added to the code. The graph reduction process can then make use of tools such as ILP (integer linear programming) to produce a tight estimate of worst-case execution time. They can also advise on the input data needed to drive the program down the path that gives rise to this estimation. For complex nested loop structures abstract interpretation methods can be used. Here analysis is performed on the intermediate code level. Pattern-matching methods exploit the fact that most compilers use the same group of machine instructions to initialise, update and test loop counters [52].

Clearly, if a process is to be analyzed for its worst-case execution time, the code itself needs to be restricted. For example, all loops and recursion must be bounded, otherwise it would be impossible to predict offline when the code terminates. Furthermore, the code generated by the compiler must also be understandable and analyzable.

The biggest challenge facing worst-case execution time analysis comes from the use of modern processors with on-chip data and instruction caches, pipelines, branch predictors, speculative and out-of-order execution etc [53,41,3,30]. All of these features aim to reduce average execution time, but their impact on worst-case behaviour can be hard to predict. If one ignores these features the resulting estimates can be very pessimistic, but to include them is not always straightforward. One approach is to assume non-preemptive execution, and hence all the benefits from caching etc can be taken into account. At a later phase of the analysis, the number of actual preemptions is calculated and a penalty applied for the resulting cache misses and pipeline refills.

The interaction between hardware features can result in complex optimisation problems that are extremely difficult to solve. For example, with an 'if' statement one branch may result in a data cache miss, whilst the other branch may cause a instruction cache miss – which is the worst? This problem is exasperated if the cache misses are conditional on the path the process took through earlier 'if' statements.

Interactions can also cause what are called *timing anomalies*. There are contra-intuitive instances where a local optimisation leads to a global penalty. An example of this is described by Heckmann et al [31]. Here a single cache hit causes a branch prediction failure that results in a prefetch that clears an area of cache that is needed later. As a result, an initial cache miss will produce a shorter execution time, and hence the cache hit sequence must be used for worst-case estimation.

Overall, to model in detail the temporal behaviour of a modern processor is non-trivial and may indeed need proprietary information that can be hard to obtain. For real-time systems one is left with the choice of either using simpler (but less powerful) processor architectures or to put more effort into measurement. Given that all high-integrity real-time systems will be subject to considerable testing, an approach that combines testing and measurement for code units (basic blocks or basic paths) but control flow analysis for the process itself seems appropriate with today's technology. This is the so called hybrid approach which aims to combine the advantages of analysis and measurement. However it does require a certain amount of instrumentation of the target platform that may or may not be problematic. Nevertheless as Bernat states (as cited in [18]) "the best model of the processor is the processor itself".

Another difficulty with current timing analysis techniques and tools is that they do not scale. Constraint satisfaction tools such as ILP cannot deal with the ten of thousands of lines of code typically found in a single component of a modern system such as a military or civil aircraft control system. Indeed code segment with close to half a million statement are not unheard of in a number of application domains. This presents a real challenge to the techniques and methods that are advocated for timing analysis.

5.1 Summary

The final form of analysis that needs to be carried out on any real-time system is the determination of the worst-case execution times of the software components of the implementation. The process by which the C values needed for schedulability analysis are obtained can involve pure analysis, measurement, or a combination of the two.

Timing analysis has itself a broad body of literature that has identified many different approaches. Early work was undertaken by Puschner [45,46]. It is beyond the scope of this paper to give a comprehensive summary of the timing analysis literature, but it is a key stage in the engineering process advocated in this paper. A recent survey [52] covers most of the current literature and tools.

One area that is gaining attention due to the scale issues noted above is to moving timing analysis onto a probabilistic foundation [8,24,17]. Clearly a simplistic approach that assumes independence between features will not work, but there are methods published that show promise [9].

6 Conclusion

This paper has described an engineering process for the development and verification of real-time systems. The process is built upon a single model of behaviour but has a number of aspects and abstractions. Firstly a system is considered to consist of a number of time bands that represent dynamic behaviour at different granularities of time. Timing properties within a band are represented by delays and deadlines. The paper has explored the verification of these properties by model checking.

From a system defined in terms of delays and deadline an implementation over the available resources must be produced and again verified. Schedulability analysis is the term used for this verification stage, in this paper we have concentrated on fixed priority scheduling (and Earliest Deadline First to some extent) of the final implementation with verification via response time analysis supported by timing analysis.

For simple systems, with periodic tasks for example, confidence in the timing statements may be easy to obtain – although effective implementation may still be difficult to ensure. The use of timed automata models and model checking does enable a high level of confidence in the temporal characteristics of applications to be gained. Although we argue that the process developed here increases the confidence with which real-time systems can be developed, the approach is not completely formal.

Space considerations have limited the coverage of issues to do with the programming of systems designed according to the model of behaviour outlined in this paper and the programming languages suitable for this approach. These issues are however address in a recently published paper [13]. Taken together that constitute an effective means of delivering real-time behaviour.

References

1. Allen, J.: Towards a general theory of actions and time. Artificial Intelligence 23, 123–154 (1984)
2. Amin, M.: Toward self-healing infrastructure systems. Computer, 44–52 (August 2000)
3. Arnold, R., Mueller, F., Whalley, D.: Bounding worst-case instruction cache performance. In: Proceedings 15th IEEE Real Time Systems Symposium, pp. 172–181. IEEE Computer Society Press, Los Alamitos (1994)
4. Audsley, N.C., Burns, A., Richardson, M., Tindell, K., Wellings, A.J.: Applying new scheduling theory to static priority preemptive scheduling. Software Engineering Journal 8(5), 284–292 (1993)
5. Audsley, N.C., Tindell, K., Burns, A.: The end of the line for static cyclic scheduling? In: Proceedings of the Fifth Euromicro Workshop on Real-Time Systems, Oulu, Finland, pp. 36–41. IEEE Computer Society Press, Los Alamitos (1993)
6. Baker, T.P.: A stack-based resource allocation policy for realtime processes. In: Proceedings 11th IEEE Real-Time Systems Symposium, pp. 191–200. IEEE Computer Society Press, Los Alamitos (1990)
7. Baker, T.P.: Stack-based scheduling of realtime processes. Real-Time Systems 3(1) (March 1991)
8. Bernat, G., Colin, A., Petters, S.M.: WCET analysis of probabilistic hard real–time systems. In: Proceedings of the 23rd Real-Time Systems Symposium, pp. 279–288 (2002)
9. Bernat, G., Newby, M., Burns, A.: Probabilistic timing analysis, an approach using Copulas. Journal of Embbedded Computing 1(2), 179–194 (2005)
10. Burns, A., Baxter, G.D.: Time bands in systems structure. In: Structure for Dependability, pp. 74–90 (2006)
11. Burns, A., Hayes, I.J., Baxter, G., Fidge, C.J.: Modelling temporal behaviour in complex socio-technical systems. Computer Science Technical Report YCS 390, University of York (2005)
12. Burns, A., Lin, T.-M.: Adding temporal annotations and associated verification to Ravenscar profile. In: Rosen, J.-P., Strohmeier, A. (eds.) Ada-Europe 2003. LNCS, vol. 2655, pp. 80–91. Springer, Heidelberg (2003)
13. Burns, A., Lin, T.-M.: An engineering process for the verification of real-time systems. Formal Aspects of Computing 19, 111–136 (2007)
14. Burns, A., Wellings, A.J.: Real-Time Systems and Programming Languages, 3rd edn. Addison Wesley Longman, Redwood City, CA, USA (2001)
15. Buttazzo, G.C.: Hard Real-Time Computing Systems. Springer, Heidelberg (2005)

16. Ciapessoni, E., Corsetti, E., Montanari, A., San Pietro, P.: Embedding time granularity in a logical specification language for synchronous real-time systems. Science of Computer Programming 20, 141–171 (1993)
17. Colin, A., Petters, S.M.: Experimental evaluation of code properties for WCET analysis. In: Proceedings 24th IEEE Real-Time Systems Symposium, IEEE Computer Society Press, Los Alamitos (2003)
18. Colin, A., Petters, S.M.: Experimental evaluation of code properties for WCET analysis. In: Proceedings of the 24rd Real-Time Systems Symposium, pp. 190–199 (2003)
19. Conn, A.P.: Time affordances: the time factor in diagnostic usability heuristics. In: Proceedings of the SIGCHI conference on Human factors in computing systems, pp. 186–193 (1995)
20. Cornhill, D., Sha, L., Lehoczky, J.P., Rajkumar, R., Tokuda, H.: Limitations of Ada for real-time scheduling. In: Proceedings of the International Workshop on Real Time Ada Issues, ACM Ada Letters, pp. 33–39. ACM Press, New York (1987)
21. Corsetti, E., Montanari, A., Ratto, E.: Dealing with different time granularities in formal specifications of real-time systems. Journal of Real-Time Systems 3(2) (1991)
22. Davis, R., Burns, A.: Hierarchical fixed priority preemptive scheduling. In: IEEE Real-Time Systems Symposium, pp. 389–398. IEEE Computer Society Press, Los Alamitos (2005)
23. Davis, R.I., Wellings, A.J.: Dual priority scheduling. In: Proceedings 16th IEEE Real-Time Systems Symposium, pp. 100–109. IEEE Computer Society Press, Los Alamitos (1995)
24. Edgar, S., Burns, A.: Statistical analysis of WCET for scheduling. In: Proceedings 22nd IEEE Real-Time Systems Symposium, IEEE Computer Society Press, Los Alamitos (2001)
25. Fidge, C.J., Hayes, I.J., Watson, G.: The deadline command. IEEE Software — Special Issue on Real-Time Systems 146(2), 104–111 (1999)
26. Finnie, G.: SPARK - the SPADE Ada kernel, Ed 3.3. Technical report, Praxis Plc (1997)
27. Fraisse, P.: The psychology of time. Harper and Row, New York (1963)
28. Friedman, W.: About time: Inventing the fourth dimension. MIT Press, Cambridge, MA (1990)
29. Ghosal, A., Henzinger, T.A., Iercan, D., Kirsch, C.M., Sangiovanni-Vincentelli, A.: A hierarchical coordination language for interacting real-time tasks. In: EMSOFT. Proceedings of the 6th International Embedded Software Conference (2006)
30. Healy, C.A., Whalley, D.B.: Integrating the timing analysis of pipelining and instruction caching. In: Proceedings Real Time Systems Symposium, pp. 288–297 (1995)
31. Heckmann, R., Langenbach, M., Thesing, S., Wilhelm, R.: IEEE Proceedings on Real-Time Systems, vol. 91, pp. 1038–1054 (2003)
32. Hollnagel, E.: Human Reliability Analysis: Context and Control. Academic Press, London (1993)
33. Hutchesson, S.G., Hayes, N.: Technology transfer and certification issues in safety critical real-time systems. In: Digest of the IEE Colloquium on Real-Time Systems, vol. 98/306 (April 1998)
34. Jones, C.B.: Reasoning about interference in an object-based design method. In: Larsen, P.G., Woodcock, J.C.P. (eds.) FME 1993. LNCS, vol. 670, pp. 1–18. Springer, Heidelberg (1993)
35. Joseph, M., Pandya, P.: Finding response times in a real-time system. BCS Computer Journal 29(5), 390–395 (1986)
36. Lauer, H., Satterwaite, E.: The impact of Mesa on system design. In: Proceedings of the 4th International Conference on Software Engineering, pp. 174–182. IEEE, Los Alamitos (1979)
37. Lehoczky, J.P., Sha, L., Strosnider, J.K.: Enhanced aperiodic responsiveness in a hard real-time environment. In: Proceedings 8th IEEE Real-Time Systems Symposium, pp. 261–270. IEEE Computer Society Press, Los Alamitos (1987)
38. Leung, J.Y.T., Whitehead, J.: On the complexity of fixed-priority scheduling of periodic, real-time tasks. Performance Evaluation (Netherlands) 2(4), 237–250 (1982)

39. Levine, R.: A geography of time. Guilford Press, New York (1997)
40. Liu, C.L., Layland, J.W.: Scheduling algorithms for multiprogramming in a hard real-time environment. JACM 20(1), 46–61 (1973)
41. Liu, J.-C., Lee, H.-J.: Deterministic upperbounds of the worst-case execution times of caches programs. In: Proceedings Real Time Systems Symposium, pp. 182–191 (1994)
42. Liu, J.W.S.: Real-Time Systems. Prentice-Hall, Englewood Cliffs (2000)
43. Newell, A.: Unified theories of cognition. Harvard University Press, Cambridge, MA (1990)
44. Paul, J.M., Thomas, D.E., Cassidy, A.S.: High-level modeling and simulation of single-chip programmable heterogeneous multiprocessors. ACM Transactions on Design Automation of Electronic Systems 10(3), 431–461 (2005)
45. Puschner, P., Koza, C.: Calculating the maximum execution time of real-time programs. The Journal of Real-Time Systems 1, 159–176 (1989)
46. Puschner, P.P., Schedl, A.V.: Computing maximum task execution times - a graph-based approach. Real-Time Systems 13(1), 67–91 (1997)
47. Roeckelein, J.E.: The concept of time in psychology: A resource book and annotated bibliography. Greenwood Press, CT (2000)
48. Sha, L., Rajkumar, R., Lehoczky, J.P.: Priority inheritance protocols: An approach to real-time synchronisation. IEEE Transactions on Computers 39(9), 1175–1185 (1990)
49. Spuri, M.: Analysis of deadline scheduled real-time systems. Technical Report RR-2772, INRIA (1996)
50. Tindell, K., Burns, A., Wellings, A.J.: An extendible approach for analysing fixed priority hard real-time tasks. Real-Time Systems 6(2), 133–151 (1994)
51. Whysall, P.J.: Object Oriented Specification and Refinement. PhD thesis, Department of Computer Science, The University of York (1991)
52. Wilhelm, R., Engblom, J., Ermedahl, A., Holsti, N., Thesing, S., Whalley, D., Bernat, G., Ferdinand, C., Heckmann, R., Mitra, T., Mueller, F., Puant, I., Puschner, P., Staschulat, J., Stenstrom, P.: The worst case execution time problem - overview of methods and survey of tools. ACMTransactions on Embedded Systems (to appear)
53. Zhang, N., Burns, A., Nicholson, M.: Pipelined processors and worst case execution time. Real-Time Systems 5(4), 319–343 (1993)

Applicative Modelling with RAISE

Chris George

United Nations University International Institute for Software Technology
(UNU-IIST), PO Box 3058, Macao SAR, China
cwg@iist.unu.edu

Abstract. In this chapter we provide an introduction to the RAISE
Specification Language and to the RAISE method. We concentrate on
the applicative style of RAISE, the style most commonly used initially
in development.

We also describe two examples. The first is a simple communication
system that allows the transmission of messages with the possibility of
higher priority messages overtaking others. The example illustrates the
use of abstract initial specification to capture vital properties, and of
more detailed concrete specification to describe a model having those
properties. The second example is a control system of a lift, and illustrates the use of model checking to gain confidence in a RAISE model.

1   The RAISE Specification Language

RAISE (Rigorous Approach to Industrial Software Engineering) was originally
developed during 1985–90 by a European collaborative project in the ESPRIT-I
programme involving four companies, two in Denmark and two in the UK. A
second project, LaCoS (Large-scale Correct Systems using Formal Methods) was
a continuation ESPRIT-II project (1990–95) involving nine companies in seven
European countries. LaCoS further developed the RAISE technology, particularly the method and tools [1], and tested RAISE on a wide range of software
development projects [2].

The RAISE Specification Language (RSL) is a formal specification language,
i.e. a language with a formal, mathematical basis [3,4,5] intended to support
the precise definition of software requirements and reliable development from
such definitions to executable implementations. Particular aims of the language
were to support large, modular specifications, to provide a range of specification styles (axiomatic and model-based; applicative and imperative; sequential
and concurrent), and to support specifications ranging from abstract (close to
requirements) to concrete (close to implementations). Complete information can
be found in the books on RSL [6] and the method [5], and a number of case
studies in [7].

RSL is a modular language. Specifications are in general collections of (related)
modules. There are two kinds of modules: *schemes* and *objects*. Schemes are
(possibly parameterised) *class expressions*, and objects are instances of classes. We
return to schemes and objects later in Sections 1.8, 1.9, and 1.10. For now, if

C. George, Z. Liu, and J. Woodcock (Eds.): Domain Modeling, LNCS 4710, pp. 51–118, 2007.

you have an intuition about classes and objects in object-oriented programming languages, then this intuition largely carries over into RSL.

1.1   Basic Class Expressions

There are several ways of making class expressions, but the most common is the *basic class expression* that consists of the keywords **class** and **end** around some *declarations* of various kinds. Each declaration is a keyword followed by one or more *definitions* of the appropriate kind (Table 1).

Table 1. Declarations and their definitions

Declaration	Kind of definition
object	Embedded modules
type	Types
value	Values: constants and functions
variable	Variables for storing values
channel	Channels for input and output
axiom	Axioms: logical properties that must always hold
test_case	Test cases: expressions to be evaluated by a translator or interpreter
transition_system	Transition systems for a model checker
ltl_assertion	Temporal assertions to be checked by a model checker

No declarations are compulsory: many classes just contain type and value declarations. The order in the table is a common one to use, but any order is allowed, and there may be more than one occurrence of a kind of declaration.

The declarations **test_case**, **transition_system**, and **ltl_assertion** were added to RSL after the publication of the two books on RAISE [6,5]. They have no semantic significance, being added solely to provide extra inputs for tools.

1.2   Types

RSL, like most specification and also programming languages, is a *typed* language. That is, it must be possible to associate each occurrence of an identifier representing a value, variable or channel with a unique type, and to check that the occurrence of the identifier is consistent with a collection of typing rules. Such rules, such as that typically prohibiting expressions like "1 + **true**", are well known from programming languages and we will not describe them further here.

Built-in Types. In order to be able to define the types of values etc. we need a collection of types to use. RSL has seven built-in types (Table 2), and a number of ways of constructing other types from these.

Equality = and inequality ≠ are also defined for all types.

Table 2. Built-in types

Type	Example values	Operators
Bool	**true, false**	$\wedge, \vee, \Rightarrow \sim$
Int	..., -1, 0, 1, ...	$+, -, *, /, \backslash, \uparrow, <, \leq, >, \geq$, **abs, real**
Nat	0, 1, ...	Same as for **Int**
Real	..., -4.3, ..., 0.0, ...	$+, -, *, /, \uparrow, <, \leq, >, \geq$, **abs, int**
Char	$'a', \ldots$	
Text	$'''', "Alice", \ldots$	As for lists of **Char**
Unit	()	

Technically, the operators for **Bool** are properly referred to as *connectives*. They differ from operators in that a "lazy" or "conditional" evaluation is used for them: see Section 1.4. $\sim$ is negation. There is no need for $\Leftrightarrow$ as it would be the same as $=$.

Nat is a *subtype* of **Int**: all **Nat** values are also **Int** values. The operators are mostly conventional: / for **Int** is *integer division*, and $\backslash$ is *remainder*. $\uparrow$ for both **Int** and **Real** is exponentiation; **abs** for both **Int** and **Real** gives the absolute value. **Int** is not a subtype of **Real**: the operator **real** converts from **Int** to **Real**, and the operator **int** from **Real** to **Int**, truncating towards zero.

Unit is a type with just one value "()", also written as **skip**. It is used mainly in imperative and concurrent specifications to provide a parameter type for functions that do not need parameters, and to provide a return type for functions that do not return values.

The operators and other symbols used to construct value expressions (which we will see later in this chapter) are listed in Table 3. They are listed in increasing order of precedence (P), so the prefix operators bind most tightly. The column headed A indicates those that are associative, either right (R) or left (L).

Type Constructors. There are a number of type constructors for creating types from other types, illustrated in Table 4.

The column headed P indicates the binding precedence of the type constructors, where 1 is the highest. The column headed A indicates the constructors that are right (R) associative; the others do not associate. So, for example:

Int $\times$ **Real-set** $\rightarrow$ **Real*** $\rightarrow$ **Bool**
means
(**Int** $\times$ (**Real-set**)) $\rightarrow$ ((**Real***) $\rightarrow$ **Bool**)

The product constructor $\times$ is used to form tuples. These may be pairs, triples, etc. of any types. This constructor is not associative. For example, the products **Int** $\times$ **Text** $\times$ **Char** and **Int** $\times$ (**Text** $\times$ **Char**) are different types: the first is a triple, the second a pair containing a singleton and a pair.

-set, * and $\overrightarrow{m}$ create finite sets, list and maps respectively. There are also the potentially infinite set (**-infset**), infinite list ($^\omega$) and infinite map ($\overset{\sim}{\overrightarrow{m}}$) constructors, but they are rarely used.

Table 3. Value expression precedences

P	Symbols	A
14	λ ∀ ∃ ∃!	R
13	≡ **post**	
12	⊓ ⊓ ‖	R
11	;	R
10	:=	
9	⇒	R
8	∨	R
7	∧	R
6	= ≠ > < ≥ ≤ ⊂ ⊆ ⊃ ⊇ ∈ ∉	
5	+ − \ ^ ∪ †	L
4	* / ° ∩	L
3	↑	
2	:	
1	~ prefix operators	

Table 4. Type constructors

Ctr	P	A	Example expressions	Operators
×	2		(1,true,'a')	
-set	1		{}, {1,2}	hd, ∈, ∉, ∪, ∩, ⊂, ⊆, ⊃, ⊇, **card**, \
*	1		⟨⟩, ⟨1,2⟩	hd, tl, ∈, ∉, ^, **len, elems, inds**
⇝	3	R	[], ['a' ↦ **true**, 'b' ↦ **false**]	**dom, rng, hd**, ∈, ∉, ∪, †, \, /, °
→	3	R	λ x : **Int** • x + 1	°
⇝̃	3	R	λ (x,y) : **Int** × **Int** • x / y	°

card gives the number of elements in a (finite) set; **len** gives the length of a (finite) list. For example:

card {} = 0
len ⟨'a', 'b', 'a'⟩ = 3

The operator ^ is the concatenation operator for lists. For example:

⟨1, 2⟩ ^ ⟨2, 3⟩ = ⟨1, 2, 2, 3⟩

Maps are relations, or associations, between pairs of values. Values on the left the pairs forming the association are said to form the *domain*, and those on the right are said to form the *range*. Finite maps (⇝) are required to be one-one or many-one, not one-many or many-many. In other words, a value in the domain must not be associated with more than one value in the range. For example, the type **Int** $\xrightarrow{\vec{m}}$ **Int** contains the value $[1 \mapsto 2, 2 \mapsto 4]$ but not the value $[1 \mapsto 2, 1 \mapsto 4]$. The **dom** operator returns the domain (a set) and **rng** returns the range (also a set). For example:

dom $[\,] = \{\}$
dom $[\,'a' \mapsto$ **true**, $'b' \mapsto$ **true**$] = \{'a', 'b'\}$
rng $[\,'a' \mapsto$ **true**, $'b' \mapsto$ **true**$] = \{$**true**$\}$

The union ($\cup$) of two maps is formed as if the maps were two sets of pairs and the union of the two sets were the result. But it only gives a finite, many-one map if the domains are disjoint: see below. The override operator $\dagger$ forms a map by taking the union of the two domains, and associating each domain value with the appropriate range value from the second map, if any, otherwise that from the first map. So the second takes precedence over, or "overrides", the first. For example:

$[\,'a' \mapsto$ **true**, $'b' \mapsto$ **true**$] \cup [\,'a' \mapsto$ **false**, $'c' \mapsto$ **false**$] =$
  $[\,'a' \mapsto$ **true**, $'a' \mapsto$ **false**, $'b' \mapsto$ **true**, $'c' \mapsto$ **false**$]$
$[\,'a' \mapsto$ **true**, $'b' \mapsto$ **true**$] \dagger [\,'a' \mapsto$ **false**, $'c' \mapsto$ **false**$] =$
  $[\,'a' \mapsto$ **false**, $'b' \mapsto$ **true**, $'c' \mapsto$ **false**$]$

We see that the union of two deterministic maps can be non-deterministic (and hence in the type of possibly infinite maps constructed by $\xrightarrow{\sim}{\vec{m}}$), unless their domains are disjoint, while override preserves determinacy. So it is good practice either to never use union, or to only use it when the domains are disjoint.

There are two ways of reducing, or restricting a map. \ (the operator also used for set difference) subtracts a set of elements from the domain. / restricts the domain to values in its second argument. For example:

$[\,1 \mapsto$ **true**, $2 \mapsto$ **false**$] \setminus \{2,3\} = [\,1 \mapsto$ **true**$]$
$[\,1 \mapsto$ **true**, $2 \mapsto$ **false**$] / \{2,3\} = [\,2 \mapsto$ **false**$]$

$\rightarrow$ is the constructor for forming *total* functions. A total function is one that always returns a value when it is applied and always returns the same value for the same argument. If a function returns some value, we say it *terminates*, and if a function always returns the same value for the same argument we say it is *deterministic*. So a total function is one that terminates and is deterministic for all arguments. Consider tossing coins on a low-gravity planet as a function, with the coin as an argument. It is non-deterministic, because each coin sometimes lands one way up, sometimes the other. If gravity is so low that very light coins are tossed into orbit, then the function does not terminate for some arguments, as we wait for ever for the coin to land. A function that is not known to be total for all arguments is called *partial*, and $\xrightarrow{\sim}$ is the constructor for partial functions.

We can define functions using "lambda-expressions" as shown in Table 4, though these are not often used. The first, total function is the "add one" function for integers. The second, partial function, is the integer division function. This is partial because it is not defined for division by zero.

The operator **hd** applied to a non-empty set returns an arbitrary value from the set. For a non-empty list, **hd** returns the first element. For a non-empty map, **hd** returns an arbitrary element from the domain of the map. **hd** is not defined when its argument is empty, so it is a partial operator. The definition of **hd** for sets and maps was added to RSL after the publication of the two books on RAISE [6,5].

For non-empty lists, **tl** returns the list obtained by removing the first element. Note that **hd** returns an element, **tl** a list. For example:

$$\textbf{hd } \langle 1,\, 2 \rangle = 1$$
$$\textbf{tl } \langle 1,\, 2 \rangle = \langle 2 \rangle$$

$\in$ and $\notin$ for sets are conventional. For a list they refer to the element set; for a map they refer to the domain. For example:

$$(1 \in \{\}) = \textbf{false}$$
$$(1 \in \langle 0,\, 2 \rangle) = \textbf{false}$$
$$(1 \notin [\, 1 \mapsto \text{'a'},\, 2 \mapsto \text{'b'} \,]) = \textbf{false}$$

The definition of $\in$ and $\notin$ for lists and maps was added to RSL after the publication of the two books on RAISE [6,5].

Lists and maps may be applied like functions. For lists, the argument is an integer in the range one to the length of the list inclusive. So an empty list cannot be applied, a list of length one can be applied only to one, a list of length two to one or two, etc. When the argument can be applied, the result is the corresponding element of the list. For example:

$$\langle \text{'a'},\, \text{'b'} \rangle (1) = \text{'a'}$$

The **elems** of a list is the set of elements of it, and the **inds** (the indexes) of a list is the set of possible integer arguments that it can be applied to. For example:

$$\textbf{elems } \langle \text{'a'},\, \text{'a'} \rangle = \{ \text{'a'} \}$$
$$\textbf{inds } \langle \text{'a'},\, \text{'a'} \rangle = \{ 1,\, 2 \}$$

For maps, the possible arguments that it can be applied to are the values in the domain, and the result is the corresponding value in the range. Since we insist that finite maps are many-one, finite map application to values in the domain is deterministic.

The operator $\circ$ is available for maps and functions, with the basic property that, for two maps or two functions f and g:

$$(f \circ g)(x) = f(g(x))$$

Type Expressions. Type expressions are defined as one of the following:

− a built-in type
− a user-defined type
− a type formed from type expression(s) using a type constructor
− a *subtype* of another type expression

Subtypes are types that contain only some of the values of another type, the ones that satisfy a predicate. For example, the type **Nat** is defined as the subtype

$$\{| \; i : \textbf{Int} \bullet i \geq 0 \; |\}$$

That is, it is a subtype of **Int**, and is the type containing those integers that are at least zero.

Subtypes are commonly defined using functions, which makes them easier to read. For example, suppose we wanted to define dates as triples of the form (day, month, year), then we might use the subtype

$$\{| \; (d, m, y) : \textbf{Nat} \times \textbf{Nat} \times \textbf{Nat} \bullet \text{is\_date}(d, m, y) \; |\}$$

where the predicate (Boolean function) *is_date* is defined elsewhere, to constrain m to the range one to twelve, and to constrain d according to m and whether y is a leap year.

Type Definitions. Users can define their own types, and there are two kinds of type definitions. *Abbreviation* definitions just define identifiers that one can use instead of the defining expression. For example, here is a type declaration containing two type abbreviation definitions:

type
    Date_base = **Nat** × **Nat** × **Nat**,
    Date = $\{| \; (d, m, y) : \text{Date\_base} \bullet \text{is\_date}(d, m, y) \; |\}$

Type abbreviation definitions take the form "identifier = type expression" and, like all kinds of definitions, are separated by commas.

The second kind of type definition introduces an identifier for a new type. This kind comes in four forms:

− abstract types, or *sorts*
− record types
− variant types
− union types

Abstract Types. These are just type identifiers. An abstract type is a type we need but whose definition we haven't decided on yet. They are commonly used for two purposes:

– There are many simple types, like identifiers for people, bank accounts, books in a library, departments of an organisation, etc., that we expect to implement very easily in the final program, perhaps as numbers, or characters, or strings. All we need is to use = to compare them, and = is defined for all types, even abstract ones. There is a standard piece of advice in specification that you don't choose a design until you have to, so we typically leave such types abstract. We may later discover during design that it is useful to distinguish between identifiers for reference books and those for books that may be borrowed, and we can then design a type with a suitable structure. An added bonus is that different abstract types are regarded as different by the type checker, so we avoid the danger of using a person's identifier for a book: the type checker will report an error.

– Sometimes we want to delay the design of a type not because it is simple, but for the opposite reason: because it is complicated and we don't yet know what the design should be. There is more on this when we discuss the RAISE method, especially in Section 1.8.

Records. Records in RSL are very much like those common in programming languages. Here is an example that might be found in a system for a bookshop:

type
    Book ::
        title : **Text**
        author : **Text**
        price : **Real** ↔ new_price

This defines a new type *Book* as a record with three components. Each component has an identifier, called a *destructor*, and a type expression. Optionally a record component can have a *reconstructor*. In our example the third component has a reconstructor *new_price*.

A record type definition also provides, implicitly, a *constructor* function for creating a record value from its component values. The identifier of the constructor is formed by putting *mk_* on the front of the identifier of the type, so in our case we have a constructor *mk_Book* of type

Text × **Text** × **Real** → Book

and we can write, say, *mk_Book*("Oliver Twist", "Charles Dickens", 9.95) as a book value. We will call this value *ot_book*.

Destructors are total functions from the record type to their component's type expression. For example, the type of *price* is

Book → **Real**

So we can apply *price* to a value of type *Book* to get its price. So we can write, for example, *price(ot_book)*, and it would evaluate to 9.95. Note we do *not* write *ot_book.price* as would be found in some languages.

Reconstructors are total functions that take their component's type expression and a record to generate a new record. The type of *new_price* is

Real × Book → Book

When we write, say, *new_price(17.95, ot_book)* we get a new book value with the same title and author as *ot_book*, but with the price component set to 17.95. We could also write this as *mk_Book*("Oliver Twist", "Charles Dickens", 17.95).

Variants. Variant types allow us to define types with a choice of values, perhaps with different structures. The simplest case is rather like the enumeration type found in some programming languages, such as:

type
    Colour == red | green | yellow

This defines a new type called *Colour* and three (different) constants (*red*, *green*, and *yellow*) of type *Colour*.

But variant types allow richer structures. For example, the following type defines binary trees holding values of some type *Val*:

type
    Tree == nil | node(left : Tree, val : Val, right : Tree)

This defines a new type *Tree*, a constant *nil* of type *Tree*, a constructor *node* of type

Tree × Val × Tree → Tree

and destructors *left*, *val* and *right*. The type of left, for example, is

Tree $\xrightarrow{\sim}$ Tree

The destructors are partial because they are not defined for *nil* trees.

Records are in fact special cases of variants: single ones. We could have defined the same type *Book* that we used as an example of a record:

type
    Book == mk_Book(title : **Text**, author : **Text**, price : **Real** ↔ new_price)

This illustrates the fact that variants, like records, can optionally include reconstructors.

The type *Tree* is recursive: trees are defined in terms of trees. Variants are the only type definitions that allow recursion.

Unions. Union type definitions allow us to make new types like variants out of existing types. Suppose types *B* and *C* are defined somewhere. Then we can define a type *A* as their union:

type
  A = B | C

This is in fact a shorthand for a variant, in which the identifier A, and the type names B, and C are used to generate constructor and destructor identifiers:

type
  A == A_from_B(A_to_B : B) | A_from_C(A_to_C : C)

In order for these constructor and destructor identifiers to be generated, the constituents of a union must be names of user-defined types, and not general type expressions.

With union types, implicit (unwritten) *coercions* are allowed from union components to the union type. Suppose, for example, a function f has A as its parameter type. Then we can apply f to a value c of type C, simply by writing $f(c)$. This is short for *f(A_from_C(c))*. We could similarly apply f to values from B.

1.3   Values

Having introduced types, we can consider the values that populate the types. We first see how to define values. We define values within value declarations, where a value declaration consists of the keyword **value** followed by one or more value definitions separated by commas.

The simplest value definition takes the form "identifier : type expression", and is called a *typing*, for example:

value
  x : **Int**

This may look like a variable declaration in a language like C (though the order of identifier and type is reversed in C) but it is really a constant declaration. x is the identifier of a value, not of a variable: a variable is a location where values can be stored, and the stored value can be changed. There is a possible confusion between the way programmers use the term variable (which is the way we use it) and the way a mathematician uses the term. The mathematician means by a variable something whose value is not known, or does not matter, not something whose value may change. The constant x defined above is more like a variable in the mathematical sense: it is a constant but we don't know, without more information, what its value is. Such constants are not allowed in programming languages, because there is not enough information about them. They are useful in specification when, for example, we want to describe a lift (elevator) system without saying how many floors the building has: the lift system can be described for an arbitrary building.

Continuing with the same example, we might want to assume that the number of floors is at least two. It is hard to imagine what a lift would do in a one storey building, or what a building with zero or a negative number of floors would look like. So we might use an *implicit value definition*:

value
> floors : **Int** • floors $\geq$ 2

(The type **Int** here could be replaced by **Nat** without changing the meaning.) *floors* is a constant, but it must satisfy the *predicate* (logical expression) that follows the bullet •. The definition is implicit in that we still don't know what the actual value of *floors* is.

Sometimes we know the value of a constant: the constant identifier is just a convenient shorthand (and, as in a program, makes things easier to maintain). We can use an *explicit value definition*:

value
> floors : **Int** = 20

All three forms of value definition start with a typing, an identifier and a type separated by a colon. The same applies if we want to define functions. First, a function definition may just be a typing, as in:

value
> name : Person $\rightarrow$ **Text**

This definition says that there is a total function from the type *Person* to the type **Text**, i.e. "every person has name". It is used typically when we haven't yet decided how to represent a person, i.e. *Person* is still an abstract type. Implicitly, it says there must be enough information in the type *Person* for a name to be extracted.

We can also define functions implicitly, with a *postcondition*:

value
> square_root : **Real** $\xrightarrow{\sim}$ **Real**
> square_root(x) **as** r **post** r $\geq$ 0.0 $\wedge$ r$*$r = x
> **pre** x $\geq$ 0.0

This defines a function to produce square roots, but without specifying how they should be calculated. It requires that the result r should satisfy the predicate following **post**: it should not be negative and its square must equal the parameter x. Since **Real** numbers only have **Real** square roots when they are not negative, it is a partial function and we give it a *precondition*.

This function illustrates the fact that the type **Real** in RSL contains the mathematical real numbers. This function is in practice not *implementable* in a programming language using limited precision arithmetic, and we might prefer a specification requiring the result r to be within some machine-dependent tolerance of the mathematical square root.

The types **Int** and **Nat** are similarly not implementable in normal computer arithmetic, because their values are unbounded. In practice this is usually not a problem because we can be sure that the values used or generated will not be so large as to cause over- or underflow. If it is a problem we would have to write a specification of how arithmetic in the actual implementation behaves.

The final kind of value definition is the *explicit function definition*. Here is an example:

value
  factorial : **Int** $\xrightarrow{\sim}$ **Int**
  factorial(n) $\equiv$ **if** n = 1 **then** 1 **else** n $*$ factorial(n−1) **end**
  pre n > 0

We need a precondition here since our version of *factorial* is non-terminating for 0 or negative numbers. The definition of *factorial* illustrates a *recursive* function, one that is defined in terms of itself. It also illustrates the **if** expression in RSL.

Overloading and Distinguishable Types. Value identifiers in definitions may be *overloaded*, i.e. the same identifier may be used to define different values, provided their types are *distinguishable* by the type checker. Types are distinguishable unless they are subtypes of the same type. For example, **Nat** is not distinguishable from **Int** (or any subtype of **Int**) because they are both subtypes of **Int**. (Any type is a subtype of itself.) Similarly $\rightarrow$ is not distinguishable from $\xrightarrow{\sim}$, nor $\xrightarrow{}{m}$ from $\xrightarrow{\sim}{m}$, nor **-set** from **-infset**, nor $*$ from $^{\omega}$. **Int** and **Real** are distinguishable.

Built-in operators may be overloaded. For example, we might define a new version of "+" as follows:

value
  + : **Real** $\times$ **Int** $\rightarrow$ **Real**
  x + y $\equiv$ x + **real** y

This is possible as the type of "+" is distinguishable from both possible types of the built-in infix operator "+", which are

Int $\times$ **Int** $\rightarrow$ **Int**
Real $\times$ **Real** $\rightarrow$ **Real**

1.4 Logic

We have seen several examples of predicates, expressions that (we hope) evaluate to **true** or **false**. But we have to clarify several issues in order to define our *logic*. In particular, we will need to define:

  − what happens when expressions do not terminate, and
  − what we mean by equality.

We know it is (unfortunately) easy enough to write programs that do not terminate. The problem is present in specification as well, but we need to be very clear about what it means. We could, for example, have written a poor definition of factorial, forgetting the precondition:

value

   poor_factorial : **Int** $\rightarrow$ **Int**

   poor_factorial(i) $\equiv$ **if** i $=$ 1 **then** 1 **else** i $*$ factorial(i$-$1) **end**

and then ask what the expression *poor_factorial(0)* means. The technical answer is **chaos**, a special expression in RSL that represents an expression whose evaluation does not terminate. We need to distinguish in general between *expressions* and *values*. Constants like **true** and 0 are expressions that evaluate to themselves. "1 $+$ 1" is an expression that evaluates to the value 2. **chaos** is an expression that does not evaluate: it does not terminate. So what about an expression like "**chaos** $+$ 1"? The general rule in RSL is "left-to-right" evaluation, which means in this case we evaluate the left argument of $+$, and if this terminates with a value, we evaluate the right argument. If this also terminates with a value, we add the two values to get the value of the whole expression. If either argument does not terminate, neither does the whole expression. So "**chaos** $+$ 1" is equivalent to **chaos**. So is "0 $*$ **chaos**" that arises when we evaluate *poor_factorial(0)*, that you might have thought should be 0. All infix operators are evaluated the same way.

   Equality, $=$, is an infix operator. So if we try to express the equivalence between "0 $*$ **chaos**" and **chaos** we should not write

$$(0 * \textbf{chaos}) = \textbf{chaos}$$

because this expression would evaluate to **chaos**, not to **true**. We write instead

$$(0 * \textbf{chaos}) \equiv \textbf{chaos}$$

where the symbol $\equiv$ is read as "is equivalent to". Technically, two expressions are equivalent when their semantics, their meanings, are equivalent. For values, and more generally for any expressions that are deterministic, terminating, and read-only (do not write to variables or do input or output on channels) equivalence and equality are the same.

   We use the equivalence symbol in explicit function definitions, and we can now explain what a function definition means, namely "when the precondition is true, the function application is equivalent to the defining expression". This definition does not say anything about the situation when the precondition is not true. So, for example, we cannot say what *factorial(0)* is. The definition tells us nothing: it may be **chaos**, or it may be some integer. We say it is *underspecified*. This does not make it a bad specification. Rather, it tells us to be careful only to use *factorial* when we are sure the argument is positive. We will see later in Section 2.7 that there is a tool, called the confidence condition generator, to help us check this.

   It seems sensible to be able to assert as true that

$$n > 1 \Rightarrow (factorial(n) = n * factorial(n-1))$$

for any integer n. This should be true for 0, so we want

$0 > 1 \Rightarrow (\text{factorial}(0) = 0 * \text{factorial}(0-1))$

to be true. That is, we want

false ⇒ chaos

to be true. This means that ⇒ should not behave like an infix operator, and in RSL it does not. We call the symbols ⇒, ∧, ∨ and ~ *connectives* and define them according to the rules, for any expressions e_1, $e2$, e:

e1 ⇒ e2 ≡ **if** e1 **then** e2 **else true end**
e1 ∧ e2 ≡ **if** e1 **then** e2 **else false end**
e1 ∨ e2 ≡ **if** e1 **then true else** e2 **end**
~e ≡ **if** e **then false else true end**

To understand these, we need the evaluation rule for **if** expressions. This is:

1. Evaluate the expression following **if**.
2. If this does not terminate, the **if** expression does not terminate.
3. If it evaluates to true, evaluate the expression following **then**.
4. If it evaluates to false, evaluate the expression following **else**.

You can check that the definitions of the connectives and the evaluation rules for **if** expressions give the same results as "classical" logic, which is only concerned with the values **true** and **false**. For example:

false ⇒ false
   ≡ **if false then false else true end**   definition of ⇒
   ≡ **true**   evaluation rule for **if** expression

But now we also know what will happen when some expressions do not terminate. For example, the following all evaluate to true:

false ⇒ chaos
~(false ∧ chaos)
true ∨ chaos

The reason for including **chaos** in RSL is not that it is needed in specifications: you normally do not want your programs to loop forever! It is a useful convenience in expressing the proof theory of RSL, which is what we mean by the logic. (And even if **chaos** were not included, you could write a variety of equivalent expressions, such as "**while true do skip end**".)

The logic in RSL is called a *conditional* logic as it is based on conditionals (if expressions). There are other approaches to the problems of non-terminating expressions, such as the "logic of partial functions" (LPF) [8,9] which is used by the specification language VDM [10]. Without going into the argument as to which is better, we note two things:

— ∨ and ∧ in RSL are only commutative if their arguments terminate. For example:

(**true** ∨ **chaos**) ≡ **true**
(**chaos** ∨ **true**) ≡ **chaos**

— The connectives in RSL are implementable, because they can be translated using if expressions in programming languages, which evaluate just like RSL if expressions.

For LPF the opposite holds: ∨ and ∧ are always commutative, but the connectives are in general only implementable when their arguments terminate.

Quantifiers. RSL includes the *quantifiers* ∀ (for all), ∃ (there exists) and ∃! (there exists exactly one). For example, the following are all true expressions:

∀ i : **Int** • (i ∗ 2) / 2 = i
∀ i : **Nat** • ∃ j : **Nat** • j = i + 1
∃! i : **Int** • i ≤ 0 ∧ i ≥ 0

The quantification is over *values* in the type. It does not include expressions like 1/0 or **chaos**.

Typings. What follows the quantifier is always a typing, just like the start of every kind of value definition. But we can have more general forms of typing than just an "identifier : type expression": the identifier can be a *binding*.

Bindings. A binding is commonly just an identifier, but it can be parentheses enclosing two or more bindings separated by commas. So the following are all bindings:

x
(x,y)
(x,(y,z))

The identifiers in a binding must all be different.

In a typing, the structure of a binding must match the structure of the type: if the binding is for a product, so must the type be. For example, if *Pair* is defined as an abbreviation for **Int** × **Int**, the possible typings include the following:

x : Pair
(x,y) : Pair
((p,q),(x,y)) : Pair × Pair

but "(x,y) : **Int**", for example, is not possible.

Bindings also occur as the *formal parameters* of implicit and explicit function definitions (like the n in factorial(n) ≡ ...). What about a function f with type

A × B → ...

Does this have two parameters or one? In RSL you can take either view: the formal application can be written f(a,b) or f((a,b)), or even f(p) (where p is a binding for a pair).

1.5   Value Expressions

We have already seen the literals, infix and prefix operators for various types in Section 1.2, the Boolean connectives, if expressions and quantified expressions in Section 1.4. There are some other value expressions that we describe in this section.

Set Expressions. Sets may be formed in three ways:

1. *enumerated* sets like {} (the empty set), or {1,3,2}.
2. *ranged* sets (for integers only) like {1..3}, which is equal to the second enumerated set example. If the second number in the range is less than the first, the ranged set is empty.
3. *comprehended* sets like { i/2 | i : **Int** • i ∈ {2..7} }, which is again equal to the second enumerated set example. The predicate following • (called a *restriction*) may be omitted, in which case it is as if it were **true**.

Other expressions may of course also represent sets. For example, a function may return a set and then an application of the function will be a set expression, an expression whose type is *T*-**set** for some type *T*. Similar remarks apply for lists and maps.

List Expressions. Lists may be formed in three ways:

1. *enumerated* lists like ⟨⟩ (the empty list), or ⟨2,1,2,3⟩.
2. *ranged lists* (for integers only) like ⟨1..3⟩, which is equal to the tail of the second enumerated list example. If the second number in the range is less than the first, the ranged list is empty.
3. *comprehended* lists like ⟨ i/2 | i in ⟨2..10⟩ • i < 8 ⟩ which is again equal to the tail of the second enumerated list example. As with enumerated sets, the restriction may be omitted. A comprehended list takes its elements from another list expression, rather than a typing as with a set, and, see below, a map.

Map Expressions. Maps may be formed in two ways:

1. *enumerated* maps like [ ] (the empty map), or [1 ↦ **true**, 3 ↦ **true**, 2 ↦ **false**].
2. *comprehended* maps like [i ↦ is_odd(i) | i : **Int** • i > 0 ∧ i < 4], which is again equal to the second enumerated map example (assuming an appropriate definition of *is_odd*). The restriction may be omitted, in which case it is as if it were **true**.

Let Expressions. Let expressions are used in two main ways:

1. to destruct a product. For example:

   let (x,y) = (1,2) **in** x + y **end**

will evaluate to 3. First we evaluate the expression following the =. Then we bind x to the first part, and y to the second. Finally we evaluate the expression following the **in**.

2. to organise an evaluation into several steps. For example, a function to sum a list of integers might be defined as:

value
    sum : **Int*** → **Int**
    sum(s) ≡
      if s = $\langle\rangle$ **then** 0
      else
        let h = **hd** s, t = **tl** s, x = sum(t) **in** h + x **end**
      end

This is particularly useful when the sub-expression like **hd** s would, without the **let**, occur more than once. But even when this would not occur, **let** expressions often improve readability.

Case Expressions. Case expressions are commonly used to express functions over lists and over variant structures. For example, the *sum* function could be written:

value
  sum : **Int*** → **Int**
  sum(s) ≡
    case s **of**
      $\langle\rangle$ → 0,
      $\langle h\rangle\hat{\ }t$ → h + sum(t)
    end

A **case** expression consists of a series of *patterns* plus associated expressions. The case patterns are tried in order, the first pattern that matches is taken, and the associated expression evaluated. The pattern $\langle\rangle$ matches the empty list. The pattern $\langle h\rangle\hat{\ }t$ matches a non-empty list, and at the same time binds h to the head and t to the tail.

An example of a **case** expression for a variant type is the body of a function to calculate the depth-first traversal of a tree (Section 1.2), returning a list of the values in the nodes of the tree:

value
  traverse : Tree → Val*
  traverse(t) ≡
    case t **of**
      nil → $\langle\rangle$,
      node(l, v, r) → traverse(l) $\hat{\ }$ $\langle v\rangle$ $\hat{\ }$ traverse(r)
    end

The bindings in patterns may be replaced by "wildcards", underscores, when their values are not needed. For example, a function to calculate the depth of a tree (assuming *max* is defined somewhere):

value
  depth : Tree → Val*
  depth(t) ≡
    case t **of**
      nil → 0,
      node(l, _, r) → 1 + max(depth(l), depth(r))
    end

The most commonly used case patterns are for lists and variants, but literals are also possible, and there is a "wildcard" pattern _ that matches anything. For example, a strange definition of *is_odd*:

value
  is_odd : **Nat** → **Bool**
  is_odd(n) ≡
    case n **of**
      0 → **false**,
      1 → **true**,
      _ → is_odd(n−2)
    end

1.6   Axioms

So far we have seen type and value declarations. There are also axiom declarations, introduced by the keyword **axiom** and consisting of axiom definitions separated by commas. Each axiom definition is a predicate, optionally preceded by an identifier in square brackets. For example, instead of defining:

value
  floors : **Int** • floors ≥ 2

we could write:

value
  floors : **Int**
axiom
  [floors_constraint] floors ≥ 2

In fact all value definitions, functions as well as constants, can be written in this style, a typing plus an axiom. There are "axiomatic" or "algebraic" specification languages, like Larch [11] and CASL [12], that use only this style, and are also restricted to abstract types. This style can be used within RAISE, but we choose also to have available the pre-defined sets, lists, maps, and products that are characteristic of the "model-based" specification languages like Z [13], B [14], and VDM [10].

1.7   Test Cases

Test cases have no semantic meaning: they are like comments directed at an interpreter or translator meaning "please provide code to evaluate these expressions and report the results".

The syntax of test cases is much like axioms, except that the test case expressions can be of any type. For example, if we wanted to test the function to sum a list of integers we might define

test_case
  [sum0] sum($\langle\rangle$),
  [sum1] sum($\langle$1,2,2,3$\rangle$)

and expect to see the results

```
[sum0]  0
[sum1]  8
```

But a perhaps more useful style of test case is to include the expected result in the test case, i.e. to write

test_case
  [sum0] sum($\langle\rangle$) = 0,
  [sum1] sum($\langle$1,2,2,3$\rangle$) = 8

so that the output for every test case should be **true**.

Test cases were added to RSL after the publication of the two books on RAISE [6,5].

Transition Systems and LTL Assertions. These are discussed in Section 5.

1.8   Modules

As we mentioned earlier, there are two kinds of module in RSL, schemes and objects. Schemes are essentially classes, and objects are instances of classes, so the basic thing is the class expression. These come in six forms: basic, extending, renaming, hiding, with, and instantiation.

Basic Class Expressions. These were introduced in Section 1.1. They consist of the keywords **class** and **end** with any number of declarations between them. The declarations (and their constituent definitions) may come in any order. There is no "define before use" rule in RSL. All the entities defined in the class expression are exported (visible outside it) by default: there is nothing like an "export" clause in RSL.

Extending Class Expressions. If C_1 and $C2$ are class expressions:

extend C1 **with** C2

is an extending class expression. The declarations of $C2$ are added to those of C_1. The declarations of $C2$ can refer to entities defined in C_1, but not vice versa. The declarations of C_1 and $C2$ must be *compatible*, which simply means that duplicate definitions are not allowed, any more than they would be in a single class expression.

Renaming Class Expressions. If C is a class expression:

use id_1' **for** id1, ..., id_n' **for** id_n **in** C $(n \geq 1)$

is a renaming class expression in which the entities id_1, ..., id_n are exported with identifiers id_1', ..., id_n': they are renamed. The entities may be types, values, variables, channels or objects.

Hiding Class Expressions. If C is a class expression:

hide id1, ..., id_n **in** C $(n \geq 1)$

is a hiding class expression from which the identifiers id_1, ..., id_n are not exported. Hiding is most commonly used to hide objects, variables, channels and *auxiliary* functions (functions only intended for use within the original class to define other functions). Hiding is used to prevent access from outside the class, and also used to hide auxiliary functions or other entities that we don't expect to use in later developments, because hidden entities do not need to be implemented.

With Class Expressions. If C is a class expression:

with O1, ..., O_n **in** C $(n \geq 1)$

is a with class expression. O_1, ..., O_n are object expressions (see Section 1.10). The meaning of **with** X **in** C is that an applied occurrence of a name N in C can mean either N or $X.N$, so that, in particular, we can write just N instead of $X.N$. (It is similar to "using namespace" in C++.)

The with class expression was added to RSL after the publication of the two books on RAISE [6,5].

Scheme Instantiations. If we define a scheme called S, say:

scheme S = C

then we can use S to mean the class expression C, for example in "**extend** S **with** ...": the occurrence of S here just means the same as C. The occurrence of S is called an *instantiation* of S.

But it is also possible to *parameterise* a scheme, and we discuss this in the following section.

1.9   Parameterised Schemes

The most common use of parameterised schemes is to make *generic* schemes. For example, we considered earlier the type of binary trees. We may want more than one kind of binary tree: one to hold integers, another to hold names, etc. But we would like to define the type *Tree* and its associated functions only once. We can proceed as follows:

– We define a class to act as the scheme parameter. Commonly we use a scheme to define this class:

scheme ELEM = **class type** Elem **end**

This is a very simple, as well as a very common scheme to define a parameter. But there are no restrictions on what we can put into a parameter's class expression. This makes the parameterisation mechanism in RSL much more powerful than, for example, templates in C++.

– We define a generic scheme *TREE* using *ELEM* as a parameter:

scheme TREE(E : ELEM) =
class
  type
    Val = E.Elem,
    Tree == nil | node(left : Tree, val : Val, right : Tree)
  ...
end

The abbreviation definition of *Val* is just a commonly used convenience. We could omit it, replacing all other occurrences of *Val* with *E.Elem*.

Technically the parameter "*E : ELEM*" is like an object definition (see Section 1.10). *E* is the identifier of an object, so *E.Elem* means the type *Elem* defined in the object *E*.

So how do we make trees of integers, say? We need to make an instantiation of *TREE*, and the actual parameter we need is an object, just as the formal parameter is an object. So we define an object *I*, say:

object I : **class type** Elem = **Int end**

and now the scheme instantiation *TREE(I)* is what we want. The formal definition of *TREE(I)* says that it is the class expression of *TREE* with every occurrence of the object identifier *E* replaced by *I*. So, in particular, the defining type expression of the type *Val* will be *I.Elem*, which we can see from the definition of *I* is just an abbreviation for **Int**.

For type checking, there is a condition between the class of the formal parameter *E* and the class of the actual parameter *I*. This is that the latter must be a *static implementation* of the former. This means that for every entity in the formal parameter there must be an entity in the actual parameter of the same kind (type, object, value, variable or channel) with the same identifier and:

– for types, if the formal type definition is an abbreviation, the actual type definition must be an abbreviation for a type that is maximally the same
– for objects, the defining class in the actual parameter must statically implement the defining class in the formal parameter

– for values, variables and channels, the types in the actual and formal parameters must be maximally the same.

Here "maximally the same" means the types must not be distinguishable (see
Section 1.3).

The actual class expression may contain more entities than the formal.

Schemes can have several parameters. For example, we might define a generic
database:

scheme DATABASE(D : ELEM, R : ELEM) =
class
  type
    Domain = D.Elem,
    Range = R.Elem,
    Database = Domain $\overrightarrow{m}$ Range
  ...
end

and we can instantiate *DATABASE* with two different objects, or the same
object twice.

Sometimes we find we have an object that defines the things we need for
the actual parameters, but with the wrong identifiers. For example, the RAISE
method (Section 2) suggests defining a number of simple types that will be
used throughout the specification in a scheme *TYPES*, and making an object
T from this. Now suppose *TYPES* defines types *Id* and *Name*, and we want to
instantiate the *DATABASE* with *Id* as the domain type and *Name* as the range
type.

We can instantiate *DATABASE* as

DATABASE(T{Id **for** Elem}, T{Name **for** Elem})

The construct $\{id_1{}'$ **for** $id_1, ..., id_n{}'$ **for** $id_n\}$ is called a *fitting*. It acts as if the
fitting had been applied to the formal parameter class as a renaming.

It is possible to have parameters which depend on each other. For example
we could define:

scheme S(E : ELEM, T : TREE(E)) = ...

Then if we define objects by, say:

object
  I : **class type** Elem = **Int end**,
  TR : TREE(I)

then S could be instantiated as *S(I, TR)*.

1.10   Object Declarations

Technically class expressions denote, or mean, classes (collections) of possible implementations of them. We get different possible implementations with abstract types (since any type can be used as an implementation) and with underspecified values. The possible implementations are called *objects*. Object declarations consist of the keyword **object** followed by one or more object definitions separated by commas.

If C is a class expression, we can define an object O by:

object
  O : C

and O denotes some object in the class C.

If x is an entity in C (and not hidden or renamed in C), then, in the scope of this object definition, x can be referred to by the *name O.x*. This is sometimes called a *qualified name*, and the prefix O the *qualifier*.

The universal access **any** can also be qualified. For example, the access clause **read** *O*.**any** in a function signature allows the function to read any variable defined in the object O (including variables defined in any objects defined in C). This is often needed to write the signatures of functions that invoke functions in imperative modules, since variable and channel names are commonly hidden.

It is also possible to define *object arrays* in RSL. The object name is given a formal parameter in the form of a (list of) typings. For example, a collection of buffers indexed by a type *Index* could be defined by

object
  B[i : Index] : BUFFER

and the expression $B[e].put(d)$, where e is an expression of type *Index*, and *put* a function defined in *BUFFER*, would be used to put data value d in the buffer indexed by the value of e.

1.11   Comments

There are two kinds of comment supported in RSL. *Block comments* are opened by /* and closed by */. They may be nested. *Line comments* are opened by -- and closed by the end of a line (or file). Both kinds of comment are allowed anywhere where white space would be allowed.

Line comments were introduced, and the original restriction on the use of block comments to only certain syntactic constructs was removed, after the publication of the two books on RAISE [6,5].

2   The RAISE Method: Writing Initial Specifications

As long as you conform to the syntax and type rules of RSL, you can describe and develop software in any way that you choose. But there are a number of ideas for using RSL that have been found useful in practice, and that collectively we describe as "the" RAISE method.

Writing the initial specification is the most critical task in software development. If it is wrong, i.e. it fails to meet the requirements, then following work will be largely wasted. It is well known that mistakes made early in the life-cycle are considerably more expensive to fix than those made later, precisely because they cause so much time and effort to be expended going in the wrong direction. But we should clarify this to say that it is mistakes made *and not quickly found* that are expensive. We can't guarantee that we won't make mistakes, but if we can discover them quickly then not too much harm is done.

What kind of errors are made at the start? The main problem is that we may not understand the requirements. They are set in some domain in which we are usually not experts, while the people who wrote them, to whom the domain is familiar, tend to forget to explain what to them is obvious.

In addition, requirements are written in a natural language, like English or Chinese, and as a result are likely to be ambiguous. They are often large documents developed by several people over a period of time. As a result they are often contradictory: what they say on one page may differ from what they say on another.

The aim of the initial specification is to capture the requirements in a formal, precise manner. Formality means that our specification has just one meaning, it is unambiguous. By *capturing* the requirements we mean rewriting them in our terms, creating our model of what the system will do. So how can we check that the model we create accurately models what the writer of the requirements has in mind?

Be Abstract. The specification should be *abstract*, it should leave out as much detail as possible. The requirements may demand that identifiers have a certain format, or that dates should be presented in a particular style, or that calculations should be done to a certain degree of accuracy, or that a user screen should have a certain appearance, but we try to extract the essential information: that there are identifiers, presumably different for each different entity they identify, that we need dates, that certain calculations need to be done, that users may be requested for certain information and as a consequence they may be presented with other information, or the system's state may be changed in certain ways. We know that we can fill in the details later: we can design the details of user screens provided the information to be presented is available or can be calculated, and provided we know what input to demand.

Use Users' Concepts. The concepts in the specification should be the same as the user's concepts. If the requirements say that each customer has an account, and an account is a record of all the customer's transactions, then that is what the specification should say. It should not refer to concepts like databases, tables, and records: these are computer concepts that describe ways of solving the problem, while what we want to do first is *describe the problem, not its solution*.

Make it Readable. Specifications are intended to be read by others: by those who are to check that they correspond to requirements, by those who are to implement them, by those who are to write test plans, by those who later want to maintain the system, etc. So we want to make them as readable as possible. The guidelines here are very much like those for programming languages: meaningful identifiers, comments, simple functions, modules that are coherent and loosely coupled, etc.

Look for Problems. We recall that what we want to do is avoid mistakes, or find them quickly. So we concentrate on the things that appear difficult, strange, or novel, and we ignore or defer things that are straightforward. We might be mistaken as to what is hard, of course, but we hope that with some experience we have a feeling for such things. In capturing requirements we are also trying to find out if the system we intend to develop is feasible, at least within our budget constraints, and so we want to be assured as early as possible that we have appropriate solutions to all the problems. If we don't, we may need to do some experimentation or research before we commit ourselves further.

Minimise the State. State information should be *minimal*. This means in particular that we try hard not to include in the state *dependent* information: information that can be calculated from other information in the state. If C can be calculated from A and B, then we should not model C as part of the state. If C is stored as part of the state, together with A and B, then we will need a *consistency* condition that what is stored for C is the same as would be calculated from the stored A and B. There is a general notion that the simpler the set of consistency conditions needed, the better the state is designed. It may be that later we decide we need to store C, to achieve sufficient speed, but this should be done as a later stage of development.

When we refer to the *state* of a system we mean the information that is stored, that persists between interactions with it. We also speak of the state of a module, where we mean the part of the state associated conceptually with that module, which will typically provide functions to change it and report on it. We use the term *global state* where necessary to refer to the state of the whole system, as opposed to that of a module, or of a group of modules that we see as a subsystem.

Identify Consistency Conditions. While we try to make the state minimal, it is still usually the case that we need *consistency* conditions and *policy* conditions. Consistency conditions are needed if some possible state values cannot correspond to reality: two users of a library borrowing the same copy of a book simultaneously, perhaps. Policy conditions are ones that might perhaps arise in reality, but we intend that they should not happen: a user borrowing too many books at one time, perhaps.

If our system's state cannot correspond to reality then it becomes essentially useless: it cannot tell us who really has the book, and we probably cannot trust any information it might give us. Preserving consistency conditions is more critical for the healthiness of our system than keeping within policy.

We identify the consistency requirements first because sometimes we can think of a state design that will reduce the need for consistency conditions. For example, if we record a borrower against a copy of a book, only one such borrower can be recorded and the inconsistency of two simultaneous borrowers cannot occur. We need to bear the consistency conditions in mind during development, as we will want our functions to maintain consistency, and our initial state to establish it.

Sometimes consistency is dealt with by a subtype: we can record the number of books someone can borrow as a **Nat**, for example, to prevent it being negative. But often consistency requirements will involve more than one module, and then it is generally better to define a function expressing it, but not try to impose it as a subtype. When there are several modules involved it may not always be true during processing: we will merely want to establish that, starting from a consistent state, every top-level function will generate another one.

There are several common sources of possible inconsistency that arise in many domains, because they relate to common data structures:

- Much data is modelled as maps, allowing us to use identifiers as references. These identifiers may then be used elsewhere, and we need to ensure that every reference is to data that exists. For example, the borrower of a copy of a book should be a registered user.
- Sometimes we have relations that relate values of some type to itself, like "child" or "part of" relations. Then we typically need to ensure that there are no cycles in the relation, or else functions using the relation are likely not to terminate.
- It may be possible to access information in two ways (which is an indication that our state is not minimal, but may be done for efficiency reasons, especially in refinements of the initial specification). Then we need to check that the two ways to access information give the same result. If we can find out borrowers from information about copies of books, and find out copies borrowed from information about borrowers, then we can state as a consistency conditions (a) that the recorded borrower of a book (if any) has a borrow record for that copy for that book, and (b) that each copy in the set of copies borrowed by a borrower has the borrower recorded.

Consistency conditions help us write functions, or at least they help us avoid mistakes in functions that would occur if we overlooked consistency. They also have a relation to preconditions. Preconditions serve two main purposes:

1. They allow us to avoid unsafe or unpredictable situations, like dividing by zero, or in general applying a function or operator when its result would be undefined or non-terminating.
2. They allow us to avoid situations where we would otherwise break consistency. So a function *borrow*, for example, might include in its precondition that the user involved is registered.

It is not usually a good idea to include consistency as part of preconditions. The reason for this is that functions at the top level, accessible by our users (people or other software), will generally need to have preconditions checked when they are invoked. Checking consistency typically involves searches through all the state and this would be too inefficient. (At the same time, including a simple check even though it is implied by consistency is sensible as part of "safety-first" style.) We instead, as we mentioned above, take steps during development to ensure that our functions all preserve consistency, and that our initial state establishes it, so we can then assume it to be true.

Policy conditions are generally separated from consistency. States that violate policy requirements are possible in the real world, and if our system is to be a faithful model of the real world it must also allow them. Such states are often used to generate warning messages, raise alarms, or instigate corrective actions, so we still need to define precisely what the policy conditions are so that we can specify how to check them.

2.1   Kinds of Module

We identify two kinds of module that we find most commonly used: *global objects* and *state components*.

Global Objects. Global objects are objects declared at the top level, in a separate file. In general, they are not advised, because they have too wide a scope. But there are typically a collection of, in particular, types that we need in many places, such as identifiers for various kinds of entity, and it is convenient to collect these in one global object. Dates and a few functions or operators like $\leq$ to compare them, and perhaps also periods modelled as pairs of dates, or a date and a duration, are other common candidates. Global objects should not include any part of the state.

Another guide to when types should be in a global object is that types visible to users, i.e. types that occur as parameters to user functions or in the results of user functions, should generally be defined in one.

State Components. Most modules will contain a type modelling (a part of) the state, together with functions to *observe* it and *generate* values of it, and we term these state components. Generators usually include functions to change state values, and perhaps also to create them. The type is often called the *type of interest* of the module. Such modules are usually defined as schemes, and typically instantiated within others, as we will see in Section 2.2. Modules should have only one type of interest.

We write separate modules for each state component because we can then enforce a discipline that the part of the state within the module is only accessed through the functions defined for it. This enables us, for example, to change the way that part is modelled without affecting anything else, so long as we maintain the original properties. Such a technique is known as *encapsulation* through *information hiding*.

Object oriented approaches to program design follow the same ideas: they typically call the observers and generators *methods*.

2.2   Module Hierarchies

There are several suggested principles in creating a collection of modules to model a system:

- Each module should have only one type of interest, defining functions to create, modify and observe values of the type.
- The modules should as far as possible form a *hierarchy*: each module below the top one should be instantiated in only one other, its *parent*, as an embedded object, and its functions should only be called from its parent.

This leads naturally to a top-down style of specification and development. As we decide on the concrete type for a module, perhaps involving several components, then as long as these component types are non-trivial we define new modules for them as children of the original.

The restriction to a hierarchy sometimes seems more complicated than, say, a collection of global objects each defining one part of the state, with objects able to call functions in any others. But such designs have definite disadvantages:

- The many interdependencies mean that changes to a module may affect many others, so maintenance is more difficult.
- They are harder to test individually. With a hierarchy there is natural testing order that tests children before parents.
- In a concurrent system it is hard to ensure that the system will not deadlock. Following the guidelines for developing concurrent systems from sequential ones in the RAISE method book [5] means that freedom from deadlock is guaranteed by a simple syntactic check.

It may not be clear why we suggested using embedded objects to link child modules to their parents. There are three possibilities to use one module (the child) in another (the parent), which we consider in turn:

1. Merging the specifications textually into a single module. This is clearly not very sensible. Apart from breaking the suggestion that there only be one type of interest per module, the resulting large module is hard to read, the child cannot be reused elsewhere, it is tedious to hide the child components (as they must be hidden individually), and there may be name clashes between the two parts.
2. Writing the parent as an extension (**extend** S **with** ... where S is the scheme defining the child). This gives two separate modules, and so is readable, and the child module S can be reused, but it still suffers from the disadvantages that it is hard to hide the child components, and there may be name clashes between the two parts. (We typically use **extend** to add definitions to an existing type of interest, or perhaps to make a subtype of it, such as defining an interest-bearing deposit account by extending a basic account specification.)
3. Instantiating the child as an object within the parent. The separate modules are small and readable, the child is reusable, the child can be hidden merely by hiding its object identifier, and name clashes cannot occur because within the parent specification all the entities from the child have an object identifier qualifier. Hence this is normally the best solution.

2.3   Sharing Child Modules

Consider the proposed module structure in Figure 1.

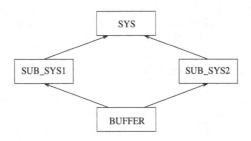

Fig. 1. Sharing a child module

If we take the advice about instantiating children as objects in parents, then in *SYS* we get two objects, called *S1* and *S2* perhaps, and in each of *SUB_SYS1* and *SUB_SYS2* we get an object *B*, say, instantiating *BUFFER*. How many buffers are there? There are two. We can see this because in *SYS* they have names *S1.B* and *S2.B*, and RSL is constructed so that different names imply different objects: there is no possibility of "aliasing", of having different names for the same variable, channel or object. Different objects will have different variables, different channels, and different embedded objects, even if they are instantiations of the same scheme.

If the buffers are intended to be different, this is fine. But what if the two sub-systems want to share one buffer, perhaps for passing information between them? This will break the normal idea of hierarchical design that child modules are independent, since a call in *SYS* of a function in *S1*, say, can result in a change in state of both *B* and *S2*. But sometimes it is necessary. We then have to be more careful than usual how we call child functions from *SYS*.

If we need such a design, there are two ways to achieve it. The first is to make a global object *B*, say, from *BUFFER*, and use this in both *SUB_SYS1* and *SUB_SYS2*. Now there is one buffer (because there is only one name for it) and so the two sub-systems must be sharing it. But other modules can also access it. What we probably want is for the buffer to be shared between the sub-systems, but be hidden within *SYS*.

The second solution us to use parameterisation. We make *BUFFER* a parameter of both *SUB_SYS1* and *SUB_SYS2*:

scheme SUB_SYS1(B : BUFFER) = ...
scheme SUB_SYS2(B : BUFFER) = ...

and in *SYS* we define the following objects:

object
  B : BUFFER,

S1 : SUB_SYS1(B),
S2 : SUB_SYS2(B)

Now we can see that there is only one buffer object B, which is defined in *SYS* and can be hidden there. The objects of the two sub-systems now share this buffer because any mention of a name prefixed by B in their specifications is now bound to that name defined in the object B in *SYS*.

2.4   Validation and Verification

Validation is the check that we have written the right specification, i.e. that we have met the requirements. It has nothing to do with internal properties: one can have a perfectly satisfactory description of a tunnel when what is wanted is a bridge, and no detailed inspection of the tunnel's description can uncover the fact that it is not what is required. Such a gross disparity between requirements and specification is unlikely, of course, but the basic fact remains: to validate a specification we must look outside it, at the requirements.

Validation therefore cannot be formalised because, usually, requirements are written in natural language. But it is a very important step: if we make mistakes in the initial specification then the following effort may be wasted! Many software projects have failed because requirements were incomplete, inconsistent, infeasible given the effort available, or misunderstood. Note that we are concerned with errors in the requirements themselves as well as with errors we make in modelling them. So we try in writing specifications to actively consider whether what we read seems sensible, complete and consistent. In creating a formal model we tend to come up with many questions, and generating these questions to ask of the people responsible for the requirements (the *customers*) has proved to be extremely beneficial in detecting problems at the start of the project. We try to be abstract, but that is not the same thing as being vague!

The main technique in validation is to check that each requirement is met. When we have written the initial specification we go back to the requirements and for each issue that we can find, we should conclude one of the following:

- It is met.
- It is not met, and we need to change the specification.
- It is not met because we think it is not a good idea (because of infeasibility, or for consistency with other parts, perhaps) and we need to discuss with the customers.
- It will be deferred to later in the development. This applies to "non-functional requirements" like the intended programming language or operating system, or performance requirements, but also to things that we have not yet designed, like aspects of the user interface or particular algorithms to be used. In this case we add it to a list of the requirements against which later development steps will be validated. We need, of course, to have in mind a development strategy that will allow such requirements to be met eventually.

There are also other validation techniques we can use:

– With experience, we can read the specification to look for properties that it will have that are not mentioned in the requirements. To take a trivial example, when we specify data storage, we naturally ask if it may become full, and if so what should happen. It may be that the user has not considered the possibility. Another example is whether a data structure should be initialised, and if so to what? This is typical of the kind of issue that may seem so obvious to the customers, who know the domain well, that they omitted to mention it. Scenarios, or use-cases, often lack essential but, to the customer, "obvious" steps. We should set up a formal procedure of queries to customers and their answers being documented.

– We should develop system tests (test cases and expected results) along with the specification. Doing this often helps to clarify the requirements, and these can also be shown to the customers, who will usually find them easier to read than the formal specification [15,16].

– It is possible to rewrite the requirements from the specification. This is an expensive task, but generally produces requirements documents that are clearer, better structured, more concise, and more complete than the originals.

– We can prototype all or part of the system, perhaps by doing a quick and simplified refinement of the abstract types in it, and using the translators to SML or C++ (see Section 2.9) in the RAISE tools to run some test cases. We can also let the customers use it to get more feedback from them.

– We can model check the system. This normally means making some changes to make the system finite (with known size parameters), adding a transition system, and defining some suitable temporal logic assertions to be checked. See Section 5 for an example.

Providing early feedback to the customers in the form of queries, test cases, rewritten requirements, or prototypes has the added advantage of committing them to what has been done so far, and helps demonstrate to them the added cost and danger of later requirement changes, the bane of every software project manager's life! We try to make the initial specification a *contract* between us and the customers.

Verification is the check that we are developing the system correctly, so that the final implementation conforms to the initial specification. It must come after validation, since it assumes the correctness of the initial specification. We discuss it as part of the next section on refinement.

2.5   Refinement

We mentioned earlier that we develop by "invent and verify": we invent a more concrete version of a module and then verify that it is correct with respect to previous one. The formal relation that must exist between the two is the *refinement relation*, sometimes also called the *implementation relation*.

The refinement relation needs to be transitive: we want to develop, say, from *A0* to *A1* and then from *A1* to *A2*, checking refinement at each step, and be assured that *A2* must refine *A0*. Additionally, refinement needs to be monotonic with respect to building modules from other modules. Suppose module A is developed through version $A0$ to the final $A2$ as above, and module B has first version $B0$ that instantiates $A0$ and is developed (perhaps by other people) to $B1$, say, that still instantiates $A0$. Now we want to integrate the final versions. We write module $B2$ that differs from $B1$ only in substituting the identifier $A2$ for the identifier $A0$: see Figure 2. We want, provided $A2$ refines $A0$ and $B1$ refines $B0$, that $B2$ should be guaranteed to refine $B1$ and hence $B0$. Monotonicity is what gives this guarantee. If this were not true we could not conveniently develop modules separately. Effectively $A0$ is a *contract* between the developers of B and the developers of A: it says to the developers of B what A will provide, and to the developers of A what they must provide. Just how the latter group does this should be of no concern to the former.

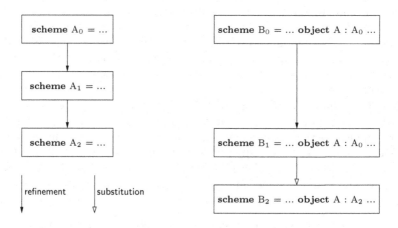

Fig. 2. Separate development

The refinement relation should also hold in instantiations of parameterised of schemes: the class of each actual parameter should be a refinement of the class of the corresponding formal parameter.

The formal definition of refinement can be found in the RAISE method book [5]. Here we give an intuition. It has two components. For $A1$ to refine $A0$ we require:

– The signature of $A1$ must include the signature of $A0$. That is, $A1$ must contain all the entities (types, values, variables, channels, and objects) with the same names and the same maximal types or, for objects, with classes that are in the same relation. This relation, termed *static implementation*, was introduced earlier in Section 1.9. The relation is necessary for the monotonicity property: we need to be able to replace references to $A0$ with references to $A1$ in other modules without causing type or scope errors. The signature we are concerned with does not include hidden entities: these do not need to be included in refinements. The relation is also one of inclusion: $A1$ may have more entities than $A0$.

− All the *properties* of *A0* must hold in *A1*. Properties may be expressed as axioms, but also include definitions of constants and functions, initial values of variables, and the restrictions in subtypes. Property preservation is clearly transitive.

The first of these conditions can be checked statically, and the RAISE tools do this as part of type checking. The second is not statically checkable, and in general requires proof for full verification. But the "R" in RAISE stands for "rigorous": the method allows for the conditions to be checked informally, by hand. The amount of proof we do will depend on how critical the system is, and how much budget we have. Proof is expensive because it involves considerable time and also skilled, experienced people to do it. It is unfortunately the case that the kinds of proofs that arise in software development are generally beyond the capabilities of automated proof tools. The RAISE tools include support for proof via a translator to the language of the proof tool PVS [17].

2.6   Lightweight Formal Methods

It is possible to use formal methods without proof, and even without refinement: the initial specification is sufficient to explore the problem and provide a basis for implementation. Such use of a formal method is sometimes called "lightweight". It is found that most of the benefit of a formal method is in analysing and capturing requirements, in identifying and resolving requirements issues at the start of development, and in providing a sound basis for implementation. If the specification is not too complicated, implementation may be done directly from it.

There are some formal techniques that we can employ, that may or may not employ proof, that we can adopt to increase confidence in specifications: confidence conditions and theorems. We consider these in turn.

2.7   Confidence Conditions

Confidence conditions are conditions that should probably be true if the module is not to be inconsistent, but that cannot in general be determined as true or false by an automatic tool. The following conditions are generated by the RAISE tools:

1. Arguments of invocations of functions and operators are in subtypes, and, for partial functions and operators, preconditions are satisfied.
2. Values supposed to be in subtypes are in the subtypes. These are generated for
   − values in explicit value definitions;
   − values of explicit function definitions (for parameters in appropriate subtypes and satisfying any given preconditions);
   − initial values of variables;
   − values assigned to variables;
   − values output on channels.

3. Subtypes are not empty.
4. Values satisfying the restrictions exist for implicit value and function definitions.
5. The classes of actual scheme parameters implement the classes of the formal parameters.
6. For an implementation relation, the implementing class implements the implemented class. This gives a means of expanding such a relation or expression, by asserting the relation in a theory and then generating the confidence conditions for the theory.
7. A definition of a partial function without a precondition (which generates the confidence condition **false**).
8. A definition of a total function with a precondition (which generates the confidence condition **false**).

Examples of all the first 4 kinds of confidence conditions listed above are generated from the following intentionally peculiar scheme (in which line numbers have been inserted so that readers can relate the following confidence conditions to their source):

```
1 scheme CC =
2 class
3   value
4     x1 : Int = hd <..>,
5     x2 : Int = f1(-1),
6     x3 : Nat = -1,
7     f1 : Nat -~-> Nat
8     f1(x) is -x
9     pre x > 0
10   type
11     None = {| i : Nat :- i < 0 |}
12   value
13     x4 : Nat :- x4 < 0,
14     f2 : Nat -> Nat
15     f2(n) as r post n + r = 0
16 end
```

This produces the following confidence conditions (which are all provably false). The first part of each condition is a reference to its source in the form file:line:column:

```
CC.rsl:4:19: CC:
-- application arguments and/or precondition
let x = <..> in x ~= <..> end

CC.rsl:5:18: CC:
-- application arguments and/or precondition
-1 >= 0 /\ let x = -1 in x > 0 end
```

```
CC.rsl:6:14: CC:
-- value in subtype
-1 >= 0

CC.rsl:8:5: CC:
-- function result in subtype
all x : Nat :- (x > 0 is true) => -x >= 0

CC.rsl:11:26: CC:
-- subtype not empty
exists i : Nat :- i < 0

CC.rsl:13:8: CC:
-- possible value in subtype
exists x4 : Nat :- x4 < 0

CC.rsl:15:5: CC:
-- possible function result in subtype
all n : Nat :- exists r : Nat :- n + r = 0
```

It is usually sufficient to carefully *inspect* confidence conditions rather than trying to prove them. Most of the time it is easy to see that the conditions are OK, but they are a good way to find errors, particularly in the first category where we apply a function forgetting its precondition.

There is a danger when proving confidence conditions, since they can indicate an inconsistency in the module. For example, scheme CC above asserts through the definition of $x3$ that -1 is in the type **Nat**. This is false, and so this definition implies the property **false**. CC is therefore inconsistent and anything can be proved about it. In particular, all the provably false confidence conditions above can also be proved true! So if we try to prove confidence conditions we must proceed with care.

2.8 Theorems

Theorems are formal statements about specifications that we state separately: they are intended to be consequences of the specifications, not part of their definitions. They can be proved, formally or by hand, or just examined carefully. Even when not proved they can be useful as part of the documentation.

Theorems can be stated in RAISE by means of a **theory** module. A theory takes the form:

theory name :
axiom

...

end

where ... is one or more axiom definitions. To support theories there are two extensions to the RAISE syntax that are useful:

- The *implementation relation* ⊢ C1 ⪯ C0, where *C1* and *C0* are class expressions. The implementation (or refinement) relation was described in Section 2.5.
- The *class scope expression* **in** C ⊢ expr, where *C* is a class expression and *expr* is a Boolean expression which may reference entities defined in *C*.

Generating confidence conditions for an implementation relation will expand it into its constituent properties, allowing us to examine them without necessarily proving them, or perhaps only proving some.

Typically if we want to do proof we will concentrate on critical properties. For example, if there are system consistency properties that should always be maintained, we can formulate as theorems the property that they are maintained by our generators (provided any preconditions hold). For example, suppose in scheme *A*, *gen* is a generator with a parameter of type *U*, *T* is the type of interest, and *can_gen* is a function expressing the precondition of *gen*, so the definition of *gen* looks like:

value
   gen : U × T $\xrightarrow{\sim}$ T
   gen(u, t) ≡ ...
   pre can_gen(u, t)

Then the theorem we would write is:

in A ⊢ ∀ u : U, t : T •
   consistent(t) ∧ can_gen(u, t) ⇒ consistent(gen(u, t))

Consistency conditions are a good choice for doing proofs. Generating the wrong result values of functions often shows up in testing, but creating inconsistencies in the system may not show up until some time after the inconsistency was created, and so it may be hard to find them in testing and hard to identify when and how an inconsistency was originally generated.

Inclusion of checking consistency is also a good thing to include in test cases. But only with a proof can one be sure that a generator will never cause an inconsistency.

Finally, one should not forget the value of code reading by peers. This is a comparatively cheap and very effective means of discovering errors, and can be applied to specifications as much as to code. In fact it is generally easier to read specifications than programming language code. They are more abstract, and are intended to be read by people rather than machines.

2.9   Generating the Executable Program

The traditional development route is from RAISE to a programming language like C++ or Java. The RAISE tools available from UNU/IIST's web site www.iist.unu.edu include a translators from a subset of RSL to C++ and SML (though the latter is intended mainly for prototyping and testing). Parts of specifications may need to be translated to SQL, say, if part of the specification is intended to specify a database. The original RAISE tools [1] also include a translator to Ada. There is advice on translation by hand, including translation of concurrency, in the RAISE method book [5].

But there are many other possibilities. The paper [18], for example, uses AWK as the implementation language.

3 When Not to Use RAISE

We do not mean to give the impression that RAISE or a similar software specification language should be used to define all software systems. There are exceptions, and we give some examples in this section.

3.1 There Is a Special-Purpose Formalism

There are many special-purpose formalisms (sometimes with associated tools) that can sometimes be used in preference to a general purpose language like RSL. For example, BNF is a standard notation for defining grammars, and has associated tools like flex and bison for generating parsers and building abstract syntax trees. BNF is well defined, and provides a well-known, convenient, and compact notation. Copying this in RSL could be done, but the result would be less concise and still require the equivalent of flex and bison to be developed.

Real-time systems, ones which depend heavily on precise timing, such as real-time schedulers and process control systems, are often better analysed using a special-purpose formalism like Duration Calculus (DC) [19]. (There is some ongoing work to add real-time features to RSL [20,21,22].)

Another example is defining semantics of languages. There are notations like Structured Operational Semantics [23] that have their own compact notations that would be much less readable in RSL.

3.2 The Effort Is Not Worth the Gain

Sometimes there is a language adapted to a particular kind of application that allows the implementation to be written at a level that is very close to how one would specify it. An example is the RAISE tools [24]. These were written in a language Gentle [25] that is a high level language intended for use by compiler constructors. The RAISE tools were written in this language without writing a specification of them. The reason is that for the type checker, for example (the first tool written and a basis for all the others) it was felt that the scope and type rules could not have been written at a much more abstract level: the actual error messages, and some details about input and output to files, which were largely copied from another system, would have been almost the only things left more abstract. So in this case the executable program (Gentle is executable in that it translates to C) is also the specification. There is, of course, a definition of the semantics of RSL (using a special-purpose formalism) that includes the static semantics (the scope and type rules) but the tools were not developed with close reference to this (and RSL has also been extended): the tool developer had a very good working knowledge of RSL having worked on its original design.

Another, rather different, example is graphical user interfaces. The top level RAISE specification of a system defines the functions that may be accessed by users, which may be people or other software. In the case of people, graphical user interfaces are common, and there are many languages and tools to aid their construction. A main feature of such interfaces is that they are functionally simple. They help users select the function they want to invoke (often with menus or buttons), they ask for the necessary inputs to be provided (by selection or on forms) and they display or output results. The top level specification describes what functions are available, shows through their signatures what inputs are needed and what results will be returned, and defines what preconditions need to be checked. All that needs to be done is the design of the graphical part, the definition of helpful messages when preconditions are violated, and perhaps the design of convenient output formats for extensive result values. There seems in practice little point in trying to specify these aspects, especially the graphical, visual ones.

4   Example 1: Message Transport

We describe a system intended to model the transport of messages. The requirements are:

- Messages can be inserted and extracted.
- There may be some delay between a message being inserted and it being available for extraction.
- The extraction order should be the same as the insertion order, except that there should be some possibility of higher priority messages "overtaking" lower priority ones.
- It is not necessary to guarantee that the next message extracted is the highest priority one in the system. This is ideal, but may not always be possible.

We will keep the "messages" completely abstract, and only assume that a "priority", for simplicity a natural number, is part of a message. Higher numbers give higher priorities.

We will model the system in terms of two buffers, one holding messages "in transit" and one holding messages that have "arrived" and are waiting to be extracted. Transfer of messages between the two will be essentially non-deterministic.

The "transit" buffer will be modelled as a FIFO buffer, a queue, and the "arrived" buffer as a priority queue.

4.1   The Initial Specification

The initial specification should try to capture the important properties of the system. If the system is small, like this one, it may be possible to do this in a single module. Otherwise, we may have to initially model the system in terms of its major components, and specify the properties of these components.

In a typical development there are a number of types and perhaps some functions over them that will be used in many components. Typical examples are identifiers and simple data structures like dates. Such types are not intended to become the state types of the imperative objects of the final system. It is convenient to place these in one or more modules that are made generally available to the other modules in the system. Such global sharing is in general not a good idea, and it is possible to define such types in modules which are then shared through parameterisation. But the number of parameters of modules can as a result grow quite alarmingly. So the method suggests that such types and their associated functions are made globally available and so can be freely referenced. Obviously, in a large development, careful control needs to be applied to changing such modules, but the advantages seem to outweigh the disadvantages.

For our system, we see the type of messages, and the notion of message priority, being candidates for such a global module and we define a scheme TYPES (figure 3).

```
scheme
   TYPES =
      class
         type Message

         value
            priority : Message → Nat,

            leq : Message × Message → Bool
            leq(m1, m2) ≡ priority(m1) ≤ priority(m2)
      end
```

Fig. 3. The scheme TYPES

TYPES illustrates the basic components of modules. They are built from *class expressions* of which the simplest is the *basic* class expression **class** ... **end** with *declarations* within. Here we have a **type** declaration and a **value** declaration. The type declaration defines a type *Message*. This is an abstract type, or *sort*: it is not defined in terms of any other types.

Values are introduced by giving their names and types. *priority* is a function value: it takes *Message* values as parameters and produces **Nat** results. Such a function obviously represents an attribute of its parameter type. **Nat**, as indicated by its bold face, is built-in to RSL. It is the type of natural numbers (the non-negative integers). Built-in types like **Nat** have associated operators like + and ≤.

The value *leq* is another function representing a relation on messages: it takes a pair of messages and returns a **Boolean**. **Bool** is another built-in type, containing the values **true** and **false**. It has associated connectives ∧ (conjunction),

∨ (disjunction), ⇒ (implication), and ∼ (negation). *leq* is given a concrete definition: the ordering on messages is the corresponding ordering on their priorities.

There are two kinds of modules in RSL, **schemes** and **objects**. A scheme is a named class expression. A class expression denotes its class of models, essentially all the things that could be used as implementations of it. A possible model of a message is a pair of a text string and a priority. Another possible model is a triple of a destination, text, and priority. And so on. An object denotes a particular model.

We want to share the notion of message and priority between other modules. So they cannot just share the scheme TYPES as it has many models. We need to share the same model. We do this by creating the object T (figure 4) from the scheme TYPES.

---

context: TYPES
object T : TYPES

Fig. 4. The object T

We define an object by giving a name and a class: TYPES is the name for its class.

There is an analogy between objects/classes and values/types, and we write "T : TYPES" just as we might write "i : Int". But objects in RSL are not the same as values, and classes are not the same as types.

Since the type *Message* in TYPES is abstract, we do not know which model T represents. But this does not matter: we can refine the type *Message* later. All we need to know for now is that all modules referring to T will refer to the same model.

Now we can write the initial specification.

Initial specifications are typically abstract: the properties are described in terms of axioms rather than constructively in terms of a concrete model. The initial specification for our system is A_MESSAGE0 (figure 5). We use a conventional prefix "A_" in the name A_MESSAGE0 to indicate an applicative module, since there will be imperative and perhaps concurrent versions developed later. We also use a conventional suffix "0" since we expect to make a more concrete version "1".

In A_MESSAGE0, we refer to the type *Message* defined in the object T as *T.Message*. The type of the second parameter of *buffered*, *T.Message**, is the type of finite lists, or sequences, of values of type *T.Message*. "*" is one of the type constructors of RSL. Others are products, or tuples (as used in the result type of *get*); sets; and maps. Each comes with syntax for creating values, like "(x,y)" for a pair (2-tuple), ⟨⟩ for the empty list, ⟨x,y⟩ for a list of two values. There are also associated operators like ∪ (set union), ⌢ (list concatenation), **hd** and **tl** for the head and tail of a (non-empty) list.

The type of *get* uses $\xrightarrow{\sim}$, which indicates that it is a *partial* function. That is, it might not be defined for all parameter values. We expect *get* not to be defined when *can_get* is false.

context: T
scheme
  A_MESSAGE0 =
    hide buffered, permutation, count **in**
      class
        type Buffer
        value
          put : T.Message $\times$ Buffer $\to$ Buffer,
          get : Buffer $\xrightarrow{\sim}$ T.Message $\times$ Buffer,
          can_get : Buffer $\to$ **Bool**,
          buffered : Buffer $\times$ T.Message* $\to$ **Bool**
        axiom
         [can_get_ax]
           $\forall$ buff : Buffer • buffered(buff, $\langle\rangle$) $\Rightarrow$ $\sim$ can_get(buff),

         [buffered_put]
           $\forall$ buff, buff$'$: Buffer, l : T.Message*, m : T.Message •
             buffered(buff, l) $\wedge$ put(m, buff) = buff$'$ $\Rightarrow$
             buffered(buff$'$, l $\frown$ $\langle$m$\rangle$)),

         [buffered_get]
           $\forall$
             buff, buff$'$: Buffer,
             l : T.Message*,
             m1, m2 : T.Message
           •
             buffered(buff, l) $\wedge$ can_get(buff) $\wedge$ get(buff) = (m1, buff$'$) $\Rightarrow$
             ($\exists$ l1, l2 : T.Message* •
               l = l1 $\frown$ $\langle$m1$\rangle$ $\frown$ l2 $\wedge$
               buffered(buff$'$, l1 $\frown$ l2) $\wedge$
               (m2 $\in$ **elems** l1 $\Rightarrow$ $\sim$ T.leq(m1, m2))),

         [no_loss_or_gain]
           $\forall$ buff : Buffer, l1, l2 : T.Message* •
             buffered(buff, l1) $\wedge$ buffered(buff, l2) $\Rightarrow$ permutation(l1, l2)

      value
        permutation : T.Message* $\times$ T.Message* $\to$ **Bool**
        permutation(l1, l2) $\equiv$
          ($\forall$ m : T.Message • count(m, l1) = count(m, l2)),

        count : T.Message $\times$ T.Message* $\to$ **Nat**
        count(m, l) $\equiv$ **card** { i | i : **Nat** • i $\in$ **inds** l $\wedge$ l(i) = m }
      end

Fig. 5. The scheme A_MESSAGE0

In making *put* a total function, we are assuming our system has unlimited capacity. A more realistic version would include a *can_put* function, initially underspecified, that we would later define in terms of maximum capacities of the queues involved. A capacity of a queue could be defined either in terms of the numbers of messages or in terms of storage consumption. For the latter we would need a size attribute of messages.

We model the state of the system by defining an abstract type *Buffer*. Values of type *Buffer* will depend on the sequence of messages input and not yet extracted. But we expect this dependency to be nondeterministic. Messages may be in transit and so not yet ready for extraction, so it may not be the case that the highest priority message input will be the next one extracted. Conversely, we do not necessarily expect to be able to discover from the state of the buffer what the actual input order of messages was. Suppose, for example, that messages *m1* and *m2* have both arrived and are ready for extraction, with *m1* of higher priority than *m2*. We cannot tell which of these messages was input first unless we add extra information not in the requirements, like including the time of sending of messages. We therefore model the connection between the input sequence of messages and the buffer state not as a function from one to the other, but as a relation, expressed by the function *buffered*. This is introduced, like the other three functions in the first value declaration of A_MESSAGE0, just by giving the name and the type.

There are a number of properties that our system must have in order to meet its requirements. These are expressed in the **axiom** declaration.

Each axiom consists of an (optional) name in square brackets, followed by a Boolean expression, a predicate.

can_get_ax asserts that if the input list of messages is empty, the buffer must be empty (i.e. nothing can be extracted from it). The converse is not necessarily true, as input messages may be in transit and not available for extraction.

buffered_put expresses the properties of a *put*. The new state is the buffering of the message appended to the end of an input list of the previous state.

buffered_get expresses the properties of a *get*. If a message is extracted it must have been input, the rest of the messages are retained, and any messages overtaken must have lower priority. **elems** is a built-in operator returning the set of elements in a list. $\in$ is set membership.

no_loss_or_gain expresses the property that messages are not lost or invented: for any given buffer state the collection of messages is fixed.

The specification is very loose in that it allows a range of implementations. At one extreme, the internal state might be just a FIFO queue, and there would be no overtaking by higher priority messages. At the other extreme, the internal state might be just a priority queue, with the highest priority message always the next one to be extracted. Our implementation will be between these two extremes. This reflects the requirements.

Since messages might be duplicates (as the requirements did not prohibit this) we have to be careful about defining the "collection" of messages. We use two extra functions to express this notion, *permutation* and *count*. **inds** is the set of index values of a list. For example, the list ⟨x, y⟩ has index values 1 and 2. Applying the list (as if it were a function) to the index value 1 returns x, the first element. And so on. **card**inality is the number of elements in a set. The argument of **card** is a *comprehended* set, in this case the set of index values i of the list l for which applying l to i gives the message m.

All types, even sorts, have equality and inequality defined automatically. This enables us to write equalities between, for example, pairs of *Message* and *Buffer* as in the *buffered_get* axiom. Equalities between tuples are defined pointwise.

There are in fact two kinds of equality in RSL: = and ≡. = just compares values, and is essentially the equality found in programming languages. ≡, as used in function definitions like that of *leq* in TYPES, is the semantic equivalence between expressions. As long as we avoid problems of undefinedness, the two are the same for applicative specifications. When we come to imperative and concurrent specifications we shall see that expressions may have *effects*, such as assigning to variables, and equivalent expressions must have the same effects as well as returning the same values, while expressions are equal if they return the same values.

Unlike many languages, RSL has no "define-before-use" restriction. *permutation*, for example, is used before it is defined. This gives useful flexibility, and modules are commonly written "top-down" as here, with details coming later.

The functions *buffered*, *permutation*, and *count* are just used to express abstract properties. We do not intend to implement them in the final system and so we **hide** them.

But before proceeding from the initial, abstract specification to a more concrete one we must *validate* the specification against the requirements. We go back to the requirements and check carefully that each requirement is either satisfied, or we have a development route in mind from the initial specification that can make it so. There are usually many requirements that should be deferred because they introduce detail that we are still leaving abstract. In a more realistic system there might be requirements about the maximum size of messages, the maximum rate at which the system should be able to deal with them, the programming language to be used, the machine architecture, the operating system, and so on.

It is almost always the case that writing the initial specification generates lots of questions about the requirements. Can there by duplicated messages? Are priorities linearly ordered? Are there limits on the buffer size? Writing specifications tends to find the inconsistencies and omissions which requirements documents in natural languages are typically full of.

This specification A_MESSAGE0 may well look rather complicated. It is not in general very easy to find such specifications. A common alternative approach is to start with the more concrete specification like the one we will present in section 4.2. More concrete specifications are generally easier to write, and allow us to explore the problem in more concrete terms. Then we can write the abstract specification later, having obtained a better grasp of the problem. Formally, since we will then show that the abstract specification is correctly implemented by the concrete one, the result is the same.

4.2 The Concrete Applicative Specification

We recall our intention to model the system in terms of a queue of messages in transit and a priority queue of messages that have arrived but are yet to be extracted. We need to create specifications of these two queues.

Modules like queues should be made generic so that they can be reused. To define such a generic module we first use a standard parameter module that gives the parameter requirements.

Parameter Classes. For the queue the parameter class ELEM (figure 6) is simple.

$$\boxed{\textbf{scheme } \text{ELEM} = \textbf{class type } \text{Elem } \textbf{end}}$$

Fig. 6. The scheme ELEM

For the priority queue we need a total ordering on elements. We could add the necessary features to ELEM by extension, but we here choose to use parameterisation to first define the scheme PARTIAL_ORDER (figure 7), and then to define TOTAL_ORDER (figure 8) by extension.

```
context: ELEM
scheme
  PARTIAL_ORDER(E : ELEM) =
    class
      value
        leq : E.Elem × E.Elem → Bool

      axiom
        [reflexive] ∀ a : E.Elem • leq(a, a),

        [transitive]
          ∀ a, b, c : E.Elem • leq(a, b) ∧ leq(b, c) ⇒ leq(a, c)
    end
```

Fig. 7. The scheme PARTIAL_ORDER

The formal parameter of PARTIAL_ORDER essentially defines an object E of class ELEM.

TOTAL_ORDER illustrates another way of making a class: by **extend**ing another class. Extension is very much like inheritance in object-oriented languages: all the declarations of the first class are inherited by the second.

There is no restriction in RSL on the classes that may be used to make parameter classes.

```
context: PARTIAL_ORDER
scheme
  TOTAL_ORDER(E : ELEM) =
    extend PARTIAL_ORDER(E) with
      class axiom [ linear ] ∀ a, b : E.Elem • leq(a, b) ∨ leq(b, a) end
```

Fig. 8. The scheme TOTAL_ORDER

Queues and Priority Queues. Queues are easily specified in terms of lists, and we have seen there is a built-in RSL list type. We present first the simpler FIFO queue A_QUEUE (figure 9).

```
context: ELEM
scheme
  A_QUEUE(E : ELEM) =
    class
      type Queue = E.Elem*

      value
        empty : Queue = ⟨⟩,

        put : E.Elem × Queue → Queue
        put(e, s) ≡ s ⁀ ⟨e⟩,

        get : Queue ⥲ E.Elem × Queue
        get(s) ≡ (hd s, tl s) pre ∼ is_empty(s),

        is_empty : Queue → Bool
        is_empty(s) ≡ s = ⟨⟩
    end
```

Fig. 9. The scheme A_QUEUE

A_QUEUE is completely concrete: the type *Queue*, the constant *empty*, and the functions *put*, *get* and *is_empty* are all defined explicitly. It is not clear that the constant *empty* is required, but we will need it later for initialising the corresponding imperative queue.

We follow Guttag [26] in using the term "type of interest" for the type *Queue* in A_QUEUE. *Buffer* is the type of interest of A_MESSAGE0. It is the type that an applicative module is trying to define, together with associated functions for generating and observing values of the type. For a module like A_QUEUE, with no subsidiary modules, the type of interest will become its state type when we make an imperative object of it.

The priority queue A_PRI_QUEUE is presented in figure 10. For its type of interest we use an ordered list of elements.

The ordering of the type *Pri_queue* is expressed using a *subtype* expression. The type *Queue* in A_QUEUE includes all finite lists of elements. The type

---

context: TOTAL_ORDER
scheme
  A_PRI_QUEUE(E : ELEM, T : TOTAL_ORDER(E)) =
    hide is_ordered **in**
      class
        type Pri_queue = {| l : E.Elem* • is_ordered(l) |}

        value
          empty : Pri_queue = ⟨⟩,

          put : E.Elem × Pri_queue → Pri_queue
          put(e, s) ≡
            case s **of**
              ⟨⟩ → ⟨e⟩,
              ⟨h⟩ ⌢ t →
                if T.leq(e, h) **then** ⟨h⟩ ⌢ put(e, t) **else** ⟨e, h⟩ ⌢ t **end**
            end,

          get : Pri_queue $\xrightarrow{\sim}$ E.Elem × Pri_queue
          get(s) ≡ (**hd** s, **tl** s) **pre** ∼ is_empty(s),

          is_empty : Pri_queue → **Bool**
          is_empty(s) ≡ s = ⟨⟩,

          is_ordered : E.Elem* → **Bool**
          is_ordered(l) ≡
            (
              ∀ i, j : **Nat** • {i, j} ⊆ **inds** l ∧ i < j ⇒ T.leq(l(j), l(i))
)
      end

Fig. 10. The scheme A_PRI_QUEUE

Pri_queue only includes those finite lists of elements that are ordered according to the function *is_ordered*.

A_PRI_QUEUE requires TOTAL_ORDER as a parameter, which in turn requires ELEM, so we need two parameters. Such a use of parameters might be considered "higher order" but causes no problems in RSL.

A_PRI_QUEUE also illustrates the use of **case** and **if** expressions.

From the type of *put* we can assume that the second parameter is an ordered list. But this type also claims that the result value will be an ordered list. Since we have an explicit definition, there is the possibility of a contradiction here, and we should check that the defining expression will indeed be an ordered list if the second parameter is. That is, we should prove the theorem

∀ l : E.Elem*, e : E.Elem •
  is_ordered(l) ⇒ is_ordered(put(e, l))

This is an example of what is called in RAISE a *confidence condition*. There is a tool in the RAISE toolset that generates such conditions. Others arising from this specification are that the empty list is ordered (from the definition of *empty*) and that the definition of *get* produces an ordered list.

The other common type of confidence condition arises from applications of functions or operators that have preconditions and/or have subtype parameters. The applications of **hd** and **tl** in the definition of *get* will generate the confidence conditions that their arguments are not empty, and perhaps remind us that a precondition is needed for *get*. In the definition of *is_ordered*, the applications of the list l to the arguments j and i will generate the conditions that these arguments are in **inds** l. Any call of *get* in another module using A_PRI_QUEUE will generate the confidence condition that its argument is ordered and not empty.

Confidence conditions can be proved formally or checked informally. The latter is often sufficient; the kinds of errors they point to are usually oversights and soon corrected once identified. We also have to beware of the danger, though it seems slight in practice, that a confidence condition can be proved precisely because there is a contradiction, from which anything can be proved.

The Concrete Applicative Message System. Having defined the two types of queue, we can use them to form the new top-level specification A_MESSAGE1 (figure 11).

We instantiate the two component queues as objects which are hidden in A_MESSAGE1. This is the most common way of using component modules. Hiding them ensures that only the upper module has access to them and so gives control over how they are used. No other part of the overall system can access them.

We can use the object T for both parameters of A_PRI_QUEUE, as the class TYPES of T meets the implementation requirements for both. We want to use *Message* for the type *Elem*, and we can achieve this with a *fitting* applied to the first actual parameter.

If we had not included an appropriate *leq* function in TYPES, or if it had been defined differently, such as by a function *higher*, say, then we could have defined an extra object in A_MESSAGE1 to use as the second parameter of A_PRI_QUEUE:

object
T1 : **class**
    value
        leq : T.Message $\times$ T.Message $\rightarrow$ **Bool**
        leq(m1, m2) $\equiv$ $\sim$ T.higher(m1, m2)
    end

We need to check that the class of the actual parameters of A_PRI_QUEUE and A_QUEUE implement the classes of the formal parameters (see section 4.3). Most of this is checked statically by tools, but we must also check that the

```
context: A_PRI_QUEUE, A_QUEUE, T
scheme
  A_MESSAGE1 =
    hide PQ, Q in
      class
        object
          PQ : A_PRI_QUEUE(T{Message for Elem}, T),
          Q : A_QUEUE(T{Message for Elem})

        type Buffer = PQ.Pri_queue × Q.Queue

        value
          put : T.Message × Buffer → Buffer
          put(m, (pq, q)) ≡ (pq, Q.put(m, q)),

          get : Buffer ⇢ T.Message × Buffer
          get(pq, q) ≡
            let (e, pq') = PQ.get(pq) in (e, (pq', q)) end
            pre can_get(pq, q),

          can_get : Buffer → Bool
          can_get(pq, q) ≡ ~ PQ.is_empty(pq),

          shift : Nat × Buffer → Buffer
          shift(n, (pq, q)) ≡
          if n = 0 ∨ Q.is_empty(q) then
            (pq, q)
          else
            let (m, q') = Q.get(q), pq' = PQ.put(m, pq) in
              shift(n − 1, (pq', q'))
            end
          end
      end
```

Fig. 11. The scheme A_MESSAGE1

definition of *leq* in TYPES satisfies the properties expressed in the axiom of
TOTAL_ORDER, plus the two axioms it inherited from PARTIAL_ORDER.

We can use the types of the component objects PQ and Q to provide the concrete type *Buffer* for the upper module, here using a product. RSL also provides
a *record* type constructor that we could have used. Records are isomorphic to
tuples, but provide a richer syntax for extracting and changing components, and
are particularly useful when there are more components.

The definition of *shift* illustrates the use of the **let** expression. The form used
is a shorthand for the nested **let**

let (e, q') = Q.get(q) in
  let pq' = PQ.put(e, pq) in

shift(n − 1, (pq′, q′))
  end
end

When a message is *put* into the combined queue it is initially added to the "transit" queue Q. Messages are extracted from the "arrived" queue PQ with *get*. We have included a function *shift* to transfer a number of messages (if available) from one queue to the other. *shift* has effectively been added to the user interface of the system. Without it the system would meet its "safety" requirements, but not its "liveness" requirements. A safety requirement is that "nothing bad happens": messages do not get lost; lower priority ones do not overtake higher priority ones. A (simple) liveness requirement is that "something good happens": input messages can eventually be extracted. We will see later how to put *shift* inside the system.

We intend A_MESSAGE1 to be correct with respect to A_MESSAGE0. What this means and how we check it is presented in the next section.

4.3   The Implementation Relation

The *implementation relation* between classes (also termed the *refinement relation*) is the relation used to define the correctness of a development step from a more abstract module to a more concrete one.

Parameterised schemes have objects as formal parameters, and objects must be used as actual parameters. There needs to be a relation between the classes of the formal and actual objects. This is also the implementation relation, as we remarked earlier.

Class B *implements* a class A (written B $\preceq$ A) if and only if

1. the signature of B includes the signature of A
2. all the properties of A hold in B

The first condition is called *static implementation*. It means that

- for every type in A there is a type of the same name in B, and with the same defining type if the type in A is not a sort
- for every value, variable, or channel in A there is a value, variable, or channel in B with the same name and same maximal type (i.e. ignoring subtypes)
- for every object in A there is an object in B of the same name with a class that statically implements the class of the object in A.[1]

---

[1] The original version of RSL [6] allowed schemes to be defined in classes, with the obvious static implementation requirement. These are disallowed in the later version [5] to simplify the logic. There are also good methodological reasons for this restriction. There is no danger in making all schemes global (not defined within a class) — unlike objects which need to be protected against global access, particularly when they are imperative. The problem with a scheme defined inside a class is that it may refer to entities defined in the rest of the class, and this is bad practice since we believe that such sharing should generally be made explicit through parameterisation.

The second condition involves the *properties* of a class, which arise from

- axioms
- value definitions
- subtype conditions on values, variables and channels
- initialisations of variables
- properties of objects defined in the class

A formal definition of the properties of a class is given in the method book [5].

We can see that if we can show that A_MESSAGE1 implements A_MESSAGE0 we will have shown that all the functions we were supposed to provide (*put* and *get*) are still supplied, and that their now concrete definitions satisfy the axioms we used to express the required properties. So, if A_MESSAGE0 met the requirements, A_MESSAGE1 will.

Checking Implementation. Static implementation can be checked by tools. For the properties part we generally need to do proof. We can choose to do it formally or (partly or wholly) informally.

It is a good idea to first document an informal argument. Then we (or, better, someone else) can decide if it is sufficiently convincing, or whether some parts, or even all of it, should be done using a proof tool.

A very informal argument is that the two queues never lose or create elements. For each, *put* adds an element and *get* may remove one, while the others remain. *put* and *get* at the top level call *put* and *get* respectively at the lower level, and therefore have similar properties to the lower level functions. Finally, *shift* transfers the same number of elements from one queue to the other. Thus we can see there is no loss or gain of messages.

A_QUEUE clearly maintains its order of elements. A_PRI_QUEUE only puts a new element in front of an existing one if the new element has a higher priority. We have to check that this means that the elements in the priority queue behind this existing one must also have elements of a lower priority than the new one, i.e. that the queue is ordered.

This very informal argument might suffice in this case. But for critical systems a formal argument is necessary. For such an argument we must first define in terms of A_MESSAGE1, i.e. in terms of a buffer consisting of a queue and a priority queue, the hidden and undefined function *buffered* of A_MESSAGE0.

The definition we use is

value
  buffered : Buffer × T.Message* → **Bool**
  buffered((pq, q), l) ≡
    ($\exists$ l1 : T.Message* • l = l1 ^ q ∧ pq = sort(l1))

where *sort* is some definition of a sorting algorithm. The question is which definition to use, and since we are just adding functions to define *buffered*, which is never actually implemented, we can use any explicit or implicit function we wish, so long as, of course, it correctly defines a sort of its input. What guides our choice is what will make the proof easiest. If we look at the axiom *buffered_get* in A_MESSAGE0, which is one of the axioms we will have to prove, then it identifies the output message *m1* as one satisfying a particular property making it the first message that should appear, and this suggests a suitable description of a sorting algorithm: find the first, put it at the front, and sort the rest:

value
    sort : T.Message* $\to$ T.Message*
    sort(l) $\equiv$
      if l = $\langle\rangle$ **then** $\langle\rangle$
      else
        let i = first(l) **in**
          $\langle l(i) \rangle$ $\frown$
          sort(sublist(l, 1, i − 1) $\frown$ sublist(l, i + 1, **len** l))
        end
      end,

    first : T.Message* $\xrightarrow{\sim}$ **Nat**
    first(l) **as** i **post**
      i $\in$ **inds** l $\wedge$
      ($\forall$ j : **Nat** •
        j $\in$ {1 .. i − 1} $\Rightarrow$ $\sim$ T.leq(l(i), l(j))) $\wedge$
      ($\forall$ j : **Nat** •
        j $\in$ {i + 1 .. **len** l} $\Rightarrow$ T.leq(l(j), l(i)))
    pre l $\neq$ $\langle\rangle$,

    sublist : T.Message* $\times$ **Nat** $\times$ **Nat** $\to$ T.Message*
    sublist(l, i, j) **as** l1 **post**
      if i < 1 $\vee$ j > **len** l $\vee$ i > j **then** l1 = $\langle\rangle$
      else
        len l1 = j − i + 1 $\wedge$
        ($\forall$ k : **Nat** •
          k $\in$ **inds** l1 $\Rightarrow$ l1(k) = l(k + i − 1))
      end

sort uses two auxiliary functions *first* and *sublist* that are specified implicitly. This is common when defining functions that we want to use in proof: their properties are typically more useful than their definitions.

Proving Implementation. We are now in a position to formally prove the implementation of A_MESSAGE0 by the extension of A_MESSAGE1 that defines the hidden functions *buffered* (as described above) and *permutation*. The latter was concrete in A_MESSAGE0, so we just copy the definition of it and the auxiliary function count in the *extension*:

scheme E_MESSAGE1 = **extend** A_MESSAGE1 **with**

class
  value
    buffered ...,
    permutation ...
end

Now we can construct the **theory** that says that E_MESSAGE1 implements A_MESSAGE0:

```
context: E_MESSAGE1, A_MESSAGE0
theory MESSAGE01 :
axiom
  [ implements ]
    ⊢ E_MESSAGE1 ⪯ A_MESSAGE0
end
```

Fig. 12. The theory MESSAGE01

This can be proved using the translator from RSL to PVS [17], together with the PVS proof tool.

5 Example 2: Lift Control

5.1 Aims of Example

The example is the specification of a simple safety-critical system, and the use of model checking to gain assurance about the design. We use the recent addition [27] to the RAISE tools of a model checker to SAL [28].

The lift control described here is developed in much more detail, through to a model as a set of concurrent processes, in the RAISE method book [5].

The safety-criticality means that we will want to be very careful to state the safety properties and justify them. Some components (like buttons, doors and the lift cage) are hardware components; our specification of them will describe the assumptions about them.

5.2 Model Checking

First we provide a little background about what we want to achieve. We assume that we have specified a number of functions that can produce a new state of a system. In the previous example these are the functions *put*, *get*, and *shift*. Now we want to check that, perhaps provided these functions are applied according to some rules, or perhaps allowing them to be applied at any time, our system will evolve in particular ways. For example, we might have a consistency condition that we want always to be true. Or we might have a condition about something eventually happening (such as a message eventually being delivered).

To model check such an applicative RAISE specification we have i general to do 4 things:

1. We have to make the system finite. Model checking is like exhaustive testing, but it can only achieve this over a finite set of possible states. So typically we might have to replace an abstract type *Message*, say, with a variant type containing only three messages:

   type Message == m1 | m2 | m3

   Similarly types that were **Int** and **Nat** might be replaced with small ranges.
2. We have to make sure all our functions are explicitly defined.
3. We have to add a *transition system* to express the rules controlling when our functions can be applied (often just whenever their preconditions are true). We will see an example of a transition system in section 5.5.
4. We have to add definitions of the conditions we want to check, which are stated in the form of assertions in Linear Temporal Logic (LTL). We will see some examples of LTL assertions in section 5.6.

5.3 Requirements

A lift is required to serve a number of floors. Each floor has doors which must only be open when the lift is stationary at the floor. Each floor except the top one has a button to request the lift to stop there and then go up; each floor except the bottom one has a button to request the lift to stop there and then go down. The lift also has a button for each floor to request the lift to go to the floor.

Simplifying Assumptions

- We do not distinguish between lift doors (if any) and floor doors.
- We do not consider the time taken for the lift to move or the doors to open or close. We will at the detailed level, however, have both "do" and "acknowledge" events for such actions and assume the hardware will tell us by the acknowledgements when the actions are completed.
- We do not consider lights on buttons or audible signals that the lift is stopping at a floor. We assume these will be done purely by hardware.
- We will also make some assumptions about the way the lift cage is controlled that will be described later.

5.4 Initial Formulation

A lift is an example of an asynchronous system, since buttons may be pressed at any time. In other words there are external stimuli that may arrive at any time, or may never happen. We have to be careful with such systems to make them "loosely coupled". We must not create the situation where a lift is waiting for a button to be pushed, or a button is waiting for the lift to take notice of it.

We handle this problem quite naturally in our development style. There will be a BUTTON module with methods allowing a user to press it and allowing the lift to see if it has been pressed and to clear it.

As usual we start by considering the objects of the system and whether they will have dynamic state:

- the cage will presumably change its position, direction and speed
- doors will be open or closed or perhaps in intermediate positions
- buttons will be pressed (and lit) or cleared (and unlit)
- a floor could be dynamically "visited" by a lift or not but this would duplicate the lift position. So floors seem only to have static attributes, like their number, whether they are above or below other floors, whether they are the top or bottom floor.

Certainly it looks as if the lift, the doors and the buttons will have dynamic state and hence be modelled as RSL objects.

Next comes the question of what attributes are necessary for these. In this case there is a question of how finely we need to model things. Are doors just open or closed, or do they also have intermediate opening and closing states? Do we need to go further and measure their current separation, their velocities and accelerations? Similar questions apply to the cage's movements.

The answers to such questions will lie in the detailed requirements (or should be clarified before we start if not stated there). For manual doors it is almost certainly enough to just distinguish "closed" (when the door is shut and locked) from "open" when it does not mater if the door is actually physically open or shut or somewhere in between. The important thing is that it is not locked shut and therefore could be opened, so the lift must be stationary at that floor. It seems that the same distinction can be made about automatic doors: they are either in a safe closed state or in some other state.

We will make similar assumptions about the cage. We will assume it can be sufficiently characterised by being halted at a floor (when the doors there may be open), or in some other state which we will call "moving". When halted it will be at a floor; it turns out to be convenient to always associate it with a floor even when moving, and this will be the (next) floor it is moving towards. When moving it must have a direction, up or down. Again it turns out to be convenient to associate a direction with the lift when it is halted, which is the direction in which it was last moving.

Simplifications for Model Checking. Normally one would make a general model first, and then decide what changes are necessary to make it capable of being model checked. But here, since the general model is available already in [5], we will go straight to a model suitable for model checking.

We obviously need to be specific about the number of floors, and three floors seems to be the minimum number to allow all the possible movements of a lift: with only two floors there would be no possibility of moving past a floor without stopping, for example.

```
scheme
  TYPES =
    class
      value
        min_floor : Nat = 0, max_floor : Nat = 2

      type
        Floor = {| n : Nat • n ∈ {min_floor .. max_floor} |},
        Door_state == open | shut,
        Button == bup0 | bup1 | bdown1 | bdown2 | blift0 | blift1 | blift2,
        Button_state == lit | clear,
        Direction == up | down,
        Movement == halted | moving,
        Requirement :: here : Bool after : Bool before : Bool

      value
        next_floor : Direction × Floor →~ Floor
        next_floor(d, f) ≡
          if d = up then f + 1 else f − 1 end
          pre is_next_floor(d, f),

        is_next_floor : Direction × Floor → Bool
        is_next_floor(d, f) ≡
          if d = up then f < max_floor else f > min_floor end,

        invert : Direction → Direction
        invert(d) ≡ if d = up then down else up end
    end
```

Fig. 13. The scheme TYPES

```
context: TYPES
object T : TYPES
```

Fig. 14. The object T

This gives us enough to formulate the type module for the system, which we will call TYPES and instantiate as the global object T:

We have chosen to model the type *Floor* directly as a subtype of **Int**. We have no indication that there will be any attributes of floors other than their numbers (and we will assume that $f+1$ is directly above floor f, and $f-1$ directly below it).

Since we have decided on three floors we can also be explicit about what buttons there will be: two "up" buttons (on floors 0 and 1), two "down" buttons (on floors 1 and 2), and a lift button (inside the lift cage) for each of the three floors. Buttons are obviously simple two-state machines: they are "lit" (pressed), or "clear".

The type *Requirement* is used to control the cage by calculating, according to the button states, the current floor, and the current direction whether the cage is required to stop *here*, *after* (i.e. at some floor further on in the current direction), or *before* (i.e. at some floor in the opposite direction). The module BUTTONS in figures 15 and 16 defines the buttons, operations to press and clear them, and the calculation of a *Requirement*.

It would be more natural to define *required_beyond* by

required_beyond(f, d, bs) ≡
  T.is_next_floor(d, f) ∧
  let f′ = T.next_floor(d, f) **in**
    required_here(d, f′, bs) ∨ required_beyond(d, f′, bs)
  end

but our model checker SAL cannot handle recursive functions, so we have unrolled the recursion, using the fact that there are only three floors.

The DOORS module, figure 17, is straightforward.

The module for the CAGE, figure 18, is also simple.

We can now construct the lift system type from the cage, doors and buttons: figure 19.

Now we define a number of functions we need to operate the lift system: figure 20.

The function *move* will move the lift from a floor to the next floor in the given direction. It also has a parameter to say whether the lift is to move from a *halted* or *moving* state. *move* changes the three components of the lift system:

1. It calls the *move* function of the CAGE object *C*, which may change the direction, movement and floor attributes of the cage.
2. If the lift is moving from *halted* it calls the *close* function of the DOORS object *DS*, else the doors are unchanged.
3. The buttons are unchanged.

The function *halt* has a similar structure to *move*:

1. The cage is halted.
2. The doors at the floor where it is halting (which is the current floor) are opened.
3. The buttons for the current floor are cleared.

The functions *check_buttons*, *is_clear*, and *press* are just means to access the corresponding functions in the BUTTONS object *BS*.

The heart of the lift specification is the function *next* which calculates what to do next in any state, according to the current requirement: figure 21.

To explain the algorithm of *next* in detail:

- We calculate the current requirement using *check_buttons*. Recall that a requirement has three Boolean components: *here*, *after*, and *before*.
- If the lift is halted:

```
context: T
scheme BUTTONS = hide required_here, required_beyond in
  class
    type
      Buttons ::
        up0 : T.Button_state ↔ re_up0
        up1 : T.Button_state ↔ re_up1
        down1 : T.Button_state ↔ re_down1
        down2 : T.Button_state ↔ re_down2
        lift0 : T.Button_state ↔ re_lift0
        lift1 : T.Button_state ↔ re_lift1
        lift2 : T.Button_state ↔ re_lift2
    value
      clear : T.Floor × Buttons → Buttons
      clear(f, bs) ≡
        case f of
          0 → re_up0(T.clear, re_lift0(T.clear, bs)),
          1 → re_down1(T.clear, re_up1(T.clear, re_lift1(T.clear, bs))),
          2 → re_down2(T.clear, re_lift2(T.clear, bs))
        end,

      press : T.Button × Buttons → Buttons
      press(b, bs) ≡
        case b of
          T.bup0 → re_up0(T.lit, bs),
          T.bup1 → re_up1(T.lit, bs),
          T.bdown1 → re_down1(T.lit, bs),
          T.bdown2 → re_down2(T.lit, bs),
          T.blift0 → re_lift0(T.lit, bs),
          T.blift1 → re_lift1(T.lit, bs),
          T.blift2 → re_lift2(T.lit, bs)
        end,

      is_clear : T.Button × Buttons → Bool
      is_clear(b, bs) ≡
        case b of
          T.bup0 → up0(bs) = T.clear,
          T.bup1 → up1(bs) = T.clear,
          T.bdown1 → down1(bs) = T.clear,
          T.bdown2 → down2(bs) = T.clear,
          T.blift0 → lift0(bs) = T.clear,
          T.blift1 → lift1(bs) = T.clear,
          T.blift2 → lift2(bs) = T.clear
        end,
```

Fig. 15. The scheme BUTTONS: part 1

```
check : T.Direction × T.Floor × Buttons → T.Requirement
check(d, f, bs) ≡
  T.mk_Requirement(
      required_here(d, f, bs),
      required_beyond(d, f, bs),
      required_beyond(T.invert(d), f, bs)),

required_here : T.Direction × T.Floor × Buttons → Bool
required_here(d, f, bs) ≡
  case f of
    0 → lift0(bs) = T.lit ∨ up0(bs) = T.lit,
    1 →
      lift1(bs) = T.lit ∨
      case d of
        T.up →
          up1(bs) = T.lit ∨
          down1(bs) = T.lit ∧ lift2(bs) = T.clear ∧ down2(bs) = T.clear,
        T.down →
          down1(bs) = T.lit ∨
          up1(bs) = T.lit ∧ lift0(bs) = T.clear ∧ up0(bs) = T.clear
      end,
    2 → lift2(bs) = T.lit ∨ down2(bs) = T.lit
  end,

required_beyond : T.Direction × T.Floor × Buttons → Bool
required_beyond(d, f, bs) ≡
  T.is_next_floor(d, f) ∧
  let f' = T.next_floor(d, f) in
    required_here(d, f', bs) ∨
    T.is_next_floor(d, f') ∧
    let f'' = T.next_floor(d, f') in
      required_here(d, f'', bs)
    end
  end
end
```

Fig. 16. The scheme BUTTONS: part 2

- if *after* is true then move off in the current direction
- else, if *before* is true then move off in the opposite direction
- else no change
- else (the lift is moving):
  - if *here* is true then halt
  - else, if *after* and *before* are both false (so the lift is wanted nowhere) then halt
  - else, if *after* is true then keep moving in the same direction
  - else, if *before* is true, move in the opposite direction

```
context: T
scheme DOORS =
  class
    type
      Doors ::
        d0 : T.Door_state ↔ re_d0
        d1 : T.Door_state ↔ re_d1
        d2 : T.Door_state ↔ re_d2

    value
      open : T.Floor × Doors → Doors
      open(f, ds) ≡
        case f of
          0 → re_d0(T.open, ds),
          1 → re_d1(T.open, ds),
          2 → re_d2(T.open, ds)
        end,

      close : T.Floor × Doors → Doors
      close(f, ds) ≡
        case f of
          0 → re_d0(T.shut, ds),
          1 → re_d1(T.shut, ds),
          2 → re_d2(T.shut, ds)
        end,

      door_state : T.Floor × Doors → T.Door_state
      door_state(f, ds) ≡
        case f of
          0 → d0(ds),
          1 → d1(ds),
          2 → d2(ds)
        end
  end
```

Fig. 17. The scheme DOORS

The precondition *can_next(l)* is necessary because *move* in CAGE is partial, and *can_next(l)* ensures that the *requirement* only suggests moving to another floor when such a floor exists.

Safety. A full hazard analysis of the lift software is beyond the scope of this chapter, but its conclusions are the following safety requirements:

1. The door at a floor should only be open when the lift is halted at that floor
2. When the lift is halted at a floor the door at that floor should be open
3. The lift should eventually halt at some floor

```
context: T
scheme CAGE =
  class
    type
      Cage ::
        direction : T.Direction
        movement : T.Movement
        floor : T.Floor

    value
      /* generators */
      move : T.Direction × Cage ⇾ Cage
      move(d', m) ≡
        mk_Cage(d', T.moving, T.next_floor(d', floor(m)))
      pre T.is_next_floor(d', floor(m)),

      halt : Cage → Cage
      halt(m) ≡ mk_Cage(direction(m), T.halted, floor(m))
  end
```

Fig. 18. The scheme CAGE

```
context: T, CAGE, DOORS, BUTTONS
scheme LIFT =
  class
    object C : CAGE, DS : DOORS, BS : BUTTONS

    type
      Lift ::
        cage : C.Cage
        doors : DS.Doors
        buttons : BS.Buttons
```

Fig. 19. The scheme LIFT: the *Lift* type

The first of these ensures that people cannot fall into the lift shaft. The second and third together ensure that people in the lift can eventually get out (regardless of whether they press any buttons).

The third safety requirement is in fact a simple liveness condition: it says that eventually something desirable will happen. The first two are "safety" conditions in the computer science sense: that something bad will never happen. We can combine them into the function *safe*: figure 22.

Recall that the equality between Boolean values in RSL is the same as "⇔".

```
value
    move : T.Direction × T.Movement × Lift ⇒̃ Lift
    move(d, m, l) ≡
        mk_Lift(
            C.move(d, cage(l)),
            if m = T.halted
            then DS.close(C.floor(cage(l)), doors(l))
            else doors(l) end,
            buttons(l))
    pre T.is_next_floor(d, C.floor(cage(l))),

    halt : Lift → Lift
    halt(l) ≡
        mk_Lift(
            C.halt(cage(l)),
            DS.open(C.floor(cage(l)), doors(l)),
            BS.clear(C.floor(cage(l)), buttons(l))),

    check_buttons : Lift → T.Requirement
    check_buttons(l) ≡
        BS.check(
            C.direction(cage(l)), C.floor(cage(l)),
            buttons(l)),

    is_clear : T.Button × Lift → Bool
    is_clear(b, l) ≡ BS.is_clear(b, buttons(l)),

    press : T.Button × Lift → Lift
    press(b, l) ≡
        mk_Lift(cage(l), doors(l), BS.press(b, buttons(l))),
```

Fig. 20. The scheme LIFT: basic functions

5.5   Transition System

To design the transition system we need to decide first on the variables we need. We have a single state variable *Lift*, so it seems natural to use just that. We will also need an initial state, and the lift halted with the doors open at floor 0, with all buttons clear, is a natural choice.

Then we need to decide what the guarded commands for the transitions are. Clearly one should be the use of *next*, and the guard will be its precondition. The other should be *press*, in fact a choice of any button being pressed. There doesn't seem to be a guard needed for *press*, but if we try it without one we will find later that our checks that the lift must make progress will fail because the transition system will allow repeated *press* transitions with no *next* transitions. A simple solution to this is to only allow a *press* transition when the button involved is clear. This gives us the transition system in figure 23.

```
next : Lift ⇴ Lift
next(l) ≡
   let
      c = cage(l),
      ds = doors(l),
      bs = buttons(l),
      r = check_buttons(l),
      d = C.direction(c)
   in
      case C.movement(c) of
         T.halted →
            case r of
               T.mk_Requirement(_, true, _) →
                  move(d, T.halted, l),
               T.mk_Requirement(_, _, true) →
                  move(T.invert(d), T.halted, l),
               _ → l
            end,
         T.moving →
            case r of
               T.mk_Requirement(true, _, _) → halt(l),
               T.mk_Requirement(_, false, false) → halt(l),
               T.mk_Requirement(_, true, _) →
                  move(d, T.moving, l),
               T.mk_Requirement(_, _, true) →
                  move(T.invert(d), T.moving, l)
            end
      end
   end
   pre can_next(l),

can_next : Lift → Bool
can_next(l) ≡
   let c = cage(l), r = check_buttons(l) in
      (T.after(r) ⇒ T.is_next_floor(C.direction(c), C.floor(c))) ∧
      (T.before(r) ⇒ T.is_next_floor(T.invert(C.direction(c)), C.floor(c)))
   end
end
```

Fig. 21. The scheme LIFT: the function *next* and its precondition

The choice "⫿ b : T.Button" in the first transition is a choice over all buttons.

5.6   LTL Assertions

Now we need to design the appropriate LTL assertions. One is immediate: the lift is always safe:

ltl_assertion

```
safe : Lift → Bool
safe(l) ≡
    let c = cage(l), ds = doors(l) in
        (∀ f : T.Floor •
            (DS.door_state(f, ds) = T.open) =
                (C.movement(c) = T.halted ∧ C.floor(c) = f))
    end
```

Fig. 22. The scheme LIFT: the function *safe*

```
transition_system
    [L]
    local
        lift : Lift :=
            mk_Lift(
                C.mk_Cage(T.up, T.halted, 0),
                DS.mk_Doors(T.open, T.shut, T.shut),
                BS.mk_Buttons(
                    T.clear, T.clear, T.clear, T.clear, T.clear,
                    T.clear, T.clear))
    in
        (⫿ b : T.Button •
         [press]
         is_clear(b, lift) ⟶ lift' = press(b, lift))
        ⫿
        [next]
        can_next(lift) ⟶ lift' = next(lift)
    end
```

Fig. 23. The scheme LIFT: the transition system

[safe] L ⊢ G(safe(lift))

This deals with the first two of our safety requirements. Here we use the LTL operator "G", which means "globally, in all states". What about the third, that the lift eventually halts somewhere. We can write this as:

ltl_assertion
    [eventually_halts] L ⊢ G(F(C.movement(cage(lift)) = T.halted))

Here we also use the LTL operator "F", meaning "now or in the future". Note the use of "G" as well. "G(F(a))" means that from whatever state we start in, "a" is true in that state or in some state in the future. "F(a)" would means that if we start in the initial state "a" is true or will eventually be true.

It would also be interesting to know if the lift goes where it is wanted. For example, if either of the buttons relevant to floor 0 (*bup0* and *lift0*) are lit, then the lift should eventually halt at floor 0 with the doors open. We can write this as:

ltl_assertion
   [arrives0]
      L ⊢ G(BS.up0(buttons(lift)) = T.lit ∨ BS.lift0(buttons(lift)) = T.lit ⇒
            F(DS.d0(doors(lift)) = T.open))

Note here that we are assuming the global truth of *safe*, so that doors open at floor 0 implies the lift is halted there.

We write similar conditions for the other two floors.

The liveness conditions so far expressed all say that something *must* happen eventually. We are also sometimes interested in conditions that *can* happen, but not necessarily. All the LTL assertions so far written would be satisfied if the guard on the first transition were (by a specification error) always false. No button could be pressed, and the lift would be permanently stationary on floor 0: safe but useless as a lift. We can check that we do not have such a system by intentionally asserting something we believe to be false, for example that the cage can never reach floor 2:

ltl_assertion
   [moves] L ⊢ G(C.floor(cage(lift)) < 2)

The model checker obligingly produces a counter example, such as that the button *lift2* is pressed and the lift moves from floor 0 to floor 1 and then continues to floor 2. Now we have some confidence that our lift is actually capable of useful behaviour, and our assertions are not vacuous.

Another interesting property of our lift is that *can_next* is in fact always true. We can see this in part by using SAL's deadlock checker: if there were states with all buttons lit in which *can_next* were false, the system could deadlock. One should always check the transition system for deadlock before checking the LTL assertions, since SAL is only sound if there are no deadlocks.

A complete check that *can_next* is always true is to write and model check the LTL assertion *G(can_next(lift))*.

Splitting the State. We were lucky that the SAL model checker could check this system without running out of memory. There is general advice to divide the state as much as possible into separate variables, especially if some transitions will then only affect some of the variables. Even though it is not necessary in this case we will show the technique.

The obvious initial division is to have variables *cagev* etc. for the cage, doors and buttons. The initialisation of each of these is obvious.

The first transition, *press*, only appears to involve buttons. But then we realise we need to compute a new *requirement*, as this will change when buttons are pressed, so we add a new variable *req*, and we get the guarded command

(⟦ b : T.Button •
   [press]

BS.is_clear(b, buttonsv) $\longrightarrow$
  buttonsv$'$ = BS.press(b, buttonsv),
  req$'$ = BS.check(C.direction(cagev), C.floor(cagev), buttonsv$'$))

Note that the updates *cagev$'$* = *cage* and *doorsv$'$* = *doors* are implicitly included.

For the other transitions we can split according to the cases in *next*. For example, one will be

[move_on]
  C.movement(cagev) = T.halted $\wedge$ T.after(req) $\longrightarrow$
  cagev$'$ = C.move(C.direction(cagev), cagev),
  doorsv$'$ = DS.close(C.floor(cagev), doorsv),
  req$'$ = BS.check(C.direction(cagev$'$), C.floor(cagev$'$), buttonsv)

We can see that the general idea is that the top level functions *move, halt, next* etc. are effectively unfolded into the transition system (and could be removed). We could go further and split *cagev* into *directionv, movementv* and *floorv*, by effectively unfolding the functions in CAGE.

Clearly we should do this splitting only when it is necessary. The rewriting involved increases the chance of making an error and invalidating the results of the model checking.

5.7   Confidence Condition Checking

The translator to SAL produces a second "CC" translation that enables confidence conditions to be checked. Confidence conditions were introduced in Section 2.7.

The basic idea is as follows:

- All types are "lifted" into a type which includes the original type and a second type *Not_a_value* (nav). Whenever a confidence condition violation is detected, a nav is generated.
- All functions and operators are made strict in that whenever a nav is received as an argument it is returned as a result. So navs cannot disappear.
- The only LTL assertions generated are
  - All constant values are not navs
  - All variables are globally not navs
- The system will therefore validate these assertions if no navs are generated, and otherwise report the violation, giving also the sequence of transitions that led to it.
- The type *Not_a_value* is generated as an enumeration of identifiers which give an indication of where the error occurred.

For example, if we remove the two occurrences of *T.is_next_floor* from *required_beyond* in the BUTTONS module, and run CC version the second version of the LIFT, we get the result

The assertion 'LIFT1_L_cc_check' is invalid.

and the assertion name indicates we are checking transition system "L" from module "LIFT1". We see from the accompanying counter example that *req* contains

Requirement_nav(Precondition_of_function_T_next_floor_not_satisfied)

so we know that function *next_floor* in module *T* was called when its precondition was false.

6   RAISE Tools

Specifications of more than a few lines need to be checked by tools for syntax, scope and type errors. It is also necessary to have tools for translation to other languages, and convenient to have pretty printers (for layout, or for translation to markup languages like LaTeX). For RAISE there is a toolset [24] of free, open source tools that will run on any platform for which C can be compiled. Features of the tools include:

- syntax, scope, and type checking
- pretty printing
- generation of confidence conditions
- generation of RSL from UML class diagrams
- translation to C++ (for testing and implementation)
- translation to SML (for prototyping and testing, including mutation testing and test coverage)
- translation to PVS (for proof)
- translation to SAL (for model checking)

7   Summary

In this chapter we have provided an introduction to the RAISE Specification Language and to the RAISE method. We concentrate on the applicative style of RAISE, the style most commonly used initially in development. Complete information can be found in the books on RSL [6] and the method [5], and a number of case studies in [7]. The RAISE tools [24] are free and open source.

We also described two examples. The first is a simple communication system that allows the transmission of messages with the possibility of higher priority messages overtaking others. The example illustrates the use of abstract initial specification to capture vital properties, and of more detailed concrete specification to describe a model having those properties. The second example is a control system of a lift, and illustrates the use of model checking to gain confidence in a RAISE model.

References

1. George, C., Prehn, S.: The RAISE Tools Users Guide. LaCoS Report DOC/7, Computer Resources International A/S (1992)
2. Chalmers, D., Dandanell, B., Gørtz, J., Pedersen, J.S., Zierau, E.: Using RAISE — First Impressions From a LaCoS User Trial. In: Prehn, S., Toetenel, H. (eds.) VDM 1991. LNCS, vol. 551, Springer, Heidelberg (1991)
3. Milne, R.: The Formal Basis for the RAISE Specification Language. In: Semantics of Specification Languages. Workshops in Computing, Springer, Heidelberg (1993)
4. Bolignano, D., Debabi, M.: On the Semantic Foundations of RSL: a Concurrent, Functional and Imperative Specification Language. In: Proceedings of FORTE '93, Boston University (1993)
5. RAISE Method Group, T.: The RAISE Development Method. BCS Practitioner Series. Prentice Hall (1995), available by ftp from `ftp://ftp.iist.unu.edu/pub/RAISE/method_book`
6. RAISE Language Group, T.: The RAISE Specification Language. BCS Practitioner Series. Prentice Hall (1992), available from Terma A/S. Contact jnp@terma.com
7. Dang Van, H., George, C., Janowski, T., Moore, R.: Specification Case Studies in RAISE. In: FACIT, Springer, Heidelberg (2002), available by ftp from `ftp://ftp.iist.unu.edu/pub/RAISE/case_studies`
8. Jones, C.B., Middelburg, K.: A typed logic of partial functions reconstructed classically. Acta Informatica 31(5), 399–430 (1994)
9. Cheng, J., Jones, C.: On the usability of logics which handle partial functions. In: Morgan, C., Woodcock, J. (eds.) Proceedings of the Third Refinement Workshop, Springer, Heidelberg (1990)
10. Jones, C., Shaw, R.: Case Studies in Systematic Software Development. Prentice Hall International, Englewood Cliffs (1990)
11. Guttag, J.V., Horning, J.J. (eds.): Larch: Languages and Tools for Formal Specification. Texts and Monographs in Computer Science. Springer, Heidelberg (with Garland, S.J., Jones, K.D., Modet, A., Wing, J.M.) (1993)
12. Mosses, P.D.: CASL: A Guided Tour of its Design. In: Fiadeiro, J.L. (ed.) WADT 1998. LNCS, vol. 1589, pp. 216–240. Springer, Heidelberg (1999)
13. Spivey, J.M.: The Z Notation: A Reference Manual, 2nd edn. Prentice Hall International Series in Computer Science (1992)
14. Abrial, J.R.: The B-Book. Cambridge University Press, Cambridge (1996)
15. Aichernig, B.K.: Test-design through abstraction, a systematic approach based on the refinement calculus. Journal of Universal Computer Science (J.UCS) 7(8) (2001)
16. Hörl, J., Aichernig, B.K.: Validating voice communication requirements using lightweight formal methods. IEEE Software, 21–27 (May/June 2000)
17. Owre, S., Rushby, J., Shankar, N., von Henke, F.: Formal verification for fault-tolerant architectures: Prolegomena to the design of PVS. IEEE Transactions on Software Engineering 21(2), 107–125 (1995)
18. Bakar, B.A., Janowski, T.: Automated Result Verification with AWK. Technical Report 205, UNU-IIST, P.O. Box 3058, Macau (June 2000) (presented at and published in the proceedings of the 6th IEEE International Conference on Engineering of Complex Computer Systems, Tokyo, Japan, IEEE Computer Society Press (September 2000))
19. ChaoChen, Z., Hoare, C.A.R., Ravn, A.P.: A Calculus of Durations. Information Proc. Letters 40(5) (1992)

20. George, C., Yong, X.: An Operational Semantics for Timed RAISE. Technical Report 149, UNU-IIST. In: Woodcock, J.C.P., Davies, J., Wing, J.M. (eds.) FM 1999. LNCS, vol. 1709, Springer, Heidelberg (1999)

21. Li, L., Jifeng, H.: Towards a Denotational Semantics of Timed RSL using Duration Calculus. Technical Report 161, UNU-IIST, P.O.Box 3058, Macau (April 1999) (publication by Chinese Journal of Advanced Software Research (2000))

22. Li, L., Jifeng, H.: A Denotational Semantics of Timed RSL using Duration Calculus. Technical Report 168, UNU-IIST, P.O.Box 3058, Macau (July 1999) (presented at and published in the proceedings of The Sixth International Conference on Real-Time Computing Systems and Applications (RTCSA'99), part of the federated 1999 International Computer Congress, December 13 - 15, 1999, Hong Kong, pp. 492–503. IEEE Computer Society Press (1999))

23. Plotkin, G.: A structured approach to operational semantics. Technical report, Comp. Sci. Dept., Univ. of Edinburgh (1981)

24. George, C.: RAISE Tools User Guide. Technical Report 227, UNU-IIST, P.O. Box 3058, Macau (February 2001), the tools are available from http://www.iist.unu.edu

25. Schroër, F.W.: The GENTLE Compiler Construction System. R. Oldenbourg (1997), available from http://www.first.gmd.de/gentle/

26. Guttag, J.: Abstract data types and the development of data structures. CACM 20(6) (June 1977)

27. Perna, J.I., George, C.: Model checking RAISE specifications. Technical Report 331, UNU-IIST, P.O.Box 3058, Macau (December 2005)

28. de Moura, L., Owre, S., Rueß, H., Rushby, J., Shankar, N., Sorea, M., Tiwari, A.: SAL 2. In: Alur, R., Peled, D.A. (eds.) CAV 2004. LNCS, vol. 3114, pp. 496–500. Springer, Heidelberg (2004)

A Theory of Duration Calculus with Application

Michael R. Hansen[1,*] and Dang Van Hung[2]

[1] Informatics and Math. Modelling, Technical University of Denmark
Ricard Petersens Plads, DK-2800 Lyngby, Denmark
mrh@imm.dtu.dk
[2] United Nations University, Institute of Software Technology
Casa Silva Mendes, Est. do Engenheiro Trigo No. 4, Macao
dvh@iist.unu.edu

Abstract. In this chapter we will present selected central elements in the theory of Duration Calculus and we will give examples of applications. The chapter will cover syntax, semantics and proof system for the basic logic. Furthermore, results on decidability, undecidability and model-checking will be presented. A few extensions of the basic calculus will be described, in particular, Hybrid Duration Calculus and Duration Calculus with iterations. Furthermore, a case study: the bi-phase mark protocol, is presented. We will not attempt to be exhaustive in our coverage of topics; but we will provide references for further study.

Keywords: Real-time systems, metric-time temporal logic, duration calculus, decidability, model-checking, application.

1 Introduction to Duration Calculus

In this chapter we will introduce *Durations Calculus* (abbreviated DC) [72], present central elements of the theory, and show examples of applications. The aim is not to make a comprehensive presentation of the logic; but rather to cover central parts of the logic in a way that readers afterwards can study research papers on the topic. We refer to the monograph [70] for a thorough introduction to DC. The chapter [25] on Duration Calculus in [6] contains an introduction to DC and states major results without proofs, and addresses approaches to modelling real-time systems.

1.1 Background

Duration Calculus is an interval logic which was introduced by Zhou Chaochen, C.A.R. Hoare and A.P. Ravn [72] in 1991, in connection this the ProCoS I project (Provably Correct Systems), ESPRIT BRA 3104, 1989 – 1991, see [5]. In that project, formal techniques for the construction of provably correct systems were studied. Case studies of embedded real-time system, e.g. the Gas Burner

---

* This work has been partially funded by The Danish Council for Strategic Research under project **MoDES**, the Danish National Advanced Technology Foundation under project **DaNES**, and ARTIST2 (IST-004527).

C. George, Z. Liu, and J. Woodcock (Eds.): Domain Modeling, LNCS 4710, pp. 119–176, 2007.

case study by E.V. Sørensen, H. Rischel and A.P. Ravn, showed that there were a collection of properties which could not be expressed using the specification languages for real-time systems, which were available at that time.

Case studies showed that time *intervals* are important in models of real-time systems. Several formalism did support modelling with intervals. But the case studies also showed the need to express the *accumulated present time* of a certain phenomenon, or state, of the systems. This accumulated present time, also called the *duration of the state*, could not be expressed by the available formalism.

This led to the introduction of DC [72] as an extension of the *Interval Temporal Logic* (ITL) of Halpern, Manna, and Moszkowski [23,46], with the difference that DC is based on intervals of real numbers, whereas ITL is based on a discrete-time domain. The reason for basing DC on a continuous-time domain is that many of the considered applications were in the area of hybrid systems where a discrete computer component interacts with a continuous environment using sensors and actuators.

1.2   Motivating Examples

We will introduce the notion of *duration* using two simple examples as in [70]. The first example comes from the Gas Burner case study [63,58].

A simple gas burner system: Consider a simple model of a gas burner where we observe three aspects over time. The aspects are:

- the *gas is flowing*,
- the *flame is burning*, and
- there is a *gas leak*,

and they can be modelled by two *state variables*:

$$\text{Gas}, \text{Flame} : \text{Time} \rightarrow \{0, 1\} \ .$$

We shall use real numbers as the *time domain*, i.e.

$$\text{Time} \mathrel{\widehat{=}} \mathbb{R} \ ,$$

and the intuition is that $\text{Gas}(t) = 1$ if and only if (abbreviated iff), gas is leaking at time t. The state variable Flame has a similar interpretation. Furthermore, the aspect that gas leaks ($\text{Leak} : \text{Time} \rightarrow \{0, 1\}$) can be expressed by a Boolean combination of the two state variables above:

$$\text{Leak}(t) \mathrel{\widehat{=}} \text{Gas}(t) \wedge \neg\text{Flame}(t) \ .$$

A Boolean combination of state variables is called a *state expression*, and it describes an aspect of a combined state in the system.

A major requirement for a gas burner system is that the amount of gas leaking should not be too much. Leaking gas cannot be prevented because gas must be flowing a little while before it can be ignited. For a given time interval $[a, b]$, the integral

$$\int_a^b \text{Leak}(t)dt$$

is the total time the system is leaking in the interval $[a, b]$, also called the *duration* of Leak in $[a, b]$.

We shall use $\mathbb{Intv}$ to denote the set of all time intervals:

$$\mathbb{Intv} \; \hat{=} \; \{ [a, b] \subseteq \mathbb{R} \mid a \leq b \} .$$

Scheduling of processes sharing a single processor: In connection with DC, scheduling and shared processors have been studied in several papers, e.g. [69,67,11]. Consider a shared processor, where n processes $\{p_1, \ldots, p_n\}$ share a single processor. To formalize the behavior of this processor, the model must capture, at least

- which processes are ready to run, and
- which process (if any) is currently running.

There are many ways in which to choose the state variables and the model below is based on [69]. For each process $p_i, 1 \leq i \leq n$, two state variables are used:

$$\mathrm{Rdy}_i : \mathrm{Time} \to \{0, 1\}$$
$$\mathrm{Run}_i : \mathrm{Time} \to \{0, 1\} ,$$

where $\mathrm{Rdy}_i(t) = 1$ iff process p_i is ready at time t, and $\mathrm{Run}_i(t) = 1$ iff process p_i is running at time t.

Since only ready processes may run and at most one process may run at a given time, the state variables must satisfy the well-formedness constraints:

$$\mathrm{Run}_i(t) \;\Rightarrow\; \mathrm{Rdy}_i(t)$$
$$\mathrm{Run}_i(t) \;\Rightarrow\; \bigwedge_{j \neq i} \neg \mathrm{Run}_j(t) .$$

Suppose that each process p_i on regular basis or demand should complete a task, and to do so it needs a certain amount $k_i \in \mathbb{R}_+$ of processing time. If p_i starts on a task at time b and finishes that task at time e, then we have that

$$\int_b^e \mathrm{Run}_i(t)dt = k_i .$$

Hence, the duration of Run_i must be k_i in the interval $[b, e]$.

1.3   Informal Introduction to Duration Calculus

Duration Calculus is an example of a *modal logic* [7], where the *possible worlds* are time intervals. A consequence of this is that formulas can be considered truth-valued functions on intervals and properties of intervals can be expressed without mentioning the intervals explicitly. An example of a formula is

$$20 \cdot \int\! \mathrm{Leak} \leq \ell ,$$

where ℓ is a special symbol denoting the length $b - a$ of the actual interval, say $[a, b]$. The formula is true on the interval $[a, b]$, iff

$$20 \int_a^b \mathrm{Leak}(t)dt \leq b - a .$$

Thus, the duration of leak should at most be a twentieth of the elapsed time.

In general, atomic formulas are constructed from constants, durations and ℓ using functions and relation of real arithmetic.

Atomic formulas are combined using connectives and quantifiers of predicate logic. Furthermore, special interval *modalities* can be used. An example is the *chop modality* (written "$\frown$") from ITL: The formula $\phi \frown \psi$ (reads "ϕ chop ψ") holds on $[b, e]$, iff there exists m, where $b \leq m \leq e$, such that ϕ holds on $[b, m]$ and ψ holds on $[m, e]$:

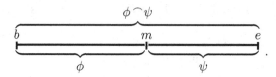

The chop modality is an example of a binary modality. Other modalities can be derived from chop using propositional logic, for example, the unary ("for some subinterval") modality $\Diamond$, and the dual modality $\Box$ ("for all subintervals"):

$$\Diamond \phi \;\;\hat{=}\;\; \text{true} \frown (\phi \frown \text{true}) \qquad \text{reads: "for some subinterval: } \phi\text{"}$$
$$\Box \phi \;\;\hat{=}\;\; \neg \Diamond \neg \phi \qquad\qquad\quad \text{reads: "for all subintervals: } \phi\text{"}.$$

Furthermore, we shall use the abbreviations:

$$\lceil S \rceil \;\hat{=}\; \int S = \ell \wedge \ell > 0$$
$$\lceil \rceil \;\hat{=}\; \ell = 0 \,.$$

The formula $\lceil S \rceil$ holds for non-point intervals where the state expression S holds (has value 1) throughout the interval except for isolated points, and $\lceil \rceil$ holds for point intervals.

Using these abbreviations on can express a decision for design of gas burners

$$\Box(\lceil \text{Leak} \rceil \Rightarrow \ell \leq 1) \,,$$

where gas is leaking for at most one time unit in every subinterval.

2   Syntax, Semantics and Proof System

This section will cover syntax, semantics and a proof system for Duration Calculus. The presentation is based on [70,25], but here we will be far less detailed.

2.1   Syntax

Duration Calculus was introduced as an extension of predicate modal logic, where the first-order part is based on real arithmetic. The first-order variables are called *global variables*, and we assume that an infinite set *GVar* of global variables ranged over by $x, y, z, \ldots$ is given. In general, we assume that there is an infinite set *FSymb* of *global function symbols* $f^n, g^m, \ldots$ equipped with arities

$n, m \geq 0$. If f^n has arity $n = 0$ then f is called a *constant*. The meaning of a global function symbol f^n, $n > 0$, will be an n-ary function, $\underline{f^n} : \mathbb{R}^n \to \mathbb{R}$. The meaning of a constant f^0 is a real number $\underline{f^0} \in \mathbb{R}$.

Similarly, we assume we that there is an infinite set $RSymb$ of *global relation symbols* $G^n, H^m, \ldots$ equipped with arities $n, m \geq 0$. The meaning of a global relation symbol G^n, $n > 0$, will be an n-ary truth-valued function, $\underline{G^n} : \mathbb{R}^n \to \{\text{tt,ff}\}$. The constants true and false are the only two global relation symbols with arity 0, and the meaning is the usual one: $\underline{\text{true}} = \text{tt}$ and $\underline{\text{false}} = \text{ff}$.

When function symbols, e.g. $+$ and $-$, and relation symbols, e.g. $\geq$ and $=$, occur in formulas they appear in the usual notation and are assumed to have their standard meaning.

We have the following syntactical categories for the time-dependent part:

- An infinite set $SVar$ of *state variables* $P, Q, R, \ldots.$ A state variable denotes a Boolean-valued function of time.
- A special symbol ℓ denoting the interval length.
- An infinite set $PLetter$ of *temporal propositional letters* $X, Y, \ldots.$ A temporal propositional letter denotes a truth-valued interval function.

The syntactical categories for *state expressions* $(S, S_i \in SExp)$, *terms* $(\theta, \theta_i \in Term)$, and *formulas* $(\phi, \psi \in Formula)$, are defined by the abstract syntax:

$$S ::= 0 \mid 1 \mid P \mid \neg S_1 \mid S_1 \vee S_2$$

$$\theta ::= x \mid \ell \mid \int S \mid f^n(\theta_1, \ldots, \theta_n)$$

$$\phi ::= X \mid G^n(\theta_1, \ldots, \theta_n) \mid \neg\phi \mid \phi \vee \psi \mid \phi \frown \psi \mid (\exists x)\phi .$$

In state expressions and formulas we shall use derived propositional connectives for conjunction $\wedge$, implication $\Rightarrow$, biimplication $\Leftrightarrow$, and standard abbreviations concerning quantifiers will be used.

Moreover, whenever $\neg, (\exists x), (\forall x), \square$ and $\diamond$ occur in formulas they have higher *precedence* than the binary connectives and the binary modalities $\frown$ and $\smile$ (defined below). The formula $(\square\phi) \Rightarrow (((\forall x)(\neg\psi)) \frown \varphi)$, for example, can be written as $\square\phi \Rightarrow ((\forall x)\neg\psi \frown \varphi)$. Furthermore, we will use standard abbreviation in connection with quantification, for example,

$$\exists x > \theta.\phi \mathrel{\widehat{=}} (\exists x)(x > \theta \wedge \phi) .$$

2.2   Semantics

In the semantics we shall shall assume fixed, standard interpretations of function and relation symbols of real arithmetic. The meaning of global variables is given by a *value assignment*, which is a function

$$\mathcal{V} : GVar \to \mathbb{R} ,$$

associating a real number with each global variable. Let Val be the set of all value assignments:

$$Val \; \hat{=} \; GVar \to \mathbb{R} \, .$$

Two value assignments $\mathcal{V}, \mathcal{V}' \in Val$ are called x-$equivalent$ if they agree on all global variables except x, i.e. if $\mathcal{V}(y) = \mathcal{V}'(y)$ for every global variable $y \neq x$.

An $interpretation$ for state variables and propositional letters is a function:

$$\mathcal{I} : \begin{pmatrix} SVar \\ \cup \\ PLetters \end{pmatrix} \to \begin{pmatrix} \text{Time} \to \{0,1\} \\ \cup \\ \mathbb{I}\text{ntv} \to \{\text{tt},\text{ff}\} \end{pmatrix} ,$$

where

- $\mathcal{I}(P) : \text{Time} \to \{0,1\}$, for every state variable P,
- $\mathcal{I}(P)$ has a finite number of discontinuity points in every interval, and
- $\mathcal{I}(X) : \mathbb{I}\text{ntv} \to \{\text{tt},\text{ff}\}$, for every propositional letter X.

Thus, each function $\mathcal{I}(P)$ has the property of $finite\ variability$, and, hence, $\mathcal{I}(P)$ is integrable in every interval.

The semantics of a state expression S, given an interpretation $\mathcal{I}$, is a function:

$$\mathcal{I}[\![S]\!] : \text{Time} \to \{0, 1\} \, ,$$

defined inductively on the structure of state expressions by:

$$\begin{aligned}
\mathcal{I}[\![0]\!](t) \quad &= 0 \\
\mathcal{I}[\![1]\!](t) \quad &= 1 \\
\mathcal{I}[\![P]\!](t) \quad &= \mathcal{I}(P)(t) \\
\mathcal{I}[\![(\neg S)]\!](t) \quad &= \begin{cases} 0 \text{ if } \mathcal{I}[\![S]\!](t) = 1 \\ 1 \text{ if } \mathcal{I}[\![S]\!](t) = 0 \end{cases} \\
\mathcal{I}[\![(S_1 \vee S_2)]\!](t) &= \begin{cases} 1 \text{ if } \mathcal{I}[\![S_1]\!](t) = 1 \text{ or } \mathcal{I}[\![S_2]\!](t) = 1 \\ 0 \text{ otherwise.} \end{cases}
\end{aligned}$$

The function $\mathcal{I}[\![S]\!]$ has a finite number of discontinuity points in any interval and is thus integrable in every interval. In the following we will use the abbreviations: $S_{\mathcal{I}} \; \hat{=} \; \mathcal{I}[\![S]\!]$ and $X_{\mathcal{I}} \; \hat{=} \; \mathcal{I}(X)$.

The $semantics\ of\ a\ term\ \theta$ in an interpretation $\mathcal{I}$ is a function:

$$\mathcal{I}[\![\theta]\!] : (Val \times \mathbb{I}\text{ntv}) \to \mathbb{R} \, ,$$

defined inductively on the structure of terms by:

$$\begin{aligned}
\mathcal{I}[\![x]\!](\mathcal{V}, [b, e]) \quad &= \mathcal{V}(x) \\
\mathcal{I}[\![\int S]\!][b, e] \quad &= \int_b^e S_{\mathcal{I}}(t)dt \\
\mathcal{I}[\![\ell]\!] \, (\mathcal{V}, [b, e]) \quad &= e - b \\
\mathcal{I}[\![f^n(\theta_1, \ldots, \theta_n)]\!] \, (\mathcal{V}, [b, e]) &= \underline{f}^n(c_1, \ldots, c_n) \\
& \quad \text{where } c_i = \mathcal{I}[\![\theta_i]\!] \, (\mathcal{V}, [b, e]), \text{ for } 1 \leq i \leq n.
\end{aligned}$$

The *semantics of a formula* ϕ in an interpretation $\mathcal{I}$ is a function:

$$\mathcal{I}[\![\phi]\!] : (\mathit{Val} \times \mathbb{Intv}) \to \{\mathrm{tt}, \mathrm{ff}\} \,,$$

defined inductively on the structure of formulas below, where the following abbreviations will be used:

$$\mathcal{I}, \mathcal{V}, [b, e] \models \phi \; \widehat{=} \; \mathcal{I}[\![\phi]\!] \, (\mathcal{V}, [b, e]) = \mathrm{tt}$$
$$\mathcal{I}, \mathcal{V}, [b, e] \not\models \phi \; \widehat{=} \; \mathcal{I}[\![\phi]\!] \, (\mathcal{V}, [b, e]) = \mathrm{ff} \,.$$

The definition of $\mathcal{I}[\![\phi]\!]$ is:

- $\mathcal{I}, \mathcal{V}, [b, e] \models X$ iff $X_{\mathcal{I}}([b, e]) = \mathrm{tt}$.

- $\mathcal{I}, \mathcal{V}, [b, e] \models G^n(\theta_1, \ldots, \theta_n)$ iff $\underline{G}^n(c_1, \ldots, c_n) = \mathrm{tt}$,
  where $c_i = \mathcal{I}[\![\theta_i]\!](\mathcal{V}, [b, e])$ for $1 \leq i \leq n$.

- $\mathcal{I}, \mathcal{V}, [b, e] \models \neg\phi$ iff $\mathcal{I}, \mathcal{V}, [b, e] \not\models \phi$.

- $\mathcal{I}, \mathcal{V}, [b, e] \models \phi \vee \psi$ iff $\mathcal{I}, \mathcal{V}, [b, e] \models \phi$ or $\mathcal{I}, \mathcal{V}, [b, e] \models \psi$.

- $\mathcal{I}, \mathcal{V}, [b, e] \models \phi ^\frown \psi$ iff $\mathcal{I}, \mathcal{V}, [b, m] \models \phi$ and $\mathcal{I}, \mathcal{V}, [m, e] \models \psi$,
  for some $m \in [b, e]$.

- $\mathcal{I}, \mathcal{V}, [b, e] \models (\exists x)\phi$ iff $\mathcal{I}, \mathcal{V}', [b, e] \models \phi$, for some $\mathcal{V}'$ x-equivalent to $\mathcal{V}$.

A formula ϕ is *valid*, written $\models \phi$, iff $\mathcal{I}, \mathcal{V}, [b, e] \models \phi$, for every interpretation $\mathcal{I}$, value assignment $\mathcal{V}$, and interval $[b, e]$. Moreover, a formula ψ is *satisfiable* iff $\mathcal{I}, \mathcal{V}, [b, e] \models \psi$, for some interpretation $\mathcal{I}$, value assignment $\mathcal{V}$, and interval $[b, e]$.

Examples: The validity of the following two formulas relies on the finite variability of states (Why?).

$$\lceil \rceil \vee (\mathrm{true} ^\frown \lceil S \rceil) \vee (\mathrm{true} ^\frown \lceil \neg S \rceil) \tag{1}$$

$$\lceil \rceil \vee (\lceil S \rceil ^\frown \mathrm{true}) \vee (\lceil \neg S \rceil ^\frown \mathrm{true}) \,. \tag{2}$$

The next three formulas express basic properties of durations:

$$\textstyle\int S + \int \neg S = \ell \,, \qquad \int S \leq \ell \quad \text{and} \quad \int S_1 \geq \int S_2, \text{ if } S_2 \Rightarrow S_1,$$

and the following formulas are valid formulas about $\lceil S \rceil$:

$$\lceil S \rceil \Leftrightarrow (\lceil S \rceil ^\frown \lceil S \rceil) \quad \text{and} \quad (\lceil S_1 \rceil \wedge \lceil S_2 \rceil) \Leftrightarrow \lceil S_1 \wedge S_2 \rceil \,,$$

where the first formula holds because we have a continuous time domain, and the last formula reflects the structure of state expressions.

2.3   Proof System

The proof system has two parts: The first part is a based on the proof system S' for IL presented and shown complete wrt. *abstract* value and time domains in [13]. The second part is proof system for state durations, which is shown relative complete wrt. IL in [27].

Proof system for interval logic: The proof system S' is a Hilbert style proof system, where we shall use the following notions. *Free (global) variables* as known from predicate logic. Furthermore, a term is called *flexible* if ℓ or a duration $\int S$ occur in the terms, and a formula is called *flexible* if ℓ, a duration $\int S$ or a propositional letter occur in the formula. A term or formula which is not flexible is also called *rigid*. Note that a rigid formula may contain the chop modality.

Furthermore, we shall use the *dual-chop* modality $\phi \smile \psi$ defined by:

$$\phi \smile \phi \mathrel{\hat{=}} \neg((\neg\phi) ^\frown (\neg\psi)) \qquad \text{reads: "}\phi \text{ dual-chop } \psi\text{"}.$$

The reading of $\phi \smile \psi$ is as follows: $\phi \smile \psi$ holds on $[b, e]$ iff, for all $m \in [b, e]$: ϕ holds on $[b, m]$ or ψ holds on $[m, e]$.

The axioms and rules below are basically those of [13], except that we use the abbreviation for the dual modality of chop. This has the advantage that certain axioms and rules can be expressed more succinctly (avoiding double negation), and some proof have a more compact form.

The axioms of are:

A0 $\quad \ell \geq 0$.

A1 $\quad \begin{aligned}((\phi ^\frown \psi) \wedge (\neg\phi \smile \varphi)) &\Rightarrow (\phi ^\frown (\psi \wedge \varphi)). \\ ((\phi ^\frown \psi) \wedge (\varphi \smile \neg\psi)) &\Rightarrow ((\phi \wedge \varphi) ^\frown \psi).\end{aligned}$

A2 $\quad ((\phi ^\frown \psi) ^\frown \varphi) \Leftrightarrow (\phi ^\frown (\psi ^\frown \varphi))$.

R $\quad \begin{aligned}(\phi ^\frown \psi) &\Rightarrow \phi \quad \text{if } \phi \text{ is a rigid formula.} \\ (\phi ^\frown \psi) &\Rightarrow \psi \quad \text{if } \psi \text{ is a rigid formula.}\end{aligned}$

E $\quad \begin{aligned}(\exists x.\phi ^\frown \psi) &\Rightarrow \exists x.(\phi ^\frown \psi) \quad \text{if } x \text{ is not free in } \psi. \\ (\phi ^\frown \exists x.\psi) &\Rightarrow \exists x.(\phi ^\frown \psi) \quad \text{if } x \text{ is not free in } \phi.\end{aligned}$

L1 $\quad \begin{aligned}((\ell = x) ^\frown \phi) &\Rightarrow ((\ell \neq x) \smile \phi). \\ (\phi ^\frown (\ell = x)) &\Rightarrow (\phi \smile (\ell \neq x)).\end{aligned}$

L2 $\quad (x \geq 0 \wedge y \geq 0) \Rightarrow ((\ell = x + y) \Leftrightarrow ((\ell = x) ^\frown (\ell = y)))$.

L3 $\quad \begin{aligned}\phi &\Rightarrow (\phi ^\frown (\ell = 0)) \\ \phi &\Rightarrow ((\ell = 0) ^\frown \phi).\end{aligned}$

The inference rules of are:

MP $\quad$ if ϕ and $\phi \Rightarrow \psi$ then ψ. $\hfill$ (modus ponens)

G $\quad$ if ϕ then $(\forall x)\phi$. $\hfill$ (generalisation)

N $\quad \begin{aligned}&\text{if } \phi \text{ then } \phi \smile \text{false.} \\ &\text{if } \phi \text{ then false} \smile \phi.\end{aligned}$ $\hfill$ (necessity)

M $\quad \begin{aligned}&\text{if } \phi \Rightarrow \psi \text{ then } (\phi ^\frown \varphi) \Rightarrow (\psi ^\frown \varphi). \\ &\text{if } \phi \Rightarrow \psi \text{ then } (\varphi ^\frown \phi) \Rightarrow (\varphi ^\frown \psi).\end{aligned}$ $\hfill$ (monotonicity)

Predicate logic: The proof system also contains axioms of first order predicate logic with equality. Extra care must be taken when universally quantified formulas are instantiated and when an existential quantifier is introduced as shown below.

A term θ is called *free for* x in ϕ if x does not occur freely in ϕ within a scope of $\exists y$ or $\forall y$, where y is any variable occurring in θ. Furthermore, a formula is called *chop free* if $\frown$ does not occur in the formula.

Two axiom schemes for quantification are:

$$\text{Q1} \quad \forall x.\phi(x) \Rightarrow \phi(\theta) \qquad \left(\begin{array}{l} \text{if } \theta \text{ is free for } x \text{ in } \phi(x), \text{ and} \\ \text{either } \theta \text{ is rigid or } \phi(x) \text{ is chop free} \end{array} \right).$$
$$\text{Q2} \quad \phi(\theta) \Rightarrow \exists x.\phi(x)$$

The proof system has to contain axioms for first order logic of real arithmetic. We will not be explicit about other axioms and rules of real arithmetic. We just write PL in proofs, when we exploit properties of real arithmetic.

Proof system for state durations: The axioms and rules for DC must reflect the structure of state expressions. The axioms are:

DCA1 $\int 0 = 0$.

DCA2 $\int 1 = \ell$.

DCA3 $\int S \geq 0$.

DCA4 $\int S_1 + \int S_2 = \int (S_1 \vee S_2) + \int (S_1 \wedge S_2)$.

DCA5 $((\int S = x) \frown (\int S = y)) \Rightarrow (\int S = x + y)$.

DCA6 $\int S_1 = \int S_2$, provided $S_1 \Leftrightarrow S_2$ holds in propositional logic.

We also need rules to formalize the finite variability of state expressions. To this end, the notion *state induction* is introduced. The main idea of state induction is the following. To prove that ϕ holds for every interval, it suffices to establish:

– The base case: ϕ holds for point intervals.
– The inductive step: it is established that ϕ holds for an interval of the form $X \frown (\lceil S \rceil \vee \lceil \neg S \rceil)$, under the assumption that $X \Rightarrow \phi$. Hence, from a arbitrary interval X on which ϕ holds:

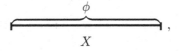

we can conclude that ϕ holds for a larger interval, where X is extended by a section throughout which either S or $\neg S$ hold:

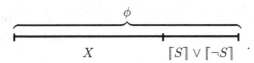

These two steps suffices since every interval can be covered by a finite sequence of sections for which either $\lceil S \rceil$ or $\lceil \neg S \rceil$ holds.

Let $H(X)$ be a formula containing the propositional letter X and let $S_1, \ldots, S_n$ be any finite collection of state expressions which are *complete* in the sense that

$$(\bigvee_{i=1}^{n} S_i) \Leftrightarrow 1 .$$

For a complete collection of state expressions: $S_1, \ldots, S_n$, there are two *induction rules*:

> IR1   If $H(\lceil \rceil)$ and $H(X) \Rightarrow H(X \vee \bigvee_{i=1}^{n}(X \frown \lceil S_i \rceil))$
> then $H(\text{true})$

and

> IR2   If $H(\lceil \rceil)$ and $H(X) \Rightarrow H(X \vee \bigvee_{i=1}^{n}(\lceil S_i \rceil \frown X))$
> then $H(\text{true})$,

where $H(\phi)$ denotes the formula obtained from $H(X)$ by replacing every occurrence of X in H with ϕ.

In these rules $H(\lceil \rceil)$ is called the *base case*, $H(X)$ is called the *induction hypothesis*, and X called the *induction letter*.

Deduction and proof: A *deduction of ϕ from a set of formulas Γ* is a sequence of formulas

$$\phi_1$$
$$\vdots$$
$$\phi_n ,$$

where ϕ_n is ϕ, and each ϕ_i is either a member of Γ, an instance of one of the above axiom schemes or obtained by applying one of the above inference rules to previous members of the sequence. We write $\Gamma \vdash \phi$ to denote that there exists a deduction of ϕ from Γ, and we write $\Gamma, \phi \vdash \psi$ for $(\Gamma \cup \{\phi\}) \vdash \psi$. When $\Gamma = \emptyset$, the deduction is called a *proof* of ϕ. In this case we call ϕ a *theorem* $\vdash \phi$.

As an example, we derive the monotonicity rules for the dual of chop:

> IL1 $\phi \Rightarrow \psi \vdash (\phi \overset{\smile}{} \varphi) \Rightarrow (\psi \overset{\smile}{} \varphi)$
> $\phi \Rightarrow \psi \vdash (\varphi \overset{\smile}{} \phi) \Rightarrow (\varphi \overset{\smile}{} \psi) .$

Proof. Here is a deduction establishing the first part:

1.	$\phi \Rightarrow \psi$	assumption
2.	$\neg\psi \Rightarrow \neg\phi$	1., PL
3.	$\neg(\psi \overset{\smile}{} \varphi) \Rightarrow \neg\psi \frown \neg\varphi$	def. $\smile$, PL
4.	$(\neg\psi \frown \neg\varphi) \Rightarrow (\neg\phi \frown \neg\varphi)$	2., M
5.	$\neg(\psi \overset{\smile}{} \varphi) \Rightarrow (\neg\phi \frown \neg\varphi)$	4., def. $\smile$, PL
6.	$(\phi \overset{\smile}{} \varphi) \Rightarrow (\psi \overset{\smile}{} \varphi)$	5., def. $\smile$, PL

The following two deduction theorems can be used to simplify proofs.

Theorem 1. *[28] If a deduction*

$$\Gamma, \phi \vdash \psi$$

involves

- *no application of the generalization rule* G *in which the quantified variable is free in* ϕ, *and*
- *no application of the induction rules,* IR1 *and* IR2, *in which the induction letter occurs in* ϕ,

then

$$\Gamma \vdash \Box \phi \Rightarrow \psi \, .$$

Theorem 2. *[70] Suppose that* $\{S_1, \ldots, S_n\}$ *is a complete set of state expressions. Then*

$$\left. \begin{array}{l} \Gamma \vdash H(\lceil \, \rceil) \text{ and} \\ \Gamma, H(X) \vdash H(X \vee \bigvee_{i=1}^{n} (X \frown \lceil S_i \rceil)) \end{array} \right\} \text{ implies } \Gamma \vdash H(true) \, ,$$

and

$$\left. \begin{array}{l} \Gamma \vdash H(\lceil \, \rceil) \text{ and} \\ \Gamma, H(X) \vdash H(X \vee \bigvee_{i=1}^{n} (\lceil S_i \rceil \frown X)) \end{array} \right\} \text{ implies } \Gamma \vdash H(true) \, ,$$

provided the deductions from $\Gamma, H(X)$ *involve no application of the induction rules, where the induction letter occurs in* $H(X)$.

Consider the formulas:

DC1 $\lceil \, \rceil \vee (true \frown \lceil S \rceil) \vee (true \frown \lceil \neg S \rceil)$

DC2 $\lceil \, \rceil \vee (\lceil S \rceil \frown true) \vee (\lceil \neg S \rceil \frown true) \, .$

The proof of DC1, for example, is by induction using $H(X) \mathrel{\hat{=}} X \Rightarrow$ DC1 as induction hypothesis and $\{S, \neg S\}$ as a complete collection of state expressions. Using Theorem 2 (and propositional logic), the proof is completed by establishing the base case $H(\lceil \, \rceil)$, i.e. $\lceil \, \rceil \Rightarrow$ DC1, which is trivial, and three easy deductions:

- $(X \Rightarrow DC1) \vdash X \Rightarrow DC1,$
- $(X \Rightarrow DC1) \vdash (X \frown \lceil S \rceil) \Rightarrow DC1,$ and
- $(X \Rightarrow DC1) \vdash (X \frown \lceil \neg S \rceil) \Rightarrow DC1.$

An essential property of a proof system is that every theorem is valid.

Theorem 3. *(Soundness)*

$$\vdash \phi \text{ implies } \models \phi \, .$$

The soundness of axioms and inference rules of IL are treated in [13] and axioms for DC are simple. The soundness of IR1 and IR2 relies on the finite variability of states and we refer to [70] for a proof.

Another important property of a proof system is that it is complete, i.e. every valid formula is provable. As DC extends real number arithmetic, and, furthermore, natural number reasoning are used in several case studies, the completeness issue is a complex matter.

We will not go into details concerning completeness issues for the arithmetical parts, but mention a few classical results. In 1951, Tarski [64] proved a completeness and decidability results for a theory of reals, where atomic formulas involve equality (=) and ordering relations ($<, \leq, >, \geq$) and terms are constructed from rational constants and (global) variables using operations for addition, subtraction, negation, and multiplication. For natural number theory, Presburger gave in 1930 a decision algorithm for linear arithmetic (excluding multiplication), while Gödel, in 1931, established his famous incompleteness theorem for a theory having addition, subtraction, negation, and multiplication as operations. Concerning theorem proving with real numbers, we refer to [29].

For DC, there is a relative completeness result with respect to ITL [27,70], which shows that there is a deduction for every valid formula, from the collection of valid ITL formulas. The completeness of IL, with abstract value and time domains, is proved in [12], and in [21] there is a completeness result for DC with respect to abstract value and time domains.

3   Basic Decidability and Undecidability Results

It is a very tedious and error-prone task to write proof by hand using a formal system. DC proofs are no exception. So there is a natural desire to get tool support. Interval logics are, however, typically very expressive logics, which often are undecidable. For example, the propositional interval logic HS with unary modalities *begins, ends* and their inverses, by Halpern and Shoham [24], is shown highly undecidable for a collection of classes of interval models. In this section we will review the first results on decidable as well as undecidable fragments of DC [71], to show limits of what we can hope for. In Sect. 5 and Sect. 6 we will provide some extensions to these results.

3.1   A Basic Decidability Results

Consider first a simple subset of DC called *Restricted Duration Calculus* (*RDC*). The formulas of *RDC* are constructed by the following abstract syntax:

$$S ::= 0 \mid 1 \mid P \mid \neg S_1 \mid S_1 \vee S_2$$
$$\phi ::= \lceil S \rceil \mid \neg \phi \mid \phi \vee \psi \mid \phi ^\frown \psi.$$

Decidability results were established both for discrete and continuous time interpretations. In a *discrete time interpretation* state variables are allowed to change value at natural number time points only. Furthermore, only intervals having natural number end points are considered, and, at last, chop points must be natural numbers.

Theorem 4. *[71] The satisfiability problem for RDC is decidable for discrete and continuous time.*

The theorem is proved by reducing the satisfiability problem for RDC to the emptiness problem for regular languages, which is decidable. The main idea of this reduction is that a letter in the alphabet describes a section of an interpretation. A letter is a conjunction of state variables or negation of state variables. $\lceil S \rceil$ is translated L^+, where L is the set of letters "for which S is true". Disjunction, negation and chop correspond to union, complement and concatenation, respectively, of regular languages.

The complexity of the satisfiability problem for RDC is non-elementary. Peter Sestoft established this result for discrete time and for continuous time the result is shown in [52].

In the tool DCVALID [50] an extension of discrete-time RDC with quantification of state variables is translated into Monadic Second-Order Logic over finite strings, which is a slight variant of the Weak Monadic Second-Order theory of one successor (WS1S) [10,14]. This second-order theory is decidable and used for instance in the MONA system [40].

There are certainly more results than those mentioned above. For example, decidable subsets are also considered in [26,42,49,17,59,36,16]. References [61,51] concern implementation of tools to check the validity of a subclass of Duration Calculus and its higher-order version. In [18], there is a bounded model construction for discrete-time Duration Calculus, which is shown NP-complete. Furthermore, in [15], a robust interpretation for a subset of Duration Calculus is considered, and a semi-decision result is obtained. Model-checking formulas wrt. automata based implementations is considered in [39,73,43,44,9,38,16], and automated proof assistance is considered in [62,60,45,56,55,54].

3.2 Basic Undecidability Results

From a point of view of tool support, a disappointing fact is that seemingly small extensions to RDC are shown undecidable in [71] by reducing the halting problem of two-counter machines to the satisfiability problem. The subsets considered were:

- RDC_1, which is defined by:

$$\phi ::= \ell = 1 \mid \lceil S \rceil \mid \neg \phi \mid \phi \vee \psi \mid \phi ^\frown \psi .$$

- RDC_2, which is defined by:

$$\phi ::= \int S_1 = \int S_2 \mid \neg \phi \mid \phi \vee \psi \mid \phi ^\frown \psi .$$

- RDC_3, which is defined by:

$$\phi ::= \ell = x \mid \lceil S \rceil \mid \neg \phi \mid \phi \vee \psi \mid \phi ^\frown \psi \mid \forall x. \phi .$$

The satisfiability problem for RDC_1 is decidable for a discrete time interpretation as the formula $\ell = 1$ is expressible in RDC as $\lceil 1 \rceil \wedge \neg (\lceil 1 \rceil ^\frown \lceil 1 \rceil)$. But for a continuous time domain, the satisfiability problem for RDC_1 is undecidable.

Theorem 5. *[71] The satisfiability problem for RDC_1 is undecidable for continuous time.*

The main idea behind the proof of this theorem is to reduce the (undecidable) halting problem for 2-counter machines to the satisfiability problem of RDC_1. In this case, a value m of a counter is represented by a state variable C which has m sections of the form $\lceil C \rceil$ separated by sections of the form $\lceil \neg C \rceil$. The continuous time domain and the formula $\ell = 1$ are used to represent any counter value on a unit interval. A full configuration of a 2-counter machine can be represented on an interval of length 4 (two units for the counters, one for the current state, and one is used as a separator). Furthermore, the formulas can express transitions of the machine from one configuration to the next.

Theorem 6. *[71] The satisfiability problems for RDC_2 and RDC_3 are undecidable for discrete and continuous time.*

The main idea behind the encoding of a 2-counter machine in RDC_2 is to have two state variables C^+ and C^- for a counter c, so that the value of c is $\int C^+ - \int C^-$ interpreted over the interval representing the computation up to the current state. The value of c is increased (decreased) by one by letting $\lceil C^+ \rceil$ ($\lceil C^- \rceil$) hold over the next section. To simulate the 2-counter machine we just need the formula $\int C^+ = \int C^-$ to test whether c's value is 0, but it is not necessary to compute the actual value of the counter. The sections representing counter operations should have equal length and RDC_2 is strong enough to express that. The proof idea works for discrete as well as a continuous time domain. We will not go into details about RDC_3, as this undecidability result just shows the well-known power of first-order logic. For further details, we refer to [71,70].

The non-elementary complexity bound of the satisfiability problem for RDC shows that very "heavy" tools are necessary to handle this seemingly simple subset. Furthermore, the simple extension with $\ell = 1$ (to RDC_2) leads to undecidability (wrt. continuus time), and so does the extension with $\int S_1 = \int S_2$ leading to RDC_3. Hence, it is not easy to find decidable extensions to RDC where you can express precise time bounds like $\ell = 1$, or make assertion about the duration of states. Before we extend the decidability results, we first show that RDC can be simplified [8].

3.3 RDC^*: A Simplification of RDC

The simplified fragment, called RDC^*, has the following abstract syntax:

$$\phi ::= P \mid \pi \mid \neg\phi \mid \phi \vee \psi \mid \phi \frown \psi \,,$$

where P is a state variable. In RDC^*, π stands for point interval and P corresponds to the formula $\lceil P \rceil$ of RDC. The simplification is that RDC^* has no syntactical category for state expressions.

The interesting point is that RDC^* has the same expressive power as RDC, as shown by the translation $\cdot^*$ from the formulas of RDC into formulas of RDC^*:

$$\begin{array}{llll}
\lceil 0 \rceil^* & = \neg T & \lceil 1 \rceil^* & = \neg \pi \\
\lceil P \rceil^* & = P & \lceil \neg S \rceil^* & = \neg \pi \wedge \Box \neg (\lceil S \rceil^*) \\
\lceil S_1 \vee S_2 \rceil^* & = \neg \pi \wedge \Box (\neg \pi \rightarrow \Diamond (\lceil S_1 \rceil^* \vee \lceil S_2 \rceil^*)) & (\neg \phi)^* & = \neg (\phi^*) \\
(\phi \vee \psi)^* & = \phi^* \vee \psi^* & (\phi ^\frown \psi)^* & = \phi^* {}^\frown \psi^* .
\end{array}$$

This translation shows that Boolean connectives in state expressions "behave like modalities. The correctness of the translation is stated in the following lemma, which says that truth is preserved by the translation $\cdot^*$. The lemma also establishes that the simpler language RDC* has the same expressive power as RDC.

Lemma 1. *[8] For all RDC formulas ϕ, interpretations $\mathcal{I}$, and intervals $[t, u]$:*

$$\mathcal{I}, [t, u] \models \phi^* \quad \text{iff} \quad \mathcal{I}, [t, u] \models \phi.$$

Discrete time: Lemma 1 holds for discrete time as well. Even in a seemingly simple fragment, some real-time properties are expressible. Observe first that the formula $\ell = 1$ can be represented in RDC as follows:

$$\ell = 1 \; \hat{=} \; \lceil 1 \rceil \wedge \neg (\lceil 1 \rceil ^\frown \lceil 1 \rceil).$$

Simple notions of durations are also expressible in RDC and hence also in RDC^*. For example, the formula $\int S = 1$ is expressed as

$$(\lceil \rceil \vee \lceil \neg S \rceil) ^\frown (\lceil S \rceil \wedge \ell = 1) ^\frown (\lceil \rceil \vee \lceil \neg S \rceil).$$

The above two formulas are not expressible in continuous-time RDC (see [71,70]). For further discussion about the expressibility of RDC we refer to [70].

4   Duration Calculus with Iterations

In this section, we present an extension of Duration Calculus, called DC*, with the modality *iteration*, also known as *Kleene star*. Iteration was introduced to DC to facilitate the reasoning about repetitive behaviour. Iteration is particularly important for the description of the repetitive behaviour of timed automata in DC. In [37] we developed a method for designing real-time hybrid systems from specifications written using a subset of DC* which consists of the so-called *simple* DC* formulas. One can reason about the correctness of designs in terms of the semantics of DC*. However, it would be more practical and interesting to be able to prove correctness syntactically. This requires the development of a proof system for DC*.

Let us return to the Gas Burner example presented earlier. The DC formula

$$S \rightleftharpoons \Box(\ell > 60 \Rightarrow (20 \int Leak \leq \ell)) \tag{3}$$

specifies that a gas burner can be in the *Leak* state for no more than one-twentieth of the time in any time interval that is at least 1 minute long. Consider the gas

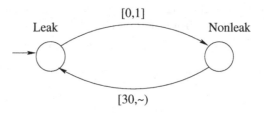

Fig. 1. A Simple Gas Burner Design

burner design described by the real-time automaton shown in Fig. 1. We assume that *Leak* is the initial state for the sake of simplicity. In this design *Leak* becomes detected within 1 second and leaks are separated by at least 30 seconds. This can be specified by the DC* formula

$$D \rightleftharpoons (([Leak] \wedge \ell \leq 1)^\frown ([Nonleak] \wedge \ell \geq 30))^* . \tag{4}$$

To show the correctness of the design, we have to prove $D \Rightarrow S$. This can be done by means of our axioms about iteration given in this section.

In this section we study the deductive power of three groups of axioms and a rule for iteration in DC which we add to the proof system presented in Sect. 2.

In the sequel, the set of the variables which have free occurrences in a formula φ is denoted by $FV(\varphi)$. For sets of formulas Γ, $FV(\Gamma)$ is defined as $\bigcup_{\varphi \in \Gamma} FV(\varphi)$. The state variables occurring freely a formula φ are assumed to be in $FV(\varphi)$ too.

4.1 Iteration Formulas

DC is extended by iteration by allowing formulas of the form φ^*. The semantics of formulas of this form is defined as:

$$\mathcal{I}, \mathcal{V}, [b, e] \models \varphi^* \text{ iff either } b = e, \text{ or there exist } m_0, m_1, \dots, m_m \text{ such that}$$
$$b = m_0 < m_1 < \dots < m_n = e \text{ and}$$
$$\mathcal{I}, \mathcal{V}, [m_i, m_{i+1}] \models \varphi \text{ for } i = 0, \dots, n-1.$$

Iteration * binds more tightly than $\frown$ and the propositional connectives.

4.2 Axioms and a Rule About Iteration in DC

From the definition of the semantics of iteration, it is obvious that the following two axioms are needed for the DC proof system:

$$(DC^*1) \qquad\qquad \ell = 0 \Rightarrow \varphi^*$$
$$(DC^*2) \qquad\qquad (\varphi^* {}^\frown \varphi) \Rightarrow \varphi^*$$

However, DC^*1 and DC^*2 are not enough to characterise the definition of iteration. In the following, we develop three axioms more named DC^*3, DC^*4 and DC^*5, and show that combining any of them with DC^*1 and DC^*2 will completely characterise the meanings of iteration.

(DC^*3) $((\varphi^* \wedge \psi)^\frown \text{true}) \Rightarrow ((\psi \wedge \ell = 0)^\frown \text{true}) \vee ((((\varphi^* \wedge \neg\psi)^\frown \varphi) \wedge \psi)^\frown \text{true})$

To understand the meaning of DC*3, assume that some non-point initial subinterval $[b, e']$ of the reference interval $[b, e]$ satisfies ψ and φ^*, and $\mathcal{I}, \mathcal{V}, [b, b] \not\models \psi$. By the definition of the semantics of iteration, for some $m_0, \ldots, m_n$ such that $b = m_0 < m_1 < \ldots < m_n = e'$ it holds that $\mathcal{I}, \mathcal{V}, [m_i, m_{i+1}] \models \varphi$. Let $j \le n$ be the least such that $\mathcal{I}, \mathcal{V}, [b, m_j] \models \psi$. From our assumption, j exists and $j > 0$. Hence, $\mathcal{I}, \mathcal{V}, [b, m_{j-1}] \models \varphi^* \wedge \neg\psi$, and consequently, $\mathcal{I}, \mathcal{V}, [b, m_j] \models ((\varphi^* \wedge \neg\psi)^\frown \varphi) \wedge \psi$.

$$(\text{DC}^*4) \qquad \Box(\ell = 0 \vee (\psi^\frown \varphi) \Rightarrow \psi) \Rightarrow (\varphi^* \Rightarrow \psi),$$

DC*4 is an expression of the fact that $\tilde{I}(\varphi^*)$ is the least set of time intervals $X \subseteq \mathbf{I}(T)$ which satisfies the inclusion

$$\tilde{I}(\ell = 0) \cup \tilde{I}(\varphi)^\frown X \subseteq X.$$

For simplicity, let us denote

$$\mathsf{f}(\varphi, Q) \rightleftharpoons \neg(((\mathrm{true}^\frown \lceil Q \rceil) \vee \ell = 0)^\frown (\lceil \neg Q \rceil \wedge \neg\varphi)^\frown (\lceil Q \rceil^\frown \mathrm{true}) \vee \ell = 0).$$

This formula $\mathsf{f}(\varphi, Q)$ means that every maximal non-trivial subinterval of the reference interval which satisfies $\lceil \neg Q \rceil$ satisfies φ. Let

$$\mathsf{g}(\varphi, P) \rightleftharpoons \mathsf{f}(\varphi, P) \wedge \mathsf{f}(\varphi, \neg P).$$

This formula means that all maximal non-trivial subintervals of the reference interval $[b, e]$ which satisfy either $\lceil P \rceil$ or $\lceil \neg P \rceil$ satisfy φ. Because of the finite variability of state variables in DC, these intervals form a finite partition of $[b, e]$. Therefore, if the model $(\mathcal{I}, \mathcal{V}, [b, e])$ satisfies $\mathsf{g}(\varphi, P)$, then it also satisfies φ^*. This observation is captured by the rule

$$(\text{DC}^*5) \quad \frac{\Gamma \vdash (\alpha^\frown \mathsf{g}(\varphi, P)^\frown \beta) \Rightarrow \psi}{\Gamma \vdash (\alpha^\frown \varphi^*{}^\frown \beta) \Rightarrow \psi}, \text{ where } P \notin FV(\Gamma \cup \{\varphi, \psi, \alpha, \beta\}).$$

If we substitute $\ell = 0$ for both α and β in the rule, we get a simpler version of this rule:

$$\frac{\Gamma \vdash \mathsf{g}(\varphi, P) \Rightarrow \psi}{\Gamma \vdash \varphi^* \Rightarrow \psi}, \text{ where } P \notin FV(\Gamma \cup \{\varphi, \psi\})$$

As mentioned above, if a reference interval $[b, e]$ satisfies $\mathsf{g}(\varphi, P)$, then the time points at which P changes its value inside φ partition it into subintervals which satisfy φ, and therefore $[b, e]$ itself satisfies φ^*. Given a *concrete* interpretation of P, the points at which P changes its value define a *concrete* finite partition of $[b, e]$, whereas for $[b, e]$ to satisfy φ^* we just need the *existence* of such a partition. Therefore, the side condition $P \notin FV(\Gamma \cup \{\varphi, \psi\})$ is needed to make the existence of such a partition independent from the interpretation of the variables that contribute to the truth value of formulas in $\Gamma \cup \{\varphi, \psi\}$.

Note that the scope of the soundness of $DC^*1 - DC^*4$ is, in fact, the extension ITL^* of ITL by iteration, because these axioms involve no DC-specific constructs.

It has been shown in [19] that with the additional axioms and rule DC*1, DC*2 and DC*5 for iteration, the proof system of DC is complete in the abstract-time domain for DC^*.

4.3   Interderivability Between DC*3, DC*4 and DC*5

The proof rule DC*5 is implicitly related to the state variable binding existential quantifier in DC*. The key ingredient in this rule is the formula $\mathbf{g}(\varphi, P)$. The proof that DC*5 is derivable from DC*1, DC*2 and DC*4 involved the proof system for the higher order Duration Calculus which is not presented in this chapter. Readers are referred to [19] for the proof details.

The relationship between the axioms introduced for iteration is formulated as follows.

Proposition 1. *[19]*

1. *DC*4 is provable in the extension of the proof system for DC by just DC*3.*
2. *DC*3 and DC*4 is provable in the extension of the proof system for DC by the axioms DC*1, DC*2 and DC*5.*

4.4   Examples of the Use of DC*1–DC*5

In this subsection we give derivations for a couple of DC* theorems of general interest and use one of them in a proof about our introductory gas-burner example in order to give some such illustration with a practical flavour.

Here are two derivations of the monotonicity of iteration. One of them involves DC*3:

$$\begin{aligned}
\alpha^* \wedge \neg\beta^* &\Rightarrow ((\neg\beta^* \wedge \ell = 0)^\frown \text{true}) \vee ((((\alpha^* \wedge \beta^*)^\frown\alpha) \wedge \neg\beta^*)^\frown\text{true}) && \text{by } DC^*3 \\
&\Rightarrow ((((\alpha^* \wedge \beta^*)^\frown\alpha) \wedge \neg\beta^*)^\frown\text{true}) && \text{by } DC^*1 \\
&\Rightarrow (\neg\beta^* \wedge \beta^*)^\frown\text{true} && \text{by } DC_2^* \\
&&& \text{and } \alpha \Rightarrow \beta \\
&\Rightarrow \text{false}
\end{aligned}$$

The other involves the proof rules ω and DC*5:

$$\begin{aligned}
&1\ \left(\frac{\lceil P \rceil \vee}{\lceil \neg P \rceil}\right)^k \Rightarrow \left(\mathbf{g}(\alpha, P) \Rightarrow \left(\Box(\varphi \Rightarrow \beta) \Rightarrow \bigvee_{l \leq k} \beta^l\right)\right) && k < \omega, \text{DC} \\
&2\ \beta^m \Rightarrow \beta^* && m < \omega, DC^*1, DC^*2, \text{DC} \\
&3\ (\lceil P \rceil \vee \lceil \neg P \rceil)^k \Rightarrow (\mathbf{g}(\alpha, P) \Rightarrow (\Box(\varphi \Rightarrow \beta) \Rightarrow \beta^*)) && k < \omega, 1, 2, \text{DC} \\
&4\ \mathbf{g}(\alpha, P) \Rightarrow (\Box(\varphi \Rightarrow \beta) \Rightarrow \beta^*) && 3, \omega \\
&5\ \alpha^* \Rightarrow (\Box(\varphi \Rightarrow \beta) \Rightarrow \beta^*) && 4, DC^*5 \\
&6\ \Box(\varphi \Rightarrow \beta) \Rightarrow (\alpha^* \Rightarrow \beta^*)
\end{aligned}$$

Here follows another useful DC* theorem:

$$\begin{aligned}
\vdash_{\text{DC}^*} &\Box(\varphi \Rightarrow \neg(\text{true}^\frown\neg\alpha) \wedge \neg(\neg\beta^\frown\text{true})) \wedge \\
&\Box(\ell = 0 \Rightarrow \alpha \wedge \beta) \wedge \Box(\beta \Rightarrow \neg(\text{true}^\frown\neg\gamma)) \Rightarrow && (5) \\
&\Rightarrow \varphi^* \Rightarrow \Box(\gamma \vee (\alpha^\frown\varphi^*{}^\frown\beta)).
\end{aligned}$$

To prove it in our system, below we give a derivation of $\varphi^* \Rightarrow \Box(\gamma \vee (\alpha^\frown\varphi^*{}^\frown\beta))$ using

$$\varphi \Rightarrow \neg(\text{true}^\frown\neg\alpha), \varphi \Rightarrow \neg(\neg\beta^\frown\text{true}), \beta \Rightarrow \neg(\text{true}^\frown\neg\gamma) \text{ and } \ell = 0 \Rightarrow \alpha, \ell = 0 \Rightarrow \beta$$

as assumptions. Then (5) will follow by the deduction theorem for DC [28].

$1\ \varphi \Rightarrow \neg(\text{true} ⌢ \neg\alpha)$ — assumption

$2\ \varphi \Rightarrow \neg(\text{true} ⌢ \neg(\alpha ⌢ \ell = 0))$ — by 1

$3\ \ell = 0 \Rightarrow \varphi^*$ — by DC_1^*

$4\ \varphi \Rightarrow \neg(\text{true} ⌢ \neg(\alpha ⌢ \varphi^*))$ — by 2, 3, $Mono_r$

$5\ \ell = 0 \Rightarrow \alpha$ — assumption

$6\ \ell = 0 \Rightarrow (\ell = 0 ⌢ \ell = 0)$ — $L2$

$7\ \ell = 0 \Rightarrow (\alpha ⌢ \varphi^*)$ — by 5, 6, DC_1^*, $Mono_l$, $Mono_r$

$8\ (\text{true} ⌢ \neg(\alpha ⌢ \varphi^*)) \Rightarrow \neg\ell = 0$ — by 7, DC

$9\ \neg((\text{true} ⌢ \neg(\alpha ⌢ \varphi^*)) \wedge \ell = 0 ⌢ \text{true})$ — by 8, N_l

$10\ (\varphi^* \wedge (\text{true} ⌢ \neg(\alpha ⌢ \varphi^*))) \Rightarrow$
$(((\text{true} ⌢ \neg(\alpha ⌢ \varphi^*)) \wedge \ell = 0) ⌢ \text{true}) \vee$
$(((\varphi^* \wedge \neg(\text{true} ⌢ \neg(\alpha ⌢ \varphi^*))) ⌢ \varphi) \wedge$
$(\text{true} ⌢ \neg(\alpha ⌢ \varphi^*))) ⌢ \text{true})$ — by DC^*3

$11\ (\varphi^* \wedge \neg(\text{true} ⌢ \neg(\alpha ⌢ \varphi^*)) ⌢ \varphi) \wedge$
$(\text{true} ⌢ \neg(\alpha ⌢ \varphi^*)) \Rightarrow$
$(\text{true} ⌢ (\alpha ⌢ \varphi^* ⌢ \varphi) \wedge \neg(\alpha ⌢ \varphi^*)) \vee$
$(\varphi \wedge (\text{true} ⌢ \neg(\alpha ⌢ \varphi^*))))$ — DC

$12\ (\alpha ⌢ \varphi^* ⌢ \varphi) \Rightarrow (\alpha ⌢ \varphi^*)$ — by DC_2^*, $Mono_r$

$13\ \neg((\alpha ⌢ \varphi^* ⌢ \varphi) \wedge \neg(\alpha ⌢ \varphi^*))$
$\vee(\varphi \wedge (\text{true} ⌢ \neg(\alpha ⌢ \varphi^*)))$ — by 4, $Mono_r$, 14

$14\ \neg(\text{true} ⌢ ((\alpha ⌢ \varphi^* ⌢ \varphi) \wedge \neg(\alpha ⌢ \varphi^*))$
$\vee(\varphi \wedge (\text{true} ⌢ \neg(\alpha ⌢ \varphi^*))))$ — by 13, N_r

$15\ \neg((\varphi^* \wedge \neg(\text{true} ⌢ \neg(\alpha ⌢ \varphi^*))) ⌢ \varphi) \wedge$
$(\text{true} ⌢ \neg(\alpha ⌢ \varphi^*)))$ — by 11, 14

$16\ \varphi^* \Rightarrow \neg(\text{true} ⌢ \neg(\alpha ⌢ \varphi^*)))$ — by 9, 10, 15, $Mono_l$

$17\ \varphi^* \wedge (\neg(\varphi^* ⌢ \neg\beta) ⌢ \text{true}) \Rightarrow$
$((((\neg(\varphi^* ⌢ \neg\beta) ⌢ \text{true}) \wedge \ell = 0) ⌢ \text{true}) \vee$
$(((\varphi^* \wedge \neg(\neg(\varphi^* ⌢ \neg\beta) ⌢ \text{true})) ⌢ \varphi) \wedge$
$(\neg(\varphi^* ⌢ \neg\beta) ⌢ \text{true})) ⌢ \text{true})$ — DC_3^*

$18\ \ell = 0 \Rightarrow \beta$ — assumption

$19\ \ell = 0 \Rightarrow \varphi^*$ — DC_1^*

$20\ \ell = 0 \Rightarrow \neg(\neg(\varphi^* ⌢ \neg\beta) ⌢ \text{true})$ — 18, 19, DC

$21\ \neg((\neg(\varphi^* ⌢ \neg\beta) ⌢ \text{true}) \wedge \ell = 0 ⌢ \text{true})$ — 20, DC

$22\ \neg(((\varphi^* \wedge \neg(\neg(\varphi^* ⌢ \neg\beta) ⌢ \text{true})) ⌢ \varphi) \wedge (\neg(\varphi^* ⌢ \neg\beta) ⌢ \text{true}) ⌢ \text{true})$ — DC

$23\ \varphi^* \Rightarrow \neg(\neg(\varphi^* ⌢ \neg\beta) ⌢ \text{true})$ — 17, 20, 22, DC

$24\ \beta \Rightarrow \neg(\text{true} ⌢ \neg\gamma)$ — assumption

$25\ \varphi^* \Rightarrow \square(\gamma \vee (\alpha ⌢ \varphi^* ⌢ \neg\beta))$ — 16, 23, 24, DC

Now let us prove the correctness of the gas-burner design from the introduction as a last example of the working of our DC* axioms and rule. We have to give a derivation for

$$((\lceil Leak \rceil \wedge \ell \leq 1) ⌢ (\lceil Nonleak \rceil \wedge \ell \geq 30))^* \Rightarrow \square(\ell \geq 60 \Rightarrow 20 \int Leak \leq \ell).$$

Let
$$\varphi \rightleftharpoons \lceil Leak \rceil \wedge \ell \leq 1 \frown \lceil \neg Leak \rceil \wedge \ell \geq 30,$$
$$\alpha \rightleftharpoons \ell = 0 \vee \lceil \neg Leak \rceil \vee (\lceil Leak \rceil \wedge \ell \leq 1 \frown \lceil \neg Leak \rceil \wedge \ell \geq 30),$$
$$\beta, \gamma \rightleftharpoons \ell = 0 \vee (\ell \leq 1 \wedge \lceil Leak \rceil \frown \ell = 0 \vee \lceil \neg Leak \rceil).$$

The formulas

$$\Box(\varphi \Rightarrow \neg(true \frown \neg \alpha) \wedge \neg(\neg \beta \frown true)), \quad \Box(\ell = 0 \Rightarrow \alpha \wedge \beta) \text{ and } \beta \Rightarrow \neg(true \frown \neg \gamma)$$

are valid in DC without iteration. Therefore we can complete our derivation using (5), provided we can derive

$$\gamma \Rightarrow 20 \int Leak \leq \ell \text{ and } (\alpha \frown \varphi^* \frown \beta) \wedge \ell \geq 60 \Rightarrow 20 \int Leak \leq \ell.$$

The first formula is straightforward to derive without DC*-specific axioms. Here follows a derivation for the second formula:

1 $\alpha \Rightarrow 31 \int Leak \leq \ell$ DC
2 $\varphi^* \wedge 31 \int Leak > \ell \Rightarrow (\varphi^* \wedge 31 \int Leak > \ell \frown true)$ DC
3 $\varphi \Rightarrow 31 \int Leak \leq \ell$ DC
4 $(\varphi^* \wedge 31 \int Leak > \ell \frown true) \Rightarrow$
  $(\ell = 0 \wedge 31 \int Leak > \ell \frown true) \vee$
  $(((\varphi^* \wedge 31 \int Leak \leq \ell \frown \varphi) \wedge 31 \int Leak > \ell) \frown true)$ by DC^*3
5 $\ell = 0 \Rightarrow 31 \int Leak \leq \ell$ DC
6 $(\varphi^* \wedge 31 \int Leak > \ell \frown true) \Rightarrow$
  $(((\varphi^* \wedge 31 \int Leak \leq \ell \frown \varphi) \wedge 31 \int Leak > \ell) \frown true)$ by 4, 5, $Mono_r$
7 $(\varphi^* \wedge 31 \int Leak \leq \ell \frown \varphi) \Rightarrow 31 \int Leak \leq \ell$ by 2, 3, DC
8 $\varphi^* \Rightarrow 31 \int Leak \leq \ell$ by 6, 7, $Mono_r$
9 $(\alpha \frown \varphi^*) \Rightarrow 31 \int Leak \leq \ell$ by 1, 8, DC
10 $\beta \Rightarrow \int Leak \leq 1$ DC
11 $(\alpha \frown \varphi^* \frown \beta) \wedge \ell \geq 60 \Rightarrow 20 \int Leak \leq \ell$ by 9, 10, DC

Iteration is known *chop-star* in Moszkowski's original discrete-time *ITL*, where it is regarded as part of the basic system. One should notice here that the axioms DC*1–DC*4 are valid in discrete-time *ITL* too and can be derived in its proof system. The rule DC*5, however, is new and DC-specific.

5   Hybrid Duration Calculus (*HDC*)

The modalities of DC are defined in terms of the chop-modality only. Hence, for every expressible modality only subintervals, of a given interval, can be reached. We also say that DC supports *contracting modalities*. In this section we study a hybrid version of *RDC** called *hybrid duration calculus (HDC)*. HDC was introduced in [8], and the results of this section comes from that paper.

"Pure" modal logics do not have a mean for referencing worlds (in our case intervals) explicitly in formulas. In hybrid modal logics worlds can be referred to in the syntax. We shall see in following, that the hybrid machinery, in the case of *RDC*, gives us increased expressiveness as expanding modalities, for example, can be expressed. Furthermore, satisfiability for *HDC* is still decidable, and that problem is still non-elementary.

5.1   Syntax of *HDC*

We extend the language of RDC* (see Sect. 3.3) with a countable collection of symbols called *nominals*. We use $a, b, \ldots$ to range over nominals. A nominal will name one and only one interval. Furthermore, we extend the language with a satisfaction operator a: for each nominal a, with the global modality E and with the down-arrow binder $\downarrow$. The grammar of *HDC* is as follows:

$$\phi ::= P \mid \pi \mid \neg\phi \mid \phi \vee \psi \mid \phi \,^\frown \psi \mid a \mid a : \phi \mid E\phi \mid \downarrow a.\phi \,.$$

The intuition with the new types of formulas are: The formula a holds at the specific interval named by a only; the formula $a : \phi$ holds if ϕ holds on the interval named by a; $E\phi$ holds if there is some interval where ϕ holds; and $\downarrow a.\phi$ holds if ϕ holds under the assumption that a names the current interval. To limit the number of required parentheses, we will use the following precedence relation on the connectives: the down-arrow binders $\downarrow a$ have the lowest precedence; $^\frown$, $\vee$ and $\wedge$ have the next lowest precedence; $\neg$, E and the satisfaction operators $a :$ have the highest precedence.

5.2   Semantics of *HDC*

In order to give semantics for *HDC*, we introduce the notion of an *assignment* G that associates a unique interval $[t_a, u_a] \subseteq \mathbb{R}_{\geq 0}$ with each nominal a. An *interpretation* $\mathcal{I}$ for *HDC* is simply as for DC. For interpretations $\mathcal{I}$, assignments G, intervals $[t, u] \subseteq \mathbb{R}_{\geq 0}$, and *HDC* formulas ϕ, we define the semantic relation $\mathcal{I}, G, [t, u] \models \phi$ below. We just give the cases which are special for *HDC*:

$$
\begin{array}{lll}
\mathcal{I}, G, [t, u] \models \pi & \text{iff} & u = t \\
\mathcal{I}, G, [t, u] \models P & \text{iff} & u > t \text{ and } P_{\mathcal{I}}(t) = 1 \text{ almost everywhere on } [t, u] \\
\mathcal{I}, G, [t, u] \models a & \text{iff} & G(a) = [t, u] \\
\mathcal{I}, G, [t, u] \models a : \phi & \text{iff} & \mathcal{I}, G, G(a) \models \phi \\
\mathcal{I}, G, [t, u] \models E\phi & \text{iff} & \text{for some interval } [v, w]: \mathcal{I}, G, [v, w] \models \phi \\
\mathcal{I}, G, [t, u] \models \downarrow a.\phi & \text{iff} & \mathcal{I}, G[a := [t, u]], [t, u] \models \phi \,,
\end{array}
$$

where $G[a := [t, u]]$ is the assignment that assigns $[t, u]$ to a and agrees with G on all other nominals.

5.3   Expressivity of HDC

We will now give examples showing the extra expressiveness of *HDC*.

Propositional neighborhood logic: The interval logic *Neighbbourhood Logic* was introduced in [68]. Neighbourhood Logic has two basic modalities $\Diamond_l$ (reads:

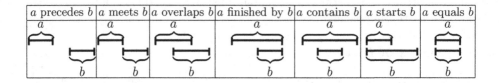

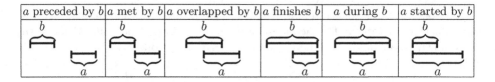

Fig. 2. The 13 possible relations between two intervals a and b

"for some left neighbourhood) and $\Diamond_r$ (reads: "for some right neighbourhood). These two modalities, which are both expanding, are defined by:

$$\mathcal{I}, [t, u] \models \Diamond_l \phi \text{ iff } \mathcal{I}, [s, t] \models \phi \text{ for some } s \leq t$$
$$\mathcal{I}, [t, u] \models \Diamond_r \phi \text{ iff } \mathcal{I}, [u, v] \models \phi \text{ for some } v \geq u,$$

and they can be expressed in *HDC* in the following way:

$$\Diamond_l \phi \text{ is defined by } \downarrow a.E(\phi \frown a)$$
$$\Diamond_r \phi \text{ is defined by } \downarrow a.E(a \frown \phi) ,$$

where the correctness is easily checked using the semantics. This shows *HDC* to be more expressive than standard *RDC*, since *RDC* cannot express the neighborhood modalities or other expanding modalities.

Allen's interval relations: Allen has shown [2], that there are 13 possible relations between a pair of intervals. All these relations can, in *HDC*, be expressed in a natural manner [8]. Allen's interval relations are presented in Fig. 2, and, in Fig. 3, we show how each of the 13 relations can be expressed in *HDC*. In the formulas, a and b are nominals denoting the two intervals in question. It is a simple exercise to check the correctness of the translations in Fig. 3.

5.4 Monadic Second-Order Theory of Order

We shall reduce satisfiability of *HDC* to satisfiability of *monadic second-order theory of order*. The following presentation of monadic second-order theory of order, named $L_2^<$, is based on [53].

Syntax of $L_2^<$: The formulas are constructed from first-order variables, ranged over by $x, y, z, \ldots$, and second-order variables, ranged over by $P, Q, R, \ldots$, as described by the following grammar:

$$\phi ::= x < y \mid x \in P \mid \phi \vee \psi \mid \neg \phi \mid \exists x \phi \mid \exists P \phi .$$

a precedes b	$a : \Diamond_r(\neg\pi \wedge \Diamond_r b)$
a meets b	$a : \Diamond_r b$
a overlaps b	$E(\downarrow c.\neg\pi \wedge a : (\neg\pi \frown c) \wedge b : (c \frown \neg\pi))$
a finished by b	$a : (\neg\pi \frown b)$
a contains b	$a : (\neg\pi \frown b \frown \neg\pi)$
a starts b	$b : (a \frown \neg\pi)$
a equals b	$a : b$
a preceded by b	$a : \Diamond_l(\neg\pi \wedge \Diamond_l b)$
a met by b	$a : \Diamond_l b$
a overlapped by b	$E(\downarrow c.\neg\pi \wedge b : (\neg\pi \frown c) \wedge a : (c \frown \neg\pi))$
a finishes b	$b : (\neg\pi \frown a)$
a during b	$b : (\neg\pi \frown a \frown \neg\pi)$
a started by b	$a : (b \frown \neg\pi)$

Fig. 3. Representation in HDC of the 13 possible relations between intervals

Semantics of $L_2^<$: A *structure* $K = (A, B, <)$ *for* $L_2^<$ consists of a set A, partially ordered by $<$, and a set B of Boolean-valued functions on A. An element $b \in B$ can be considered a, possibly infinite, subset of A: $\{a \in A : b(a) = \text{true}\}$.

An *interpretation* $\mathcal{I}$ associates a member $P_{\mathcal{I}}$ of B to every second-order variable P and a *valuation* ν is a function assigning a member $\nu(x)$ of A to every first-order variable x. The semantic relation $\mathcal{I}, \nu \models \phi$ is defined by:

$$\mathcal{I}, \nu \models x < y \text{ iff } \nu(x) < \nu(y)$$
$$\mathcal{I}, \nu \models x \in P \text{ iff } \nu(x) \in P_{\mathcal{I}}$$
$$\mathcal{I}, \nu \models \neg\phi \quad \text{iff } \mathcal{I}, \nu \not\models \phi$$
$$\mathcal{I}, \nu \models \phi \vee \psi \text{ iff } \mathcal{I}, \nu \models \phi \text{ or } \mathcal{I}, \nu \models \psi$$
$$\mathcal{I}, \nu \models \exists x\phi \quad \text{iff for some } a \in A: \mathcal{I}, \nu[x := a] \models \phi$$
$$\mathcal{I}, \nu \models \exists P\phi \quad \text{iff for some } b \in B: \mathcal{I}[P := b], \nu \models \phi .$$

In the following we will assume that we have standard abbreviations for derived relations, propositional connectives and quantifiers. Furthermore, we use the following abbreviations:

$$x \geq y \mathrel{\widehat{=}} \neg(x < y) \qquad \text{and} \qquad x = y \mathrel{\widehat{=}} x \geq y \wedge y \geq x ,$$

as we will just consider sets A with a linear order.

We shall exploit the following two decidability results for $L_2^<$ to obtain our decidability results for discrete and continuous-time HDC.

The first result is a classical result by Buchi. Let ω denote the $L_2^<$ structure $(\mathbb{N}, 2^{\mathbb{N}}, <)$, where $2^{\mathbb{N}}$ denotes the set of Boolean-valued functions on natural numbers. The logic $L_2^<$ interpreted over the structure ω will be denoted $L_2^<(\omega)$.

Theorem 7. *[10] $L_2^<(\omega)$ is decidable.*

The second result is by Rabinovich [53] for so-called signal structures corresponding to interpretations of continuous-time DC. A Boolean-valued function

h from $\mathbb{R}_{\geq 0}$ is called a *signal* [53] if there exists an unbounded increasing sequence $\tau_0 = 0 < \tau_1 < \tau_2 < \cdots < \tau_n < \cdots$ such that h is constant on every open interval $]\tau_i, \tau_{i+1}[, i \geq 0$. Let *SIGNAL* denote the set of all signals, and let *Sig* denote the signal structure $(\mathbb{R}_{\geq 0}, SIGNAL, <)$. The logic $L_2^<$ interpreted over the structure *Sig* will be denoted $L_2^<(Sig)$.

Theorem 8. *[53] $L_2^<(Sig)$ is decidable.*

5.5   Translation of *HDC* to $L_2^<$

The translation is strongly inspired by the translation of Quantified Discrete-Time DC to Monadic Logic over Finite Words, which is used in the tool DC-VALID [50]. The language of second order theory of one successor (called S1S) is $L_2^<$ extended by the successor function. For the structure ω, the successor function is definable in $L_2^<$, while for continuous structures S1S is more expressive, e.g. the validity of S1S is undecidable for signal structures [53]. In WS1S the interpretations of the second-order variables are restricted to finite sets. Since we have the global modality E where intervals of arbitrary size can be reached from any given interval we must base our results on $L_2^<$.

The translation – discrete time: In the translation, each state variable P corresponds to a second-order variable denoted by P also. The intuition with the formula $i \in P$ is that in the *HDC* interpretation $P(t) = 1$ in the interval $]i, i + 1[$. Furthermore, for each nominal a we associate two unique first-order variables x_a and y_a, where the intuition is that a names the interval $[x_a, y_a]$.

The translation is defined recursively with respect to two first-order variables x and y naming the current interval $[x, y]$. These must be distinct from all the variables of the form x_a and y_a, where a is a nominal:

$$\begin{aligned}
\mathcal{T}_{x,y}(\pi) &= x = y \\
\mathcal{T}_{x,y}(P) &= x < y \wedge \forall z(x \leq z < y \to z \in P) \\
\mathcal{T}_{x,y}(\neg\phi) &= \neg\mathcal{T}_{x,y}(\phi) \\
\mathcal{T}_{x,y}(\phi \vee \psi) &= \mathcal{T}_{x,y}(\phi) \vee \mathcal{T}_{x,y}(\psi) \\
\mathcal{T}_{x,y}(\phi \frown \psi) &= \exists z(\mathcal{T}_{x,z}(\phi) \wedge \mathcal{T}_{z,y}(\psi) \wedge x \leq z \wedge z \leq y) \\
\mathcal{T}_{x,y}(a) &= x = x_a \wedge y = y_a \\
\mathcal{T}_{x,y}(a : \phi) &= \mathcal{T}_{x_a,y_a}(\phi) \\
\mathcal{T}_{x,y}(E\phi) &= \exists x \exists y(x \leq y \wedge \mathcal{T}_{x,y}(\phi)) \\
\mathcal{T}_{x,y}(\downarrow a.\phi) &= \exists x_a \exists y_a(x = x_a \wedge y = y_a \wedge \mathcal{T}_{x,y}(\phi)) \,.
\end{aligned}$$

In the translation for chop we assume that z is a "fresh" variable and distinct from x_a and y_a for all nominals a.

The translation – continuous time: In the continuous-time case, the formulas of $L_2^<$ are interpreted in signal structures and [53] contains a translation from *RDC* to $L_2^<$. We can adapt the translation above to a translation for continuous-time *HDC* by changing the translation of P only. The translation $\mathcal{T}_{x,y}(P)$ is:

$$x < y \wedge \forall z(x < z < y \to \exists v(x < v < z \wedge \forall t(v < t < z \to t \in P)))$$
$$\wedge \forall z(x < z < y \to \exists v(z < v < y \wedge \forall t(z < t < v \to t \in P))) \,.$$

The idea behind this translation is: P is 1 almost everywhere in $[x, y]$ ($x < y$) iff for every $z \in]x, y[$ there are left and right neighborhoods of z where P is constant and equal to 1.

We will just refer to [8] for the correctness proofs for the translations. The main result only is stated here.

Theorem 9. *[8] HDC is decidable for discrete and continuous-time domains.*

Since neighbourhood modalities are expressible in *HDC* this result shows that a propositional neighbourhood logic based on *RDC* is decidable.

6   Model-Checking: Using Priced Timed Automata

In this section we will present the model-checking result described in [16]. In particular, we shall address the model-checking problem:

$$ A \models \neg\phi \, , $$

where A is an arbitrary timed automaton. The formula ϕ is a negation-free formulas where linear duration constraints can occur in an arbitrary positive Boolean context as described by the grammar:

$$ S ::= 0 \mid 1 \mid P \mid \neg S \mid S_1 \vee S_2 $$
$$ \phi ::= \ell \bowtie k \mid \lceil S \rceil \mid \sum_{i=1}^{m} c_i \int S_i \bowtie k \mid \phi \vee \psi \mid \phi \wedge \psi \mid \phi ^\frown \psi \, , $$

where $k, m, c_i \in \mathbb{N}$, and $\bowtie \in \{<, \leq, =, \geq, >\}$. We shall assume that formulas contain only upper-bound constraints on durations, i.e. where $\bowtie \in \{<, \leq\}$, and where exactly one duration constraint is a strict inequality. Such formulas are called *negation-free formula* in this section. Adding general negation to this fragment would lead to one of the undecidable fragments described in Sect. 3.

In a model-checking problem of the form $A \models \neg\phi$, the formula ϕ is a specification of an undesired situation – a counter example – and $A \models \neg\phi$ expresses that no run of A exist where this undesired situation occurs. This idea is, for example, pursued in [47,30], where ϕ can have the restricted form of a *DC implementable* [57], thus abandoning accumulated durations and replacing chop by more restricted, operationally inspired operators.

6.1   Multi-priced Timed Automata

We shall reduce the satisfiability problem for negation-free formulas above to a problem of computing minimal costs in *multi-priced timed automata* (MPTA) [41]. MPTA are an extension of timed automata [3,4], where *prices* are associated with edges and locations. The cost of taking an edge is the price of that edge, and the cost of staying in a location is given by the product of the *cost-rate* for that location and the time spent in the location.

Let $\mathbb{C}$ be a finite set of clocks. An *atomic constraint* is a formula of the form: $x \bowtie n$, where $x \in \mathbb{C}$, $\bowtie \in \{\leq, =, \geq, <, >\}$, and $n \in \mathbb{N}$. A *clock constraint* over $\mathbb{C}$ is a conjunction of atomic constraints. Let $B(\mathbb{C})$ denote the set of clock constraints over $\mathbb{C}$ and let $B(\mathbb{C})^*$ denote the set of clock constraints over $\mathbb{C}$ involving only upper bounds, i.e. $\leq$ or $<$. Furthermore, let $2^{\mathbb{C}}$ denote the power set of $\mathbb{C}$.

A *clock valuation* $v : \mathbb{C} \to R_{\geq 0}$ is a function assigning a non-negative real number with each clock. The valuation v *satisfies* a clock constraint $g \in B(\mathbb{C})$, if each conjunct of g is true in v. In this case we write $v \in g$. Let $\mathbb{R}_{\geq 0}^{\mathbb{C}}$ denote the set of all clock valuations.

Definition 1. *([41]) A multi-priced timed automaton A over clocks $\mathbb{C}$ is a tuple (L, l_0, E, I, P), where L is a finite set of locations, l_0 is the initial location, $E \subseteq L \times B(\mathbb{C}) \times 2^{\mathbb{C}} \times L$ is the set of edges, where an edge contains a source, a guard, a set of clocks to be reset, and a target. $I : L \to B(\mathbb{C})^*$ assigns invariants to locations, and $P : (L \cup E) \to \mathbb{N}^m$ assigns a vector of prices to both locations and edges. In the case of $(l, g, r, l') \in E$, we write $l \xrightarrow{g,r} l'$.*

A *multi-priced transition system* is a structure $T = (S, s_0, \Sigma, \longrightarrow)$, where S is a, possibly infinite, set of states, $s_0 \in S$ is the initial state, Σ is a finite set of labels, and $\longrightarrow$ is a partial function from $S \times \Sigma \times S$ to $\mathbb{R}_{\geq 0}^m$, defining the possible transitions and their associated costs. The notation $s \xrightarrow{a}_p s'$ means that $\longrightarrow (s, a, s')$ is defined and equal to p.

An *execution* of T is a finite sequence $\alpha = s_0 \xrightarrow{a_1}_{p_1} s_1 \cdots s_{n-1} \xrightarrow{a_n}_{p_n} s_n$, and the associated *cost* of α is $\text{cost}(\alpha) = \sum_{i=1}^n p_i$.

For a given state s and a vector $u = (u_1, \ldots, u_{m-1}) \in \mathbb{R}_{\geq 0}^{m-1}$, let $\text{mincost}_{T,u}(s)$ denote the *minimum cost* wrt. the last component of the price vector of reaching s while respecting the upper bound constraints to the other prices which are given by u. This is defined as the infimum of the cost of all executions ending in s and respecting price constraint u, i.e.

$$\text{mincost}_{T,u}(s) = \inf \left\{ \text{cost}(\alpha)_m \,\middle|\, \begin{array}{l} \alpha \text{ an execution of } T \text{ ending in } s, \\ \forall i \in \mathbb{N}_{<m}.\text{cost}(\alpha)_i \leq u_i \end{array} \right\}.$$

Furthermore, for a set of states $G \subseteq S$, let $\text{mincost}_{T,u}(G)$ denote the minimal cost of reaching some state in G while respecting the upper price bounds u.

The semantics of a linearly multi-priced timed automaton $A = (L, l_0, E, I, P)$ is a *multi-priced transition system* $T_A = (S, s_0, \Sigma, \longrightarrow)$, where

- $S = L \times \mathbb{R}_{\geq 0}^{\mathbb{C}}$,
- $s_0 = (l_0, v_0)$, where v_0 is the (clock) valuation assigning 0 to every clock,
- $\Sigma = E \cup \{\delta\}$, where δ indicates a delay and $e \in E$ the edge taken, and
- the partial transition function $\longrightarrow$ is defined as follows:

  - $(l, v) \xrightarrow{\delta}_p (l, v+d)$ if $\forall e.0 \leq e \leq d : v + e \in I(l)$, and $p = d \cdot P(l)$,
  - $(l, v) \xrightarrow{e}_p (l', v')$ if $(l, g, r, l') \in E, v \in g, v' = v[r \mapsto 0]$ and $p = P(e)$,

  where $v + d$ means the clock valuation where the value of x is $v(x) + d$, for $x \in \mathbb{C}, d \in R_{\geq 0}$, and $v[r \mapsto 0]$ is the valuation which is as v except that clocks in r are mapped to 0.

In case T_A performs a δ step $(l, v) \xrightarrow{\delta}_p (l, v + d)$, we say that the *duration of the step* is d. All other steps, i.e. those labelled $e \in E$, have duration 0.

The main results that we shall exploit concerning linearly multi-priced timed automata is that the minimum cost of reaching some target location is computable for any (set of) target location(s) and any upper bound on the remaining prices: Given an MPTA $A = (L, l_0, E, I, P)$, a target $G \subset L$, and some cost constraint $\boldsymbol{u} \in \mathbb{R}_{\geq 0}^{m-1}$, we define the *minimum cost* $\mathrm{mincost}_{A,\boldsymbol{u}}(G)$ to be $\mathrm{mincost}_{T_A,\boldsymbol{u}}(G \times \mathbb{R}_{\geq 0}^C)$.

Theorem 10. *[41] For any MPTA $A = (L, l_0, E, I, P)$, any set $G \subset L$, and any cost constraint $\boldsymbol{u} \in \mathbb{R}_{\geq 0}^{m-1}$, the minimum cost $\mathrm{mincost}_{A,\boldsymbol{u}}(G)$ is computable.*

6.2 Representing Negation-Free Formulas by MPTA

In the construction of a MPTA for a negation-free formula ϕ, we represent ϕ by a tuple $(L, s, E, I, P, f, \Lambda)$ denoted A_ϕ, where (L, s, E, I, P) is a multi-priced timed automaton, f is a special *final location* to be reached, and Λ is a function associating a state expression S (of DC) with every location. The automaton will not spend (positive) time in the final location, and the idea is that the runs of A_ϕ from the start location s to f represent the models of ϕ. Durational constraints $\sum_{i=1}^m c_i \int S_i \bowtie k$ are, however, treated in a special way: for any run from s to f, the value of $\sum_{i=1}^m c_i \int S_i$ is the cost of the execution, and an analysis of minimal costs will be used decide the satisfaction of $\sum_{i=1}^m c_i \int S_i \bowtie k$.

The construction [16]: We shall use the following conventions: the cost of an edge is always 0, the cost-rate of a location is 0 unless otherwise stated, the invariant of a location is true unless otherwise stated, the mark of a location l is the state expression 1, i.e. $\Lambda(l) = 1$, unless otherwise stated. Furthermore, we assume that the formula ϕ contains n distinct state variables $P_1, \ldots, P_n$ and m subformulas $\sum_{i=1}^{m_j} c_{i,j} \int S_{i,j} \bowtie_j k_j$, where $\bowtie_m = <$ and $\bowtie_j = \leq$ for every $j < m$. The construction follows the structure of the formula.

The case $\phi = \ell \bowtie k$. (See Fig. 4(a).) Let $A_\phi = (L, s, E, I, P, f, \Lambda)$, where

- $L = \{s, f\}$,
- $E = \{(s, x \bowtie k, \{x\}, f)\}$, and
- $I(f) = x \leq 0$.

The case $\phi = \lceil S \rceil$. (See Fig. 4(b).) Let $A_\phi = (L, s, E, I, P, f, \Lambda)$, where

- $L = \{s, l_1, f\}$,
- $E = \{e_1, e_2, e_3\}$, where $e_1 = (s, \mathrm{true}, \{\}, l_1)$, $e_2 = (l_1, y > 0, \{y\}, s)$, and $e_3 = (l_1, x > 0, \{x\}, f)$,
- $I(s) = y \leq 0$ and $I(f) = x \leq 0$, and
- $\Lambda(l_1) = S$.

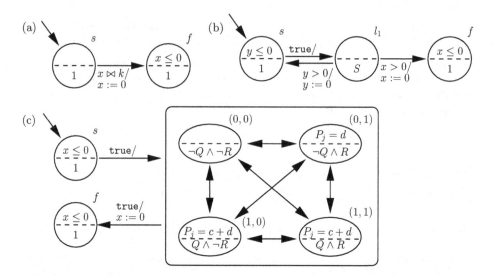

Fig. 4. MPTA encoding of atomic formulas: (a) $\ell \bowtie k$, (b) $\lceil S \rceil$, (c) $c \int Q + d \int Q \vee R \bowtie k$. State decorations above the dashed line denote invariants and cost assignments (both omitted if trivial), while those below the dashed line denote the labeling function Λ.

The case $\phi = \sum_{i=1}^{m_j} c_{i,j} \int S_{i,j} \bowtie_j k_j$. (See Fig. 4(c).) Let $A_\phi = (L, s, E, I, P, f, \Lambda)$, where $L = \{s, f\} \cup \{0,1\}^n$ and E, I, P and Λ are defined below. Each bit-vector $\boldsymbol{b} = (b_1, \ldots, b_n) \in \{0,1\}^n$ is such that $b_i = 1$ iff P_i is 1 in that state. The edges $E = E_1 \cup E_2 \cup E_3$, where

- $E_1 = \{(s, \text{true}, \emptyset, \boldsymbol{b}) \mid \boldsymbol{b} \in \{0,1\}^n\}$,
- $E_2 = \{(\boldsymbol{b}, \text{true}, \emptyset, \boldsymbol{b}') \mid \boldsymbol{b}, \boldsymbol{b}' \in \{0,1\}^n \wedge \boldsymbol{b} \neq \boldsymbol{b}'\}$, and
- $E_3 = \{(\boldsymbol{b}, \text{true}, \{x\}, f) \mid \boldsymbol{b} \in \{0,1\}^n\}$.

For $\boldsymbol{b} \in \{0,1\}^n$, we define two sets: $\boldsymbol{b}^+ = \{l \in \mathbb{N} \mid 1 \leq l \leq n \wedge b_l = 1\}$ and $\boldsymbol{b}^- = \{l \in \mathbb{N} \mid 1 \leq l \leq n \wedge b_l = 0\}$. Let $F(\boldsymbol{b})$ denote the state expression:

$$\bigwedge_{l \in \boldsymbol{b}^-} \neg P_l \wedge \bigwedge_{l \in \boldsymbol{b}^+} P_l \, .$$

For each state expression $S_{i,j}$ occurring in the summation $\sum_{i=1}^{m_j} c_{i,j} \int S_{i,j}$, we define the cost rate as follows:

$$C(\boldsymbol{b})(S_{i,j}) = \begin{cases} c_{i,j}, & \text{if } F(\boldsymbol{b}) \Rightarrow S_{i,j}, \\ C(\boldsymbol{b})(S_{i,j}) = 0 & \text{otherwise.} \end{cases}$$

The invariants of locations are as follows: $I(s) = x \leq 0, I(f) = x \leq 0$, and for all other locations the invariant is true.

The cost assignment $P : L \cup E \to \mathbb{N}^m$ is defined as follows:

$$P(l)_k = \begin{cases} 0 & \text{if } l = s \text{ or } l = f \text{ or } k \neq j \text{ or } l \in E \\ \sum_{i=1}^{m_j} C(l)(S_{i,j}) & \text{otherwise.} \end{cases}$$

The definition Λ is $\Lambda(l) = 1$ if $l = s$ or $l = f$, and $F(l)$ otherwise.

In the recursive cases: $\phi \vee \psi$, $\phi \wedge \psi$ and $\phi \frown \psi$ below, we will assume that $A_\phi = (L_1, s_1, E_1, I_1, P_1, f_1, \Lambda_1)$ and $A_\psi = (L_2, s_2, E_2, I_2, P_2, f_2, \Lambda_2)$, have disjoint sets of locations and clocks, respectively. These constructions are generalization of standard constructions on finite automata.

The case $\phi \vee \psi$. Assume that s and f are two new locations and that x is a new clock. Let $A_{\phi \vee \psi} = (L, s, E, I, P, f, \Lambda)$, where

- $L = \{s, f\} \cup L_1 \cup L_2$,
- $E = \{e_1, e_2, e_3, e_4\} \cup E_1 \cup E_2$, where $e_1 = (s, \text{true}, \{\}, s_1)$, $e_2 = (s, \text{true}, \{\}, s_2)$, $e_3 = (f_1, \text{true}, \{x\}, f)$, and $e_4 = (f_2, \text{true}, \{x\}, f)$.
- $I(s) = I(f) = x \leq 0$, $I(l) = I_1(l)$, for $l \in L_1$, and $I(l) = I_2(l)$, for $l \in L_2$,
- $P(l) = P_1(l)$, for $l \in L_1$, and $P(l) = P_2(l)$, for $l \in L_2$, and
- $\Lambda(l) = \Lambda_1(l)$, for $l \in L_1$, and $\Lambda(l) = \Lambda_2(l)$, for $l \in L_2$.

The case: $\phi \wedge \psi$. Let $A_{\phi \wedge \psi} = (L, (s_1, s_2), E, I, P, (f_1, f_2), \Lambda)$, where

- $L = \{(l_1, l_2) \in L_1 \times L_2 \mid \Lambda_1(l_1) \wedge \Lambda_2(l_2) \text{ is satisfiable}\}$,

- $E = \left\{ ((l_1, l_2), g_1 \wedge g_2, r_1 \cup r_2, (l_1', l_2')) \;\middle|\; \begin{array}{l} (l_1, l_2), (l_1', l_2') \in L \\ \wedge \, (l_1, g_1, r_1, l_1') \in E_1 \\ \wedge \, (l_2, g_2, r_2, l_2') \in E_2 \end{array} \right\} \quad \cup$

  $\{((l_1, l_2), g_1, r_1, (l_1', l_2)) \mid (l_1, l_2), (l_1', l_2) \in L \wedge (l_1, g_1, r_1, l_1') \in E_1\} \cup$
  $\{((l_1, l_2), g_1, r_1, (l_1, l_2')) \mid (l_1, l_2), (l_1, l_2') \in L \wedge (l_2, g_2, r_2, l_2') \in E_2\}$
- $I(l_1, l_2) = I_1(l_1) \wedge I_2(l_2)$, for $(l_1, l_2) \in L$,
- $P(l_1, l_2)_k = P_1(l_1)_k + P_2(l_2)_k$, for $(l_1, l_2) \in L$ and $1 \leq k \leq m$ and
- $\Lambda(l_1, l_2) = \Lambda_1(l_1) \wedge \Lambda_2(l_2)$, for $(l_1, l_2) \in L$.

The case: $\phi \frown \psi$. Let $A_{\phi \frown \psi} = (L_1 \cup L_2, s_1, E, I, P, f_2, \Lambda)$, where

- $E = \{(f_1, \text{true}, C_2, s_2)\} \cup E_1 \cup E_2$, where C_2 is the set of clocks used by A_ψ,
- $I(l) = I_1(l)$, for $l \in L_1$, and $I(l) = I_2(l)$, for $l \in L_2$,
- $P(l) = P_1(l)$, for $l \in L_1$, and $P(l) = P_2(l)$, for $l \in L_2$.
- $\Lambda(l) = \Lambda_1(l)$, for $l \in L_1$, and $\Lambda(l) = \Lambda_2(l)$, for $l \in L_2$.

The transition from f_1 to s_2 is taken immediately when f_1 is reached, as the clock constraints in $I_1(f_1)$ does not permit durational stays in f_1.

In order to reduce the satisfiability problem for negation-free formulas to computation of minimal costs for MPTA, a correspondence between interpretations for formulas and runs of MPTA must be established: consider a transition $(l, v) \xrightarrow{\delta}_p (l, v + d)$, where the location l is labelled with the state expression S. This transition corresponds to a set of interpretations (of length δ) for which S is 1 almost everywhere. The set of interpretations corresponding to an execution is obtained by concatenation of the interpretations for the individual transitions. For further details we just refer to [16], and assume for now that for every run α of A_ϕ, there is a set of *observations* $Intp(\alpha)$ corresponding to α, where an observation is a pair consisting of an interpretation and an interval. The correspondence between runs and observations is stated in the following lemma.

Lemma 2. *[16] Let ϕ be a negation-free formula. Then $\mathcal{I}, [0, e] \models \phi$ iff there exists a run α of A_ϕ with $(\mathcal{I}, [0, e]) \in Intp(\alpha)$ and $\mathrm{cost}(\alpha)_j \bowtie_j k_j$ for $1 \leq j \leq m$.*

The main result follows from this lemma.

Theorem 11. *[16] Let ϕ be a negation-free formula, $A_\phi = (L, s, E, I, P, f, \Lambda)$, and $\boldsymbol{u} = (k_1, \ldots, k_{m-1})$. Then $\mathrm{mincost}_{(L,s,E,I,P),\boldsymbol{u}}(f) < k_m$ iff ϕ is satisfiable.*

The above construction can also be used for model-checking a timed automaton wrt. a negation of a negation-free formula, as stated in the next theorem.

Theorem 12. *[16] Let $A = (L_1, s_1, E_1, I_1, \Lambda_1)$ be a timed automaton (L_1, s_1, E_1, I_1) extended by a location labelling $\Lambda_1 : L_1 \rightarrow S$, ϕ a negation-free formula, $A_\phi = (L_2, s_2, E_2, I_2, P_2, f_2, \Lambda_2)$, and $\boldsymbol{u} = (k_1, \ldots, k_{m-1})$.*
Then $A \models \neg\phi$ iff $\mathrm{mincost}_{(L,s,E,I,P),\boldsymbol{u}}(f \times L_1) \geq k_m$, where

- *$B = (L_1, s_1, E_1, I_1, P_0, s, \Lambda_1)$ is A converted to an MPTA by extension with the trivial cost function $P_0 \equiv \mathbf{0}$ and an irrelevant terminal state $s \in L_1$,*
- *$(L, s, E, I, P, f, \Lambda) = A_\phi \otimes B$ is the MPTA-product from case $\phi \wedge \psi$.*

7 Model-Checking: Linear Duration Invariants

In this section, we present a model checking technique for a class of chop-free formulas of DC called *linear duration invariants* which is different from the technique presented in the previous section. From now on in this chapter, we restrict ourselves to the class of DC formulas that do not have global (rigid) variables. Therefore, the valuation $\mathcal{V}$ is irrelevant in DC models and will be dropped out from them.

Let $\mathbf{S}$ ranged over by $s, u, v, \ldots$, be a finite set of state variables of the DC language. A linear duration invariant is a DC formula of the form

$$\psi \,\hat{=}\, (A \leq \ell \leq B \Rightarrow \textstyle\sum_{s \in \mathbf{S}} c_s \int s \leq M)$$

where $A, B, c_s, M, (A \leq B)$ are fixed real numbers (B may be ∞).

We address in this section the problem of checking if a timed automaton satisfies a linear duration invariant. To simplify our presentation and to make the problem easier, we restrict ourselves to the class of timed automata whose behaviour can be represented by a class of so-called Timed Regular Expressions (TRE) that has been introduced in [1] and also from our earlier work [34,43]. The relationship between TRE's and timed automata was presented in [1] which says that the class of timed languages recognised by timed automata can be received from that of timed regular languages with renaming.

A DC model represents an observation of the behaviour of states in $\mathbf{S}$ in an interval of time. It consists of an interval $[0, T]$ and an interpretation $\mathcal{I}$ in the interval $[0, T]$ of the states in $\mathbf{S}$.

Timed Regular Expressions are defined as follows. For a TRE R, let $state(R)$ denote the set of states occurring in R.

Definition 2. TRE *are defined recursively by*

1. ϵ *is a* TRE *and* $state(\epsilon) = \emptyset$.
2. *For any* $s \in \mathbf{S}$, s *is a* TRE *and* $state(s) = \{s\}$.
3. *If* R *is a* TRE, *for any real numbers* a, b, $0 \le a \le b$ *(b may be ∞), the pair* $(R, [a, b])$ *is a* TRE, *and* $state(R, [a, b]) = state(R)$.
4. *If* R_1, R_2 *are* TRE*'s, then* R_1^*, $R_1 {}^\frown R_2$, $R_1 \oplus R_2$ *are* TRE*'s, and* $state(R_1^*) = state(R_1)$; $state(R_1 {}^\frown R_2) = state(R_1 \oplus R_2) = state(R_1) \cup state(R_2)$.
5. *If* R_1, R_2 *are* TRE*'s, and* $state(R_1) \cap state(R_2) = \emptyset$, *then* $R_1 \otimes R_2$ *is a* TRE, *and* $state(R_1 \otimes R_2) = state(R_1) \cup state(R_2)$.

Here we overload the operator ${}^\frown$ to be defined in TRE's because the meaning we are going to give to it is similar to its meaning in DC. The operator ${}^\frown$ is for sequential composition, the operator $\otimes$ for parallel composition, and $*$ for repetition.

To see how TRE's are used as abstract model for real-time systems, we associate a set of Duration Calculus model to each TRE. Each TRE R defines a class of DC models $\mathcal{M}(R)$ as:

1. A model $\sigma = (\mathcal{I}, [0, T])$ is in $\mathcal{M}(\epsilon)$ iff $T = 0$.
2. A model $\sigma = (\mathcal{I}, [0, T])$ is in $\mathcal{M}(s)$ iff $0 \le T$, and for all $t \in [0, T]$ $s_{\mathcal{I}}(t) = 1$, and for all $s' \neq s$ $s'_{\mathcal{I}}(t) = 0$.
3. A model $\sigma = (\mathcal{I}, [0, T])$ is in $\mathcal{M}(R, [a, b])$ iff $\sigma = (\mathcal{I}, [0, T]) \in \mathcal{M}(R)$ and $a \le T \le b$.
4. A model $\sigma = (\mathcal{I}, [0, T])$ is in $\mathcal{M}(R_1 {}^\frown R_2)$ iff there are $0 \le T' \le T$, $\sigma_1 = (\mathcal{I}_1, [0, T']) \in \mathcal{M}(R_1)$, $\sigma_2 = (\mathcal{I}_2, [0, T - T']) \in \mathcal{M}(R_2)$ such that for all $s \in state(R_1) \cup state(R_2)$, $s_{\mathcal{I}_1}(t) = s_{\mathcal{I}}(t)$ for all $t \in [0, T')$ and $s_{\mathcal{I}_2}(t - T') = s_{\mathcal{I}}(t)$ for all $t \in [T', T]$, and for all $s' \notin state(R_1) \cup state(R_2)$, $s'_{\mathcal{I}}(t) = 0$ for all $t \in [0, T]$. We also define $\sigma = \sigma_1 {}^\frown \sigma_2$.
5. A model $\sigma = (\mathcal{I}, [0, T])$ is in $\mathcal{M}(R_1 \otimes R_2)$ iff there are $\sigma_1 = (\mathcal{I}_1, [0, T]) \in \mathcal{M}(R_1)$, $\sigma_2 = (\mathcal{I}_2, [0, T]) \in \mathcal{M}(R_2)$ such that for all $t \in [0, T]$, $s_{\mathcal{I}_1}(t) = s_{\mathcal{I}}(t)$ for all $s \in state(R_1)$, and $s_{\mathcal{I}_2}(t) = s_{\mathcal{I}}(t)$ for all $s \in state(R_2)$, and $s'_{\mathcal{I}}(t) = 0$ for all $s' \notin state(R_1) \cup state(R_2)$, and then we define $\sigma_1 \otimes \sigma_2$ as σ.
6. A model $\sigma = (\mathcal{I}, [0, T]) \in \mathcal{M}(R_1 \oplus R_2)$ iff $\sigma \in \mathcal{M}(R_1)$ or $\sigma \in \mathcal{M}(R_2)$
7. A model $\sigma = (\mathcal{I}, [0, T]) \in \mathcal{M}(R^*)$ iff there is an integer $k \ge 0$ such that $\sigma \in \mathcal{M}(R^k)$, where $R^0 \cong \epsilon$, and for $k > 0$, $R^k \cong R {}^\frown R^{k-1}$. Or, equivalently, either $\sigma = (\mathcal{I}, [0, 0])$ or there are models $\sigma_1, \ldots, \sigma_k \in \mathcal{M}(R)$ such that $\sigma = \sigma_1 {}^\frown \sigma_2 {}^\frown \ldots {}^\frown \sigma_k$. (It should be noted here that ${}^\frown$ is associative).

So, if we consider R as the abstract model of a real-time system, a model $\sigma \in \mathcal{M}(R)$ represents a behaviour of the system. Our checking problem in this subsection is to decide if $\sigma \models \psi$ for all $\sigma \in \mathcal{M}(R)$ for a given TRE R and a given LDI ψ.

The algorithm for solving this problem is presented via a series of lemmas and theorems. Therefore, for the readability, we also give a proof for some theorems in this section.

For simplicity, let $d_s(\sigma)$ denote the accumulated time (duration) of state $s \in \mathbf{S}$ over the interval $[0, T]$ under the interpretation $\mathcal{I}$, i.e. $d_s(\sigma) = \int_0^T s_{\mathcal{I}}(t)dt$, let $d(\sigma)$

denote the length of the interval $[0, T]$, i.e. T, and let $inv(\sigma)$ denote $\sum_{s \in \mathbf{S}} c_s d_s(\sigma)$ (i.e. $\sum_{s \in \mathbf{S}} c_s \int s$ evaluated over σ). Hence, $\sigma \models \psi$ iff $A \leq d(\sigma) \leq B \Rightarrow inv(\sigma) \leq M$.

Lemma 3. *[34] Let σ, $\sigma_1 = (\mathcal{I}_1, [0, T_1])$, $\sigma_2 = (\mathcal{I}_2, [0, T_2]) \in \mathcal{M}(R_2)$ be DC models. Then,*

1. *if $\sigma = \sigma_1 \frown \sigma_2$ then $d_s(\sigma) = d_s(\sigma_1) + d_s(\sigma_2)$ for all $s \in \mathbf{S}$, $d(\sigma) = d(\sigma_1) + d(\sigma_2)$ and $inv(\sigma) = inv(\sigma_1) + inv(\sigma_2)$, and*
2. *if $\sigma = \sigma_1 \otimes \sigma_2$ then $d_s(\sigma) = d_s(\sigma_1) + d_s(\sigma_2)$ for all $s \in \mathbf{S}$, $d(\sigma) = d(\sigma_1) = d(\sigma_2)$, and $inv(\sigma) = inv(\sigma_1) + inv(\sigma_2)$.*

We will not distinguish the TRE's that define the same set of DC models.

Definition 3. *For arbitrary TRE's R_1, R_2, we say $R_1 \equiv R_2$ iff $\mathcal{M}(R_1) = \mathcal{M}(R_2)$.*

The following theorem can be proved by direct check.

Theorem 13. *For arbitrary TRE's R, R_1, R_2*

1. $(R_1 \oplus R_2) \frown R \equiv (R_1 \frown R) \oplus (R_2 \frown R)$ *and* $R \frown (R_1 \oplus R_2) \equiv (R \frown R_1) \oplus (R \frown R_2)$
2. $(R_1 \oplus R_2) \otimes R \equiv (R_1 \otimes R) \oplus (R_2 \otimes R)$ *and* $R \otimes (R_1 \oplus R_2) \equiv (R \otimes R_1) \oplus (R \otimes R_2)$
3. $(R_1 \oplus R_2)^* \equiv ((R_1^*) \frown (R_2^*))^*$

Theorem 13 implies that any TRE $\mathcal{R}$ can be written as $\mathcal{R}_1 \oplus \mathcal{R}_2 \oplus \ldots \oplus \mathcal{R}_k$, where each $\mathcal{R}_i$ is a TRE in which there is no occurrence of $\oplus$.

Since we are interested in checking a TRE for the linear duration invariant ψ, we will not distinguish the TRE's of which the sets of models satisfy ψ at the same time, and define:

Definition 4. *R_1 and R_2 are ψ-equivalent, denoted by $R_1 \equiv_\psi R_2$, iff $R_1 \models \psi$ if and only if $R_2 \models \psi$.*

Of course, if $R_1 \equiv R_2$ then $R_1 \equiv_\psi R_2$. The following theorem follows immediately from Lemma 3.

Theorem 14. *For arbitrary TRE's R_1, R_2*

1. $R_1 \frown R_2 \equiv_\psi R_2 \frown R_1$
2. $(R_1 \oplus R_2)^* \equiv_\psi (R_1^*) \frown (R_2^*)$
3. $((R_1^*) \frown R_2)^* \equiv_\psi (R_1^*) \frown R_2^*$
4. $(R_1^* \otimes R_2^*)^* \equiv (R_1^* \otimes R_2^*)$

Definition 5.

- *A TRE R in which there is no occurrence of the operator $*$ is said to be finite. Otherwise, R is said to be infinite.*
- *A simple TRE is a finite TRE in which there is no occurrence of the operator $\oplus$.*

First we show how to decide for a finite TRE R, $R \models \psi$. We will only have to consider the simple TRE's because any finite TRE R can be written as $R_1 \oplus \ldots \oplus R_k$, where each R_i is a simple TRE's, and $R \models \psi$ iff for all i ($i \leq k$), $R_i \models \psi$.

Let R be a simple TRE. We associate a set of linear constraints $\mathcal{C}(R)$, the set of durations $\{d_s(R) \mid s \in \mathbf{S}\}$ and execution time $d(R)$ to R as follows. Let $Var(\mathcal{C}(R))$ denote the set of (real) variables occurring in $\mathcal{C}(R)$.

Definition 6.

- Let $R = s$. Then $\mathcal{C}(R) = \emptyset$, $d_s(R) = t$, $d(R) = t$ where t is a real variable, and $d_{s'}(R) = 0$ for all $s' \neq s$.
- Let $R = (R_1, [a, b])$. Then $\mathcal{C}(R) = \mathcal{C}(R_1) \cup \{a \leq d(R_1) \leq b\}$, $d_s(R) = d_s(R_1)$ for all s, and $d(R) = d(R_1)$.
- Let $R = R_1 \frown R_2$. By renaming the variables if necessary, we can assume that $Var(\mathcal{C}(R_1)) \cap Var(\mathcal{C}(R_2)) = \emptyset$. Then, $\mathcal{C}(R) = \mathcal{C}(R_1) \cup \mathcal{C}(R_2)$, $d_s(R) = d_s(R_1) + d_s(R_2)$ and $d(R) = d(R_1) + d(R_2)$.
- Let $R = R_1 \otimes R_2$. Assume that $Var(\mathcal{C}(R_1)) \cap Var(\mathcal{C}(R_2)) = \emptyset$. Then, $\mathcal{C}(R) = \mathcal{C}(R_1) \cup \mathcal{C}(R_2) \cup \{d(R_1) = d(R_2)\}$, $d_s(R) = d_s(R_1) + d_s(R_2)$ for all $s \in \mathbf{S}$, and $d(R) = d(R_1)$.

Let $inv(R)$ denote $\sum_{s \in S} c_s d_s(R)$.

For instance, let R be

$$((s, [1, 5]) \frown (u, [1, 7])) \otimes (v, [3, 10]) .$$

Then, we can associate to each primitive in R a variable, say to $(s, [1, 5])$ variable x, to $(u, [1, 7])$ variable y and to $(v, [3, 10])$ variable z. Then, $\mathcal{C}(R) = \{1 \leq x \leq 5, 1 \leq y \leq 7, 3 \leq z \leq 10, x + y = z\}$, $d(R) = z$, $d_s(R) = x$, $d_u(R) = y$, and $d_v(R) = z$.

For a solution w of the system of linear constraints $\mathcal{C}(R)$, denote by $d_s(R)(w)$, $d(R)(w)$ and $inv(R)(w)$ respectively, the value of $d_s(R)$, $d(R)$ and $inv(R)$ evaluated over w. For vectors $w_1 = (t_1, t_2, \ldots, t_p)$ and $w_2 = (u_1, u_2, \ldots, u_q)$, we denote by (w_1, w_2) the vector $(t_1, t_2, \ldots, t_p, u_1, u_2, \ldots, u_q)$, and if $p = q$ we denote by $w_1 + w_2$ the vector $(t_1 + u_1, t_2 + u_2, \ldots, t_p + u_p)$.

Let $\psi(R)$ denote $\max\{inv(R)\}$ subject to $\mathcal{C}(R) \cup \{A \leq d(R) \leq B\}$.

Theorem 15. *[34] For a simple TRE R, $R \models \psi$ iff $\psi(R) \leq M$.*

From Theorem 15, for a simple TRE R, checking $R \models \psi$ can be done by solving the linear programming problem to find $\psi(R)$ and comparing it to M.

Example 1. Let

$$R = ((s, [1, 5]) \frown (u, [1, 7])) \otimes (v, [3, 10])$$
$$\psi = 4 \leq \ell \leq 8 \Rightarrow 2 \int s - \int v \leq 5q$$

Let x, y, z be variables associated to the primitives $(s, [1, 5]), (u, [1, 7])$, $(v, [3, 10])$ respectively. $R \models \psi$ can be checked by solving the linear programming problem

$$\max\{2x - z\} \text{ subject to } 1 \le x \le 5$$
$$1 \le y \le 7$$
$$3 \le z \le 10$$
$$z = x + y$$
$$4 \le z \le 8$$

and checking whether it is less than 5. It is easy to see that the solution of the linear programming problem is $x = 5$, $y = 1$, $z = 6$ and the maximal value of the objective function is 4, which is less than 5.   □

Let R be an infinite TRE. By replacing each occurrence of the operator $*$ (repetition) with a fresh integer variable k_i, we obtain a finite TRE and can associate a finite number of linear programming problems to it. However, because the set of values of k_i's is infinite, the number of linear programming problems is also infinite. It is therefore impossible to solve all of these problems.

   In the following sections, we will introduce a technique to reduce an infinite TRE to a finite TRE which is ψ-equivalent to it, and therefore an infinite TRE could be checked for ψ. This technique was first introduced by Zhou et al [73] and was generalized by us in [43] and [34].

Reducing TRE's to finite TRE's. From now on we assume that any subexpression of TRE R is not of the form $(R', [0,0])$ because removing the subexpressions of that form from R does not change the set $\mathcal{M}(R)$.

   Let R, R' be TRE's. If there is an occurrence of R' in R, then R' is called *sub-expression* of R. For example, let $R = ((s, [1, 5])\frown(u, [1, 7])) \otimes (v, [3, 10])^*$. Then $(s, [1, 5])$, $(u, [1, 7])$, $(v, [3, 10])$, $(s, [1, 5])\frown(u, [1, 7])$, $(v, [3, 10])^*$ and R are sub-expressions of R. A sub-expression R' of R can occur at many different positions in R. In the sequel, when we talk about a subexpression of R, we mean an occurrence of its in R.

   An TRE R for which $\mathcal{M}(R) = \emptyset$ is said to be *empty* TRE and denoted by Λ. For example, $(s, [3, 5]) \otimes (v, [6, 9])$ is an empty TRE. We will show how to recognise an empty expression later in the section.

   For any TRE R in which there is no occurrence of an empty sub-expression, we associate with the numbers $m(R)$, $M(R)$ as follows. Roughly speaking, $m(R)$ is a lower bound and $M(R)$ is an upper bound of the set $\{d(\sigma) \mid \sigma \in \mathcal{M}(R)\}$.

Definition 7.

- If $R = \epsilon$, then $m(R) = 0$ and $M(R) = 0$.
- If $R = (R_1, [a, b])$, then $m(R) = \min\{m(R_1), a\}$ and $M(R) = \max\{M(R_1), b\}$ (b may be ∞).
- If $R = R_1^*$, then $m(R) = 0$ and $M(R) = \infty$.
- If $R = R_1\frown R_2$, then $m(R) = m(R_1) + m(R_2)$ and $M(R) = M(R_1) + M(R_2)$.
- If $R = R_1 \oplus R_2$,
  then $m(R) = \min(m(R_1), m(R_2))$ and $M(R) = \max(M(R_1), M(R_2))$.
- If $R = R_1 \otimes R_2$,
  then $m(R) = \max(m(R_1), m(R_2))$ and $M(R) = \min(M(R_1), M(R_2))$.

From Definition 7, it is easy to see that if R is a simple TRE and $M(R) < \infty$ then $m(R), M(R)$ are minimum and maximum of the set $\{d(\sigma) \mid \sigma \in \mathcal{M}(R)\}$. Furthermore, for any TRE R, for any $\sigma \in \mathcal{M}(R)$, $m(R) \leq d(\sigma) \leq M(R)$.

For example, let

$$R = ((s, [1, 5])^\frown(u, [1, 7])) \otimes (v, [3, 10]).$$

Then, $m(R) = 3$ and $M(R) = 10$. This means that for any $\sigma \in \mathcal{M}(R)$, $3 \leq d(\sigma) \leq 10$.

An important remark should be made here is that for any simple TRE R, for any real number r such that $m(R) \leq r \leq M(R)$, there is a model $\sigma \in \mathcal{M}(R)$ for which $d(\sigma) = r$. Therefore, checking the emptiness of a simple TRE R is trivial. Hence, for a simple TRE R, $m(R) = 0$ means that for any constrained expression $(R_1, [a, b])$ occurring in R the lower bound a should be 0.

Note that for any non empty TRE's R_1, R_2, the expression $R_1 \otimes R_2$ may be empty although the expressions $R_1^\frown R_2, R_1 \oplus R_2, R_1^*$ cannot be empty.

If R is not an empty TRE, we can find out R_1 such that R_1 has no empty sub-expression and that $\mathcal{M}(R) = \mathcal{M}(R_1)$. Thus, from now on, unless otherwise stated, we assume that all TRE's under our consideration are not empty TRE's and do not have any empty sub-expression.

Let R_1, R_2 be TRE's. As discussed earlier, if $R = R_1 \otimes R_2$ then any $\sigma \in \mathcal{M}(R)$ is constructed from models $\sigma_1 \in \mathcal{M}(R_1)$ and $\sigma_2 \in \mathcal{M}(R_2)$ such that $d(\sigma_1) = d(\sigma_2)$. Hence, the execution time of R_1 is limited by the execution time of R_2 and vice-versa. In general, the execution time of R', where R' is an arbitrary sub-expression of R_1, is not only bounded by $m(R')$ and $M(R')$ but also by $m(R_2)$ and $M(R_2)$. This means that the execution time of a sub-expression R' in a TRE R is constrained by the operator $\otimes$ and by its occurrence position in R. To capture these constraints we define the quantities $m(R', R)$ and $M(R', R)$ as lower and upper bounds of the time execution of R' when it occurs at fixed position in R. $m(R', R)$ and $M(R', R)$ are defined recursively as follows.

Definition 8.

- Let $R = R'$. $m(R', R) = 0$ and $M(R', R) = \infty$ (no additional constraint).
- Let $R = R_1 \star R_2$ $(R_2 \star R_1, R_1^*)$, where $\star \in \{^\frown, \oplus\}$ and R' occurs in R_1. Then $m(R', R) = m(R', R_1)$ and $M(R', R) = M(R', R_1)$ (no additional constraint).
- Let $R = R_1 \otimes R_2$ $(R_2 \otimes R_1)$, and let R' occur in R_1. Then $m(R', R) = max(m(R', R_1), m(R_2))$ and $M(R', R) = min(M(R', R_1), M(R_2))$ (additional constraint enforced by the operator $\otimes$).

For example, let

$$R = ((s, [1, 5])^\frown(u, [1, 7])) \otimes (v, [3, 10])^*.$$

Let $R' = (s, [1, 5])^\frown(u, [1, 7])$ then $m(R', R) = 0$ and $M(R', R) = \infty$.
Let $R' = (v, [3, 10])^*$. Then $m(R', R) = 2$ and $M(R', R) = 12$.

Denote $\mathcal{M}(R', R) = \{\sigma \in \mathcal{M}(R') \mid m(R', R) \leq d(\sigma) \leq M(R', R)\}$. From the above discussion, it can be seen that only the models in $\mathcal{M}(R', R)$ can participate in constructing models of R. Therefore, from now on, if R' is considered as a sub-expression (occurring at a fixed position) of R then we can use $\mathcal{M}(R', R)$ for $\mathcal{M}(R')$.

By induction on the structure of TRE's, we can prove the following lemmas.

Lemma 4. *Let R_1, R_2, R' be arbitrary TRE's. If for any model $\sigma_1 \in \mathcal{M}(R_1)$, there exists a model $\sigma_2 \in \mathcal{M}(R_2)$ such that $d(\sigma_1) = d(\sigma_2)$ and $inv(\sigma_1) \leq inv(\sigma_2)$ then for any model $\sigma_1' \in \mathcal{M}(R_1 \frown R')$ ($\mathcal{M}(R_1 \oplus R')$, $\mathcal{M}(R_1 \otimes R')$, $\mathcal{M}(R_1^*)$) there exists a model $\sigma_2' \in \mathcal{M}(R_2 \frown R')$ ($\mathcal{M}(R_2 \oplus R')$, $\mathcal{M}(R_2 \otimes R')$, $\mathcal{M}(R_2^*)$) such that $d(\sigma_1') = d(\sigma_2')$ and $inv(\sigma_1') \leq inv(\sigma_2')$.*

Lemma 5. *Let R, R_1, R_2 be arbitrary TRE's. If*

1. *For any model $\sigma_1 \in \mathcal{M}(R_1)$, there exists a model $\sigma_2 \in \mathcal{M}(R_2)$ such that $d(\sigma_1) = d(\sigma_2)$ and $inv(\sigma_1) \leq inv(\sigma_2)$, and*
2. *For any model $\sigma_2 \in \mathcal{M}(R_2)$, there exists a model $\sigma_1 \in \mathcal{M}(R_1)$ such that $d(\sigma_2) = d(\sigma_1)$ and $inv(\sigma_2) \leq inv(\sigma_1)$,*

then by replacing an occurrence of R_1 in R with R_2, we obtain a new expression R' which is ψ-equivalent to R, i.e. $R' \equiv_\psi R$.

Let $\lfloor x \rfloor$ be the floor of a real variable x, which is the maximal integer which are not greater than x.

Theorem 16. *[34] Let R_1 be a simple TRE with $m(R_1) = 0$. Let R_1' be the TRE obtained from R_1 by replacing each subexpression of the form $(R'', [0, b])$ of R_1 with $(R'', [0, \infty))$ (remember that $b > 0$ as assumed earlier). Then, by replacing an occurrence of R_1^* in a TRE R with R_1', we obtain a new expression R' which is ψ-equivalent to R.*

Theorem 17. *[34] Let R_1 be a simple TRE with $m(R_1) > 0$. Let R_1^* be an occurrence of the TRE R_1^* in a TRE R for which $M(R_1^*, R) < \infty$ or $B < \infty$ (recall that B is the upper bound of the observation time period in the premise $A \leq \ell \leq B$ of the linear duration invariant ψ). Let $R_1' = \oplus_{i=0}^{k} R_1^i$, where $k = \lfloor min \{M(R_1^*, R), B\}/(m(R_1)\rfloor + 1)$. Then by replacing the occurrence R_1^* in R with R_1', we obtain a new expression R' which is ψ-equivalent to R.*

Let R' be a sub-expression of R. R' is said to be under $\otimes$ if there is a sub-expression of form $R_1 \otimes R_2$ of R such that R' occurs either in R_1 or in R_2. If A^* is not under $\otimes$, then by definition 8, $M(A^*, R) = \infty$.

Given a simple TRE R_1. Let $maxinv(R_1)$ denote the maximal value of $\{inv(\sigma) \mid \sigma \in \mathcal{M}(R_1)\}$. $maxinv(R_1)$ can be computed by solving the linear programming problem: finding the maximum of the objective function $\sum_{s \in \mathbf{S}} c_s d_s$ (R_1) subject to the set of constraints $\mathcal{C}(R_1)$.

Lemma 6. *Let K be a real number, R_1^* be a sub-expression of R which is not under $\otimes$, where R_1 is a simple TRE with $m(R_1) > 0, maxinv(R_1) \leq 0$. Assume* that $B = \infty$. Furthermore, let R' be obtained from R by replacing the occurrence R_1^* in R by $R_1' = \bigoplus_{i=0}^{k} R_1^i$ with $k = \lfloor K/m(R_1) \rfloor + 1$.

Then, for any model $\sigma \in \mathcal{M}(R)$ such that $d(\sigma) \geq K$, there exists a model $\sigma' \in \mathcal{M}(R')$ such that $d(\sigma') \geq K$, and $inv(\sigma) \leq inv(\sigma')$.

Theorem 18. *[34] Let $B = \infty$, and R_1^* be a sub-expression of R such that R_1^* is not under $\otimes$, where R_1 is a simple* TRE *with $m(R_1) > 0$. Then*

1. *If $maxinv(R_1) \leq 0$, then by replacing R_1^* in R with $R_1' = \bigoplus_{i=0}^{k} R_1^i$, where $k = \lfloor A/m(R_1) \rfloor + 1$, we obtain a new expression R' such that $R' \equiv_\psi R$.*
2. *If $maxinv(R_1) > 0$, then $R \not\models \psi$.*

Proof.

1. It is obviously that $\mathcal{M}(R_1') \subset \mathcal{M}(R_1^*)$. Hence, by Lemma 4, for any model $\sigma' \in \mathcal{M}(R')$, there exists model $\sigma \in \mathcal{M}(R)$ such that $d(\sigma) = d(\sigma')$ and $inv(\sigma) \leq inv(\sigma')$. By Lemmas 4 and 5, it follows that $R \models \psi$ implies $R' \models \psi$. The other direction is proved as follows. By lemma 6, for any $\sigma \in \mathcal{M}(R)$ such that $d(\sigma) \geq A$ there is $\sigma' \in \mathcal{M}(R')$ such that $d(\sigma') \geq A$ and $inv(\sigma') \geq inv(\sigma)$. Hence, as a result, $R' \models \psi$ implies $R \models \psi$.

2. Assume that $maxinv(R_1) > 0$ and R_1^* is not under $\otimes$. By induction on the structure of R, it can be seen easily that for any subexpression R_1 of R if there exists a sequence of models $\sigma_i \in \mathcal{M}(R_1)$, $i \geq 1$ such that $\lim inv(\sigma_i) = \infty$, then there exists a sequence of models $\sigma_i' \in \mathcal{M}(R)$, $i \geq 1$ such that $\lim_{i \to \infty} inv(\sigma_i') = \infty$. Let w_0 be the optimal solution of the linear programming problem: $\max \sum_{s \in \mathbf{S}} c_s d_s(R_1)$ subject to $\mathcal{C}(R_1)$. Let $\sigma_0 \in \mathcal{M}(R_1)$ be the model corresponding to w_0 then $inv(\sigma_0) = maxinv(R_1) > 0$. Hence, for the sequence $\sigma_i = \sigma_0 \frown \sigma_0 \frown \ldots \frown \sigma_0$ (i times), $i \geq 1$, we have for all i, $\sigma_i \in \mathcal{M}(R_1^*)$ and $inv(\sigma_i) = i \times inv(\sigma_0) \to \infty$ when $i \to \infty$. Since R_1^* is a sub-expression of R, we can construct a sequence of models σ_i', $i \geq 1$ such that $\sigma_i' \in \mathcal{M}(R)$ and $inv(\sigma_i') \to \infty$ (when $i \to \infty$). Hence, we can find a model $\sigma \in R$ satisfying that $A \leq d(\sigma) \leq \infty$ and $inv(\sigma) > M$. In the other words, $R \not\models \psi$.   □

By Theorems 16, 17 and 18, we can remove a star in a TRE R without introducing a new star, without increasing the number of stars under $\otimes$ for the following cases:

- a star of the form R_1^*, where R_1 is a simple TRE with $m(R_1) = 0$ (Theorem 16),
- a star of the form R_1^*, where R_1 is a simple TRE with $m(R_1) > 0$ for the case that either $M(R_1^*, R)$ or B is finite (Theorem 17),
- a star of the form R_1^*, where R_1 is a simple TRE with $m(R_1) > 0$ for the case that B is infinite and R_1^* is not under $\otimes$ (Theorem 18).

Therefore, if the linear duration ψ is of the form $A \leq \ell \leq B \Rightarrow \sum_{s \in \mathbf{S}} c_s \int s \leq M$ for which $B < \infty$ or if the TRE R has no sub-expression of the form R_1^*, where R_1 is a simple TRE with $m(R_1) > 0$ and $M(R_1^*, R) = \infty$, then checking $R \models \psi$ can be reduced to solving a finite number of linear programming problems.

As said earlier, what we still need to do in using this technique is to check the emptiness of TRE's. Checking the emptiness of a TRE in which the star does

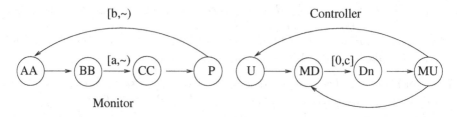

Fig. 5. A Railroad Crossing Monitor. Transitions from AA to BB and from U to MD are synchronised, and transitions from CC to P and from Dn to MU are synchronised.

not occur under $\otimes$ is so trivial. However, the problem becomes difficult when the star occurs in the operands of a $\otimes$. Let for example

$$R = ((s_1, [a_1, b_1])^* \frown (s_2, [a_2, b_2])^*) \otimes$$
$$((s_3, [a_3, b_3])^* \frown (s_4, [a_4, b_4])^*)$$

Replacing each star $*$ with an integral variable, we get

$$R = \bigoplus_{m_1, m_2, m_3, m_4 \geq 0} \left(\begin{array}{c} ((s_1, [a_1, b_1])^{m_1} \frown (s_2, [a_2, b_2])^{m_2}) \\ \otimes \\ ((s_3, [a_3, b_3])^{m_3} \frown (s_4, [a_4, b_4])^{m_4}) \end{array} \right).$$

Thus, R is not empty iff the inequalities

$$m_1 a_1 + m_2 a_2 \leq m_3 b_b + m_4 b_4$$
$$m_3 a_3 + m_4 a_4 \leq m_1 b_1 + m_2 b_2$$
$$m_1 \geq 0, m_2 \geq 0, m_3 \geq 0, m_4 \geq 0$$

has an integral solution. In order to make the problem easier, we assume in this section that all the real constants occurring in a TRE are rational. Thus, checking the emptiness of TRE's leads to checking the emptiness of $\{\mathbf{A}\mathbf{x} \leq \mathbf{b} | \mathbf{x} \text{ integral}\}$, where $\mathbf{A}$ is a rational matrix, $\mathbf{b}$ is a rational vector, which is an integer linear programming problem and can be solved in polynomial time.

For the TRE's in which there are occurrences of the operator $*$ under $\otimes$ and $B = \infty$ in the LDI D, the problem is difficult, and we have to use mixed integer linear programming techniques ([39,34]) to solve the problem.

Example 2. Let us take the railroad crossing system [66] as an example to illustrate the checking technique. We have trains, a railroad crossing monitor, and a gate controller which are subject to the following constraints (see Figure 5).

1. The monitor has four states to express the positions of train: state AA for train approaching beyond 1/2 mile, state BB for train approaching within 1/2 mile, state CC for train crossing, and state P for train just passed.
2. The controller has four states to express the positions of the gate: state U for the gate being up, state MD for the gate moving down, state Dn for the gate being down and MU for the gate moving up.

When the system starts, the monitor is in state AA and the controller is in state U. In state AA, when the monitor detects that a train approaching within $1/2$ mile, it enters state BB, and at the same time if the controller is in state U or state MU, it must enters state MD. Namely, when the gate is up or is moving up, and detects that the monitor enters state BB, it must start moving down. When the train enters the crossing, the monitor enters state CC, and when the train has passed, it enters state P. When the monitor changes its state from CC to P then at the same time the monitor changes its state from Dn to MU. This means, when the gate is down, and detects that the monitor enters state P, it begins to move up. In addition, due to the speed of trains and the safety distance between trains, it takes at least a time units for a train to go to the crossing, after entering state BB, and when a train has passed, a new train could come after at least b time units. That means that the monitor stays in BB at least a time units each time and in P at least b time units each time. Furthermore, assume that it takes the gate at most c time units to move down, and hence, the controller stays at MD at most c time units each time, where $c \leq a$. The automata modelling the railroad crossing system are depicted in Figure 5. Intuitively, the parallel behaviour of the system is now can be described by the following TRE RCM:

$$
\begin{aligned}
&(AA \otimes U)^\frown \\
&(((BB, [a, \infty))^\frown CC \otimes (MD, [0, c])^\frown Dn)^\frown \\
&((P, [b, \infty))^\frown AA \otimes (MU^\frown U \oplus MU)))^* {}^\frown \\
&(\epsilon \oplus \\
&(BB \oplus (BB, [a, \infty))^\frown CC) \otimes ((MD, [0, c]) \oplus (MD, [0, c])^\frown Dn) \oplus \\
&((BB, [a, \infty))^\frown CC \otimes (MD, [0, c])^\frown Dn)^\frown \\
&((P \oplus P^\frown AA) \otimes (MU \oplus MU^\frown U)))
\end{aligned}
$$

Now we verify that the railroad crossing monitor satisfies the requirement for the system. That is to check $RCM \models D$, where D is $0 \leq \ell \leq \infty \Rightarrow \int CC - \int Dn \leq 0$.

Because the subexpression under $*$ is not a simple one, in order to use Theorem 18, we transform RCM into the following expression $RCM1$ using Theorem 14:

$$
\begin{aligned}
RCM1 \equiv\ &(AA \otimes U)^\frown \\
&(((BB, [a, \infty))^\frown CC \otimes (MD, [0, c])^\frown Dn)^\frown \\
&((P, [b, \infty))^\frown AA \otimes MU^\frown U))^* {}^\frown \\
&(((BB, [a, \infty))^\frown CC \otimes (MD, [0, c])^\frown Dn)^\frown \\
&((P, [b, \infty))^\frown AA \otimes MU))^* {}^\frown \\
&(\epsilon \oplus \\
&(BB \oplus (BB, [a, \infty))^\frown CC) \otimes \\
&\quad ((MD, [0, c]) \oplus (MD, [0, c])^\frown Dn) \oplus \\
&((BB, [a, \infty))^\frown CC \otimes (MD, [0, c])^\frown Dn)^\frown \\
&((P \oplus P^\frown AA) \otimes (MU \oplus MU^\frown U)))
\end{aligned}
$$

Let

$$R_1 = (((BB, [a, \infty))^\frown CC \otimes (MD, [0, c])^\frown Dn)^\frown$$
$$((P, [b, \infty))^\frown AA \otimes MU^\frown U))$$
$$R_2 = (((BB, [a, \infty))^\frown CC \otimes (MD, [0, c])^\frown Dn)^\frown$$
$$((P, [b, \infty))^\frown AA \otimes MU))$$

By Definition 7, $m(R_1) > 0$ and $m(R_2) > 0$. Furthermore,

$$maxinv(R_1) = \max\{inv(\sigma)|\sigma \in \mathcal{M}(R_1)\}$$
$$= \max\{t_2 - t_4\} \text{ subject to}$$
$$a \leq t_1, \ 0 \leq t_2$$
$$0 \leq t_3 \leq c, \ 0 \leq t_4$$
$$t_1 + t_2 = t_3 + t_4, \ b \leq t_5$$
$$0 \leq t_6, \ 0 \leq t_7$$
$$0 \leq t_8, \ t_5 + t_6 = t_7 + t_8$$
$$= c - a$$

Similarly, we have $maxinv(R_2) = c - a$ as well. Since $c \leq a$, we have $maxinv(R_1)$ ≤ 0 and $maxinv(R_2) \leq 0$. By applying Theorem 18 twice with noticing that $k = 1$, we have that $RCM \models D$ is now equivalent to $RCM2 \models D$, where

$$RCM2 = (AA \otimes U)^\frown$$
$$(\epsilon \oplus$$
$$(((BB, [a, \infty))^\frown CC \otimes (MD, [0, c])^\frown Dn)^\frown$$
$$((P, [b, \infty))^\frown AA \otimes MU^\frown U)))^\frown$$
$$(\epsilon \oplus$$
$$(((BB, [a, \infty))^\frown CC \otimes (MD, [0, c])^\frown Dn)^\frown$$
$$((P, [b, \infty))^\frown AA \otimes MU)))^\frown$$
$$(\epsilon \oplus$$
$$(BB \oplus (BB, [a, \infty))^\frown CC) \otimes ((MD, [0, c]) \oplus$$
$$(MD, [0, c])^\frown Dn) \oplus$$
$$(BB^\frown CC \otimes (MD, [0, c])^\frown Dn)^\frown$$
$$((P \oplus P^\frown AA) \otimes (MU \oplus MU^\frown U)))$$

$RCM2$ is a finite TRE, and checking $RCM2 \models D$ is so simple for this case using Theorem 15.   □

For the class of real time systems whose behaviours are described by general timed automata, if the constants occurring in the linear Duration Invariant are integer, then checking can also be done by investigating the region graph of the timed automaton modelling the system. Readers are referred to [38,65] for the details of the technique.

8   A Case Study: Modeling and Verification of the Bi-phase Mark Protocol in Duration Calculus

It is natural and convenient to model time as non-negative real numbers. However, during the development of a real-time computing system, we may have to use the set of natural numbers for time. This is specially true when dealing with the implementation of the system in computer which running in discrete time. In this section, we introduce some techniques for using Duration Calculus in modelling and specification of some discrete time structures. These techniques demonstrate how to use temporal propositional letters with specific meanings in additional to state variables in modelling and specification. We then use these techniques for modelling and verifying the correctness of the well-known case study "Biphase Mark Protocol".

For our convenience, we extend DC with the formula $\lceil P \rceil^0$ that has been introduced by Pandya in his early work [49]. The semantic for $\lceil P \rceil^0$ is defined by $\mathcal{I}, [a, b] \models \lceil P \rceil^0$ iff $a = b$ and $P_{\mathcal{I}}(a) = 1$.

8.1   Discrete Duration Calculus Models

Recall that discrete models of Duration Calculus use the set of natural numbers $\mathbb{N}$, which is a subset of $\mathbb{R}^+$, for time (we assume that $0 \in \mathbb{N}$). We can embed the discrete time models into continuous time models by considering a state variable in discrete DC models as a state in continuous models that can change its value only at the integer points. For that purpose, we introduce several fresh temporal propositional letters and state variables with specific meaning. Let int be a temporal propositional letter with the meaning that int is interpreted as 1 for an interval if and only if the interval is from an integer to an integer, i.e. for any interpretation $\mathcal{I}$, $int_{\mathcal{I}}([a, b]) = 1$ iff $a, b \in \mathbb{N}$. The axioms to characterise the properties of the temporal propositional letter int can be given as follows. First, the integer intervals have integral endpoints, and remain integer intervals when extended by 1 time unit:

$$int \Rightarrow ((int \wedge \ell = 0) \frown (int \wedge \ell = 1)^*) \wedge$$
$$((int \wedge \ell = 1)^* \frown (int \wedge \ell = 0)) \tag{6}$$
$$int \frown (\ell = 1) \Rightarrow int \tag{7}$$

Second, $int \wedge \ell = 1$ should be a unique partition of the greatest integral subinterval of any interval with length 2 or more, i.e.

$$\ell \geq 2 \Rightarrow \ell < 1 \frown ((int \wedge \ell = 1)^* \wedge \tag{8}$$
$$\neg(true \frown (int \wedge \ell = 1) \frown \neg(int \wedge \ell = 1)^*) \wedge$$
$$\neg(\neg(int \wedge \ell = 1)^* \frown (int \wedge \ell = 1) \frown true)) \frown$$
$$\ell < 1$$

Similarly to Lemma 3.2 in [20] we can show that the axiom 8 is equivalent to the fact that any interval $[b, e]$ that have the length 2 or longer has the unique set of time points $b \leq \tau_0 < \tau_1 < \ldots < \tau_m \leq e$ such that $\mathcal{I}, [\tau_i, \tau_{i+1}] \models int \wedge \ell = 1$, $\tau_0 - b < 1$ and $e - \tau_m < 1$, and $[\tau_i, \tau_{i+1}]$ are the only subintervals of $[b, e]$ that that satisfy $(int \wedge \ell = 1)$.

Let $\mathcal{ID}$ denote the set of these three axioms 6, 7 and 8. $\mathcal{ID}$ specifies all the properties of integer intervals except that their endpoints are integer as formulated by:

Proposition 2. *[31]*

1. *Let $\mathcal{I}$ be an interpretation satisfying that $int_{\mathcal{I}}([b, e]) = true$ iff $[b, e]$ is an integer interval. Then $\mathcal{I}, [b, e] \models D$ for any integer interval $[b.e]$, and for any formula $D \in \mathcal{ID}$.*
2. *Let $\mathcal{I}$ be an interpretation satisfying that $\mathcal{I}, [b, e] \models D$ for any interval $[b.e]$, and for any formula $D \in \mathcal{ID}$. Then, $int_{\mathcal{I}}([0, 0]) = true$ implies that for $int_{\mathcal{I}}([b, e]) = true$ iff $[b, e]$ is an integer interval.*

Proof. The item 1 is obvious, and we only give a proof of Item 2 here. Let us consider an interval $[0, n]$ with $n > 100$. From the fact that $\mathcal{I}, [0, n] \models D$ where D is the formula 8, we have that there are points $0 \leq \tau_0 < \tau_1 < \ldots < \tau_m \leq e$ such that $\mathcal{I}, [\tau_i, \tau_{i+i}] \models int \wedge \ell = 1$, $\tau_0 < 1$ and $n - \tau_m < 1$, and

$$\mathcal{I}, [\tau_0, \tau_m] \models (\neg(true^\frown(int \wedge \ell = 1)^\frown\neg(int \wedge \ell = 1)^*) \wedge \\ \neg(\neg(int \wedge \ell = 1)^*{}^\frown(int \wedge \ell = 1)^\frown true))$$

If $\tau_0 > 0$, from the axiom 7, it follows that $\mathcal{I}, [0, k] \models int$ for all $k \in \mathbb{N}$ and $k \leq n$ and $k < \tau_k < k + 1$. Applying the axiom 6 for the interval $[0, k]$ implies that $\mathcal{I}, [k, k + 1] \models int \wedge \ell = 1$. Consequently, $\mathcal{I}, [m - 1, \tau_m] \models \neg(int \wedge \ell = 1)^*$ and $\mathcal{I}, [m - 2, m_1] \models (int \wedge \ell = 1)$. This is a contradiction to $\mathcal{I}, [\tau_0, \tau_m] \models \neg(true^\frown(int \wedge \ell = 1)^\frown\neg(int \wedge \ell = 1)^*)$. $\qquad\square$

Note that Item 2 of Proposition 2 can be generalised as

Let $\mathcal{I}$ be an interpretation satisfying that $\mathcal{I}, [b, e] \models D$ for any interval $[b.e]$, and for any formula $D \in \mathcal{ID}$. Let $h \in \mathcal{R}^+$, $h < 1$. Then, $int_{\mathcal{I}}([h, h]) = true$ implies that for $int_{\mathcal{I}}([b, e]) = true$ iff $[b, e]$ is of the form $[h + n, h + m]$, $m, n \in \mathbb{N}$ and $n \leq m$.

So, $\mathcal{ID}$ is a set of formulas specifying the set of intervals of a discrete time obtained by shifting $\mathbb{N}$ by h time units ($h < 1$).

Another way to express integer intervals is to use a state variable C be that changes its value at each natural number which represents a tick of the real-time clock, i.e. $C_{\mathcal{I}}(t) = 1$ iff $\lfloor t \rfloor$ is odd.

The state variable C can also express if an interval is an integer interval. Namely, we have

$$(\lceil C \rceil \vee \lceil \neg C \rceil) \wedge \ell = 1 \Rightarrow int$$
$$int \wedge \ell = 1 \Rightarrow (\lceil C \rceil \vee \lceil \neg C \rceil)$$
$$\lceil C \rceil^\frown\lceil \neg C \rceil \Rightarrow true^\frown int^\frown true$$
$$\lceil \neg C \rceil^\frown\lceil C \rceil \Rightarrow true^\frown int^\frown true$$
$$(int \wedge \ell = 1)^\frown(int \wedge \ell = 1) \Rightarrow$$
$$((\lceil C \rceil \wedge \ell = 1)^\frown(\lceil \neg C \rceil \wedge \ell = 1)) \vee$$
$$((\lceil \neg C \rceil \wedge \ell = 1)^\frown(\lceil C \rceil \wedge \ell = 1))$$

Let $\mathcal{CC}$ denote the set of these formulas. $\mathcal{CC}$ specifies all the properties of the special clock state variable C. Any interval satisfying $int \wedge \ell > 0$ can be expressed precisely via a DC formula with state variable C (without int). Perhaps $int \wedge \ell = 0$ is the only formula that cannot be expressed by a formula via state variable

C without *int*. CC can also be used as a means to define the variable C via *int* and vice-versa. If we use CC to define *int*, the axioms for C simply are:

$$\lceil C \rceil \vee \lceil \neg C \rceil \Rightarrow \ell \le 1 \tag{9}$$
$$((\lceil C \rceil ^\frown \lceil \neg C \rceil ^\frown \lceil C \rceil) \vee (\lceil \neg C \rceil ^\frown \lceil C \rceil ^\frown \lceil \neg C \rceil)) \Rightarrow \ell \ge 1 \tag{10}$$

The relationship between these axioms and the axioms for *int* presented earlier is formulated as:

Proposition 3. *[31] Let interpretation $\mathcal{I}$ be such that the formulas in CC and axioms (6) and (7) are satisfied by all intervals.*

1. *If the axioms (9) and (10) are satisfied by all intervals, the axiom (8) is satisfied by all intervals.*
2. *If the axiom (8) is satisfied by all intervals then the axioms (9) and (10) are satisfied by all intervals, too.*

Proof.

  Proof of Item 1. The axioms (9) and (10) implies that the formula

$$(\lceil \neg P \rceil ^\frown \lceil P \rceil ^\frown \lceil \neg P \rceil)) \Rightarrow (\lceil \neg P \rceil ^\frown (\lceil P \rceil \wedge \ell = 1) ^\frown \lceil \neg P \rceil))$$

is satisfied for any interval when P is either C or $\neg C$. For any interval $[b, e]$, if $e - b \ge 2$ then there are $b = \tau_0 < \ldots < \tau_n = e$ such that $[\tau_i, \tau_{i+1}]$ satisfies $\lceil C \rceil \vee \lceil \neg C \rceil$, and $\tau_i, 0 < i < n$ are the points the state C changes its value. Therefore, from (3), (4) and CC the formula $int \wedge \ell = 1$ is satisfied by $[\tau_i, \tau_{i+1}]$ when $0 < i < n - 1$, and $\tau_1 - \tau_0 < 1$ and $\tau_n - \tau_{n-1} < 1$. Furthermore, from $int \wedge \ell = 1 \Rightarrow (\lceil C \rceil \vee \lceil \neg C \rceil)$ it follows that $[\tau_i, \tau_{i+1}], 0 < i < n - 1$ are the only intervals satisfying $int \wedge \ell = 1$. Hence, (8) is satisfied by $[b, e]$.

  Proof of Item 2. Let $h > 0$ be the first time point that state C changes its value. From the axioms (6), (7) and (8) it follows that $h \le 1$ and $int \wedge \ell = 1$ is satisfied by and only by the intervals of the form $[n + h, n + 1 + h]$, $n \in \mathbb{N}$. Hence, if CC is satisfied by all intervals, the axioms (9) and (10) are also satisfied by all intervals. $\qquad \square$

So, with the assumption that 0 is an integer point, the axioms (9) and (10) are equivalent to the axiom (8).

  Let *step* be a temporal propositional letter that represents two consecutive state changes of the system under consideration. When there are several state changes at a time point t, *step* evaluates to 1 over interval $[t, t]$. When two consecutive state changes are at t and t' such that $t \ne t'$, *step* is true for the interval $[t, t']$, and for any state variable P, either $\lceil P \rceil$ or $\lceil \neg P \rceil$ holds for the interval $[t, t']$. This is represented by:

$$step \wedge \ell > 0 \Rightarrow (\lceil P \rceil \vee \lceil \neg P \rceil) \text{ for any state variable } P$$
$$step \wedge \ell > 0 \Rightarrow \neg((step \wedge \ell > 0) ^\frown (step \wedge \ell > 0))$$

Let SC denote this class of formulas.

Now consider two kinds of Duration Calculus semantics which are different from the original one defined earlier for continuous time, and called discrete semantics and discrete step time semantics.

Discrete Duration Calculus semantics are defined in the same way as for continuous time semantics except that all intervals are integer intervals. So, a, b, m and m_i in the definition should be integers instead of reals, and an interpretation $\mathcal{I}$ should assign to each state variable P a function from $\mathbb{N}$ to $\{0, 1\}$, and then expanded to a function from $\mathcal{R}^+$ to $\{0, 1\}$ by letting $\mathcal{I}_P(t) = \mathcal{I}_P(\lfloor t \rfloor)$ which is right continuous, and could be discontinuous only at integer time points. Let us use $\models_{DDC}$ to denote the modelling relation in these semantics.

Similarly, discrete step time Duration Calculus semantics are defined by restricting the set of intervals to that of intervals between state change time points. So, a, b, m and m_i in the definition should be time points where states change, and an interpretation $\mathcal{I}$ should assign to each state variable P a function from $\mathcal{S}$ to $\{0, 1\}$, where $\mathcal{S}$ is a countable subset of $\mathcal{R}^+$ intended to be the set of time points for state changes that includes the set $\mathbb{N}$. $\mathcal{I}_P$ is then expanded to a function from $\mathcal{R}^+$ to $\{0, 1\}$ by letting $\mathcal{I}_P(t) = \mathcal{I}_P(t_s)$, where $t \in \mathcal{R}^+$ and $t_s = \max\{t' \in \mathcal{S} \mid t' \leq t\}$. Then $\mathcal{I}_P(t)$ is also right continuous, and could be discontinuous only at a point in $\mathcal{S}$. Let us use $\models_{SDC}$ to denote the modelling relation in this semantics.

To express that states are interpreted as right continuous functions, we can use formula called $\mathcal{RC}$

$$\lceil P \rceil \Rightarrow \lceil P \rceil^0 {}^\frown \lceil P \rceil \text{ for any state variable } P$$

In [48], Pandya also proposed a semantics using only the intervals of the form $[0, t]$. This semantics is often used in model checking when only the properties in the intervals of that form is specified, and we have to check if an automata model of the system satisfied those properties during its life. We can also specify this interval model with a temporal propositional letter Pre. Pre is interpreted as true only for the interval of the form $[0, t]$. Pre is specified by the set of formulas $Pref$ defined as

$$Pre {}^\frown true \Rightarrow Pre$$
$$\neg(\ell > 0 {}^\frown Pre)$$
$$Pre \wedge D \Rightarrow (Pre \wedge \ell = 0) {}^\frown D$$
$$Pre \wedge (D1 {}^\frown D2) \Rightarrow (Pre \wedge D1) {}^\frown D2$$

Proposition 4. *[31] Let $\mathcal{I}$ be an interpretation that validates the set of formulas $Pref$ and $\mathcal{I}, [0, 0] \models Pre$. Then, $\mathcal{I}, \mathcal{V}, [a, b] \models Pre$ iff $a = 0$.*

Proof. Straightforward   □

Then, a formula D is valid in the prefix time interval model if and only if $Pre \Rightarrow D$ is a valid formula in the original model of time interval.

So far, we have introduced special temporal propositional letters int, $step$ and Pre together with DC formulas specifying their special features. We are going to show that with these propositional letters we can provide a complete description of many useful time models.

Integer Time Model. To specify that a state can only change at an integer time point, we can use the formula $\mathcal{IS}$:

$$step \Rightarrow int$$

Let $\mathcal{DL}$ be the union of $\mathcal{SC}, \mathcal{IS}, \mathcal{ID}, \mathcal{RC}$. $\mathcal{DL}$ forms a relative complete specification for the discrete time structure. Let φ be a formula which does not have any occurrence of temporal variables int ans $step$. Let $intemb(\varphi)$ be a formula that obtained from φ by replacing each proper subformula ψ of φ by $\psi \wedge int$. For example $intemb(\phi^\frown \neg \psi) = (\phi \wedge int)^\frown(int \wedge \neg(\psi \wedge int))$.

Theorem 19. *[31] Let φ be a DC formula with no occurrence of temporal proposition letters. Then, $\mathcal{DL} \vdash int \Rightarrow intemb(\varphi)$ exactly when $\models_{DDC} \varphi$.*

Proof. Any discrete time model $\mathcal{I}, [a, b]$ can be extended to a model that satisfies the formulas in $\mathcal{DL}$ in the obvious way, namely with the interpretation for int and $step$ with the intended meanings for them. By induction on the structure of the formula φ, it is easy to prove that $\mathcal{I}, [a, b] \models_{DDC} \varphi$ if and only $\mathcal{I}, [a, b] \models intemb(\varphi)$.

Then, the "only if" part follows directly from the soundness of the proof of the DC system that $intemb(\varphi)$ is satisfied by any integer model that satisfies $\mathcal{DL}$.

The "if" part is proved as follows. From the above observation, if $\models_{DDC}$ φ then $int \Rightarrow intemb(\varphi)$ is a valid formula in DC with the assumption $\mathcal{DL}$. Consequently, from the relative completeness of DC, $intemb(\varphi)$ is provable in DC with the assumption $\mathcal{DL}$. □

Discrete Step Time Model. As it was said earlier, a discrete step time model consists of all time points at which there is a the state change. Since we have assumed that the special state variable C for the clock ticks is present in our system that changes its value at every integer point, this model of time should also include the set of natural numbers. This is the reason that we include $\mathbb{N}$ as a subset of $\mathcal{S}$. This time model was defined and used by Pandya et al in [48]. To represent a time point in this model, we introduce a temporal propositional letter pt, pt holds for an interval $[t, t']$ iff $t = t'$ and t is a time point at which there is a state change. pt should satisfy:

$$pt \Rightarrow \ell = 0$$
$$step \Rightarrow pt^\frown true^\frown pt$$
$$int \Rightarrow pt^\frown true^\frown pt$$
$$int \Rightarrow pt^\frown step^*$$

Let $\mathcal{DP}$ denote this set of formulas. The last formula in this set expresses our assumption that no Zeno computation is allowed, i.e. in any time interval, there are only a finite number of state changes. Let us define a DC formula dis as

$$dis \mathrel{\widehat{=}} (pt^\frown true^\frown pt)$$

dis represents an interval between two discrete points. When considering the Discrete Step Time Models, the chop point should satisfy *pt*.

The sublanguage $\mathcal{DSL}$, which is the union of $\mathcal{SC}$, $\mathcal{ID}$, $\mathcal{CC}$, $\mathcal{DP}$ $\mathcal{DC}$ and $\mathcal{RC}$, forms a relatively complete specification for the discrete time structure.

Let $disemb(\varphi)$ be a formula that is obtained from φ by replacing each proper subformula ψ of φ by $\psi \wedge dis$. For example $disemb(\phi \frown \neg\psi) = (\phi \wedge dis)\frown(dis \wedge \neg(\psi \wedge dis))$.

Theorem 20. *[31] Let φ be a DC formula with no occurrence of temporal proposition letters. Then, $\mathcal{DSL} \vdash dis \Rightarrow disemb(\varphi)$ exactly $\models_{SDC} \varphi$.*

Proof. The proof works in exactly the same way as the proof of Theorem 19.

Any discrete step time model $\mathcal{I}, [a, b]$ can be extended to a model that satisfies formulas in $\mathcal{DL}$ in the obvious way, namely with the interpretation for *int* and *step* with the intended meanings for them. By induction on the structure of the formula φ, it is easy to prove that $\mathcal{I}, [a, b] \models_{SDC} \varphi$ if and only $\mathcal{I}, [a, b] \models intemb(\varphi)$.

Then, the "only if" part follows directly from the soundness of the proof of the DC system that $intemb(\varphi)$ is satisfied by any discrete step time model that satisfies $\mathcal{DL}$.

For the "if" part, notice that if $\models_{SDC} \varphi$ then $dis \Rightarrow intemb(\varphi)$ is a valid formula in DC with the assumption $\mathcal{DL}$. Consequently, from the relative completeness of DC, $disemb(\varphi)$ is provable in DC with the assumption $\mathcal{DL}$.   □

Sampling Time Models. A sampling time model consists of the time points where we sample the data. Assume that the samplings are frequent enough and that any state change should be at a sampling point. To specify this time model, we can use $\mathcal{DSL}$ and an additional assumption

$$step \Rightarrow \ell = 1/h$$

where $h \in \mathbb{N}$, $h > 0$, i.e. $1/h$ is the sampling time step. Let $\mathcal{SL}_h$ be the language for the sampling time model with the sampling time step $1/h$.

8.2   Specifying Sampling, Periodic Task Systems

Sampling. Sampling and specifying periodic task systems are immediate applications of the results presented in the previous section.

We have built a language for sampling time models based on the continuous time DC. Hence, we can use the proof system of DC to reason about validity of a formula in that time and state model. How to relate the validity of a formula D in that time and state model with the validity of a formula D' in the original DC? In our early work [35], we have considered that relation, but had to formulate the results in a natural meta language due to the use of different semantic models. With the help from the time modeling language, we can also formulate the relationship as formulas in DC.

Let P be a state variable. Let P_h be a state in the sampling time model with the sampling time step $1/h$ such that P_h is interpreted the same as P at any sampling time point, i.e. $\square(pt \Rightarrow (\lceil P \rceil^0 \Leftrightarrow \lceil P_h \rceil^0)$ (denoted by $samp(P, P_h)$), and $\square(step \wedge \ell > 0 \Rightarrow (\lceil P_h \rceil \vee \lceil \neg P_h \rceil))$ (denoted by $dig(P_h)$). Let $stable(P, d)$ denote the formula $\square((\lceil \neg P \rceil \frown \lceil P \rceil \frown \lceil \neg P \rceil) \Rightarrow \ell \geq d)$.

Theorem 21. *Let $d > 1/h$. The following formulas are valid in DC:*

1. $(stable(P, d) \wedge samp(P, P_h) \wedge dig(P_h)) \Rightarrow$
   $(\int P = m \Rightarrow |\int P_h - m| \leq \min\{\ell, (\ell/d + 1)1/h\}$

2. $(stable(P, d) \wedge samp(P, P_h) \wedge dig(P_h)) \Rightarrow$
   $(\int P = m \wedge dis) \Rightarrow |\int P_h - m| \leq \min\{\ell, 1/h\ell/d\}$

3. $(stable(P, d) \wedge samp(P, P_h) \wedge dig(P_h)) \Rightarrow$
   $\int P_h = m \Rightarrow |\int P - m| \leq (\ell/d + 1)1/h$

4. $(stable(P, d) \wedge samp(P, P_h) \wedge dig(P_h)) \Rightarrow$
   $\int P_h < m \Rightarrow \int P < m + 1/h(\ell/d + 1)$

5. $(stable(P, d) \wedge samp(P, P_h) \wedge dig(P_h)) \Rightarrow$
   $\int P < m \Rightarrow \int P_h < m + 1/h(\ell/d + 1)$

6. $(stable(P, d) \wedge samp(P, P_h) \wedge dig(P_h)) \Rightarrow$
   $\int P_h > m \Rightarrow \int P > m - 1/h(\ell/d + 1)$

7. $(stable(P, d) \wedge samp(P, P_h) \wedge dig(P_h)) \Rightarrow$
   $\int P > m \Rightarrow \int P_h > m - 1/h(\ell/d + 1)$

8. $(stable(P, d) \wedge samp(P, P_h) \wedge dig(P_h)) \Rightarrow$
   $dis \Rightarrow (\lceil P_h \rceil \Leftrightarrow \lceil P \rceil)$

Proof. This is just a reformulation of Theorem 1 in [35]. $\qquad\qquad\square$

This theorem is useful for deriving a valid formula in the original DC from valid formulas in discrete time model. It can be used in approximate reasoning, especially in model checking: to check if a system S satisfies a DC property D, we can check a sampling system S_h of S whether it satisfies a discrete DC property D_h. D_h is found such that $S_h \models D_h$ implies $S \models D$. This technique has been used in [48].

Periodic Task System. Now we return to the scheduler mentioned in the introduction of the paper. Recall that a periodic task system T consists of n processes $\{1, \ldots, n\}$. Each process i raises its request periodically with period T_i, and for each period it requests a constant amount of processor time C_i. A specification of system T in DC has been given in many works, see e.g [70], which assume that all the processes raise their request at time 0. Now we can give a complete specification of the system without this assumption using the same technique that was introduced for temporal variable int in the previous section. To specify periodic behaviour of process i, we also use temporal variable $dLine\_i$

as in [70] whose behavior is similar to temporal variable int, and specified by:

$$dLine\_i \Rightarrow ((dLine\_i \land \ell = 0)^\frown(dLine\_i \land \ell = T_i)^*) \land \qquad (11)$$
$$((dLine\_i \land \ell = T_i)^*{}^\frown(dLine\_i \land \ell = 0))$$

$$dLine\_i^\frown(\ell = T_i) \Rightarrow dLine_i \qquad (12)$$

$$\ell \geq 2T_i \Rightarrow \ell < T_i^\frown((dLine\_i \land \ell = T_i)^* \land \qquad (13)$$
$$\neg(true^\frown(dLine\_i \land \ell = T_i)^\frown\neg(dLine\_i \land \ell = T_i)^*) \land$$
$$\neg(\neg(dLine\_i \land \ell = T_i)^*{}^\frown(dLine\_i \land \ell = T_i)^\frown true))^\frown$$
$$\ell < T_i$$

Let Run_i be a state variable saying that process i is running on the processor, i.e. $Run_i(t) = 1$ if process i is running on the processor, and $Run_i(t) = 0$ otherwise. Let $Stand_i$ be a state variable saying that the current request of process i has not been fulfilled. The behaviour of process i is fully specified by the following formula $\mathcal{B}_i$:

$$dLine\_i \land \ell = T_i \Rightarrow (((\textstyle\int Run_i < C_i \Leftrightarrow \lceil Stand_i \rceil)^\frown true) \land$$
$$(\textstyle\int Run_i = C_i^\frown \ell > 0 \Rightarrow \int Run_i = C_i^\frown\lceil\neg Stand_i\rceil))$$

The requirement REQ of system T is simply specified by:

$$\bigwedge_{i \leq n} dLine\_i \land \ell = T_i \Rightarrow \textstyle\int Run_i = C_i$$

Denote by $PERIOD$ the conjunction of formulas 11, 12 and 13. $PERIOD$ forms a complete specification of temporal propositional variables $dLine_i$, $i \leq n$, and are useful in proving the correctness of a scheduler for system T.

A priority-based scheduler $\mathcal{S}$ for system T with single processor is characterised by state variables $HiPri_{ij}$ ($i, j \leq n, i \neq j$) which specify the dynamic priority among the processes defined by $\mathcal{S}$, and the following state formulas characterising its behaviour:

$$\bigwedge_{i \neq j}((Run_i \land Stand_j) => HiPri_{ij})$$
$$\bigwedge_{i \leq n}(Run_i => Stand_i)$$
$$\bigwedge_{i \neq j}(HiPri_{ij} \Rightarrow \neg HiPri_{ji})$$
$$\bigwedge_{i \neq j}\neg(Run_i \land Run_j)$$
$$\bigvee_{i \leq n} Stand_i \Rightarrow \bigvee_{i \leq n} Run_i$$

The first formula says that a standby process j is not running because there is a process i with higher priority is running. The second formulas says that only standby process can run, the third formula characterises that the priority relation is totally defined, and the last formula specifies that only if there is a standby process then at least one process should be running. Let SCH denote the conjunction of these five formulas.

Deadline driven scheduler is a priority-based scheduler that considers process i to have a higher priority than process j (i.e. the value of $HiPri_{ij}$ at the current time point is 1) iff the deadline for process i is nearer than the deadline for

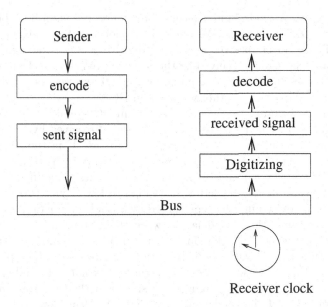

Fig. 6. Communication Protocol Model

process j. The deadline driven scheduler can be modelled with the additional formula specifying the behaviour of state variables $HiPri_{ij}$ $(i,j \leq n)$:

$$\wedge_{i \neq j} \lceil HiPri_{ij} \rceil \cap \ell = T_i \Rightarrow (\neg \Diamond dLine_j) \cap dLine_i \cap true$$

Denote this formula by DDS. The interesting thing here is that variables $HiPri_{ij}$ can be defined in DC, without any quantification on rigid variables, via temporal propositional variables $dLine_i$ $(i \leq n)$ which are completely specified by formulas 11, 12 and 13. Note that with defining $HiPri_{ij}$ in this way, we don't have to assume that all the processes raise their request at time 0. Hence, reasoning about the correctness of the scheduler for the general case can be done with the proof system of DC. For example, the correctness of deadline-driven scheduler (included in Liu and Layland's Theorem for the feasibility of the deadline-driven scheduler) is formalised as:

$$\{PERIOD, \wedge_{i \leq n} \mathcal{B}_i, SCH, DDS, \sum_{i \leq n}(C_i/T_i) \leq 1\} \models REQ$$

This can be proved by using the proof system of DC.

8.3   Modelling Communication Protocols with Digitizing in DC

In this section, we show that with discrete time structure formalised, we can model communication protocols using Duration Calculus (DC) in a very convenient way without any extension for digitising. This model has been presented in our earlier work [32,33]. Consider a model for communication at the physical layer (see Fig. 6). A sender and a receiver are connected via a bus. Their clocks are running at different rates. We refer to the clock of the receiver as the time reference. The receiver receives signals by digitising. Since the signals sent by the sender and the signals received by the receiver are functions from the set $\mathbb{R}^+$ to $\{0, 1\}$ (1 represents that the signal is *high*, and 0 represents that the signal is *low*), we can model them as state variables in DC.

The communication protocols are modelled in DC as follows. The signal sent by the sender is modelled by a state X. The signal received by the receiver by sampling the signal on the bus is modelled by a state Y in the sampling time model with the sampling time step 1. So, $step \Leftrightarrow int \wedge \ell = 1$. However, it is not the case that $samp(X, Y)$ due to the fact that it takes a significant amount of time to change the signal on the bus from high to low or vice-versa, and hence, the signal on the bus cannot be represented by a Boolean function. Without loss of generality, assume that the delay between the sender and the receiver is 0. Assume also that when the signal on the bus is neither high nor low, the receiver will choose an arbitrary value from $\{0, 1\}$ for the value of Y. The phenomenon is depicted in Fig. 7. Assume that it takes r (r is a natural number) receiver-clock cycles for the sender to change the signal on the bus from high to low or vice-versa. Then if the sender changes the signal from low to high or from high to low, the receiver's signal will be unreliable for r cycles starting from the last tick of the receiver clock and during this period it can be any value chosen nondeterministically from 0 and 1. Otherwise, the signal received by the receiver is the same as the signal sent by the sender (see Figure 7). This relationship between X and Y is formalised as

$$(\lceil X \rceil \wedge (\ell \geq r + 1)) \Rightarrow (\ell \leq r) \frown (\lceil Y \rceil \wedge int) \frown (\ell < 1),$$
$$(\lceil \neg X \rceil \wedge (\ell \geq r + 1)) \Rightarrow (\ell \leq r) \frown (\lceil \neg Y \rceil \wedge int) \frown (\ell < 1).$$

Since the behaviour of a state can be specified by a DC formula, a communication protocol can be modelled as consisting of a coding function f, which maps a sequence of bits to a DC formula expressing the behaviour of X, and a decoding function g, which maps a DC formula expressing the behaviour of Y to a sequence of bits. The protocol is correct iff for any sequence w of bits, if the sender puts the signal represented by $f(w)$ on the bus then by digitising the receiver must receive and receives only the signals represented by a DC formula D for which $g(D) = w$.

8.4   Biphase Mark Protocols

In the Biphase Mark Protocols (BMP) the sender encodes a bit as a cell consisting of a mark subcell of length b and a code subcell of length a. The sender keeps the signal stable in each subcell (hence either $\lceil X \rceil$ or $\lceil \neg X \rceil$ holds for the interval representing a subcell). For a cell, if the signal in the mark subcell is the same as the signal in the code subcell, the information carried by the cell is 0; otherwise, the information carried by the cell is 1. There is a phase reverse between two consecutive cells. This means that, for a cell, the signal of the mark subcell of the following cell is held as the negation of the signal of the code

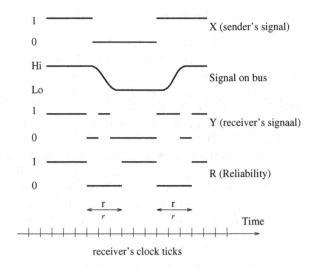

Fig. 7. Signal patterns

subcell of the cell. The receiver, on detecting a state change (of Y), knows that it is the beginning of a cell, and skips d cycles (called the *sampling distance*) and samples the signal. If the sampled signal is the same as the signal at the beginning of the cell, it decodes the cell as 0; otherwise it decodes the cell as 1.

At the beginning of the transmission, the signal is low for a cycles (this means, $\lceil \neg X \rceil$ holds for the interval of length a starting from the beginning). When the sender finishes sending, it keeps the signal stable for cc time units which is longer than the code subcell. We use HLS, LHS to denote the formulas representing intervals consisting of the code subcell of a cell and the mark subcell of the next one for the sender, and use $HLR^\frown(\ell = d)$, $LHR^\frown(\ell = d)$ to denote the formulas representing the intervals between the two consecutive sampling points (from the time the receiver samples the signal of a code subcell to the next one. Formally,

$$HLS \,\widehat{=}\, (\lceil X \rceil \wedge \ell = a)^\frown(\lceil \neg X \rceil \wedge \ell = b)\,,$$
$$LHS \,\widehat{=}\, (\lceil \neg X \rceil \wedge \ell = a)^\frown(\lceil X \rceil \wedge \ell = b)\,,$$
$$HLR \,\widehat{=}\, (\lceil Y \rceil \wedge int \wedge 1 \leq \ell \leq \rho)^\frown(\lceil \neg Y \rceil \wedge \ell = 1)\,,$$
$$LHR \,\widehat{=}\, (\lceil \neg Y \rceil \wedge int \wedge 1 \leq \ell \leq \rho)^\frown(\lceil Y \rceil \wedge \ell = 1)\,.$$

Now, we are ready to formalise the BMP in DC. What we have to do is write down the encoding function f and the decoding function g. From the informal description of the protocol, we can define f inductively as follows.

1. $f(\epsilon) \,\widehat{=}\, (\lceil \neg X \rceil \wedge \ell = c)$
2. If $f(w) = D^\frown(\lceil X \rceil \wedge \ell = c)$, then

$$f(w0) \,\widehat{=}\, D^\frown HLS^\frown(\lceil \neg X \rceil \wedge \ell = c)$$
$$f(w1) \,\widehat{=}\, D^\frown HLS^\frown(\lceil X \rceil \wedge \ell = c)$$

3. If $f(w) = D^\frown(\lceil \neg X \rceil \wedge \ell = c)$, then

$$f(w0) \; \hat{=} \; D^\frown LHS^\frown(\lceil X \rceil \wedge \ell = c)$$
$$f(w1) \; \hat{=} \; D^\frown LHS^\frown(\lceil \neg X \rceil \wedge \ell = c)$$

For example, $f(1) = LHS^\frown(\lceil \neg X \rceil \wedge \ell = c)$, $f(10) = LHS^\frown LHS^\frown(\lceil X \rceil \wedge \ell = c)$, and $f(101) = LHS^\frown LHS^\frown HLS^\frown(\lceil X \rceil \wedge \ell = c)$.

Because the decoding function g is a partial function, we have to describe its domain first, i.e. what kind of DC formulas on the state Y are detected (received) by the receiver. According to the behaviour of the receiver, first it skips r cycles. Then it begins to scan for an edge (HLR or LHR). When an edge is detected, it skips d cycles and repeats this procedure until it detects that the transmission has completed (Y is stable for more than ρ cycles). Thus, a DC formula D is received by the receiver iff D is of the form $A_0{}^\frown A_1{}^\frown \ldots {}^\frown A_n$, $n \geq 1$, where

- $A_0 = (1 \geq \ell \wedge \ell > 0)^\frown(int \wedge (\ell = r - 1)))$
- and either $A_n = (int \wedge \lceil Y \rceil \wedge (\ell > \rho))^\frown(\ell < 1))$,
  or $A_n = (int \wedge \lceil \neg Y \rceil \wedge (\ell > \rho))^\frown(\ell < 1))$
- and for $j = 1, \ldots, n - 1$ either $A_j = LHR^\frown(\ell = d)$ or $A_j = HLR^\frown(\ell = d)$
- and if $n = 1$ then $A_n = (int \wedge \lceil \neg Y \rceil \wedge (\ell > \rho))^\frown(\ell < 1))$ and if $n > 1$ then $A_1 = LHR^\frown(\ell = d)$ (since at the beginning the signal is low).

Now, the decoding function g can be written as follows. Let D be a formula received by the receiver.

- If $D = (\ell \leq 1 \wedge \ell > 0)^\frown(int \wedge \ell = r - 1)^\frown(\lceil \neg Y \rceil \wedge \ell > \rho \wedge int)^\frown \ell < 1$ then $g(D) = \epsilon$.
- Let $g(D)$ be defined.

  • If $D = D'^\frown(\lceil Y \rceil \wedge int \wedge \ell \geq \rho)^\frown \ell < 1$ then
  $g(D'^\frown HLR^\frown(\ell = d)^\frown(\lceil Y \rceil \wedge int \wedge \ell \geq \rho)^\frown \ell < 1) = g(D)1$, and
  $g(D'^\frown HLR^\frown(\ell = d)^\frown(\lceil \neg Y \rceil \wedge int \wedge \ell \geq \rho)^\frown \ell < 1) = g(D)0$.
  • If $D = D'^\frown(\lceil \neg Y \rceil \wedge int \wedge \ell \geq \rho)^\frown \ell < 1$, then
  $g(D'^\frown LHR^\frown(\ell = d)^\frown(\lceil Y \rceil \wedge int \wedge \ell \geq \rho)^\frown \ell < 1) = g(D)0$, and
  $g(D'^\frown LHR^\frown(\ell = d)^\frown(\lceil \neg Y \rceil \wedge int \wedge \ell \geq \rho)^\frown \ell < 1) = g(D)1$.

For example, let D be $(\ell \leq 1 \wedge \ell > 0)^\frown(int \wedge \ell = r-1)^\frown LHR^\frown(\ell = d)^\frown LHR^\frown(\ell = d)^\frown HLR^\frown(\ell = d)^\frown(\lceil Y \rceil \wedge \ell > \rho \wedge int)^\frown(\ell < 1))$. Then,

$$
\begin{aligned}
g(D) &= g((\ell \leq 1 \wedge \ell > 0)^\frown(int \wedge \ell = r - 1)^\frown LHR^\frown(\ell = d) \\
&\quad {}^\frown LHR^\frown(\ell = d)^\frown(\lceil Y \rceil \wedge \ell > \rho \wedge int)^\frown(\ell < 1))\,1 \\
&= g((\ell \leq 1 \wedge \ell > 0)^\frown(int \wedge \ell = r - 1)^\frown LHR^\frown(\ell = d)^\frown \\
&\quad (\lceil \neg Y \rceil \wedge \ell > \rho \wedge int)^\frown(\ell < 1))\,01 \\
&= g((\ell \leq 1 \wedge \ell > 0)^\frown(int \wedge \ell = r - 1) \\
&\quad {}^\frown(\lceil \neg Y \rceil \wedge \ell > \rho \wedge int)^\frown(\ell < 1))\,101 \\
&= \epsilon 101\,.
\end{aligned}
$$

8.5   Verification of BMP

As said earlier, we have to verify that for any sequence of bits w, if the sender puts on the bus the signal represented by DC formula $f(w)$, then the receiver must receive and receives only the signals represented by a DC formula D for which $g(D) = w$. We can only prove this requirement with some condition on the values of the parameter r, a, b, c, ρ and d. The requirement is formalised as:

For all sequence of bits w,

- there exists a DC formula D received by the receiver such that $f(w) \Rightarrow D$, and
- for all D receivable by the receiver, if $f(w) \Rightarrow D$ then $g(D) = w$.

Since in BMP g is a deterministic function, for any sequence of bits w there is no more than one receivable formula D for which $f(w) \Rightarrow D$. Thus we can have a stronger requirement which is formalised as:

For all sequences of bits w there exists uniquely a receivable formula D such that $f(w) \Rightarrow D$ and $g(D) = w$.

Our verification is done by proving the following two theorems.

Theorem 22. *[31] For any receivable formulas D and D', if D is different from D' syntactically then $\models ((D \wedge D') \Rightarrow ff)$.*

This theorem says that each time at most one receivable formula D is received by the receiver.

Theorem 23. *[31] Assume that $r \geq 1$, $b \geq r+1$, $a \geq r+1$, $c \geq \rho+a$, $d \geq b+r$, $d \leq a+b-3-r$, and $\rho \geq a+1$. Then for any sequence of bits w there exists a receivable formula D for which $f(w) \Rightarrow D$ and $g(D) = w$.*

In [33] we proved these two theorems, with PVS proof checker, with the encoding of the proof system for Duration Calculus.

We have seen in this section that by using temporal propositional letters we can specify many classes of time models that are suitable for our applications. The properties of the introduced temporal propositional letters are then specified by a class of Duration Calculus formulas. Using this class of formulas and the proof system of the original Duration Calculus we can reason about the behaviour of our real-time systems in different time domains.

9   Conclusion

We have presented in this chapter a theory of Duration Calculus with applications. This theory contains the main components of the calculus such as its syntax, semantics and proof system. We also present some extensions of DC which are convenient for specification and give more expressive power to DC. We give a brief summary of the decidability and undecidability results and present some techniques for doing model-check for a sub-class of the calculus that have been published in the literatures, and for specifying real-time properties of computing systems via some well-known examples. The materials presented in this chapter is fundamental for researching and practicing in Duration Calculus. The research in this area is on the way, and we believe that many newly developed results in Duration Calculus are not covered in this chapter.

References

1. Asarin, E., Caspi, P., Maler, O.: A Kleene Theorem for Timed Automata. In: LICS'97. International Symposium on Logics in Computer Science, pp. 160–171. IEEE Computer Society Press, Los Alamitos (1997)
2. Allen, J.F.: Towards a general theory of action and time. Artificial Intelligence 23, 123–154 (1984)
3. Alur, R., Dill, D.L.: A theory of timed automata. Theoretical Comput. Sci. 126(2), 183–235 (1994)
4. Bengtsson, J., Larsen, K.G., Larsson, F., Pettersson, P., Yi, W.: Uppaal – a tool suite for automatic verification of real-time systems. In: Alur, R., Sontag, E.D., Henzinger, T.A. (eds.) Hybrid Systems III. LNCS, vol. 1066, pp. 232–243. Springer, Heidelberg (1996)
5. Bjørner, D.: Trusted computing systems: the ProCoS experience. In: Proceedings of the 14th international conference on Software engineering, Melbourne, Australia, pp. 15–34. ACM Press, New York (1992)
6. Bjørner, D., Hensson, M. (eds.): Logics of Specification Languages. EATCS Monographs in Theoretical Computer Science. Springer, Heidelberg (to appear, 2007)
7. Blackburn, P., de Rijke, M., Venema, Y.: Modal Logic, Cambridge (2001)
8. Bolander, B., Hansen, J.U., Hansen, M.R.: Decidability of hybrid duration calculus. ENTCS 174(6), 113–133 (2006)
9. Braberman, V.A., Hung, D.V.: On checking timed automata for linear duration invariants. In: Proceedings of the 19th IEEE Real-Time Systems Symposium, pp. 264–273. IEEE Computer Society Press, Los Alamitos (1998)
10. Buchi, J.R.: Weak second-order arithmetic and finite automata. Z. Math. Logik Grundl. Math. 6, 66–92 (1960)
11. Chan, P., Hung, D.V.: Duration calculus specification of scheduling for tasks with shared resources. In: Kanchanasut, K., Levy, J.-J. (eds.) Algorithms, Concurrency and Knowledge. LNCS, vol. 1023, pp. 365–380. Springer, Heidelberg (1995)
12. Dutertre, B.: Complete proof systems for first order interval temporal logic. In: Tenth Annual IEEE Symp. on Logic in Computer Science, pp. 36–43. IEEE Press, Los Alamitos (1995)
13. Dutertre, B.: On first order interval temporal logic. Technical report, Report no. CSD-TR-94-3, Department of Computer Science, Royal Holloway, University of London, Eghan, Surrey TW20 0EX, England (1995)
14. Elgot, C.C.: Decision problems of finite automata design and related arithmetics. Transactions of the American Mathematical Society 98, 21–52 (1961)
15. Fränzle, M., Hansen, M.R.: A Robust Interpretation of Duration Calculus. In: Van Hung, D., Wirsing, M. (eds.) ICTAC 2005. LNCS, vol. 3722, pp. 257–271. Springer, Heidelberg (2005)
16. Fränzle, M., Hansen, M.R.: Deciding an Interval Logic with Accumulated Durations. In: Grumberg, O., Huth, M.D.V. (eds.) TACAS 2007. LNCS, vol. 4424, pp. 201–215. Springer, Heidelberg (2007)

17. Fränzle, M.: Synthesizing controllers from duration calculus. In: Jonsson, B., Parrow, J. (eds.) Formal Techniques in Real-Time and Fault-Tolerant Systems. LNCS, vol. 1135, pp. 168–187. Springer, Heidelberg (1996)

18. Fränzle, M.: Take it np-easy: Bounded model construction for duration calculus. In: Damm, W., Olderog, E.-R. (eds.) FTRTFT 2002. LNCS, vol. 2469, pp. 245–264. Springer, Heidelberg (2002)

19. Guelev, D.P., Van Hung, D.: On the completeness and decidability of duration calculus with iteration. Theor. Comput. Sci. 337(1-3), 278–304 (2005)

20. Guelev, D.P.: A Complete Proof System for First Order Interval Temporal Logic with Projection. Technical Report 202, UNU-IIST, P.O.Box 3058, Macau (June 2000) (A revised version of this report was published in the Journal of Logic and Computation 14(2), 215–249, Oxford University Press (April 2004))

21. Guelev, D.P.: A calculus of durations on abstract domains: Completeness and extensions. Technical report, UNU/IIST 139 (1998)

22. Guelev, D.P., Hung, D.V.: On the completeness and decidability of duration calculus with iteration. In: Thiagarajan, P.S., Yap, R.H.C. (eds.) ASIAN 1999. LNCS, vol. 1742, pp. 139–150. Springer, Heidelberg (1999)

23. Halpern, J., Moskowski, B., Manna, Z.: A hardware semantics based on temporal intervals. In: Díaz, J. (ed.) Automata, Languages and Programming. LNCS, vol. 154, pp. 278–291. Springer, Heidelberg (1983)

24. Halpern, J., Shoham, Y.: A propositional modal logic of time intervals. Journal of the ACM 33(4), 935–962 (1991)

25. Hansen, M.R.: Duration Calculus. Chapter in [6], pp. 293–441 (2007)

26. Hansen, M.R.: Model-checking discrete duration calculus. Formal Aspects of Computing 6A, 826–845 (1994)

27. Hansen, M.R., Zhou, C.: Semantics and completeness of duration calculus. In: Huizing, C., de Bakker, J.W., Rozenberg, G., de Roever, W.-P. (eds.) Real-Time: Theory in Practice. LNCS, vol. 600, pp. 209–225. Springer, Heidelberg (1992)

28. Hansen, M.R., Zhou, C.: Duration calculus: Logical foundations. Formal Aspects of Computing 9, 283–330 (1997)

29. Harrison, J.: Theorem Proving with the Real Numbers. Springer, Heidelberg (1998)

30. Hoenicke: Combination of Processes, Data and Time. Dissertation, Carl von Ossietzky Universität, Oldenburg, Germany (2006)

31. Van Hung, D.: Specifying Various Time Models with Temporal Propositional Variables in Duration Calculus. Research Report 377, UNU-IIST, P.O.Box 3058, Macau (June 2007)

32. Hung, D.V., Il, K.-K.: Verification via Digitized Model of Real-Time Systems. Research Report 54, UNU-IIST, P.O.Box 3058, Macau (February 1996) (published in the Proceedings of Asia-Pacific Software Engineering Conference 1996 (APSEC'96), pp. 4–15, IEEE Computer Society Press (1996))

33. Hung, D.V.: Modelling and verification of biphase mark protocols in duration calculus using pvs/dc⁻. In: CSD'98. Application of Concurrency to System Design, pp. 88–98. IEEE Computer Society Press, Los Alamitos (1998)

34. Hung, D.V., Thai, P.H.: Checking a Regular Class of Duration Calculus Models for Linear Duration Invariants. Technical Report 118, UNU/IIST, P.O.Box 3058, Macau (July 1997) (presented at and published in Kramer, B., Uchihira, N., Croll, P., Russo, S. (eds.) The Proceedings of the International Symposium on Software Engineering for Parallel and Distributed Systems (PDSE'98), April 20-21, 1998, Kyoto, Japan, pp. 61–71. IEEE Computer Society Press (1998))

35. Hung, D.V., Giang, P.H.: A sampling semantics of duration calculus. In: Jonsson, B., Parrow, J. (eds.) Formal Techniques in Real-Time and Fault-Tolerant Systems. LNCS, vol. 1135, pp. 188–207. Springer, Heidelberg (1996)
36. Hung, D.V., Guelev, D.P.: Completeness and decidability of a fragment of duration calculus with iteration. In: Thiagarajan, P.S., Yap, R.H.C. (eds.) ASIAN 1999. LNCS, vol. 1742, pp. 139–150. Springer, Heidelberg (1999)
37. Hung, D.V., Ji, W.: On design of hybrid control systems using i/o automata models. In: Chandru, V., Vinay, V. (eds.) Foundations of Software Technology and Theoretical Computer Science. LNCS, vol. 1180, pp. 156–167. Springer, Heidelberg (1996)
38. Zhao, J., Hung, D.V.: On checking real-time parallel systems for linear duration properties. In: Ravn, A.P., Rischel, H. (eds.) FTRTFT 1998. LNCS, vol. 1486, pp. 241–250. Springer, Heidelberg (1998)
39. Kesten, Y., Pnueli, A., Sifakis, J., Yovine, S.: Integration graphs: A class of decidable hybrid systems. In: Grossman, R.L., Ravn, A.P., Rischel, H., Nerode, A. (eds.) Hybrid Systems. LNCS, vol. 736, pp. 179–208. Springer, Heidelberg (1993)
40. Klarlund, N., Moller, A.: MONA Version 1.4: User Manual. BRICS, Department of Computer Science, University of Aarhus, Denmark (2001)
41. Larsen, K.G., Rasmussen, J.I.: Optimal conditional reachability for multi-priced timed automata. In: Sassone, V. (ed.) FOSSACS 2005. LNCS, vol. 3441, pp. 230–244. Springer, Heidelberg (2005)
42. Li, X.: A Mean Value Calculus. PhD Thesis, Software Institute, Academia Sinica (1993)
43. Li, X., Hung, D.V.: Checking linear duration invariants by linear programming. In: Jaffar, J., Yap, R.H.C. (eds.) ASIAN 1996. LNCS, vol. 1179, pp. 321–332. Springer, Heidelberg (1996)
44. Li, X., Hung, D.V., Zheng, T.: Checking hybrid automata for linear duration invariants. In: Suciu, D., Vossen, G. (eds.) WebDB 2000. LNCS, vol. 1997, pp. 166–180. Springer, Heidelberg (2001)
45. Mao, X., Xu, Q., Hung, D.V., Wang, J.: Towards a proof assistant for interval logics. Technical report, UNU/IIST Report No. 77, UNU/IIST, International Institute for Software Technology, Macau (1996)
46. Moszkowski,: A temporal logic for multilevel reasoning about hardware. IEEE Computer 18(2), 10–19 (1985)
47. Olderog, E.R., Dierks, H.: Decomposing real-time specifications. In: de Roever, W.-P., Langmaack, H., Pnueli, A. (eds.) COMPOS 1997. LNCS, vol. 1536, Springer, Heidelberg (1998)
48. Pandya, P.K., Krishna, S.N., Loya, K.: On Sampling Abstraction of Continuous Time Logic with Duration Calculus. Technical Report TIFR-PKP-GM-2006/1, Tata Institute of Fundamental Research, India (2006)
49. Pandya, P.K.: Some extensions to propositional mean value calculus: Expressiveness and decidability. In: Kleine Büning, H. (ed.) CSL 1995. LNCS, vol. 1092, pp. 434–451. Springer, Heidelberg (1996)
50. Pandya, P.K.: Specifying and deciding quantified discrete-time duration calculus formulae using DCVALID. Tata Institute of Fundamental Research, India. Technical report, TCS00-PKP-1 (2000)
51. Pandya, P.K.: Dcvalid 1.3: The user manual. Technical report, Computer Science Group, TIFR, Bombay, Technical Report TCS-99/1 (1999)
52. Rabinovich, A.: Non-elementary lower bound for propositional duration calculus. Information Processing Letters, pp. 7–11 (1998)

53. Rabinovich, A.: On the decidability of continuous time specification formalism. Journal of logic and computation 8(5), 669–678 (1998)

54. Rasmussen, T.M.: Automated proof support for interval logics. In: Nieuwenhuis, R., Voronkov, A. (eds.) LPAR 2001. LNCS (LNAI), vol. 2250, pp. 317–326. Springer, Heidelberg (2001)

55. Rasmussen, T.M.: Labelled natural deduction for interval logics. In: Fribourg, L. (ed.) CSL 2001 and EACSL 2001. LNCS, vol. 2142, pp. 308–323. Springer, Heidelberg (2001)

56. Rasmussen, T.M.: Interval Logic: Proof Theory and Theorem Proving. PhD Thesis, Informatics and Mathematical Modelling, Technical University of Denmark (2002)

57. Ravn, A.P.: Design of Embedded Real-Time Computing Systems. Doctoral Dissertation, Department of Computer Science, Technical University of Denmark (1995)

58. Ravn, A.P., Rischel, H., Hansen, K.M.: Specifying and verifying requirements of real-time systems. IEEE Trans. Softw. Eng. 19(1), 41–55 (1993)

59. Satpathy, M., Hung, D.V., Pandya, P.K.: Some results on the decidability of duration calculus under synchronous interpretation. In: Ravn, A.P., Rischel, H. (eds.) FTRTFT 1998. LNCS, vol. 1486, pp. 186–197. Springer, Heidelberg (1998)

60. Skakkebæk, J.U.: A Verification Assistant for a Real-Time Logic. PhD Thesis, Department of Computer Science, Technical University of Denmark (1994)

61. Skakkebæk, J.U., Sestoft, P.: Checking validity of duration calculus formulas. Technical report, ProCoS II, ESPRIT BRA 7071, report no. ID/DTH JUS 3/1, Department of Computer Science, Technical University of Denmark (1994)

62. Skakkebæk, J.U., Shankar, N.: Towards a duration calculus proof assistant in pvs. In: Langmaack, H., de Roever, W.-P., Vytopil, J. (eds.) Formal Techniques in Real-Time and Fault-Tolerant Systems. LNCS, vol. 863, pp. 660–679. Springer, Heidelberg (1994)

63. Sørensen, E.V., Ravn, A.P., Rischel, H.: Control program for a gas burner: Part 1: Informal requirements, procos case study 1. Technical report, ProCoS Rep. ID/DTH EVS2 (1990)

64. Tarski, A.: A decision method for elementary algebra and geometry. RAND Corporation, Santa Monica, California (1948)

65. Thai, P.H., Hung, D.V.: Verifying Linear Duration Constraints of Timed Automata. In: Liu, Z., Araki, K. (eds.) ICTAC 2004. LNCS, vol. 3407, pp. 295–309. Springer, Heidelberg (2005)

66. Wang, F., Mok, A.K., Emerson, E.A.: Distributed Real-Time System Specification and Verification in APTL. ACM Transactions on Software Engineering and Methodology 2(4), 346–378 (1993)

67. Zheng, Y., Zhou, C.: A formal proof of the deadline driven scheduler. In: Langmaack, H., de Roever, W.-P., Vytopil, J. (eds.) Formal Techniques in Real-Time and Fault-Tolerant Systems. LNCS, vol. 863, pp. 756–775. Springer, Heidelberg (1994)

68. Zhou, C., Hansen, M.R.: An adequate first order logic of intervals. In: de Roever, W.-P., Langmaack, H., Pnueli, A. (eds.) COMPOS 1997. LNCS, vol. 1536, pp. 584–608. Springer, Heidelberg (1998)

69. Zhou, C., Hansen, M.R., Ravn, A.P., Rischel: Duration specifications for shared processors. In: Vytopil, J. (ed.) Formal Techniques in Real-Time and Fault-Tolerant Systems. LNCS, vol. 571, pp. 21–32. Springer, Heidelberg (1991)

70. Zhou, C., Hansen, M.R.: Duration Calculus: A formal approach to real-time systems. Springer, New York (2004)

71. Zhou, C., Hansen, M.R., Sestoft, P.: Decidability and undecidability results for duration calculus. In: Enjalbert, P., Wagner, K.W., Finkel, A. (eds.) STACS 93. LNCS, vol. 665, pp. 58–68. Springer, Heidelberg (1993)
72. Zhou, C., Hoare, C.A.R., Ravn, A.P.: A calculus of durations. Information Processing Letters 40(5), 269–276 (1991)
73. Zhou, C., Zhang, J., Yang, L., Li, X.: Linear duration invariants. In: Langmaack, H., de Roever, W.-P., Vytopil, J. (eds.) Formal Techniques in Real-Time and Fault-Tolerant Systems. LNCS, vol. 863, pp. 86–109. Springer, Heidelberg (1994)

Understanding Programming Language Concepts Via Operational Semantics

Cliff B. Jones

School of Computing Science, University of Newcastle, NE1 7RU, UK

Abstract. The origins of "formal methods" lie partly in language description (although applications of methods like VDM, RAISE or B to areas other than programming languages are probably more widely known). This paper revisits the language description task but uses operational (rather than denotational) semantics to illustrate that the crucial idea is thinking about an abstract model of something that one is trying to understand or design. A "story" is told which links together some of the more important concepts in programming languages and thus illustrates how formal semantics deepens our understanding.

1 Introduction

One objective of this paper is to show how the concept of "abstract modelling" of any computer system applies to programming languages. The position taken is that a description of the semantics of such a language can not only aid understanding but can also be used to design a language which is likely to satisfy the needs of both users and compiler writers.

Computers are normally programmed in "high-level" (programming) languages (HLLs). Two important problems are

1. the correctness of programs (i.e. whether or not a program satisfies its specification) written in such a language; and
2. the correctness of the compiler that translates "source programs" into "object programs" (in "machine code").

At the root of both of these problems is the far more important issue of the design of the high-level language itself.

The designer of a programming language faces several engineering challenges — one balance that must be sought is the "level" of the language: too low a level of language increases the work of every programmer who writes programs in that language; too high a level (far from the realities of the machines on which the object programs will run) and not only is the compiler writer's task harder but it is also likely that any compiler will produce less efficient code than a programmer with closer access to the machine. A badly designed language will impair the effectiveness of both user and implementer.

The essence of what this paper addresses is the *modelling* of *concepts* in programming languages based on the firm conviction that most language issues can

C. George, Z. Liu, and J. Woodcock (Eds.): Domain Modeling, LNCS 4710, pp. 177–235, 2007.
© Springer-Verlag Berlin Heidelberg 2007

–and should– be thought out in terms of a semantic model long before the task of designing a complier is undertaken.

A thread –partly historical– through some of the more important concepts of programming languages is created. Little time is spent on details of the (concrete) syntax of how a concept is expressed in one or another programming language. The interest here is in concepts like "strong typing", the need for –and support of– abstract types, ways of composing programs and documenting interfaces to components, modes of parameter passing, constraining "side-effects", deciding where to allow non-determinacy, the need for files/databases, the (lack of) integration of database access languages into programming languages, and the role of objects. A particular emphasis is on issues relating to concurrency.

The main focus is not, however, on the specific features selected for study; it is the modelling concept which is promoted. Modelling tools like "environments", choosing a "small state" and (above all) *abstraction* are taught by application. The interest here is in *modelling* — not in theory for its own sake. The methods can be applied to almost any language. They are not limited to the specific language features discussed here — but an attempt has been made to provide a "thread" through those features chosen. Indeed, another objective of the paper is to show relationships between language concepts that are often treated separately.

This paper uses VDM notation for objects/functions etc. — the choice is not important and the material could be presented in other notations. The story of the move from VDL [LW69] to VDM [BBH$^+$74, BJ78, BJ82] is told in [Jon01b]. This author's decision to move back to operational semantics is justified in [Jon03b].

1.1   Natural vs. Artificial Languages

The distinction between natural and formal languages is important. All humans use languages when they speak and write "prose" (or poetry). These "natural" languages have evolved and each generation of humans pushes the evolution (if not "development") further. The natural language in which this paper is written incorporates ideas and words from the languages of the many invaders of "England".[1]

In contrast to the evolving natural languages, humans have designed formal or artificial languages to communicate with computers. Different though the history –and objectives– of natural and formal languages are, there are ideas in common in the way one can study languages in either class.

The languages that are spoken by human beings were not designed by committee; they just evolved[2] — and they continue to change. The evolution process is all too obvious from the irregularities in natural languages. The task of describing natural languages is therefore very challenging but, because they have been around longer, it is precisely with natural languages that one first finds a

---

[1] No slight to the rest of the United Kingdom – just to make the link to "English" which is the name of our common language.

[2] Of course, there are a small number of exceptions like Volapük and Esperanto.

systematic study. Charles Sanders Peirce (1839-1914) used the term "Semiotics". Crucially, he divided the study the study of languages into:

- syntax: structure
- semantics: meaning
- pragmatics: intention

Heinz Zemanek applied the terminology to programming languages in [Zem66].

It is not difficult to write syntax rules for parts of natural languages but because of their irregularity, a complete syntax is probably not a sensible objective.

It is far harder to give a semantics to a language (than to write syntactic rules). If one knows a language, another language might be explained by translating it into the known language (although nuances and beauty might be lost).

Within one language, a dictionary is used to give the meanings of words. But there is clearly a danger of an infinite loop here.

1.2   Formal Languages

People designed "formal" (or artificial) languages long before computers existed (a relevant example is Boole's logic [Boo54]); but the main focus here is on languages used to communicate with (mostly – program) computers. These languages are "formal" because they are designed (often by committees); the term artificial is used to emphasize the distinction from the evolutionary process that gives us "natural languages".

When digital computers were first programmed, it was by writing instructions in the code of the machine (indeed, in the world's first "stored program electronic computer" –the Manchester "Baby"– (1948), the program was inserted in binary via switches). Assembler programs gave some level of convenience/abstraction (e.g. offering names for instructions; later, allocating addresses for variables).

FORTRAN ("formula translator") is generally credited as the first successful programming language. It was conceived in the early 1950s and offered a number of conveniences (and some confusions) to people wanting to have a computer perform numerical computations.

The creation of FORTRAN led to the need for a translator (or compiler). The first such was built by an IBM team led by John Backus (1924–2007) in 1954–57.

There is an enormous number of high-level programming languages.[3] Jean Sammet wrote a book on "500 Programming Languages" but gave up trying to update it; a very useful history of the main languages is [Wex81]. I take the position that existing languages are *mostly poor and sometimes disastrous!* Just think for a minute about how many billions of pounds have been wasted by

---

[3] Some interesting points along the history of "imperative" languages are FORTRAN, COMTRAN, COBOL, ALGOL 60, ALGOL W, PL/I, Pascal, Simula, CPL, Modula (1, 2 and 3), BCPL, C, C++, Eiffel, Java and Csharp.

programs that can index outside the limits of a "stack". It is clear that these imperative[4] languages are *crucial* in the effective use of computers.[5]

- few encourage clear expression of ideas
- almost all offer gratuitous traps for the unwary
- almost none maximize the cases where a static process (compilation) can detect errors in programs

Apart from programming languages, there are many other classes of artificial languages associated with computers including those for databases. So one can see readily that there is an enormous advantage in designing good languages.

1.3   Goals of This Paper

Engineers use models to understand things *before* they build them. The essence of a model is that it abstracts away from detail that might be irrelevant and facilitates focus on some specific aspect of the system under discussion.

It is possible to design a language by writing a compiler for that language but it is likely –even for a small language– to be a wasteful exercise because the writer of a compiler has to work at a level of detail that prevents seeing "the wood for the trees". It might be *slightly* easier to start by writing an interpreter for the language being designed but this still requires a mass of detail to be addressed and actually introduces a specific technical danger (lack of static checking) that is discussed in more detail in Section 2.2.

In fact, many languages have been designed by a mixture of writing down example programs and sketching how they might be translated (it is made clear above that language design requires that engineering trade-offs are made between ease of expression and ease of translation). But in many cases, the first formal manifestation of a language has been its (first) compiler or interpreter.

The idea of writing a formal (syntax or) semantics is to model the language without getting involved in the detail of translation to some specific machine code. With a short document one can experiment with options. If that document is in some useful sense "formal" one can reason about the consequences of a language design.

A repeated "leitmotiv" of this paper is the need to abstract. In fact, the simplest semantic descriptions will be just *abstract interpreters*: the first descriptions in Section 3 are interpreters that are made easier to write because they abstract from much irrelevant detail. Even the syntax descriptions chosen in Section 2 are abstract in the sense that they (constructively) ignore many details of parsing etc.

---

[4] As the qualification "imperative" suggests, there are other classes of HLLs. This paper mostly ignores "functional" and "logic" programming languages here.

[5] This author was on a panel on the history of languages and semantics in CMU during 2004; Vaughan Pratt asked: "(i) how much money have high-level programming languages saved the world? (ii) is there a Nobel prize in economics for answering part (i)?".

1.4   A Little History

The history of research on program verification is outlined in [Jon03a] (a slightly extended TR version is also available [Jon01a]) but that paper barely mentions the equally interesting story about research on the semantics of programming languages.[6] Some material which relates directly to the current paper can be found in [Jon01b, Plo04a].

There are different approaches to describing the semantics of programming languages. It is common practice to list three approaches but there are actually four and it is, perhaps, useful to split the approaches into two groups:

− model oriented
− implicit

Model-oriented approaches build a more-or-less explicit model of the state of the program; these approaches can be further divided into

− operational
− denotational

This paper emphasizes the operational semantics approach. Any operational approach can be compared with the task of interpreting the language in question. This comparison is very clear in Section 3 below but is also the essence of the generalization explained in Section 3.1 (and applied to more language features in Sections 4–4.5). The denotational approach is akin to translating one language into another and is discussed further in Section 7.

Many authors equate "implicit" language descriptions with "axiomatic semantics" but it is actually worth also dividing this class of descriptions into

− axiomatic
− equivalences

Axiomatic descriptions provide a way of reasoning about programs written *in* a language; these approaches –and the link to model-oriented semantics– are discussed in Section 7. The idea of characterizing a programming language by equivalence laws goes back to the 1960s but is achieving more notice again in recent years.

McCarthy's paper [McC66] at the 1964 Baden-bei-Wien conference was a key step in the development of ideas on describing a language by way of an "abstract interpreter". His paper was one of the major influences on VDL [LW69]. Interestingly, McCarthy also introduced a notion of "abstract syntax" in that same paper.

There are many useful texts [Gor79, Gor88, Hen90, NN92, Win93]; books which also look at implementation aspects include [Rey98, Sco00, Wat04].

2   Delimiting the Language to Be Defined

The ultimate interest here is in describing (or designing) the semantics of programming languages. Before one can describe a language, one needs to know

---

[6] There is a wealth of source material all the way from [Ste66] to recent events organized under the aegis of the (UK) "Computer Conservation Society" — see http://vmoc.museophile.org/pvs01 and http://vmoc.museophile.org/pvs04

what are its valid "texts". The concern with the content (as opposed to the meaning) of a language is termed syntax. In general, there will be an infinite number of possible "utterances" in any interesting language so they cannot be simply enumerated. Consequently a syntactic description technique must be capable of showing how any text in the infinite class can be generated.

Section 2.1 discusses how a *concrete syntax* can be used to define the strings of symbols which are plausible programs in a language. A concrete syntax can also tell us something about the structure the strings are trying to represent. A carefully designed concrete syntax can also be used in parsing.

Most authors define semantics in terms of concrete representations of programs but experience with defining larger languages (e.g. PL/I or Ada) –or languages with many ways of expressing same thing (e.g. C or Java)– makes clear that this becomes messy and brings gratuitous difficulties into the part of the description (the semantics) where one wants to focus on deeper questions. Therefore, *abstract syntax* descriptions are used because these focus on structure and remove the need to worry about those symbols that are only inserted in order to make parsing possible.

This is not quite the end of the story since both concrete and abstract syntax descriptions allow too many possibilities and Section 2.2 explains how to cut down the set of "valid" programs before attempting to give their semantics.

2.1   Syntax

There are many variants of notation for describing the *Concrete Syntax* of a language. It is not difficult to devise ways of specifying valid strings and most of the techniques are equivalent to Chomsky "context free" syntax notation. Most publications follow the Algol 60 report [BBG+63] and use the notation which is known as "Backus Normal Form" (also known as "Backus Naur Form").[7] Such a grammar can be used to *generate* or *recognize* sentences in the language. *Parsing* also uses the grammar to associate a tree structure with the recognized sentences.

A concrete syntax gives both a way of producing the texts of programs and of parsing programs. But even for this rather simple language the concrete syntax is "fussy" in that it is concerned with those details which make it possible to parse strings (e.g. the commas, semicolons, keywords and –most notably– those things that serve to bracket strings that occur in recursive definitions). For a programming language like C or Java where there are many options, the concrete syntax becomes tedious to write; the task has to be done but, since the syntactic variants have nothing to do with semantics, basing the semantics on a concrete syntax complicates it in an unnecessary way. The first big dose of abstraction is deployed and all of the subsequent work is based on an "abstract syntax".

An abstract syntax defines a class of *objects*. In most cases, such objects are tree-like in that they are (nested) VDM composite objects. But to achieve the abstraction objective, sets, sequences and maps are used whenever appropriate.

---

[7] In passing, it is hard to believe that so many programming language books today are published without a full concrete syntax for the language!.

This section builds up the Abstract Syntax of "Base" (see Appendix A where the description of the "Base" Language is presented in full).

A simple language ("Base") can be built where a program is rather like a single Algol block (with no nested blocks). A *Program* contains declarations of *Id*s as (scalar[8]) variables and a sequence of *Stmt*s which are to be executed.[9] The declarations of the variables (*vars*) maps the identifiers to their types.

$$Program :: vars : Id \xrightarrow{m} ScalarType$$
$$body : Stmt^*$$

Notice that has –at a stroke– removed worries about the (irrelevant) order of declarations; this also ignores the delimiters between identifiers and statements since they are not an issue in the semantic description. The parsability of a language has to be sorted out; but it is not a semantic question. Here and elsewhere it is preferable to deal with issues separately and get things out of the way rather than complicate the semantic description. The abstraction in an abstract syntax does precisely this.

According to this abstract syntax, the smallest possible *Program* declares no variables and contains no statements, thus

$$mk\text{-}Program(\{\,\}, [\,]) \in Program$$

Not much more useful is a program which declares one variable but still has no statements.

$$mk\text{-}Program(\{i \mapsto \text{INTTP}\}, [\,]) \in Program$$

More interesting programs are given below.

There are exactly two types in this base language:

$$ScalarType = \text{INTTP} \mid \text{BOOLTP}$$

Three forms of statement will serve to introduce most concepts

$$Stmt = Assign \mid If \mid While$$

$$Assign :: lhs : Id$$
$$rhs : Expr$$

Thus, if $e \in Expr; i \in Id$

$$mk\text{-}Assign(i, e) \in Assign$$

One of the major advantages of the VDM record notation is that the *mk-Record* constructors make the sets disjoint.

Conditional execution can be defined in an *If* statement.

$$If :: test : Expr$$
$$th : Stmt^*$$
$$el : Stmt^*$$

---

[8] The adjective "scalar" appears superfluous for now but compound variables like arrays are discussed below.

[9] Section 4 introduces *Blocks* and a program can then be said to contain a single *Block* – but this is not yet needed.

Thus,

$$mk\text{-}If(e, [\,], [\,]) \in If$$

A common form of repetitive execution is achieved by a *While* statement.

While :: *test* : *Expr*
          body : *Stmt**

Thus,

$$mk\text{-}While(e, [\,]) \in While$$

It is possible to illustrate the key semantic points with rather simple expressions.

$$Expr = ArithExpr \mid RelExpr \mid Id \mid ScalarValue$$

ArithExpr :: *opd*1   : *Expr*
               operator : PLUS | MINUS
               *opd*2   : *Expr*

RelExpr :: *opd*1   : *Expr*
             operator : EQUALS | NOTEQUALS
             *opd*2   : *Expr*

$$ScalarValue = \mathbb{Z} \mid \mathbb{B}$$

No definition is provided for *Id* since one can abstract from such (concrete) details.

Thus,

$1 \in ScalarValue$
$i \in Id$
$mk\text{-}ArithExpr(i, \text{MINUS}, 1) \in Expr$
$mk\text{-}RelExpr(i, \text{NOTEQUALS}, 1) \in Expr$

And then with

$s_1 = mk\text{-}If(mk\text{-}RelExpr(i, \text{NOTEQUALS}, 1),$
$\qquad [mk\text{-}Assign(i, mk\text{-}ArithExpr(i, \text{MINUS}, 1))],$
$\qquad [mk\text{-}Assign(i, mk\text{-}ArithExpr(i, \text{PLUS}, 1))])$
$s_1 \in Stmt$

And, finally

$$mk\text{-}Program(\{i \mapsto \text{INTTP}\}, [s_1]) \in Program$$

It it worth noting that the supposed distinction between arithmetic and relational expressions is not policeable at this point; this gets sorted out in the next section when type information is used.

2.2   Eliminating Invalid Programs

Before moving to look at semantics, it is worth eliminating as many invalid programs as possible. For example, it is easy to recognize that

$$mk\text{-}ArithExpr(i, \text{Minus}, \textbf{true})$$

contains an error of types. This is easy to check because it requires no "context" but in a program which (like the final one in the preceding section) declares only the identifier i, one would say that

$$mk\text{-}Assign(j, mk\text{-}ArithExpr(i, \text{Minus}, 1))$$

has no meaning because it uses an undeclared variable name. Similarly, uses of variables should match their declarations and, if i is declared to be an integer,

$$mk\text{-}Assign(i, \textbf{true})$$

makes no sense.

A function is required which "sorts the sheep from the goats": a program which is type correct is said to be "well formed". A function which delivers either **true** or **false** is a predicate. It is not difficult to define a predicate which delivers **true** if type information is respected and **false** otherwise.

In order to bring the type information down from the declarations, the signature of the inner predicates must be

$$wf\text{-}Stmt : Stmt \times TypeMap \to \mathbb{B}$$

$$wf\text{-}Stmt(s, tpm) \;\;\triangleq\;\; \cdots$$

(all of these predicates are given names starting $wf\text{-}\cdots$ as a reminder that they are concerned with well-formedness) with the following "auxiliary objects"

$$TypeMap = Id \xrightarrow{\;m\;} ScalarType$$

The top-level predicate is defined

$$wf\text{-}Program : Program \to \mathbb{B}$$

$$wf\text{-}Program(mk\text{-}Program(vars, body)) \;\;\triangleq\;\; wf\text{-}StmtList(body, vars)$$

All that remains to be done is to define the subsidiary predicates. Those for $Stmt$ (and for $Expr$) have to be recursive because the objects themselves are recursive. Thus

$$wf\text{-}StmtList : (Stmt^*) \times TypeMap \to \mathbb{B}$$

$$wf\text{-}StmtList(sl, tpm) \;\;\triangleq\;\; \forall i \in \textbf{inds}\, sl \cdot wf\text{-}Stmt(sl(i), tpm)$$

Then:

$$wf\text{-}Stmt : Stmt \times TypeMap \to \mathbb{B}$$

$$wf\text{-}Stmt(s, tpm) \;\;\triangleq\;\; \cdots$$

is most easily given by cases below[10]

$wf\text{-}Stmt(mk\text{-}Assign(lhs, rhs), tpm) \quad \triangleq$
$\quad lhs \in \mathbf{dom}\ tpm\ \wedge$
$\quad c\text{-}tp(rhs, tpm) = tpm(lhs)$

$wf\text{-}Stmt(mk\text{-}If(test, th, el), tpm) \quad \triangleq$
$\quad c\text{-}tp(test, tpm) = \textsc{BoolTp}\ \wedge$
$\quad wf\text{-}StmtList(th, tpm) \wedge wf\text{-}StmtList(el, tpm)$

$wf\text{-}Stmt(mk\text{-}While(test, body), tpm) \quad \triangleq$
$\quad c\text{-}tp(test, tpm) = \textsc{BoolTp}\ \wedge$
$\quad wf\text{-}StmtList(body, tpm)$

The auxiliary function to compute the type of an expression ($c\text{-}tp$ used above) is defined as follows

$c\text{-}tp : Expr \times TypeMap \rightarrow (\textsc{IntTp} \mid \textsc{BoolTp} \mid \textsc{Error})$

$c\text{-}tp(e, tpm) \quad \triangleq \quad$ given by cases below

$c\text{-}tp(mk\text{-}ArithExpr(e1, opt, e2), tpm) \quad \triangleq$
$\quad \mathbf{if}\ c\text{-}tp(e1, tpm) = \textsc{IntTp} \wedge c\text{-}tp(e2, tpm) = \textsc{IntTp}$
$\quad \mathbf{then}\ \textsc{IntTp}$
$\quad \mathbf{else}\ \textsc{Error}$

$c\text{-}tp(mk\text{-}RelExpr(e1, opt, e2), tpm) \quad \triangleq$
$\quad \mathbf{if}\ c\text{-}tp(e1, tpm) = \textsc{IntTp} \wedge c\text{-}tp(e2, tpm) = \textsc{IntTp}$
$\quad \mathbf{then}\ \textsc{BoolTp}$
$\quad \mathbf{else}\ \textsc{Error}$

For the base cases:

$e \in Id \ \Rightarrow\ c\text{-}tp(e, tpm) = tpm(e)$

$e \in \mathbb{Z} \ \Rightarrow\ c\text{-}tp(e, tpm) = \textsc{IntTp}$

$e \in \mathbb{B} \ \Rightarrow\ c\text{-}tp(e, tpm) = \textsc{BoolTp}$

Because they are dealing with the type information in the context of single statements and expressions, such a collection of predicates and functions are referred to as the "context conditions" of a language. They correspond to the type checking done in a compiler. Just as there, it is not always so clear how far to go with static checking (e.g. would one say that a program which included an infinite loop had no meaning?)

The issue of whether or not a language is "strongly typed" is important and this issue recurs repeatedly.

---

[10] This is using the VDM pattern matching trick of writing a "constructor" in a parameter list.

3   Semantics and Abstract Interpreters

This section explains the essential idea of presenting semantics via an abstract interpreter. This is first done in terms of functions. The need –and notation– for generalizing this to relations follows.

3.1   Presenting Operational Semantics by Rules

The essence of any imperative language is that it changes some form of "state": programs have an effect. For a procedural programming language the state notion normally contains an association (sometimes indirect) between variable names and their values (a "store"). In the simple language considered in this section, the main "semantic object" is

$$\Sigma = Id \xrightarrow{m} ScVal$$

Thus $\sigma \in \Sigma$ is a single "state"; Σ is the set of all "States".

The fundamental idea is that executing a statement will transform the state — this can be most obviously modelled as a function:

$$exec : Stmt \times \Sigma \to \Sigma$$

$$exec(s, \sigma) \quad \triangleq \quad \ldots$$

Such a function can be presented one case at a time by using the VDM constructors as pattern matching parameters.

Expression evaluation has the type

$$eval : Expr \times \Sigma \to ScVal$$

$$eval(e, \sigma) \quad \triangleq \quad \ldots$$

and can again be defined one case at a time.

Remember that only *Program*s that satisfy the context conditions are to be given semantics. This restriction implies that types of arguments match the operators "during execution"; similarly, the type of the expression of the value evaluated in *rhs* must match the *lhs* variable and the type of any value in a conditional or while statement must be Boolean.

The recursive function style is intuitive but there is a serious limitation: it does not handle non-determinism! Non-determinism can arise in many ways in programming languages:

– order of expression evaluation is a nasty example
– specific non-deterministic constructs
– parallelism

It is really the third of these which is most interesting and is the reason for facing non-determinism from the beginning.

The issues can be illustrated with a tiny example language. Later sections (notably, Sections 5.4, and 6) make clear that key concepts are establishing threads (of computation), the atomicity with which threads can merge and explicit synchronization between threads. In the simple language that follows, a

Program consists of exactly two threads, assignment statements are (unrealistically) assumed to be atomic and no explicit thread synchronization mechanisms are offered. This gives rise to the following abstract syntax.

$$Program :: left \quad : \ Assign^*$$
$$right \ : \ Assign^*$$

In order to give a semantics for any such language, one needs to accept that it is necessary to think in terms of relations: one starting state can legitimately give rise to (under the same program) different final states. Moreover, the semantic relation has to be between "configurations" which record, as well as the store, the program which remains to be executed. Thus:

$$\xrightarrow{p} : \mathcal{P}((Program \times \Sigma) \times (Program \times \Sigma))$$

The two semantic rules which follow show exactly how nondeterminism arises because a program which has non-empty statement lists in both branches will match the hypotheses of both rules.

$$\frac{(s, \sigma) \xrightarrow{s} \sigma'}{mk\text{-}Program([s] \ \frown restl, r), \sigma) \xrightarrow{p} mk\text{-}Program(restl, r), \sigma')}$$

$$\frac{(s, \sigma) \xrightarrow{s} \sigma'}{(mk\text{-}Program(l, [s] \ \frown restr), \sigma) \xrightarrow{p} (mk\text{-}Program(l, restr), \sigma')}$$

Finally, a program is complete when both of its branches have terminated.

$$\frac{}{mk\text{-}Program([\,], [\,]), \sigma) \longrightarrow \sigma}$$

The interleaving of the two threads is achieved by the semantics being "small step": the whole configuration is subject to matching of the rules after each step.

Alternatively, one might want to add to the language an explicit construct with which a programmer can determine the level of atomicity:

$$Program :: left \quad : \ (Assign \mid Atomic)^*$$
$$right \ : \ (Assign \mid Atomic)^*$$

$$Atomic :: Assign^*$$

The relevant semantic rule becomes:

$$\frac{(sl, \sigma) \xrightarrow{sl} \sigma'}{(mk\text{-}Program([mk\text{-}Atomic(sl)] \ \frown restl, r), \sigma) \xrightarrow{p} (mk\text{-}Program(restl, r), \sigma')}$$

The semantic transition relation for expressions could be given as:

$$\xrightarrow{e} : \mathcal{P}((Expr \times \Sigma) \times ScVal)$$

Strictly, there are no constructs in this language that make expression evaluation non-deterministic so it would be possible to stick with functions.

It would also be possible to illustrate how it is necessary to extend the idea of a functional semantics (to one using relations) by looking at a specific non-deterministic construct such as Dijkstra's "guarded command" [Dij76]. Just as with the concurrent assignment threads, an explicit relation $((Stmt \times \Sigma) \times \Sigma)$ has to be used.

This way of presenting operational semantics rules follows Plotkin's [Plo81][11] and is often referred to as "Plotkin rules". Using this style for an entirely deterministic language gives the first full semantics in this paper: the attentive reader ought be able to understand the definition in Appendix A.

3.2   Ways of Understanding the Rules

There are several different views of the operational semantics rules used in the previous section. For a given starting store and program text, the rules can be used to construct a diagram whose root is that initial program and store. Each rule that matches a particular configuration can then be used to define successor configurations. Because more than one rule might match, the inherent non-determinism is seen where there is more than one outgoing arc from a particular configuration.

For our purposes, it is more interesting to view the rules as providing an inductive definition of the $\xrightarrow{s}$ relation. This leads on naturally to the use of such rules in proofs. At the specific level one might write:

$$\textbf{from } \sigma_0 = \{x \mapsto 9, y \mapsto 1\}; \ \sigma_1 = \{x \mapsto 3, y \mapsto 1\}$$

1	$(3, \sigma_0) \xrightarrow{e} 3$	$\xrightarrow{e}$
2	$(mk\text{-}Assn(x,3), \sigma_0) \xrightarrow{s} \sigma_1$	$1, \xrightarrow{s}$
3	$(x, \sigma_1) \xrightarrow{e} 3$	$\xrightarrow{e}$
4	$(mk\text{-}Assn(y,x), \sigma_1) \xrightarrow{s} \{x \mapsto 3, y \mapsto 3\}$	$3, \xrightarrow{s}$

$$\textbf{infer } ([mk\text{-}Assn(x,3), mk\text{-}Assn(y,x)], \sigma_0) \xrightarrow{sl} \{x \mapsto 3, y \mapsto 3\} \qquad 2, 4, \xrightarrow{sl}$$

but it is more interesting to produce general proofs of the form:

$$\textbf{from } pre\text{-}prog(\sigma_0); (prog, \sigma_0) \xrightarrow{p} \sigma_f$$

n $\vdots$

$$\textbf{infer } post\text{-}prog(\sigma_0, \sigma_f)$$

where the intermediate steps are justified either by a semantic rule or by rules of the underlying logic. This is essentially what is done in [CM92, KNvO$^+$02] and very clearly in [CJ07].

3.3   Developments from This Base

There are many ways to extend the language description in Appendix A that do not require any further modelling concepts — they would just constitute applications of the ideas above to cover other programming language concepts. There are a few topics, however, which deserve mention before moving on to Section 4.

Looking back at the semantic rule for $(mk\text{-}Program(vars, body)) \xrightarrow{p}$ DONE in Appendix A it could be observed that there is no point in running a program!

---

[11] Republished as [Plo04b] — see also [Plo04a, Jon03b].

Execution leaves no visible trace in the world outside the program because the block structure "pops all of the variables off the stack" at the end of execution. Adding input/output is however a simple exercise. For the abstract syntax:

$Stmt = \ldots \mid Write$

$Write :: value : Expr$

The relevant context condition is:

$$wf\text{-}Stmt(mk\text{-}Write(value), tps) \quad \triangleq \quad tp(value, tps) = \text{INT}\textsc{Tp}$$

The essence of modelling an imperative language is to put in the "state" those things that can be changed. So for output the state needs to be a composite object that embeds the "store" in "state" but adds an abstraction of an output file.

$$\Sigma :: \begin{array}{ll} vars : & Id \xrightarrow{m} ScVal \\ out : & \mathbb{Z}^* \end{array}$$

The semantic rule for the new statement is:

$$\frac{(value, \sigma) \xrightarrow{e} v}{(mk\text{-}Write(value), \sigma) \xrightarrow{s} mk\text{-}\Sigma(\sigma.vars, \sigma.out \curvearrowright [v])}$$

Unfortunately, some other rules have to be revised because of the change in Σ — but only a few (routine) changes.

$$\frac{(rhs, \sigma) \xrightarrow{e} v}{(mk\text{-}Assign(lhs, rhs), \sigma) \xrightarrow{s} mk\text{-}\Sigma(\sigma.vars \dagger \{lhs \mapsto v\}, \sigma.out)}$$

$$\frac{e \in Id}{(e, \sigma) \xrightarrow{e} \sigma.vars(e)}$$

Covering input statements should be obvious and an extension to linking programs to more complex file stores –or even databases– not difficult. (The whole question of why programming languages do not directly embed database concepts is interesting. It is certainly not difficult to view relations as datatypes and concepts of typing could be clarified thereby. The most interesting aspects concern the different views of concurrency and locking: this is briefly touched on in Section 5.4.)

Another topic that offers interesting language design trade-offs is statements for repetition. Whilst it is true that **while** statements suffice in that they make a language "Turing complete", many other forms of repetitive statement are found in programming languages.

The intuition here is that programmers want to deal with regular collections of data in analogous ways. Thus, it would be useful to study **for** statements in connection with arrays. (But the more interesting possibilities for the semantics of arrays come after parameter passing by location (aka by reference) has been covered in Section 4.) A simple statement might be:

$Stmt = \cdots \mid For$

$$
\begin{array}{llll}
For & :: & control & : Id \\
& & limit & : Expr \\
& & body & : Stmt^*
\end{array}
$$

$$
\dfrac{(limit, \sigma) \xrightarrow{\ e\ } limitv \qquad ((control, limitv, body), \sigma \dagger \{control \mapsto 1\}) \xrightarrow{\ i\ } \sigma'}{(mk\text{-}For(control, limit, body), \sigma) \xrightarrow{\ s\ } \sigma'}
$$

Where, the auxiliary concept of iteration is defined as follows:

$$
\xrightarrow{\ i\ }: \mathcal{P}(((Id \times \mathbb{Z} \times (Stmt^*)) \times \Sigma) \times \Sigma)
$$

$$
\dfrac{\sigma(control) > limitv}{((control, limitv, body), \sigma) \xrightarrow{\ i\ } \sigma}
$$

$$
\dfrac{\begin{array}{l}\sigma(control) \le limitv \\ (body, \sigma) \xrightarrow{\ sl\ } \sigma' \\ ((control, limitv, body), \sigma' \dagger \{control \mapsto \sigma'(control) + 1\}) \xrightarrow{\ i\ } \sigma''\end{array}}{((control, limitv, body), \sigma) \xrightarrow{\ s\ } \sigma''}
$$

Not only are there many alternative forms of **for** construct to be investigated but they also point to both questions of scoping (e.g. should the control variable be considered to be a local declaration) and interesting semantic issues of equivalences a programmer might expect to hold between different forms. It is also tempting to look at parallel forms because –from their earliest manifestation in FORTRAN– **for** statements have frequently over-specified irrelevant sequential constraints.

4   Scopes and Parameter Passing

This section considers the problem of variables having scope and some different ways in which parameters can be passed to functions. The language ("Blocks") used is still in the ALGOL/Pascal family because it is here that these problems were first thought out. A firm understanding of these concepts makes for greater appreciation of what is going on in an object-oriented language (see Section 6). A bonus of this study is that one of the key modelling techniques is explained (in the setting where is first arose).

4.1   Nested Blocks

Sections 4.2–4.5 cover the modelling of functions and procedures which facilitate the use of the same piece of code from different places in a program containing them. Before addressing this directly, nested blocks can be added to the language of Section 3. Here the pragmatics of the feature are the ability to use the same identifier with different meaning within the same program (a nested block might

```
program
  begin
  bool a; int i; int j;
  if i = j then
    begin
    int a;
    a : = 1
    end
  fi
  a : =  false
  end
end
```

Fig. 1. Scope for *Block*

for example be designed by a different programmer than the one who wrote the containing text; it would be tedious and error prone to have to change all identifiers to be unique throughout a program).

In the examples throughout Section 4, a concrete syntax is used that surrounds the declarations and statements with **begin** $\cdots$ **end**. Consider the example (concrete) program in Figure 1. The inner block defines its own scope and the *a* declared (to be of type **integer**) there is distinct from the variable of the same name (declared to be of type **bool**) in the outer block. Although the two assignments to the name *a* imply that the type is different, both are correct because two different variables are in play. One could insist that programmers avoid the reuse of names in this way but this would not be a kind restriction.

It is easy to add an option to *Stmt* that allows such nesting

$$Stmt = \cdots \mid Block$$

One might then expect to say that a *Program* is a *Block* but allowing it to be a single *Stmt* leaves that possibility open and adds a slight generalization. Thus the abstract syntax might change (from Section 3) in the following ways:

$$Program = Stmt$$

$$Stmt = Assign \mid If \mid While \mid Block$$

$$Block :: vars : Id \xrightarrow{m} ScalarType$$
$$\qquad\quad body : Stmt^*$$

The context conditions only change as follows:

$$wf\text{-}Program : Program \to \mathbb{B}$$

$$wf\text{-}Program(s) \;\triangleq\; wf\text{-}Stmt(s, \{\,\})$$

$$wf\text{-}Block : Block \times TypeMap \to \mathbb{B}$$

$$wf\text{-}Block(mk\text{-}Block(vars, body), tpm) \;\triangleq\; wf\text{-}StmtList(body, tpm \dagger vars)$$

Notice that it is obvious from this that all statements in a list are checked (for type correctness) against the same *TypeMap*: even if the ith statement is a block, the $i + 1$st statement has the same potential set of variables as the $i - 1$st statement.

The semantics for a *Block* have to show that local variables are distinct from those of the surrounding text. On entry to $mk\text{-}Block(vars, body)$ this just requires that each identifier in the domain of *vars* gets initialized. Leaving the block is actually more interesting. After the execution of *body* has transformed σ_i into σ_i', the state after execution of the whole block contains the values of the (not re-declared) local variables from σ_i' but it is also necessary to recover the values from σ of variables which were masked by the local names.

$$\{id \mapsto \sigma_i'(id) \mid id \in \mathbf{dom}\,\sigma \land id \notin \mathbf{dom}\,vars\} \cup$$
$$\{id \mapsto \sigma(id) \mid id \in \mathbf{dom}\,\sigma \land id \in \mathbf{dom}\,vars)\}$$

Thus (using the VDM map restriction operator):

$$\sigma_i = \sigma \dagger (\{id \mapsto 0 \mid id \in \mathbf{dom}\,vars \land vars(id) = \textsc{IntTp}\} \cup$$
$$\{id \mapsto \mathbf{true} \mid id \in \mathbf{dom}\,vars \land vars(id) = \textsc{BoolTp}\})$$

$$\frac{(body, \sigma_i) \xrightarrow{sl} \sigma_i'}{(mk\text{-}Block(vars, body), \sigma) \xrightarrow{s}}$$
$$((\mathbf{dom}\,\sigma - \mathbf{dom}\,vars) \lhd \sigma_i') \cup (\mathbf{dom}\,vars \lhd \sigma)$$

Notice that $\mathbf{dom}\,\sigma$ is unchanged by any *Stmt* (even a *Block*).

4.2   Avoiding Non-deterministic Side Effects

The pragmatics for adding functions (or procedures) to a language are for re-use of code: one can pull out a piece of algorithm to be used frequently — not so much for space since a compiler might anyway "in-line" it — but as a way of making sure that it is modified everywhere at once if it has to be changed.

Functions again bring a form of local naming. Unless a language designer is careful, they can also bring a very messy side effect problem. If a function can reference non-local variables, a call to the function can give rise to side effects. In cases where there is more than one function call in an expression, the order in which the function calls occur can influence the final result of the program.[12]

An obvious way to avoid the non-determinism caused by functions referring to non-local variables is to set up the context conditions to ban global access: the only identifiers to which a function can refer are either names of the parameters or those of newly defined local variables.

The form of *Function* here has an explicit result clause[13] at the end of its text:

---

[12] Pascal's rule that such a program would be in error is the worst of all worlds for the language specifier: one has to show the non-determinism in order to ban it!

[13] This avoids a goto-like jump out of phrase structure.

```
program
  begin
  bool a;
  function f(int a) int
    a := 1; ...
    result(7)
  end
    ...
  a := true
  end
end
```

Fig. 2. Scope for *Fun*

function f(**int** a) **int**
  $a := 1;$
  result$(a + 7)$
end

A small program to illustrate scope definition in functions might be as in Figure 2. As in Figure 1, there are two distinct uses of the name a and the arguments against asking the programmer to take the strain are stronger since functions might well be taken from another source.

One might build such a definition around an abstract syntax:

$Block$ :: $vars$: $Id \xrightarrow{m} ScalarType$
         fns : $Id \xrightarrow{m} FnDefn$
         $body$: $Stmt^*$

$FnDefn$ :: $type$: $ScalarType$
           $parml$: $ParmInfo^*$
           $body$: $Stmt^*$
           $result$: $Expr$

$ParmInfo$ :: $name$: Id
             $type$: $ScalarType$

$Expr = \cdots \mid FnCall$

$FnCall$ :: fn : Id
           $argl$: $Expr^*$

There are interesting semantic issues even with such a restrictive form of function call. First, there is the language decision about how to return a value from a function: different languages introduce a statement **return**(e); or assign to the name of the function as in $f \leftarrow e$; or just allow that an expression is written in place of a statement. Notice that all of these approaches only support the return of a single value. One can mitigate the impact of this restriction with the introduction of "records" (see Section 5.1). Another way around the restriction is by using an appropriate parameter passing mechanism (e.g. pass by location) — see Section 4.3.

There is a whole collection of questions around modes of parameter passing, but these are deferred to Sections 4.3–4.5.

Turning next to the description of such a language, the result of banning side effects is that the semantic transition relation for expressions remains:

$$\xrightarrow{e}: \mathcal{P}((\mathit{Expr} \times \Sigma) \times \mathit{ScVal})$$

(rather than also having a Σ on the right of the main relation).

When writing a semantics for any feature that can use a named piece of text from many places, there is the question of how that text is located when it is "called". Here, it is stored in some form of environment (*Env* in Section 4.3); a slightly different approach is illustrated for the object-oriented language in Section 6.

It has however been made clear by the title of this section that a major language design issue around functions is finding ways to avoid unpredictable side effects. An alternative way of avoiding the non-determinism from side-effects is to have "procedure calls" (rather than functions which can be referenced in an expressions).

4.3   Parameter Passing

In Section 3.1, variables were declared for the whole *Program*; Section 4.1 introduced nested blocks and Section 4.2 looked at functions with no external references. It is now time to move on to begin a look at various forms of parameter passing — call-by-location (call by reference) is covered first followed by a look at other modes in Section 4.5.

There are real engineering trade-offs here. Passing parameters by location offers a way to change values in the calling environment.[14] This is particularly useful for programs which manipulate and reshape tree structures. But passing parameters by location introduces aliasing problems which complicate formal reasoning and debugging alike.

So the Abstract Syntax for Function definitions might be

$$
\begin{array}{llll}
\mathit{Fun} :: & \mathit{returns} & : & \mathit{ScalarType} \\
& \mathit{params} & : & \mathit{Id}^* \\
& \mathit{paramtps} & : & \mathit{Id} \xrightarrow{m} \mathit{ScalarType} \\
& \mathit{body} & : & \mathit{Stmt}^* \\
& \mathit{result} & : & \mathit{Expr}
\end{array}
$$

and the relevant context condition[15]

---

[14] In passing, it is worth noting that this facilitates returning more than one value from a single function call.

[15] The function *uniquel* can be defined:

$$\mathit{uniquel} : (X^*) \to \mathbb{B}$$

$$\mathit{uniquel}(l) \;\;\triangleq\;\; \forall i,j \in \mathbf{inds}\, l \cdot i \neq j \;\Rightarrow\; l(i) \neq l(j)$$

$wf\text{-}Fun : Fun \times Types \to \mathbb{B}$

$wf\text{-}Fun(mk\text{-}Fun(returns, params, paramtps, body, result), tps) \quad \triangle$
    $uniquel(params) \land$
    elems $params = $ **dom** $paramtps \land$
    $tp(result) = returns \land$
    $wf\text{-}StmtList(body, tps \dagger paramtps)$

To define the way that a *Block* builds the extended *Types*

$Types = Id \xrightarrow{m} Type$

$Type = ScalarType \mid FunType$

one needs

$FunType :: \quad returns \quad : \; ScalarType$
               $paramtpl \; : \; ScalarType^*$

The Abstract Syntax for *Block* is

$Block :: \quad vars \; : \; Id \xrightarrow{m} ScalarType$
            $funs \; : \; Id \xrightarrow{m} Fun$
            $body \; : \; Stmt^*$

and the resulting Context Condition is[16]

$wf\text{-}Stmt : Block \times Types \to \mathbb{B}$

$wf\text{-}Stmt(mk\text{-}Block(vars, funs, body), tps) \quad \triangle$
    dom $vars \cap$ **dom** $funs = \{\,\} \land$
    let $var\text{-}tps = tps \dagger vars$ **in**
    let $fun\text{-}tps =$
        $\{f \mapsto mk\text{-}FunType(funs(f).returns,$
               $apply(funs(f).params, funs(f).paramtps)) \mid$
        $f \in$ **dom** $funs\}$ **in**
    $\forall f \in$ **dom** $funs \cdot wf\text{-}Fun(funs(f), var\text{-}tps)$
    $wf\text{-}StmtList(body, var\text{-}tps \dagger fun\text{-}tps)$

The next task is to look closely at parameter passing. As indicated at the beginning of this section, this is done in an ALGOL (or Pascal) framework.

A small program which illustrates the way functions are handled in the "Blocks" language is given in Figure 3. Functions are declared to have a type;

---

[16] The auxiliary function *apply* is defined:

$apply : (X^*) \times (X \xrightarrow{m} Y) \to (Y^*)$

$apply(l, m) \quad \triangle$
    if $l = [\,]$
    then $[\,]$
    else $[m(\mathbf{hd}\; l)] \frown apply(\mathbf{tl}\; l, m)$

```
program
  begin
  int i, j, k;
  function f(int x, int y) int
      i := i + 1; x := x + 1; y := y + 1 /* print(x, y) */
      result(7)
  end
  ...
  i := 1; j := 4;
  k := f(i, j) /* print(i, j) */
  end
end
```

Fig. 3. Parameter example (i)

their definition text contains a body which is a sequence of statements to be executed; the text ends with an explicit result expression.

Here, the non-determinism discussed in Section 4.2 can be avoided by limiting functions to be called only in a specific way.

$$v := f(i)$$

So the Abstract Syntax for a *Call* statement is:

$$Call :: lhs \ : \ Id$$
$$fun \ : \ Id$$
$$args \ : \ Id^*$$

The Context Condition is

$$wf\text{-}Stmt(mk\text{-}Call(lhs, fun, args), tps) \ \triangleq$$
$$\quad lhs \in \mathbf{dom} \ tps \ \wedge$$
$$\quad fun \in \mathbf{dom} \ tps \ \wedge$$
$$\quad tps(fun) \in FunType \ \wedge$$
$$\quad tps(lhs) = (tps(fun)).returns \ \wedge$$
$$\quad \mathbf{len} \ args = \mathbf{len} \ (tps(fun)).paramtpl \ \wedge$$
$$\quad \forall i \in \mathbf{inds} \ args \cdot tp(args(i), tps) = ((tps(fun)).paramtpl)(i)$$

In Figure 3, within f, both x, i refer to the same "location". Changing the call to be as in Figure 4 results in the situation, within f, that all of x, y, i refer to the same "location". Notice that $j := f(i + j, 3)$ cannot be allowed for "by location".

The basic modelling idea is to split Σ of Section 3.1 into two mappings: *Env* and Σ:

$$Env = Id \ \xrightarrow{m} \ Den$$

$$Den = ScalarLoc \ | \ FunDen$$

$$\Sigma = ScalarLoc \ \xrightarrow{m} \ ScalarValue$$

```
program
  begin
  int i, j, k;
  function f(int x, int y) int
    i := i + 1; x := x + 1; y := y + 1 /* print(x, y) */
      result(7)
  end

  ...

  i := 1; j := 4;
  k := f(i, i) /* print(i, j) */
  end
end
```

Fig. 4. Parameter example (ii)

So now the basic semantic relations become:

$$\xrightarrow{s} : \mathcal{P}((Stmt \times Env \times \Sigma) \times \Sigma)$$

$$\xrightarrow{e} : \mathcal{P}((Expr \times Env \times \Sigma) \times ScalarValue)$$

One can now talk about the left-hand (of an assignment) value of an identifier and separating this out will pay off in Section 4.4 when dealing with references to elements of arrays. Left-hand values occur elsewhere so it is worth having a way of deriving them.

$$\xrightarrow{lhv} : \mathcal{P}((VarRef \times Env \times \Sigma) \times ScalarLoc)$$

$$\frac{e \in Id}{(e, env, \sigma) \xrightarrow{lhv} env(e)}$$

in terms of which, accessing the "right hand value" can be defined:

$$\frac{e \in Id \quad (e, env, \sigma) \xrightarrow{lhv} l}{(e, env, \sigma) \xrightarrow{e} \sigma(l)}$$

The left hand value is used to change a value in –for example– assignments:

$$\frac{(lhs, env, \sigma) \xrightarrow{lhv} l \quad (rhs, env, \sigma) \xrightarrow{e} v}{(mk\text{-}Assign(lhs, rhs), env, \sigma) \xrightarrow{s} \sigma \dagger \{l \mapsto v\}}$$

Most rules just pass on env:

$$\xrightarrow{sl} : \mathcal{P}(((Stmt^*) \times Env \times \Sigma) \times \Sigma)$$

$$\frac{(s, env, \sigma) \xrightarrow{s} \sigma' \quad (rest, env, \sigma') \xrightarrow{sl} \sigma''}{([s] \frown rest, env, \sigma) \xrightarrow{sl} \sigma''}$$

```
program
  begin
  int a;
  function f() int
      a := 2 result(7) end
  . . .
  a := 1
      begin
      int a;
      a := 5;
      a := f()
      end
  /* what is the value of a */
  end
end
```

Fig. 5. Function static scoping

Similarly

$$\overset{e}{\longrightarrow}: \mathcal{P}((Expr \times Env \times \Sigma) \times ScalarValue)$$

$$\frac{(e1, env, \sigma) \overset{e}{\longrightarrow} v1 \qquad (e2, env, \sigma) \overset{e}{\longrightarrow} v2}{(mk\text{-}ArithExpr(e1, \text{PLUS}, e2), env, \sigma) \overset{e}{\longrightarrow} v1 + v2}$$

We now look at how to create and modify *env*. Postponing the question of functions for a moment, the overall shape of the meaning of a *Block* is:

$$\frac{\begin{array}{l}(varenv, \sigma') = /* \text{ find and initialize free locations } */\\ funenv = /* \text{ create function denotations } */\\ env' = env \dagger varenv \dagger funenv\\ (body, env', \sigma') \overset{sl}{\longrightarrow} \sigma''\end{array}}{(mk\text{-}Block(vars, funs, body), env, \sigma) \overset{s}{\longrightarrow} (\mathbf{dom}\, \sigma) \lhd \sigma''}$$

The cleaning up of the locations from σ'' might look "fussy" but it pays off in compiler proofs where the designer will probably want to re-use locations in a stack discipline. The first hypothesis of this rule can be completed to

$$(varenv, \sigma') = newlocs(vars, \sigma)$$

where the auxiliary function *newlocs* creates an initial state for the initial values of a sufficient number of locations for each identifier declared in *vars*: each is initialized appropriately (a formal definition is in Appendix B).

Function denotations contain the information about a function which is needed for its execution. There is one final issue here: consider the program in Figure 5. The non-local reference to *a* within the function *f* must refer to the lexically embracing variable and not to the one at the point of call. (This is handled by the *FunDen* containing the *Env* from the point of declaration.)

$$FunDen :: parms \quad : Id^*$$
$$body \quad : Stmt^*$$
$$result \quad : Expr$$
$$context : Env$$

These are easy to build by selecting some components of the declaration of a *Fun*. (The reason for storing the declaring *Env* is explained below.)

$b\text{-}Fun\text{-}Den : Fun \times Env \rightarrow FunDen$

$b\text{-}Fun\text{-}Den(mk\text{-}Fun(returns, params, paramtps, body, result), env) \quad \triangleq$
$\quad mk\text{-}FunDen(params, body, result, env)$

Putting this all together gives:

$(varenv, \sigma') = newlocs(vars, \sigma)$
$funenv =$
$\quad \{f \mapsto b\text{-}FunDen(funs(f), env \dagger varenv) \mid f \in \textbf{dom } funs\}$
$env' = env \dagger varenv \dagger funenv$
$$\frac{(body, env', \sigma') \xrightarrow{sl} \sigma''}{(mk\text{-}Block(vars, funs, body), env, \sigma) \xrightarrow{s} (\textbf{dom } \sigma) \lhd \sigma''}$$

The key point in the semantic rule for *Call* statements is the creation of *arglocs* which holds the locations of the arguments:

$(lhs, env, \sigma) \xrightarrow{lhv} l$
$mk\text{-}FunDen(parms, body, result, context) = env(f)$
$\textbf{len } arglocs = \textbf{len } args$
$\forall i \in \textbf{inds } arglocs \cdot (args(i), env, \sigma) \xrightarrow{lhv} arglocs(i)$
$parm\text{-}env = \{parms(i) \mapsto arglocs(i) \mid i \in \textbf{inds } parms\}$
$$\frac{(body, (context \dagger parm\text{-}env), \sigma) \xrightarrow{sl} \sigma'}{(result, (context \dagger parm\text{-}env), \sigma') \xrightarrow{e} res}$$
$$\overline{(mk\text{-}Call(lhs, f, args), env, \sigma) \xrightarrow{s} (\sigma' \dagger \{l \mapsto res\})}$$

At this point a complete definition of the language so far can be presented — see Appendix B.

If one were to allow side effects in functions, the type of the semantic relation for *Expressions* would have to reflect this decision.

Both *Env* and "surrogates" like *ScalarLoc* are general modelling tools.

4.4   Modelling Arrays

It is interesting to pause for a moment to consider two possible models for adding arrays to the language in Appendix B. Looking firstly at one dimensional arrays (vectors), one might be tempted to use:

$Env = Id \xrightarrow{m} Loc$

$\Sigma = Loc \xrightarrow{m} (ScalarValue \mid ArrayValue)$

$$ArrayVal = \mathbb{N} \xrightarrow{m} ScalarValue$$

This would make passing of array elements by-location very messy. A far better model is:

$$Env = Id \xrightarrow{m} Den$$

$$Den = ScalarLoc \mid ArrayLoc \mid FunDen$$

$$ArrayLoc = \mathbb{N} \xrightarrow{m} ScalarLoc$$

$$\Sigma = ScalarLoc \xrightarrow{m} ScalarValue$$

Thinking about alternatives for multi-dimensional arrays, symmetry points us at:

$$ArrayLoc = (\mathbb{N}^*) \xrightarrow{m} ScalarLoc$$

Rather than

$$ArrayLoc = \mathbb{N} \xrightarrow{m} (ScalarLoc \mid ArrayLoc)$$

It is possible to add a data type invariant:

$$ArrayLoc = (\mathbb{N}^*) \xrightarrow{m} ScalarLoc$$
$$\textbf{inv } (m) \triangleq \exists ubl \in (\mathbb{N}^*) \cdot \textbf{dom } m = sscs(ubl)$$

The semantics of Appendix B requires minimal changes.[17] They are sketched here, starting with the abstract syntax:

$$Assign :: lhs \ : \ VarRef$$
$$rhs \ : \ Expr$$

$$VarRef = ScalarRef \mid ArrayElRef$$

$$ScalarRef :: name \ : \ Id$$

$$ArrayElRef :: array \ : \ Id$$
$$sscs \ \ : \ Expr^*$$

$$Call :: lhs \ \ : \ VarRef$$
$$fun \ \ : \ Id$$
$$args \ : \ VarRef^*$$

$$Expr = ArithExpr \mid RelExpr \mid VarRef \mid ScalarValue$$

The semantics requires a revision to the computation of left hand values.[18]

$$\xrightarrow{lhv} : \mathcal{P}((VarRef \times Env \times \Sigma) \times ScalarLoc)$$

$$\overline{(mk\text{-}ScalarRef(id), env, \sigma) \xrightarrow{lhv} env(id)}$$

---

[17] In fact, the most extensive change is coding up a way to select distinct *ScalarLocs* for each array element.

[18] The issue of dynamic errors is here impossible to avoid — see Section 5.5.

$$\frac{\begin{array}{c} \textbf{len } sscvl = \textbf{len } sscs \\ \forall i \in sscs \cdot (sscs(i), env, \sigma) \xrightarrow{e} sscvl(i) \\ sscvl \in \textbf{dom } (env(id)) \end{array}}{(mk\text{-}ArrayElRef(id, sscs), env, \sigma) \xrightarrow{lhv} (env(id))(sscvl)}$$

$$\frac{\begin{array}{c} e \in VarRef \\ (e, env, \sigma) \xrightarrow{lhv} l \end{array}}{(e, env, \sigma) \xrightarrow{e} \sigma(l)}$$

One interesting issue that can be considered at this point is array "slicing" (i.e. the ability to define locations for (arbitrary) sub-parts of arrays).

4.5   Other Parameter Passing Mechanisms

Many other parameter passing mechanisms have been devised. Since what happens in object-oriented languages is fairly simple, a full account is not presented here; but a few brief notes might encourage the reader to experiment.

The simplest and most obvious mechanism is probably parameter passing by value. This is modelled as though one were creating a block with initialization via the argument of the newly created locations. Here, of course, arguments in calls can be general expressions.

As pointed out at the beginning of Section 4.3, there are clear dangers in parameter passing by-location. These are tolerated because the other side of the engineering balance is that certain programs are significantly more efficient if addresses are passed without creating new locations and copying values. The other advantage of being able to affect the values in the calling code can, however, be achieved without introducing all of the disadvantages of aliasing. The parameter passing mechanism known as by-value/return copies the values at call time but also copies the values back at the end of the called code. Not surprisingly, the formal model is a hybrid of call-by-name and call-by-value.

These three methods by no means exhaust the possibilities: for example, Algol 60 [BBG+63] offered a general "call-by-name" mechanism which essentially treated the argument like a function (which therefore required evaluation in an appropriateenvironment).Itisimportanttonotethatthisisnotthesameasparameter passing "by text" where the raw text is passed and evaluated in the called context.

It is not difficult to see how functions can be passed as arguments. It should be noted that returning functions as results is more delicate because the context in which they were declared might no longer exist after the return. For similar reasons, this author has never accepted arguments about "making functions first class objects" (cf. [vWSM+76]) and adding function variables to a language (they also add confusionsinreasoningaboutprogramswhichareakintothosewithgotostatements).

5   Modelling More Language Features

There are many aspects of programming languages that could be explored at this point: here, only to those that relate to our objective of understanding object-oriented languages in Section 6 are considered.

5.1   Records

Algol-W [WH66] provided support for a "record" construct (in other languages sometimes called "structures"). Records are like arrays in that they collect together several values but in the case of records the "fields" need not be of the same type. Reference to individual fields is by name (rather than numerical index) and it is straightforward to offer a "strong typing" approach so that correct reference is a compile time question but this does require a notion of declaring record types if the matching is done by name rather than by shape. (Some languages –including Pascal– somewhat complicated this issue by offering "variant records".)

Having studied arrays in Section 4.4, it is fairly clear how to model structures. Their type checking is straightforward. The semantic model revolves around

$$RecordLoc = Id \xrightarrow{m} Loc$$

Unlike *ArrayLoc*, there is no virtue in providing the symmetrical access to any nested field and one has:

$$Loc = ScalrLoc \mid RecordLoc$$

An interesting scoping extension is the Pascal **with** construct that can be used to open up the naming of the fields of a record.

Extensions to cope with arrays of structures or record elements which are arrays are straightforward.

5.2   Heap Storage

The block structured languages up to this point can be implemented with a "stack discipline": that is, the most recently allocated storage is always the next to be released. Making this work for languages of the Algol family is non-trivial but Dijkstra's "display" idea showed that it was possible and there have been subsequent developments (e.g. [HJ71]).

Storage which is allocated and freed by the programmer poses many dangers but heap storage in one form or another is available in all but the most restrictive languages. The need is clear: programs such as those for B-Trees need to allocate and free storage at times that do not match the phrase structure of a program. In fact, forms of dynamic storage manipulation were simulated in arrays from FORTRAN onwards and, of course, LISP was built around pointers. The concept of records made it possible for the programmer to describe structures that contained fields which were pointers (to record types). Pascal offered a **new** statement which was implemented by keeping a pool of free storage and allocating on request.

Once one has a model of records as in the preceding section, it is not difficult to build a model for heap storage: the set of *ScValues* has to include *Pointers*. In fact, this is an area where the abstract model is perhaps too easy to construct in the sense that the ease hides considerable implementation detail. One can however discuss issues like "garbage collection" and "dangling pointers" in terms of a carefully constructed model.

5.3   Abstract Data Types

The whole subject of "abstract data types" deserves a history in its own right. For the key contribution made by the "CLU" language, see [Lis96]. Here, it is sufficient to observe that it was realized that programmers needed the ability to change the implementation of a collection of functions and/or procedures by redefining the underlying data structures *without* changing their syntactic or semantic interface. It was thus essential to have language constructs which fixed interfaces but hid internal details.

5.4   More on Concurrency

There are many concurrency extensions which can be made to the language developed to this point.[19] Interesting exercises include the addition of a "parallel For statement". As in Section 3.1, one quickly becomes aware of the dangers of interference between concurrent threads of execution. It is argued in Section 6 that one of the advantages of object-oriented languages is that they offer a way to marshal concurrency.

For now, the key questions to be noted are:

– How are threads created?
– How does one synchronize activity between threads?
– What is the level of granularity? (or atomicity)

Each of these questions can be studied and described using operational semantics and the question of atomicity in particular is returned to in Section 7.

A study of the different views of locking taken by the programming language and database communities (cf. [JLRW05]) can also be based on operational semantic descriptions.

5.5   Handling Run-Time Errors

Context conditions are used to rule out programs which can be seen to be incorrect statically: the classic example of such errors is mismatch between type declarations of variables and their use. Many errors can, however, only be detected when a program is executed — at least in general. Access to uninitialized variables (especially those declared to contain pointers) is one class of such errors: obvious cases might be spotted statically, but in general one can only know about control flow issues with the actual values in a state.

A better example –and the one used in this section– might be indexing outside the bounds of an array. As those who have suffered from "stack overflow" attacks know to their cost, this can be an effective way to corrupt a program. It is not difficult to mark the detection of such errors in operational semantic descriptions; the bigger question is what action should be described when run-time errors are detected. In Section 4.4, the rule

---

[19] In fact, it is instructive to model even primitive concepts like "semaphores".

$$\frac{\begin{array}{l}\textbf{len } sscvl = \textbf{len } sscs \\ \forall i \in sscs \cdot (sscs(i), env, \sigma) \xrightarrow{e} sscvl(i) \\ sscvl \in \textbf{dom } (env(id))\end{array}}{(mk\text{-}ArrayElRef(id, sscs), env, \sigma) \xrightarrow{lhv} (env(id))(sscvl)}$$

clearly shows in its last hypothesis that access is only defined for valid subscript lists. In effect, there is no rule for invalid subscripts so the computation "stalls". For emphasis, one could add a rule that states an error has occurred but there is a meta-issue about what a language standard has to say about whether such errors must be detected or whether an implementation is free to deliver any result from the time of the error onwards. This latter course might appear to be a denigration of responsibility but one must accept that checking for arbitrary rune time errors can be expensive. This is one reason for seeking as strong a type discipline as possible.

More promising are the languages which define what should be done on encountering errors. A language might, for example, require that an out-of-bounds exception be raised. Essentially, the idea is to make semantic functions deliver either a normal or abnormal result. This idea originated in [HJ70] and was fully worked out in [ACJ72]; Nipkow [KNvO+02] uses a more economical way of defining the union of the possibilities.

6   Understanding Objects

All of the modelling tools to understand –and record our understanding of– an interesting language are to hand. Furthermore, it is possible to look at how object-oriented languages resolve some of the key engineering tensions relating to the design of programming languages. The strands of our story coalesce here.

The language introduced in this section is referred to as "COOL". It is not intended to be a complete OOL (extensions are sketched in Section 6.6). The reader is referred to [KNvO+02] for a description of Java.

Section 5.2 discusses the need to create storage dynamically (on a heap); the necessity to dispose of unwanted items; and resulting issues of garbage collection. Objects collect together data fields for their "instance variables" in a way that gives the power or records. Objects can be dynamically created (and garbage collected).

Locality of reference to the fields of an object by the methods of that class offers a way to resolve the (abstract data type — cf. Section 5.3) issues in a way which lets the implementation of an object be changed without changing its interface.

In one sense, the pure object view that everything (even a constant) is an object sweeps away the distinctions in parameter passing: everything is passed by location — but some objects are immutable.

Most importantly for our concern about concurrency, object-oriented languages provide a natural way to marshal threads. The view is taken here that each object should comprise a thread of control. Because instance variables can only be referred to by the methods of that class[20], there is a natural insulation against interference. Sharing can be established by the passing of object references but this is under clear programmer control. In COOL, the restrictive view is taken that only one method can be active in an object and this eliminates local race conditions. This combination of decisions means that the programmer is also in control of the level of atomicity (of interference).

(Space does not permit a discussion of (the important) issues of why objects work well in design and point the reader at excellent books such as [DW99] for such material.)

6.1   Introducing COOL

It is easiest to get into the spirit of COOL by considering a programming example. The class *Sort* in Figure 6 provides a (sequential) facility for maintaining a sequence of integers in ascending order. (One could add a method that returns –and deletes– the first item but the *insert* and *test* let us show the interesting features.)

```
Sort class
vars v: ℕ ← 0; l: unique ref(Sort) ← nil
insert(x: ℕ) method
   begin
      if is-nil(l) then (v ← x; l ← new Sort)
      elif v ≤ x then l.insert(x)
      else (l.insert(v); v ← x)
      fi
      ;
      return
   end
test(x: ℕ) method : 𝔹
   if is-nil(l) ∨ x < v then return false
   elif x = v then return true
   else return l.test(x)
   fi
```

Fig. 6. Example Program *Sort* – sequential

A class is a template for object structure and behaviour: it lists the instance variables with their corresponding types and defines the parameters for each method, its result type and its implementation. An instance variable can have one of three types: integer, Boolean or (typed) reference (or "handle"). A reference value is the "handle" of another object; the special value nil is used to indicate when no reference is being held.[21]

---

[20] Avoiding the use of Java's **public** fields.

[21] To justify some interesting equivalences (see below) any variable declared to be a reference is identified as either shared or private (unique). The latter is written as a keyword (unique); the default is shared. A variable marked as unique can only be assigned a handle of a newly created object and it is prohibited to duplicate its

Objects of a class (objects corresponding to the class description) can be generated by executing a new statement that creates a new object with which a unique reference is associated, and returns this reference as a result. As implied above, all objects of a class share the same structure and behaviour, however, each possesses its own copy of the instance variables; it is on these copies that the methods operate.

An object can attempt to invoke[22] a method of any object to which it holds a handle. The concrete syntax for method invocation is $\alpha.m(\tilde{x})$, where α is the identity of the object, m is the method name and $\tilde{x}$ is the list of parameters. When an object accepts a method invocation the client is held in a *rendezvous*. The *rendezvous* is completed when a value is returned; in the simplest case this is by a return statement.[23]

In addition to the statements described above, COOL provides a normal repertoire of simple statements.

It follows from the above that an object can be in one of three states: *quiescent* (idle), *waiting* (held in *rendezvous*) or *active* (executing a method body). Methods can only be invoked in an object which is in the quiescent state; therefore –in COOL– at most one method can be active at any one time in a given object.

These comments should help to clarify most aspects of the sequential version of *Sort*.[24]

The implementation of both these methods is sequential: at most one object is active at any one time. Concurrency can be introduced into this example by applying two equivalences. The *insert* method given in Figure 6 is sequential because its client is held in a *rendezvous* until the effect of the insert has passed down the list structure to the appropriate point and the return statements have been executed in every object on the way back up the list. If the return statement of *insert* is commuted to the beginning of the method as in Figure 7, it becomes a release in which the client is able to continue its computation concurrently with the activity of the insertion. Furthermore, as the insertion progresses down the list, objects 'up stream' of the operation are free to accept further method calls. One can thus imagine a whole series of *insert* operations trickling down the list structure concurrently.

It is not possible to apply the return commutation equivalence to the *test* method because the client must be held until a result can be returned. It is,

---

contents: unique variables cannot appear on the right hand side of an assignment statement, be passed as arguments to a method or be returned as a result. These restrictions ensure that the object reference being held is unknown to any other object.

[22] The terms "method invocation" and "method call" are used interchangeably.

[23] The delegate statement allows an object to transfer the responsibility for answering a method call to another object, without itself waiting for the result – see below.

[24] The return statement in Figure 6 has a method call in the place of an expression, which strictly does not conform to the syntax of COOL. One simple remedy would be to assign the result of this call to a temporary variable and return the value of that variable. Since this is straightforward, and adds nothing to the language, it is preferred here to rely on the reader's comprehension.

```
Sort class
vars v: ℕ ← 0; l: unique ref(Sort) ← nil
insert(x: ℕ) method
    begin
        release;
        if is-nil(l) then (v ← x; l ← new Sort)
        elif v ≤ x then l.insert(x)
        else (l.insert(v); v ← x)
        fi
    end
test(x: ℕ) method : 𝔹
    if is-nil(l) ∨ x < v then return false
    elif x = v then return true
    else delegate l.test(x)
    fi
```

Fig. 7. The concurrent implementation of *Sort*

however, possible to avoid the entire list being 'locked' throughout the duration of a *test* method. In the sequential implementation, invocations of the *test* method in successive instances of *Sort* run down the list structure until either the value being sought is found or the end of the list is reached; at this point the Boolean result is passed back up the list; when the result reaches the object at the head of the list it is passed to the client. If instead each object has the option to *delegate* the responsibility of answering the client, it is possible for the first object in the list to accept further method calls. Again one can imagine a sequence of *test* method calls progressing down the list concurrently.[25] The transformed implementation of *test* is given in Figure 7. A more telling example with trees is given in [Jon96].

Because release statements do not have to come at the end of methods and the use of delegate statements, COOL is already an object-based language which permits concurrency. Other ways in which concurrency can be added are mentioned in Section 6.6.

Sections 6.3–6.5 outline the parts of a formal description. Appendix C fills in the details and collects the description in the same order as Appendix B. But first the overall modelling strategy is discussed.

6.2 Modelling Strategy

At one level, objects are just pieces of storage (not unlike records) that can be dynamically created by executing a **new** statement. One can thus anticipate that

---
[25] Notice however that although the linear structure of the list prevents overtaking, it is possible for invocations to be answered in a different order from that in which they were accepted. For example –in the situation – if two invocations are accepted in the order *test*(4) followed by *test*(1), it is possible for the result of the second call to be returned before the first has completed. Although this would constitute a modified behaviour when viewed from an all-seeing spectator, no COOL program can detect the difference.

there will have to be –in our semantic model– a mapping from some *Reference* to the local values. But this does not completely bring out the nature of objects. I owe to the late Ole-Johan Dahl the observation that objects are best understood as "blocks" that can be instantiated multiple times (in contrast to the Algol model where their existence is governed by when control flows through their text). A class defines instance variables and methods just like the local variables and functions/procedures of a block. The instance variables are known only to those methods. One oddity is that the scope of the method names is external to the class (but this is precisely so that they become the access points to actions on the instances (objects) of the class). As mentioned already, the real difference from an Algol block is that instances of classes can be created at will.[26]

This understanding gives us our basic modelling strategy: the run-time information about objects will be stored in a mapping (*ObjMap* in Section 6.5). The *ObjInfo*s stored in this mapping have –as might be expected– a field (*state*) in which the values of the instance variables for the object in question are stored. Because the threads are running interleaved, *ObjInfo* is also keeping track of what text remains to be executed in each active thread. In essence, *ObjInfo* replaces the notion of a "configuration" discussed in Section 3.1. (Section 6.5 discusses the other fields in *ObjInfo*.) Notice that there is no notion of global state here although one might need one if input/output to files were considered.

Section 4.2 points out the need to have access to the text of any program unit which can be used from many places. In COOL, this applies both to the shape (in terms of its instance variables) of a class and the text of the methods of a class for when they are invoked. In Section 6.5 the program text is always available in *Classes*. This leads us to an overall semantic relation:

$$\overset{s}{\longrightarrow} : \mathcal{P}((\textit{Classes} \times \textit{ObjMap}) \times \textit{ObjMap})$$

Returning to the question of relating the parameter passing in COOL to what has gone before, it is clear that object references are passed by-reference. This is precisely what lets a programmer set up sharing patterns (which can in turn introduce race conditions).

6.3   Abstract Syntax

The aim here is to build up the definition of "COOL" in Appendix C where the description is organized by language construct. Here, the whole abstract syntax is presented at once.

A *Program* contains a collection of named *ClassBlock*s; it is assumed that execution begins with a single (parameterless) method call.

$$
\begin{aligned}
\textit{Program} :: \ &cm &&: \textit{Classes} \\
&\textit{start-class} &&: \textit{Id} \\
&\textit{start-meth} &&: \textit{Id}
\end{aligned}
$$

$$\textit{Classes} = \textit{Id} \overset{m}{\longrightarrow} \textit{ClassBlock}$$

---

[26] Postponing a discussion of nesting until Section 6.6.

Notice that there is (unlike in the *Block* language) no body in a *ClassBlock*; having one would provide another natural concurrency extension – see Section 6.6.

$$ClassBlock :: \; vars \quad : \; Id \xrightarrow{m} Type$$
$$meths \; : \; Id \xrightarrow{m} Meth$$

$$Type = Id \mid ScalarType$$

$$ScalarType = \textsc{IntTp} \mid \textsc{BoolTp}$$

Methods are very like function definitions.

$$Meth :: \; returns \quad : \; Type$$
$$params \quad : \; Id^*$$
$$paramtps \; : \; Id \xrightarrow{m} Type$$
$$body \qquad : \; Stmt^*$$

All of the points to be illustrated can be made with the following list of statements.

$$Stmt = Assign \mid If \mid New \mid MethCall \mid Return \mid Release \mid Delegate$$

$$Assign :: \; lhs \; : \; Id$$
$$rhs \; : \; Expr$$

$$If :: \; test : Expr$$
$$th \quad : \; Stmt^*$$
$$el \quad : \; Stmt^*$$

$$New :: \; targ \; : \; Id$$
$$class \; : \; Id$$

$$MethCall :: \; lhs \quad : \; Id$$
$$obj \quad : \; Id$$
$$meth \; : \; Id$$
$$args \; : \; Id^*$$

$$Return :: \; val \; : \; (Expr \mid \textsc{self})$$

$$Release :: \; val \; : \; (Expr \mid \textsc{self})$$

$$Delegate :: \; obj \quad : \; Id$$
$$meth \; : \; Id$$
$$args \; : \; Id^*$$

The syntax of expression is presented only in the appendix.

6.4   Context Conditions

The context conditions are straightforward (and are given in the appendix). Well-formed COOL programs are statically checked to have only syntactically correct method calls.

6.5   Semantics

Dynamic information about Objects is stored in:

$$ObjMap = Reference \xrightarrow{m} ObjInfo$$

$$
\begin{array}{llll}
ObjInfo & :: & class & : Id \\
& & state & : VarState \\
& & status & : Status \\
& & remaining & : Stmt^* \\
& & client & : [Reference]
\end{array}
$$

For any object, the *class* field is the name of the class to which it belongs. This can be used on invocation of a method to locate its *body*.

The *state* field for an object contains the values of its instance variables.

$$VarState = Id \xrightarrow{m} Val$$

$$Val = Reference \mid \mathbb{Z} \mid \mathbb{B}$$

There is some redundancy in the way the *status* of an object is recorded but it is in all cases essential to be able to distinguish between an object which presents an active thread from one which is idle (methods can only be invoked in idle threads). Furthermore, when an object is waiting for a value to returned, the *Wait* field records where that value will be stored.

$$Status = \text{ACTIVE} \mid \text{IDLE} \mid Wait$$

$$Wait :: lhs : Id$$

For an ACTIVE thread (object), the text remaining to be executed in its method is recorded in the *remaining* field and the identity of the client who is awaiting a returned value from any object is recorded in that object's *client* field.

The types of the required relations are

$$\xrightarrow{s} : \mathcal{P}((Classes \times ObjMap) \times ObjMap)$$

and

$$\xrightarrow{e} : \mathcal{P}((Expr \times VarState) \times Val)$$

Each rule in the semantics for a statement needs to locate an active thread awaiting execution of a statement of that type: thus the general shape of all of the $\xrightarrow{s}$ rules is:

$$O(a) = mk\text{-}ObjInfo(c, \sigma, \text{ACTIVE}, [mk\text{-}Stmt\text{-}Type(\ldots)] \curvearrowright rl, co)$$

$$\vdots$$

$$\overline{(C, O) \xrightarrow{s} O \dagger \cdots}$$

For **new**, all that is needed is a thread ready to execute $mk\text{-}New(targ, c')$. The execution of that statement is reflected by its removal and a new object (with a brand new *Reference* — and in **Idle** status) is created with appropriate initial values for the instance variables:

$$O(a) = mk\text{-}ObjInfo(c, \sigma, \text{ACTIVE}, [mk\text{-}New(targ, c')] \curvearrowright rl, co)$$
$$b \in (Reference - \textbf{dom } O)$$
$$aobj' = mk\text{-}ObjInfo(c, \sigma \dagger \{targ \mapsto b\}, \text{ACTIVE}, rl, co)$$
$$\sigma_b = \text{initial values}$$
$$nobj = mk\text{-}ObjInfo(c', \sigma_b, \text{IDLE}, [\,], \textbf{nil})$$
$$\overline{(C, O) \xrightarrow{s} O \dagger \{a \mapsto aobj', b \mapsto nobj\}}$$

In order for thread a to invoke a method in another thread, the latter must be quiescent (its *status* field must be IDLE). The statements to be executed for the called method are found in C and parameters are passed in an obvious way.

$$O(a) =$$
$$\quad mk\text{-}ObjInfo(c, \sigma, \text{ACTIVE}, [mk\text{-}MethCall(lhs, obj, meth, args)] \curvearrowright rl, co)$$
$$O(\sigma(obj)) = mk\text{-}ObjInfo(c', \sigma', \text{IDLE}, [\,], \text{NIL})$$
$$C(c') = mk\text{-}ClassBlock(vars, meths)$$
$$aobj' = mk\text{-}ObjInfo(c, \sigma, mk\text{-}Wait(lhs), rl, co)$$
$$\sigma'' = \sigma' \dagger \{(meths(meth).params)(i) \mapsto \sigma(args(i)) \mid i \in \textbf{inds } args\}$$
$$sobj = mk\text{-}ObjInfo(c', \sigma'', \text{ACTIVE}, meths(meth).body, a)$$
$$\overline{(C, O) \xrightarrow{s} O \dagger \{a \mapsto aobj', \sigma(obj) \mapsto sobj\}}$$

When a method finishes (remember the *Release* can have occured earlier) it reverts to the quiescent status.

$$O(a) = mk\text{-}ObjInfo(c, \sigma, \text{ACTIVE}, [\,], co)$$
$$aobj' = mk\text{-}ObjInfo(c, \sigma, \text{IDLE}, [\,], \textbf{nil})$$
$$\overline{(C, O) \xrightarrow{s} O \dagger \{a \mapsto aobj'\}}$$

Returning values makes the server object IDLE. The thread to which the value is to be returned is found from the *client* field of the completing method. The place to which the returned value should be assigned is found in $mk\text{-}Wait(lhs)$ which was placed there at the time of the method invocation. The server object a becomes idle.

$$O(a) = mk\text{-}ObjInfo(c, \sigma, \text{ACTIVE}, [mk\text{-}Return(e)] \curvearrowright rl, co)$$
$$e \in Expr$$
$$(e, \sigma) \xrightarrow{e} v$$
$$O(co) = mk\text{-}ObjInfo(c', \sigma', mk\text{-}Wait(lhs), sl, co')$$
$$aobj' = mk\text{-}ObjInfo(c, \sigma, \text{IDLE}, [\,], \textbf{nil})$$
$$cobj' = mk\text{-}ObjInfo(c', \sigma' \dagger \{lhs \mapsto v\}, \text{ACTIVE}, sl, co')$$
$$\overline{(C, O) \xrightarrow{s} O \dagger \{a \mapsto aobj', co \mapsto cobj'\}}$$

If SELF is being returned, replace the second line with $v = a$.

Releasing a *rendez vous* is similar except that the a thread remains active:

$$O(a) = mk\text{-}ObjInfo(c, \sigma, \text{ACTIVE}, [mk\text{-}Release(e)] \curvearrowright rl, co)$$
$$(e, \sigma) \xrightarrow{e} v$$
$$O(co) = mk\text{-}ObjInfo(c', \sigma', mk\text{-}Wait(lhs), sl, co')$$
$$aobj' = mk\text{-}ObjInfo(c, \sigma, \text{ACTIVE}, rl, \textbf{nil})$$
$$\underline{cobj' = mk\text{-}ObjInfo(c', \sigma' \dagger \{lhs \mapsto v\}, \text{ACTIVE}, sl, co')}$$
$$(C, O) \xrightarrow{s} O \dagger \{a \mapsto aobj', co \mapsto cobj'\}$$

If SELF is being returned, one again replaces the second line with $v = a$.

The delegate statement is interesting because it works like a combination of method invocation and a release statement:

$$O(a) =$$
$$\quad mk\text{-}ObjInfo(c, \sigma, \text{ACTIVE}, [mk\text{-}Delegate(obj, meth, args)] \curvearrowright rl, co)$$
$$O(\sigma(obj)) = mk\text{-}ObjInfo(c', \sigma', \text{IDLE}, [\,], \text{NIL})$$
$$C(c') = mk\text{-}ClassBlock(vars, meths)$$
$$aobj' = mk\text{-}ObjInfo(c, \sigma, \text{ACTIVE}, rl, \textbf{nil})$$
$$\sigma'' = \sigma' \dagger \{(meths(meth).params)(i) \mapsto \sigma(args(i)) \mid i \in \textbf{inds } args\}$$
$$\underline{sobj = mk\text{-}ObjInfo(c', \sigma'', \text{ACTIVE}, meths(meth).body, co)}$$
$$(C, O) \xrightarrow{s} O \dagger \{a \mapsto aobj', \sigma(obj) \mapsto sobj\}$$

Rules For *Assign* etc. should be obvious (and are in the appendix).

6.6   Developments from Here

There are an enormous number of developments that one can make from the definition in Appendix C. It is straightforward to add new data types (such as strings) or new statement types. A(n OO) purist would point out that COOL is not fully OO (in the sense of Smalltalk) since it uses integer and Boolean values. (There is a subtlety in removing Booleans from the language itself: in order to give a semantics to any statement requiring a truth-valued result, one ends up needing some form of "closure".) Adding arrays is also interesting in as much as it highlights the lack of a location concept for the instance variables (see also below).

More subtly, it is not difficult to partially lift the restriction on "one method active per object" and provide some form of "call back" without introducing race conditions.

Much more interesting is to add to COOL new ways of creating concurrency. In Appendix C, concurrency is achieved by use of **release** (and **delegate**); as an alternative (or addition), a parallel *For* statement could be added and one could, for example, program a parallel version of the "Sieve of Eratosthenes" [Jon96].

A useful extension would be to add "creation code" to each class by including code in the body of the class.

$$
\begin{array}{llll}
ClassBlock & :: & vars & : Id \xrightarrow{m} Type \\
& & meths & : Id \xrightarrow{m} Meth \\
& & constructor & : [CMeth] \\
\end{array}
$$

$$
\begin{array}{llll}
CMeth & :: & params & : Id^* \\
& & paramtps & : Id \xrightarrow{m} Type \\
& & body & : Stmt^* \\
\end{array}
$$

One could then have the **new** statement pass arguments to the creation code

$$New :: \quad targ \quad : \quad Id$$
$$class \quad : \quad Id$$
$$args \quad : \quad Id^*$$

Having a creation body in a Class makes it an autonomous locus of control; one could then fire off many processes at once (cf. [Ame89]). Thus the semantic rule for the **new** statement might become:

$$O(a) = mk\text{-}ObjInfo(c, \sigma, \text{ACTIVE}, [mk\text{-}New(targ, c', args)] \curvearrowright rl, co)$$
$$b \in (Reference - \textbf{dom } O)$$
$$aobj' = mk\text{-}ObjInfo(c, \sigma \dagger \{targ \mapsto b\}, \text{ACTIVE}, rl, co)$$
$$mk\text{-}ClassBlock(vars, meths, cons) = C(c')$$
$$mk\text{-}CMeth(parms, parmts, cbody) = cons$$
$$\sigma_b = \{parms(i) \mapsto \sigma(args(i)) \mid i \in \textbf{inds } parms\}$$
$$nobj = mk\text{-}ObjInfo(c', \sigma_b, \text{ACTIVE}, cbody, \textbf{nil})$$
$$\overline{(C, O) \xrightarrow{s} O \dagger \{a \mapsto aobj', b \mapsto nobj\}}$$

COOL's "one method per object" rule means that the constructor will block other method calls until construction is finished.

Another interesting extension would be to allow some access to the instance variables of an object (as in Java's **public**). It would be safe to do this for IDLE objects; permitting such access within an ACTIVE object would introduce the danger of race conditions.

One could go further and add some form of process algebraic notation for controlling permissible orders of method activation.[27]

Object-oriented purists would also object that COOL offers no form of inheritance. This is –at least in part– intentional because of the confusions surrounding the idea. One useful handle on the semantics of inheritance is to go back to the observation that classes are like blocks that can be instantiated at will. A nested block offers all of the facilities (variables and functions) of its surrounding block except where overridden. If one thinks of inheritance as creating instances of an inner block, one begins to see what the semantic implications might be (including some doubt about "multiple inheritance").

7   Conclusions

It is hoped that the reader now sees the extent to which semantic models can elucidate and record the understanding of the features of programming languages. There are descriptions of many real languages (full citations are omitted here for space reasons)

---

[27] One could derive intuition from similar ideas in the meta-language as in [FL98], [But00] or [WC02]. My own preference would be to use pi-calculus and have the ν operator create objects (I have given talks on this but not yet written anything).

- (operational and denotational) of ALGOL 60
- (denotational) of Pascal
- SOS for ML
- (denotational) of PL/I ECMA/ANSI standard
- (denotational) of Ada
- Modula-2 standard
- Java description [KNvO+02]

In fact, the obvious duplication involved in writing descriptions where there is a considerable amount of overlap in the features of the languages has led to attempts to look for ideas that make it possible to document language concepts in a way which facilitates their combination. Early steps towards this are visible in the "combinators" of the Vienna PL/I description [BBH+74]; Mosses' "action semantics" [Mos92] took this much further and he has more recently been studying "Modular SOS" [Mos06].

There is no doubt that reasoning about language descriptions is extremely important. This goes beyond using a semantics to establish facts about particular programs as discussed in Section 3.2. A simple example of a general result is that a well-formed program cannot give rise to run-time type errors. An important class of proofs is the consistency of Floyd-Hoare-like proof rules with respect to a model-oriented semantics. The paper [CJ07] is an example of this (and it contains references to earlier material in this vein) which establishes the soundness of rely/guarantee rules.

The potential that originally took this author to the IBM Vienna Laboratory in 1968 was the use of formal language descriptions as a base for compiler design.[28] A description from the research at that time is [JL71] (but much of the material is only available as Technical Reports). An important historical reference is [MP66].

A knowledgeable reader might question why this text has been based on operational –rather than denotational [Sto77]– semantics. It is claimed in Section 1.3 that the message is "abstraction, abstraction, abstraction" and there is a clear technical sense in which denotational semantics are more abstract than operational. The reasons are largely pedagogic (cf. [CJJ06]) but it is this author's conviction that once concurrency has to be tackled, the cost of extra mathematical apparatus does not present an adequate return.

The other omitted topic that might give rise to comment is that of process algebras such as CSP [Hoa78], CCS [Mil89] or the pi-calculus [MPW92, SW01]. The topic of their semantics and proof methods is itself fascinating.

One topic that links closely with the material above is the mapping of object-oriented languages to process algebras (cf. [Wal91, Jon93]). These semantics have been used to justify the equivalences used in transforming OO programs in Section 6 — see [Wal93, Jon94, San99] and references therein.

---

[28] Notice that post-facto proofs were seen even then as pointless: the pay off of formalism is in the design process.

Acknowledgments

The author gratefully acknowledges the EPSRC support for his research under the "Splitting (software) atoms safely" grant.

References

[ACJ72]   Allen, C.D., Chapman, D.N., Jones, C.B.: A formal definition of ALGOL 60. Technical Report 12.105, IBM Laboratory Hursley (August 1972)

[Ame89]   America, P.: Issues in the design of a parallel object-oriented language. Formal Aspects of Computing 1(4) (1989)

[BBG⁺63]   Backus, J.W., Bauer, F.L., Green, J., Katz, C., McCarthy, J., Naur, P., Perlis, A.J., Rutishauser, H., Samelson, K., Vauquois, B., Wegstein, J.H., van Wijngaarden, A., Woodger, M.: Revised report on the algorithmic language Algol 60. Communications of the ACM 6(1), 1–17 (1963)

[BBH⁺74]   Bekič, H., Bjørner, D., Henhapl, W., Jones, C.B., Lucas, P.: A formal definition of a PL/I subset. Technical Report 25.139, IBM Laboratory Vienna (December 1974)

[BJ78]   Bjørner, D., Jones, C.B. (eds.): The Vienna Development Method: The Meta-Language. LNCS, vol. 61. Springer, Heidelberg (1978)

[BJ82]   Bjørner, D., Jones, C.B.: Formal Specification and Software Development. Prentice Hall International, Englewood Cliffs (1982)

[Boo54]   Boole, G.: An Investigation of the Laws of Thought. Macmillan (1854) (reprinted by Dover (1958))

[But00]   Butler, M.J.: CSP2B: A practical approach to combining CSP and B. Formal Aspects of Computing 12(3), 182–198 (2000)

[CJ07]   Coleman, J.W., Jones, C.B.: Guaranteeing the soundness of rely/guarantee rules (revised). Journal of Logic and Computation (accepted for publication, 2007)

[CJJ06]   Coleman, J.W., Jefferson, N.P., Jones, C.B.: Comments on several years of teaching of modelling programming language concepts. Technical Report CS-TR-978, Newcastle University (2006)

[CM92]   Camilleri, J., Melham, T.: Reasoning with inductively defined relations in the HOL theorem prover. Technical Report 265, Computer Laboratory, University of Cambridge (August 1992)

[Dij76]   Dijkstra, E.W.: A Discipline of Programming. Prentice-Hall, Englewood Cliffs (1976)

[DW99]   D'Souza, D.F., Wills, A.C.: Objects, components, and frameworks with UML: the catalysis approach. Addison-Wesley Longman Publishing Co., Inc., Boston, MA, USA (1999)

[Eng71]   Engeler, E.: Symposium on Semantics of Algorithmic Languages. Lecture Notes in Mathematics, vol. 188. Springer, Heidelberg (1971)

[FL98]   Fitzgerald, J., GormLarsen, P.: Modelling systems: practical tools and techniques in software development. Cambridge University Press, Cambridge (1998)

[Gor79]   Gordon, M.J.C.: The Denotational Description of Programming Languages: An Introduction. Springer, Heidelberg (1979)

[Gor88]   Gordon, M.J.C.: Programming Language Theory and its Implementation. Prentice-Hall International, Englewood Cliffs (1988)

[Hen90]   Hennessy, M.: The Semantics of Programming Languages: an elementary introduction using structural operational semantics. Wiley, Chichester (1990)

[HJ70]   Henhapl, W., Jones, C.B.: On the interpretation of GOTO statements in the ULD. Technical Report LN 25.3.065, IBM Laboratory, Vienna (March 1970)

[HJ71]   Henhapl, W., Jones, C.B.: A run-time mechanism for referencing variables. Information Processing Letters 1, 14–16 (1971)

[Hoa78]   Hoare, C.A.R.: Communicating sequential processes. Communications of the ACM 21, 666–677 (1978)

[JL71]   Jones, C.B., Lucas, P.: Proving correctness of implementation techniques. In: [Eng71], pp. 178–211 (1971)

[JLRW05]   Jones, C.B., Lomet, D., Romanovsky, A., Weikum, G.: The atomicity manifesto (2005)

[Jon93]   Jones, C.B.: A pi-calculus semantics for an object-based design notation. In: Best, E. (ed.) CONCUR 1993. LNCS, vol. 715, pp. 158–172. Springer, Heidelberg (1993)

[Jon94]   Jones, C.B.: Process algebra arguments about an object-based design notation. In: Classical, A. (ed.) A Classical Mind: Essays in Honour of C. A. R. Hoare, ch. 14, Prentice-Hall, Englewood Cliffs (1994)

[Jon96]   Jones, C.B.: Accommodating interference in the formal design of concurrent object-based programs. Formal Methods in System Design 8(2), 105–122 (1996)

[Jon01a]   Jones, C.B.: On the search for tractable ways of reasoning about programs. Technical Report CS-TR-740, Newcastle University, Superceded by [Jon03a] (2001)

[Jon01b]   Jones, C.B.: The transition from VDL to VDM. JUCS 7(8), 631–640 (2001)

[Jon03a]   Jones, C.B.: The early search for tractable ways of reasonning about programs. IEEE, Annals of the History of Computing 25(2), 26–49 (2003)

[Jon03b]   Jones, C.B.: Operational semantics: concepts and their expression. Information Processing Letters 88(1-2), 27–32 (2003)

[KNvO+02]   Klein, G., Nipkow, T., von Oheimb, D., Nieto, L.P., Schirmer, N., Strecker, M.: Java source and bytecode formalisations in Isabelle (2002)

[Lis96]   Liskov, B.: A history of CLU. In: History of programming languages—II, pp. 471–510. ACM Press, New York (1996)

[LW69]   Lucas, P., Walk, K.: On The Formal Description of PL/I. Annual Review in Automatic Programming Part 3, vol. 6. Pergamon Press, Oxford (1969)

[McC66]   McCarthy, J.: A formal description of a subset of ALGOL. In: [Ste66], pp. 1–12 (1966)

[Mil89]   Milner, R.: Communication and Concurrency. Prentice-Hall, Englewood Cliffs (1989)

[Mos92]   Mosses, P.D.: Action Semantics. Cambridge Tracts in Theoretical Computer Science, vol. 26. Cambridge University Press, Cambridge (1992)

[Mos06]   Mosses, P.D.: Teaching semantics of programming languages with Modular SOS. In: Teaching Formal Methods: Practice and Experience. Electr. Workshops in Comput. BCS (2006)

[MP66]   McCarthy, J., Painter, J.: Correctness of a compiler for arithmetic expressions. Technical Report CS38, Computer Science Department, Stanford University (April 1966) (see also Proc. Symp. in Applied Mathematics, vol.19, pp. 33–41, Mathematical Aspects of Computer Science, American Mathematical Society (1967))

[MPW92]   Milner, R., Parrow, J., Walker, D.: A calculus of mobile processes. Information and Computation 100, 1–77 (1992)

[NN92]   Nielson, H.R., Nielson, F.: Semantics with Applications: A Formal Introduction. Wiley, Chichester (1992), available on the WWW as http://www.daimi.au.dk/bra8130/Wiley_book/wiley.html

[Plo81]   Plotkin, G.D.: A structural approach to operational semantics. Technical report, Aarhus University (1981)

[Plo04a]   Plotkin, G.D.: The origins of structural operational semantics. Journal of Logic and Algebraic Programming 60–61, 3–15 (July–December, 2004)

[Plo04b]   Plotkin, G.D.: A structural approach to operational semantics. Journal of Logic and Algebraic Programming 60–61, 17–139 (July–December, 2004)

[Rey98]   Reynolds, J.C.: Theories of Programming Languages. Cambridge University Press, Cambridge (1998)

[San99]   Sangiorgi, D.: Typed π-calculus at work: a correctness proof of Jones's parallelisation transformation on concurrent objects. Theory and Practice of Object Systems 5(1), 25–34 (1999)

[Sco00]   Scott, M.L.: Programming Language Pragmatics. Morgan Kaufmann, San Francisco (2000)

[Ste66]   Steel, T.B.: Formal Language Description Languages for Computer Programming. North-Holland, Amsterdam (1966)

[Sto77]   Stoy, J.E.: Denotational Semantics: The Scott-Strachey Approach to Programming Language Theory. MIT Press, Cambridge (1977)

[SW01]   Sangiorgi, D., Walker, D.: The π-calculus: A Theory of Mobile Processes. Cambridge University Press, Cambridge (2001)

[vWSM$^+$76]   van Wijngaarden, A., Sintzoff, M., Mailloux, B.J., Lindsey, C.H., Peck, J.E.L., Meertens, L.G.L.T., Koster, C.H.A., Fisker, R.G.: Revised report on the Algorithmic Language ALGOL 68, Mathematisch Centrum, Amsterdam. Mathematical Centre Tracts 50 (1976)

[Wal91]   Walker, D.: π-calculus semantics for object-oriented programming languages. In: Ito, T., Meyer, A.R. (eds.) TACS 1991. LNCS, vol. 526, pp. 532–547. Springer, Heidelberg (1991)

[Wal93]   Walker, D.: Process calculus and parallel object-oriented programming languages. In: Casavant, T. (ed.) Parallel Computers: Theory and Practice, Computer Society Press (1993)

[Wat04]   Watt, D.A.: Programming Language Design Concepts. John Wiley, Chichester (2004)

[WC02]   Woodcock, J., Cavalcanti, A.: The semantics of circus. In: Bert, D., Bowen, J.P., Henson, M.C., Robinson, K. (eds.) B 2002 and ZB 2002. LNCS, vol. 2272, pp. 184–203. Springer, Heidelberg (2002)

[Wex81]   Wexelblat, R.L. (ed.): History of Programming Languages. Academic Press, London (1981)

[WH66]   Wirth, N., Hoare, C.A.R.: A contribution to the development of algol. Commun. ACM 9(6), 413–432 (1966)

[Win93]   Winskel, G.: The Formal Semantics of Programming Languages. MIT Press, Cambridge (1993)

[Zem66]   Zemanek, H.: Semiotics and programming languages. Communications of the ACM 9, 139–143 (1966)

A   Base Language

Notice that the formulae in this appendix separate abstract syntax, context conditions and semantics. This is not the order used in other appendices[29] but it serves at this stage to emphasize the distinctions.

A.1   Abstract Syntax

$Program :: vars : Id \xrightarrow{m} ScalarType$
$\qquad\qquad body : Stmt^*$

$ScalarType = \text{INTTP} \mid \text{BOOLTP}$

$Stmt = Assign \mid If \mid While$

$Assign :: lhs : Id$
$\qquad\qquad rhs : Expr$

$If :: test : Expr$
$\quad\ th \quad : Stmt^*$
$\quad\ el \quad : Stmt^*$

$While :: test \ : Expr$
$\qquad\qquad body : Stmt^*$

$Expr = ArithExpr \mid RelExpr \mid Id \mid ScalarValue$

$ArithExpr :: opd1 \qquad : Expr$
$\qquad\qquad\quad operator : \text{PLUS} \mid \text{MINUS}$
$\qquad\qquad\quad opd2 \qquad : Expr$

$RelExpr :: opd1 \qquad : Expr$
$\qquad\qquad\ operator : \text{EQUALS} \mid \text{NOTEQUALS}$
$\qquad\qquad\ opd2 \qquad : Expr$

$ScalarValue = \mathbb{Z} \mid \mathbb{B}$

A.2   Context Conditions

In order to define the Context Conditions below, an auxiliary object is required in which the types of declared identifiers can be stored.

$TypeMap = Id \xrightarrow{m} ScalarType$

$wf\text{-}Program : Program \to \mathbb{B}$

$wf\text{-}Program(mk\text{-}Program(vars, body)) \ \triangle \ wf\text{-}StmtList(body, vars)$

---

[29] For reference purposes, this is normally most convenient. There remains the decision whether to present the parts of a language in a top-down (from *Program* to *Expr*) order or bottom-up: this decision is fairly arbitrary. What is really needed is an interactive support system!

$$wf\text{-}StmtList : (Stmt^*) \times TypeMap \to \mathbb{B}$$

$$wf\text{-}StmtList(sl, tpm) \quad \triangleq \quad \forall i \in \mathbf{inds}\ sl \cdot wf\text{-}Stmt(sl(i), tpm)$$

$$wf\text{-}Stmt : Stmt \times TypeMap \to \mathbb{B}$$

$$wf\text{-}Stmt(s, tpm) \quad \triangleq \quad \text{given by cases below}$$

$$wf\text{-}Stmt(mk\text{-}Assign(lhs, rhs), tpm) \quad \triangleq$$
$$\quad lhs \in \mathbf{dom}\ tpm\ \wedge$$
$$\quad c\text{-}tp(rhs, tpm) = tpm(lhs)$$

$$wf\text{-}Stmt(mk\text{-}If(test, th, el), tpm) \quad \triangleq$$
$$\quad c\text{-}tp(test, tpm) = \textsc{BoolTp} \wedge$$
$$\quad wf\text{-}StmtList(th, tpm) \wedge wf\text{-}StmtList(el, tpm)$$

$$wf\text{-}Stmt(mk\text{-}While(test, body), tpm) \quad \triangleq$$
$$\quad c\text{-}tp(test, tpm) = \textsc{BoolTp} \wedge$$
$$\quad wf\text{-}StmtList(body, tpm)$$

An auxiliary function $c\text{-}tp$ is defined

$$c\text{-}tp : Expr \times TypeMap \to (\textsc{IntTp} \mid \textsc{BoolTp} \mid \textsc{Error})$$

$$c\text{-}tp(e, tpm) \quad \triangleq \quad \text{given by cases below}$$

$$c\text{-}tp(mk\text{-}ArithExpr(e1, opt, e2), tpm) \quad \triangleq$$
$$\quad \mathbf{if}\ c\text{-}tp(e1, tpm) = \textsc{IntTp} \wedge c\text{-}tp(e2, tpm) = \textsc{IntTp}$$
$$\quad \mathbf{then}\ \textsc{IntTp}$$
$$\quad \mathbf{else}\ \textsc{Error}$$

$$c\text{-}tp(mk\text{-}RelExpr(e1, opt, e2), tpm) \quad \triangleq$$
$$\quad \mathbf{if}\ c\text{-}tp(e1, tpm) = \textsc{IntTp} \wedge c\text{-}tp(e2, tpm) = \textsc{IntTp}$$
$$\quad \mathbf{then}\ \textsc{BoolTp}$$
$$\quad \mathbf{else}\ \textsc{Error}$$

For the base cases:

$$e \in Id\ \Rightarrow\ c\text{-}tp(e, tpm) = tpm(e)$$

$$e \in \mathbb{Z}\ \Rightarrow\ c\text{-}tp(e, tpm) = \textsc{IntTp}$$

$$e \in \mathbb{B}\ \Rightarrow\ c\text{-}tp(e, tpm) = \textsc{BoolTp}$$

A.3 Semantics

An auxiliary object is needed to describe the Semantics — this "Semantic Object" (Σ) stores the association of identifiers and their values.

$$\Sigma = Id \xrightarrow{\ m\ } ScalarValue$$

$$\sigma_0 = \{id \mapsto 0 \mid id \in \mathbf{dom}\ vars \wedge vars(id) = \text{INTTP}\} \cup$$
$$\{id \mapsto \mathbf{true} \mid id \in \mathbf{dom}\ vars \wedge vars(id) = \text{BOOLTP}\}$$

$$\frac{(body, \sigma_0) \xrightarrow{sl} \sigma'}{(mk\text{-}Program(vars, body)) \xrightarrow{p} \text{DONE}}$$

The semantic transition relation for statement lists is

$$\xrightarrow{sl}: \mathcal{P}((Stmt^* \times \Sigma) \times \Sigma)$$

$$\frac{}{([\,], \sigma) \xrightarrow{sl} \sigma}$$

$$\frac{(s, \sigma) \xrightarrow{s} \sigma'}{(rest, \sigma') \xrightarrow{sl} \sigma''}{([s] \frown rest, \sigma) \xrightarrow{sl} \sigma''}$$

The semantic transition relation for single statements is

$$\xrightarrow{s}: \mathcal{P}((Stmt \times \Sigma) \times \Sigma)$$

$$\frac{(rhs, \sigma) \xrightarrow{e} v}{(mk\text{-}Assign(lhs, rhs), \sigma) \xrightarrow{s} \sigma \dagger \{lhs \mapsto v\}}$$

$$\frac{(test, \sigma) \xrightarrow{e} \mathbf{true}}{(th, \sigma) \xrightarrow{sl} \sigma'}{(mk\text{-}If(test, th, el), \sigma) \xrightarrow{s} \sigma'}$$

$$\frac{(test, \sigma) \xrightarrow{e} \mathbf{false}}{(el, \sigma) \xrightarrow{sl} \sigma'}{(mk\text{-}If(test, th, el), \sigma) \xrightarrow{s} \sigma'}$$

$$\frac{(test, \sigma) \xrightarrow{e} \mathbf{true}}{(body, \sigma) \xrightarrow{sl} \sigma'}{(mk\text{-}While(test, body), \sigma') \xrightarrow{s} \sigma''}{(mk\text{-}While(test, body), \sigma) \xrightarrow{s} \sigma''}$$

$$\frac{(test, \sigma) \xrightarrow{e} \mathbf{false}}{(mk\text{-}While(test, body), \sigma) \xrightarrow{s} \sigma}$$

The semantic transition relation for expressions is

$$\xrightarrow{e}: \mathcal{P}((Expr \times \Sigma) \times ScalarValue)$$

$$\frac{(e1, \sigma) \xrightarrow{e} v1}{(e2, \sigma) \xrightarrow{e} v2}{(mk\text{-}ArithExpr(e1, \text{PLUS}, e2), \sigma) \xrightarrow{e} v1 + v2}$$

$$\frac{(e1,\sigma) \xrightarrow{e} v1 \quad (e2,\sigma) \xrightarrow{e} v2}{(mk\text{-}ArithExpr(e1, \text{MINUS}, e2),\sigma) \xrightarrow{e} v1 - v2}$$

$$\frac{(e1,\sigma) \xrightarrow{e} v1 \quad (e2,\sigma) \xrightarrow{e} v2 \quad v1 = v2}{(mk\text{-}RelExpr(e1, \text{EQUALS}, e2),\sigma) \xrightarrow{e} \textbf{true}}$$

$$\frac{(e1,\sigma) \xrightarrow{e} v1 \quad (e2,\sigma) \xrightarrow{e} v2 \quad v1 = v2}{(mk\text{-}RelExpr(e1, \text{NOTEQUALS}, e2),\sigma) \xrightarrow{e} \textbf{false}}$$

$$\frac{e \in Id}{(e,\sigma) \xrightarrow{e} \sigma(e)}$$

$$\frac{e \in ScalarValue}{(e,\sigma) \xrightarrow{e} e}$$

B   The Language "Blocks"

This appendix summarizes one of the definitions discussed in Section 4 and shows a useful way in which a complete definition can be ordered. The "Blocks" language is described here with parameter passing by-location.

B.1   Auxiliary Objects

The context conditions use:

$$Types = Id \xrightarrow{m} Type$$

$$Type = ScalarType \mid FunType$$

$$FunType :: \quad returns \quad : \quad ScalarType$$
$$paramtpl : ScalarType^*$$

The semantic rules use:

$$Env = Id \xrightarrow{m} Den$$

$$Den = ScalarLoc \mid FunDen$$

Where $ScalarLoc$ is an infinite set chosen from $Token$.
    The types of the semantic relations are

$\xrightarrow{p}: \mathcal{P}(Program \times \Sigma$

$\xrightarrow{sl}: \mathcal{P}(((Stmt^*) \times Env \times \Sigma) \times \Sigma)$

$\xrightarrow{s}: \mathcal{P}((Stmt \times Env \times \Sigma) \times \Sigma)$

$\xrightarrow{e}: \mathcal{P}((Expr \times Env \times \Sigma) \times ScalarValue)$

Abbreviations

$\sigma \in \Sigma$	a single "state"
Σ	the set of all "States"
Arith	Arithmetic
Def	Definition
Den	Denotation
env	a single "environment"
Env	the set of all "Environments"
Expr	Expression
Proc	Procedure
opd	operand
Rel	Relational
Sc	Scalar
Seq	Sequence
Stmt	Statement
...	

B.2   Programs

Abstract Syntax

$Program :: Block$

$wf\text{-}Program : Program \to \mathbb{B}$

Context conditions $wf\text{-}Program(mk\text{-}Program(b)) \triangleq wf\text{-}Block(b, \{\})$

Semantics $\dfrac{(b, \{\}, \{\}) \xrightarrow{s} \sigma'}{(mk\text{-}Program(b)) \xrightarrow{p} \sigma'}$

B.3   Blocks

$Block :: vars : Id \xrightarrow{m} ScalarType$
$\qquad\quad funs : Id \xrightarrow{m} Fun$
$\qquad\quad body : Stmt^*$

Abstract syntax $ScalarType = \text{INTTP} \mid \text{BOOLTP}$

$wf\text{-}Block : Block \times Types \rightarrow \mathbb{B}$

Context conditions $wf\text{-}Block(mk\text{-}Block(vars, funs, body), tps)$ $\triangleq$
   $\mathbf{dom}\ vars \cap \mathbf{dom}\ funs = \{\ \} \wedge$
   $\mathbf{let}\ var\text{-}tps = tps \dagger vars\ \mathbf{in}$
   $\mathbf{let}\ fun\text{-}tps =$
      $\{f \mapsto mk\text{-}FunType(funs(f).returns,$
                $apply(funs(f).params, funs(f).paramtps)) \mid$
         $f \in \mathbf{dom}\ funs\}\ \mathbf{in}$
   $\forall f \in \mathbf{dom}\ funs \cdot wf\text{-}Fun(funs(f), var\text{-}tps)$
   $wf\text{-}StmtList(body, var\text{-}tps \dagger fun\text{-}tps)$

Notice that this rules out recursion.

Semantics $\dfrac{\begin{array}{l}(varenv, \sigma') = newlocs(vars, \sigma) \\ funenv = \\ \quad \{f \mapsto b\text{-}FunDen(funs(f), env \dagger varenv) \mid f \in \mathbf{dom}\ funs\} \\ env' = env \dagger varenv \dagger funenv \\ (body, env', \sigma') \xrightarrow{sl} \sigma''\end{array}}{(mk\text{-}Block(vars, funs, body), env, \sigma) \xrightarrow{s} (\mathbf{dom}\ \sigma) \lhd \sigma''}$

$newlocs\ (vars: (Id \xrightarrow{m} ScalarType), \sigma: \Sigma)\ varenv: Env, \sigma': \Sigma$

post $\mathbf{dom}\ varenv = \mathbf{dom}\ vars\ \wedge$
       $disj(\mathbf{rng}\ varenv, \mathbf{dom}\ \sigma)\ \wedge$
       $one\text{-}one(varenv)\ \wedge$
       $\sigma' = \sigma \cup \{varenv(id) \mapsto 0 \mid id \in \mathbf{dom}\ vars \wedge vars(id) = \textsc{IntTp}\} \cup$
          $\{varenv(id) \mapsto \mathbf{true} \mid id \in \mathbf{dom}\ vars \wedge vars(id) = \textsc{BoolTp}\}$

30

B.4   Function Definitions

$Fun\ ::\ returns\quad :\ ScalarType$
       $params\quad :\ Id^*$
       $paramtps\ :\ Id \xrightarrow{m} ScalarType$
       $body\quad\ \ :\ Stmt^*$
       $result\quad\ :\ Expr$

Abstract syntax

---

[30] The auxiliary function $one\text{-}one$ is defined:

$one\text{-}one : (X \xrightarrow{m} Y) \rightarrow \mathbb{B}$

$one\text{-}one(m)\quad \triangleq\quad \forall a, b \in \mathbf{dom}\ m \cdot m(a) = m(b)\ \Rightarrow\ a = b$

$wf\text{-}Fun : Fun \times Types \to \mathbb{B}$

Context conditions

$wf\text{-}Fun(mk\text{-}Fun(returns, params, paramtps, body, result), tps) \quad \triangleq$
$uniquel(params) \land$
elems $params = $ **dom** $paramtps \land$
$tp(result) = returns \land$
$wf\text{-}StmtList(body, tps \dagger paramtps)$

$b\text{-}Fun\text{-}Den : Fun \times Env \to FunDen$

$b\text{-}Fun\text{-}Den(mk\text{-}Fun(returns, params, paramtps, body, result), env) \quad \triangleq$
$mk\text{-}FunDen(params, body, result, env)$

B.5   Statement Lists

$wf\text{-}StmtList : Stmt^* \times Types \to \mathbb{B}$

Context conditions $wf\text{-}StmtList(sl, tps) \quad \triangleq$
$\forall i \in \textbf{inds}\ sl \cdot wf\text{-}Stmt(sl(i), tps)$

Semantics $\dfrac{}{([\,], env, \sigma) \xrightarrow{sl} \sigma}$

$$\frac{(s, env, \sigma) \xrightarrow{s} \sigma' \quad (rest, env, \sigma') \xrightarrow{sl} \sigma''}{([s] \frown rest, env, \sigma) \xrightarrow{sl} \sigma''}$$

B.6   Statements

Abstract syntax $Stmt = Block \mid Assign \mid If \mid Call$

B.7   Assignments

$Assign :: lhs : Id$
$\qquad\quad\ rhs : Expr$

Abstract syntax

Context conditions $wf\text{-}Stmt(mk\text{-}Assign(lhs, rhs), tps) \quad \triangleq$
$tp(rhs, tps) = tp(lhs, tps)$

Semantics $\dfrac{(lhs, env, \sigma) \xrightarrow{lhv} l \quad (rhs, env, \sigma) \xrightarrow{e} v}{(mk\text{-}Assign(lhs, rhs), env, \sigma) \xrightarrow{s} \sigma \dagger \{l \mapsto v\}}$

B.8   If Statements

$If ::$ $test$: $Expr$
th : $Stmt^*$
el : $Stmt^*$

Abstract syntax

Context conditions $wf\text{-}Stmt(mk\text{-}If(test, th, el), tps)$ $\triangleq$
$tp(test, tps) = \text{BoolTp} \land$
$wf\text{-}StmtList(th, tps) \land wf\text{-}StmtList(el, tps)$

Semantics
$$\frac{\begin{array}{c}(test, env, \sigma) \xrightarrow{e} \textbf{true} \\ (th, env, \sigma) \xrightarrow{sl} \sigma'\end{array}}{(mk\text{-}If(test, th, el), env, \sigma) \xrightarrow{s} \sigma'}$$

$$\frac{\begin{array}{c}(test, env, \sigma) \xrightarrow{e} \textbf{false} \\ (el, env, \sigma) \xrightarrow{sl} \sigma'\end{array}}{(mk\text{-}If(test, th, el), env, \sigma) \xrightarrow{s} \sigma'}$$

B.9   Call Statements

$Call ::$ lhs : $VarRef$
fun : Id
$args$: Id^*

Abstract syntax

Context conditions $wf\text{-}Stmt(mk\text{-}Call(lhs, fun, args), tps)$ $\triangleq$
$fun \in \textbf{dom}\ tps \land$
$tps(fun) \in FunType \land$
$tp(lhs, tps) = (tps(fun)).returns \land$
$\textbf{len}\ args = \textbf{len}\ (tps(fun)).paramtpl \land$
$\forall i \in \textbf{inds}\ args \cdot tp(args(i), tps) = ((tps(fun)).paramtpl)(i)$

Semantics
$$\frac{\begin{array}{c}(lhs, env, \sigma) \xrightarrow{lhv} l \\ mk\text{-}FunDen(parms, body, result, context) = env(f) \\ \textbf{len}\ arglocs = \textbf{len}\ args \\ \forall i \in \textbf{inds}\ arglocs \cdot (args(i), env, \sigma) \xrightarrow{lhv} arglocs(i) \\ parm\text{-}env = \{parms(i) \mapsto arglocs(i) \mid i \in \textbf{inds}\ parms\} \\ (body, (context \dagger parm\text{-}env), \sigma) \xrightarrow{sl} \sigma' \\ (result, (context \dagger parm\text{-}env), \sigma') \xrightarrow{e} res\end{array}}{(mk\text{-}Call(lhs, f, args), env, \sigma) \xrightarrow{s} (\sigma' \dagger \{l \mapsto res\})}$$

B.10   Expressions

Abstract syntax $Expr = ArithExpr \mid RelExpr \mid Id \mid ScalarValue$

$ArithExpr :: opd1 \quad : Expr$
$\qquad\qquad\ operator : \text{PLUS}$
$\qquad\qquad\ opd2 \quad\ : Expr$

$RelExpr :: opd1 \quad : Expr$
$\qquad\qquad operator : \text{EQUALS}$
$\qquad\qquad opd2 \quad\ : Expr$

$ScalarValue = \mathbb{Z} \mid \mathbb{B}$

Semantics
$$\frac{(e1, env, \sigma) \xrightarrow{e} v1 \quad (e2, env, \sigma) \xrightarrow{e} v2}{(mk\text{-}ArithExpr(e1, \text{PLUS}, e2), env, \sigma) \xrightarrow{e} v1 + v2}$$

$$\frac{\begin{array}{l}(e1, env, \sigma) \xrightarrow{e} v1 \\ (e2, env, \sigma) \xrightarrow{e} v2 \\ v1 = v2\end{array}}{(mk\text{-}RelExpr(e1, \text{EQUALS}, e2), env, \sigma) \xrightarrow{e} \textbf{true}}$$

$$\frac{\begin{array}{l}e \in Id \\ (id, env, \sigma) \xrightarrow{lhv} l\end{array}}{(e, env, \sigma) \xrightarrow{e} \sigma(l)}$$

$$\frac{e \in ScalarValue}{(e, env, \sigma) \xrightarrow{e} e}$$

C   COOL

Reordered definition from Section 6.

C.1   Auxiliary Objects

The objects required for both Context Conditions and Semantic Rules are given first.

Objects Needed for Context Conditions

The following objects are needed in the description of the Context Conditions.

$$ClassTypes = Id \xrightarrow{m} ClassInfo$$

$$ClassInfo = Id \xrightarrow{m} MethInfo$$

The only information required about methods is about their types (arguments and results):

$MethInfo :: return : Type$
$\qquad\qquad\ parms : Type^*$

$Type = Id \mid ScalarType$

$ScalarType = \text{INTTP} \mid \text{BOOLTP}$

When checking for the well-formedness of the body of a *Method*, information about its instance variables is also needed

$VarEnv = Id \xrightarrow{m} Type$

Semantic Objects

In addition to the abstract syntax of *Classes* (see below), the following objects are needed in the description of the Semantics.

$ObjMap = Reference \xrightarrow{m} ObjInfo$

$$ObjInfo :: \begin{array}{ll} class & : Id \\ state & : VarState \\ status & : Status \\ remaining & : Stmt^* \\ client & : [Reference] \end{array}$$

$VarState = Id \xrightarrow{m} Val$

$Val = [Reference] \mid \mathbb{Z} \mid \mathbb{B}$

The set *Reference* is infinite and **nil** $\notin Reference$.

$Status = \text{ACTIVE} \mid \text{IDLE} \mid Wait$

$Wait :: lhs : Id$

The types of the semantic relations are

$\xrightarrow{p} : \mathcal{P}(Program \times \text{DONE})$

$\xrightarrow{s} : \mathcal{P}((Classes \times ObjMap) \times ObjMap)$

$\xrightarrow{e} : \mathcal{P}((Expr \times VarState) \times Val)$

Abbreviations

Arith	Arithmetic
Expr	Expression
Obj	Object
opd	operand
Meth	Method
Rel	Relational
Stmt	Statement
Var	Variable

C.2   Programs

Abstract Syntax

$Program :: cm \qquad : Classes$
$\qquad\qquad\quad start\text{-}class : Id$
$\qquad\qquad\quad start\text{-}meth : Id$

$Classes = Id \xrightarrow{m} ClassBlock$

Context Conditions

$wf\text{-}Program : Program \to \mathbb{B}$

$wf\text{-}Program(mk\text{-}Program(cm, start\text{-}c, start\text{-}m)) \quad \triangle$
$\qquad start\text{-}c \in \mathbf{dom}\ cm\ \wedge$
$\qquad start\text{-}m \in \mathbf{dom}\ (cm(start\text{-}c).meths)\ \wedge$
$\qquad \mathbf{let}\ ctps = \{c \mapsto c\text{-}tp(cm(c))\mid c \in \mathbf{dom}\ cm\}$
$\qquad \mathbf{in}\ \forall c \in \mathbf{dom}\ cm \cdot wf\text{-}ClassBlock(cm(c), ctps)$

The following two functions extract *ClassInfo* and *MethInfo* respectively.

$c\text{-}tp : ClassBlock \to ClassInfo$

$c\text{-}tp(mk\text{-}ClassBlock(tpm, mm)) \quad \triangle$
$\qquad \{m \mapsto c\text{-}minfo(mm(m)) \mid m \in \mathbf{dom}\ mm\}$

$c\text{-}minfo : Meth \to MethInfo$

$c\text{-}minfo(mk\text{-}Meth(ret, pnl, ptm, b)) \quad \triangle$
$\qquad mk\text{-}MethInfo(ret, apply(pnl, ptm))$

Semantics

With no input/output statements, the execution of a *Program* actually leaves no trace. One might say that, for $mk\text{-}Program(cm, init\text{-}class, init\text{-}meth)$, the initial O is such that

$a \in Reference$
$mk\text{-}ClassBlock(vars_0, meths_0) = cm(init\text{-}class)$
$\sigma_0 = \{v \mapsto \mathbf{nil} \mid v \in \mathbf{dom}\ (vars_0) \wedge vars_0(v) \notin ScalarType\}\ \cup$
$\qquad\qquad \{v \mapsto \mathbf{false} \mid v \in \mathbf{dom}\ (vars_0) \wedge vars_0(v) = \mathrm{BOOLTP}\}\ \cup$
$\qquad\qquad\qquad \{v \mapsto 0 \mid v \in \mathbf{dom}\ (vars_0) \wedge vars_0(v) = \mathrm{INTTP}\}$
$sl_0 = meths_0(init\text{-}meth).body$
$O = \{a \mapsto mk\text{-}ObjInfo(init\text{-}class, \sigma_0, \mathrm{ACTIVE}, sl_0, \mathbf{nil})\}$

and that execution ceases when there are no more "threads" active. It would, of course, be more useful to look at running a program against an "object store" from the file system; such an extension is straightforward but somewhat outside the realm of the language itself.

C.3   Classes

Abstract Syntax

$$ClassBlock :: vars \quad : Id \xrightarrow{m} Type$$
$$meths : Id \xrightarrow{m} Meth$$

Context Conditions

$wf\text{-}ClassBlock : ClassBlock \times ClassTypes \to \mathbb{B}$

$wf\text{-}ClassBlock(mk\text{-}ClassBlock(tpm, mm), ctps) \quad \triangle$
$\quad \forall id \in \mathbf{dom}\, tpm \cdot (tpm(id) \in ScalarType \lor tpm(id) \in \mathbf{dom}\, ctps) \land$
$\quad \forall m \in \mathbf{dom}\, mm \cdot wf\text{-}Meth(mm(m), ctps, tpm)$

Semantics

There are no semantics for classes as such — see the semantics of *New* in Section C.8.

C.4   Methods

Abstract Syntax

$$Meth :: returns \quad : Type$$
$$params \quad : Id^*$$
$$paramtps : Id \xrightarrow{m} Type$$
$$body \quad\ : Stmt^*$$

Context Conditions

$wf\text{-}Meth : Meth \times ClassTypes \times VarEnv \to \mathbb{B}$

$wf\text{-}Meth(mk\text{-}Meth(ret, pnl, ptm, b), ctps, v\text{-}env) \quad \triangle$
$\quad (ret \in ScalarType \lor ret \in \mathbf{dom}\, ctps)) \land$
$\quad \forall id \in \mathbf{dom}\, ptm \cdot (ptm(id) \in ScalarType \lor ptm(id) \in \mathbf{dom}\, ctps) \land$
$\quad \mathbf{elems}\, pnl \subseteq \mathbf{dom}\, ptm \land$
$\quad \forall i \in \mathbf{inds}\, b \cdot wf\text{-}Stmt(b(i), ctps, v\text{-}env \dagger ptm)$

Semantics

There are no semantics for methods as such — see the semantics of method invocation in Section C.9.

C.5   Statements

$Stmt = Assign \mid If \mid New \mid MethCall \mid Return \mid Release \mid Delegate$

Context Conditions

$wf\text{-}Stmt : Stmt \times ClassTypes \times VarEnv \to \mathbb{B}$

$wf\text{-}Stmt(s, ctps, v\text{-}env) \quad \triangle \quad$ by cases below

C.6   Assignments

Remember that method calls cannot occur in an *Assign* – method invocation is covered in Section C.9.

Abstract Syntax

$Assign$ :: lhs : Id
$\qquad\qquad rhs$: $Expr$

Context Conditions

$wf\text{-}Stmt(mk\text{-}Assign(lhs, rhs), ctps, v\text{-}env)$ $\triangleq$
$\qquad lhs \in \textbf{dom}\ v\text{-}env\ \wedge$
$\qquad tp(rhs, ctps, v\text{-}env) = v\text{-}env(lhs)$

Semantics

$O(a) = mk\text{-}ObjInfo(c, \sigma, \text{ACTIVE}, [mk\text{-}Assign(lhs, rhs)] \curvearrowright rl, co)$
$(rhs, \sigma) \xrightarrow{e} v$
$aobj' = mk\text{-}ObjInfo(c, \sigma \dagger \{lhs \mapsto v\}, \text{ACTIVE}, rl, co)$
$$\overline{(C, O) \xrightarrow{s} O \dagger \{a \mapsto aobj'\}}$$

C.7   If Statements

Abstract Syntax

If :: $test$: $Expr$
$\qquad th$: $Stmt^*$
$\qquad el$: $Stmt^*$

Context Conditions

$wf\text{-}Stmt(mk\text{-}If(test, th, el), ctps, v\text{-}env)$ $\triangleq$
$\qquad tp(test, ctps, v\text{-}env) = \text{BOOLTP}\ \wedge$
$\qquad \forall i \in \textbf{inds}\ th \cdot wf\text{-}Stmt(th(i), ctps, v\text{-}env)\ \wedge$
$\qquad \forall i \in \textbf{inds}\ el \cdot wf\text{-}Stmt(el(i), ctps, v\text{-}env)$

Semantics

$O(a) = mk\text{-}ObjInfo(c, \sigma, \text{ACTIVE}, [mk\text{-}If(test, th, el)] \curvearrowright rl, co)$
$(test, \sigma) \xrightarrow{e} \textbf{true}$
$aobj' = mk\text{-}ObjInfo(c, \sigma, \text{ACTIVE}, [th] \curvearrowright rl, co)$
$$\overline{(C, O) \xrightarrow{s} O \dagger \{a \mapsto aobj'\}}$$

$O(a) = mk\text{-}ObjInfo(c, \sigma, \text{ACTIVE}, [mk\text{-}If(test, th, el)] \curvearrowright rl, co)$
$(test, \sigma) \xrightarrow{e} \textbf{false}$
$aobj' = mk\text{-}ObjInfo(c, \sigma, \text{ACTIVE}, [el] \curvearrowright rl, co)$
$$\overline{(C, O) \xrightarrow{s} O \dagger \{a \mapsto aobj'\}}$$

C.8   Creating Objects

Abstract Syntax

New :: $targ$: Id
 $class$: Id

Context Conditions

$wf\text{-}Stmt(mk\text{-}New(targ, class), ctps, v\text{-}env)$ $\triangle$
$\quad class \in \textbf{dom } ctps \wedge$
$\quad class = v\text{-}env(targ)$

Semantics

$O(a) = mk\text{-}ObjInfo(c, \sigma, \text{ACTIVE}, [mk\text{-}New(targ, c')] \curvearrowright rl, co)$
$b \in (Reference - \textbf{dom } O)$
$aobj' = mk\text{-}ObjInfo(c, \sigma \dagger \{targ \mapsto b\}, \text{ACTIVE}, rl, co)$
$\sigma_b =$
$\quad \{v \mapsto 0 \mid v \in \textbf{dom }(C(c').vars) \wedge (C(c').vars)(v) = \text{INTTP}\} \cup$
$\quad \{v \mapsto \textbf{false} \mid v \in \textbf{dom }(C(c').vars) \wedge (C(c').vars)(v) = \text{BOOLTP}\} \cup$
$\quad \{v \mapsto \textbf{nil} \mid v \in \textbf{dom }(C(c').vars) \wedge (C(c').vars)(v) \notin ScalarType\}$
$nobj = mk\text{-}ObjInfo(c', \sigma_b, \text{IDLE}, [\,], \textbf{nil})$
$$\overline{(C, O) \overset{s}{\longrightarrow} O \dagger \{a \mapsto aobj', b \mapsto nobj\}}$$

C.9   Invoking and Completing Methods

Abstract Syntax

$MethCall$ :: lhs : Id
 obj : Id
 $meth$: Id
 $args$: Id^*

Context Conditions

$wf\text{-}Stmt(mk\text{-}MethCall(lhs, obj, meth, args), ctps, v\text{-}env)$ $\triangle$
$\quad obj \in \textbf{dom } ctps \wedge$
$\quad meth \in \textbf{dom }(ctps(obj)) \wedge$
$\quad ((ctps(obj))(meth)).return = v\text{-}env(lhs) \wedge$
$\quad \textbf{len } args = \textbf{len }((ctps(obj))(meth)).parms \wedge$
$\quad \forall i \in \textbf{inds } args \cdot$
$\qquad tp(args(i), ctps, v\text{-}env) = (((ctps(obj))(meth)).parms)(i)$

Semantics

$O(a) =$
   $mk\text{-}ObjInfo(c, \sigma, \text{ACTIVE}, [mk\text{-}MethCall(lhs, obj, meth, args)] \frown rl, co)$
$O(\sigma(obj)) = mk\text{-}ObjInfo(c', \sigma', \text{IDLE}, [\,], \text{NIL})$
$C(c') = mk\text{-}ClassBlock(vars, meths)$
$aobj' = mk\text{-}ObjInfo(c, \sigma, mk\text{-}Wait(lhs), rl, co)$
$\sigma'' = \sigma' \dagger \{(meths(meth).params)(i) \mapsto \sigma(args(i)) \mid i \in \textbf{inds } args\}$
$sobj = mk\text{-}ObjInfo(c', \sigma'', \text{ACTIVE}, meths(meth).body, a)$

$$(C, O) \xrightarrow{s} O \dagger \{a \mapsto aobj', \sigma(obj) \mapsto sobj\}$$

When a method has no more statements to execute (remember the *Release* can
have occured earlier) it returns to the quiescent status.

$O(a) = mk\text{-}ObjInfo(c, \sigma, \text{ACTIVE}, [\,], co)$
$aobj' = mk\text{-}ObjInfo(c, \sigma, \text{IDLE}, [\,], \textbf{nil})$

$$(C, O) \xrightarrow{s} O \dagger \{a \mapsto aobj'\}$$

C.10   Returning Values

Abstract Syntax

$Return :: val : (Expr \mid \text{SELF})$

Context Conditions

$wf\text{-}Stmt(mk\text{-}Return(val), ctps, v\text{-}env) \;\;\triangle$
   incomplete

Semantics

The cases of an *Expr* and SELF separately.

$O(a) = mk\text{-}ObjInfo(c, \sigma, \text{ACTIVE}, [mk\text{-}Return(e)] \frown rl, co)$
$e \in Expr$
$(e, \sigma) \xrightarrow{e} v$
$O(co) = mk\text{-}ObjInfo(c', \sigma', mk\text{-}Wait(lhs), sl, co')$
$aobj' = mk\text{-}ObjInfo(c, \sigma, \text{IDLE}, [\,], \textbf{nil})$
$cobj' = mk\text{-}ObjInfo(c', \sigma' \dagger \{lhs \mapsto v\}, \text{ACTIVE}, sl, co')$

$$(C, O) \xrightarrow{s} O \dagger \{a \mapsto aobj', co \mapsto cobj'\}$$

$O(a) = mk\text{-}ObjInfo(c, \sigma, \text{ACTIVE}, [mk\text{-}Return(e)] \frown rl, co)$
$e = \text{SELF}$
$O(co) = mk\text{-}ObjInfo(c', \sigma', mk\text{-}Wait(lhs), sl, co')$
$aobj' = mk\text{-}ObjInfo(c, \sigma, \text{IDLE}, [\,], \textbf{nil})$
$cobj' = mk\text{-}ObjInfo(c', \sigma' \dagger \{lhs \mapsto a\}, \text{ACTIVE}, sl, co')$

$$(C, O) \xrightarrow{s} O \dagger \{a \mapsto aobj', co \mapsto cobj'\}$$

Release is more general than a *Return* in the sense that the former does not
have to terminate a method.

Abstract Syntax

$Release$ :: val : ($Expr$ | SELF)

Context Conditions

$wf\text{-}Stmt(mk\text{-}Release(val), ctps, v\text{-}env)$ $\;\triangleq\;$
    incomplete

Semantics

The cases of an $Expr$ and SELF are considered separately.

$$\frac{\begin{array}{l} O(a) = mk\text{-}ObjInfo(c, \sigma, \text{ACTIVE}, [mk\text{-}Release(e)] \curvearrowright rl, co) \\ e \in Expr \\ (e, \sigma) \xrightarrow{e} v \\ O(co) = mk\text{-}ObjInfo(c', \sigma', mk\text{-}Wait(lhs), sl, co') \\ aobj' = mk\text{-}ObjInfo(c, \sigma, \text{ACTIVE}, rl, \textbf{nil}) \\ cobj' = mk\text{-}ObjInfo(c', \sigma' \dagger \{lhs \mapsto v\}, \text{ACTIVE}, sl, co') \end{array}}{(C, O) \xrightarrow{s} O \dagger \{a \mapsto aobj', co \mapsto cobj'\}}$$

$$\frac{\begin{array}{l} O(a) = mk\text{-}ObjInfo(c, \sigma, \text{ACTIVE}, [mk\text{-}Release(e)] \curvearrowright rl, co) \\ e = \text{SELF} \\ O(co) = mk\text{-}ObjInfo(c', \sigma', mk\text{-}Wait(lhs), sl, co') \\ aobj' = mk\text{-}ObjInfo(c, \sigma, \text{ACTIVE}, rl, \textbf{nil}) \\ cobj' = mk\text{-}ObjInfo(c', \sigma' \dagger \{lhs \mapsto a\}, \text{ACTIVE}, sl, co') \end{array}}{(C, O) \xrightarrow{s} O \dagger \{a \mapsto aobj', co \mapsto cobj'\}}$$

C.11   Delegation

Abstract Syntax

$Delegate$ :: obj : Id
           $meth$: Id
           $args$: Id^*

Context Conditions

$wf\text{-}Stmt(mk\text{-}Delegate(obj, meth, args), ctps, v\text{-}env)$ $\;\triangleq\;$
    incomplete

Semantics

$$O(a) =$$
$$mk\text{-}ObjInfo(c, \sigma, \text{ACTIVE}, [mk\text{-}Delegate(obj, meth, args)] \frown rl, co)$$
$$O(\sigma(obj)) = mk\text{-}ObjInfo(c', \sigma', \text{IDLE}, [\,], \textbf{nil})$$
$$C(c') = mk\text{-}ClassBlock(vars, meths)$$
$$aobj' = mk\text{-}ObjInfo(c, \sigma, \text{ACTIVE}, rl, \textbf{nil})$$
$$\sigma'' = \sigma' \dagger \{(meths(meth).params)(i) \mapsto \sigma(args(i)) \mid i \in \textbf{inds } args\}$$
$$\underline{sobj = mk\text{-}ObjInfo(c', \sigma'', \text{ACTIVE}, meths(meth).body, co)}$$
$$(C, O) \overset{s}{\longrightarrow} O \dagger \{a \mapsto aobj', \sigma(obj) \mapsto sobj\}$$

C.12 Expressions

Abstract Syntax

$$Expr = ArithExpr \mid RelExpr \mid TestNil \mid Id \mid ScalarValue \mid \textbf{nil}$$

$$
\begin{aligned}
ArithExpr :: \quad & opd1 \quad && : Expr \\
& operator && : \text{PLUS} \\
& opd2 && : Expr
\end{aligned}
$$

$$
\begin{aligned}
RelExpr :: \quad & opd1 \quad && : Expr \\
& operator && : \text{EQUALS} \\
& opd2 && : Expr
\end{aligned}
$$

$$TestNil :: \quad obj \;\; : \; Id$$

$$ScalarValue = \mathbb{Z} \mid \mathbb{B}$$

Author Index

Lecture Notes in Computer Science

Sublibrary 1: Theoretical Computer Science and General Issues

For information about Vols. 1–4431
please contact your bookseller or Springer

Vol. 4600: H. Comon-Lundh, C. Kirchner, H. Kirchner (Eds.), Rewriting, Computation and Proof. XVI, 273 pages. 2007.

Vol. 4599: S. Vassiliadis, M. Berekovic, T.D. Hämäläinen (Eds.), Embedded Computer Systems: Architectures, Modeling, and Simulation. XVIII, 466 pages. 2007.

Vol. 4598: G. Lin (Ed.), Computing and Combinatorics. XII, 570 pages. 2007.

Vol. 4596: L. Arge, C. Cachin, T. Jurdziński, A. Tarlecki (Eds.), Automata, Languages and Programming. XVII, 953 pages. 2007.

Vol. 4595: D. Bošnački, S. Edelkamp (Eds.), Model Checking Software. X, 285 pages. 2007.

Vol. 4590: W. Damm, H. Hermanns (Eds.), Computer Aided Verification. XV, 562 pages. 2007.

Vol. 4588: T. Harju, J. Karhumäki, A. Lepistö (Eds.), Developments in Language Theory. XI, 423 pages. 2007.

Vol. 4583: S.R. Della Rocca (Ed.), Typed Lambda Calculi and Applications. X, 397 pages. 2007.

Vol. 4580: B. Ma, K. Zhang (Eds.), Combinatorial Pattern Matching. XII, 366 pages. 2007.

Vol. 4576: D. Leivant, R. de Queiroz (Eds.), Logic, Language, Information and Computation. X, 363 pages. 2007.

Vol. 4547: C. Carlet, B. Sunar (Eds.), Arithmetic of Finite Fields. XI, 355 pages. 2007.

Vol. 4546: J. Kleijn, A. Yakovlev (Eds.), Petri Nets and Other Models of Concurrency – ICATPN 2007. XI, 515 pages. 2007.

Vol. 4545: H. Anai, K. Horimoto, T. Kutsia (Eds.), Algebraic Biology. XIII, 379 pages. 2007.

Vol. 4533: F. Baader (Ed.), Term Rewriting and Applications. XII, 419 pages. 2007.

Vol. 4528: J. Mira, J.R. Álvarez (Eds.), Nature Inspired Problem-Solving Methods in Knowledge Engineering, Part II. XXII, 650 pages. 2007.

Vol. 4527: J. Mira, J.R. Álvarez (Eds.), Bio-inspired Modeling of Cognitive Tasks, Part I. XXII, 630 pages. 2007.

Vol. 4525: C. Demetrescu (Ed.), Experimental Algorithms. XIII, 448 pages. 2007.

Vol. 4514: S.N. Artemov, A. Nerode (Eds.), Logical Foundations of Computer Science. XI, 513 pages. 2007.

Vol. 4513: M. Fischetti, D.P. Williamson (Eds.), Integer Programming and Combinatorial Optimization. IX, 500 pages. 2007.

Vol. 4510: P. Van Hentenryck, L.A. Wolsey (Eds.), Integration of AI and OR Techniques in Constraint Programming for Combinatorial Optimization Problems. X, 391 pages. 2007.

Vol. 4507: F. Sandoval, A.G. Prieto, J. Cabestany, M. Graña (Eds.), Computational and Ambient Intelligence. XXVI, 1167 pages. 2007.

Vol. 4501: J. Marques-Silva, K.A. Sakallah (Eds.), Theory and Applications of Satisfiability Testing – SAT 2007. XI, 384 pages. 2007.

Vol. 4497: S.B. Cooper, B. Löwe, A. Sorbi (Eds.), Computation and Logic in the Real World. XVIII, 826 pages. 2007.

Vol. 4494: H. Jin, O.F. Rana, Y. Pan, V.K. Prasanna (Eds.), Algorithms and Architectures for Parallel Processing. XIV, 508 pages. 2007.

Vol. 4493: D. Liu, S. Fei, Z. Hou, H. Zhang, C. Sun (Eds.), Advances in Neural Networks – ISNN 2007, Part III. XXVI, 1215 pages. 2007.

Vol. 4492: D. Liu, S. Fei, Z. Hou, H. Zhang, C. Sun (Eds.), Advances in Neural Networks – ISNN 2007, Part II. XXVII, 1321 pages. 2007.

Vol. 4491: D. Liu, S. Fei, Z.-G. Hou, H. Zhang, C. Sun (Eds.), Advances in Neural Networks – ISNN 2007, Part I. LIV, 1365 pages. 2007.

Vol. 4490: Y. Shi, G.D. van Albada, J.J. Dongarra, P.M.A. Sloot (Eds.), Computational Science – ICCS 2007, Part IV. XXXVII, 1211 pages. 2007.

Vol. 4489: Y. Shi, G.D. van Albada, J.J. Dongarra, P.M.A. Sloot (Eds.), Computational Science – ICCS 2007, Part III. XXXVII, 1257 pages. 2007.

Vol. 4488: Y. Shi, G.D. van Albada, J.J. Dongarra, P.M.A. Sloot (Eds.), Computational Science – ICCS 2007, Part II. XXXV, 1251 pages. 2007.

Vol. 4487: Y. Shi, G.D. van Albada, J.J. Dongarra, P.M.A. Sloot (Eds.), Computational Science – ICCS 2007, Part I. LXXXI, 1275 pages. 2007.

Vol. 4484: J.-Y. Cai, S.B. Cooper, H. Zhu (Eds.), Theory and Applications of Models of Computation. XIII, 772 pages. 2007.

Vol. 4475: P. Crescenzi, G. Prencipe, G. Pucci (Eds.), Fun with Algorithms. X, 273 pages. 2007.

Vol. 4474: G. Prencipe, S. Zaks (Eds.), Structural Information and Communication Complexity. XI, 342 pages. 2007.

Vol. 4459: C. Cérin, K.-C. Li (Eds.), Advances in Grid and Pervasive Computing. XVI, 759 pages. 2007.

Vol. 4449: Z. Horváth, V. Zsók, A. Butterfield (Eds.), Implementation and Application of Functional Languages. X, 271 pages. 2007.

Vol. 4448: M. Giacobini (Ed.), Applications of Evolutionary Computing. XXIII, 755 pages. 2007.

Vol. 4447: E. Marchiori, J.H. Moore, J.C. Rajapakse (Eds.), Evolutionary Computation, Machine Learning and Data Mining in Bioinformatics. XI, 302 pages. 2007.

Vol. 4446: C. Cotta, J.I. van Hemert (Eds.), Evolutionary Computation in Combinatorial Optimization. XII, 241 pages. 2007.

Vol. 4445: M. Ebner, M. O'Neill, A. Ekárt, L. Vanneschi, A.I. Esparcia-Alcázar (Eds.), Genetic Programming. XI, 382 pages. 2007.

Vol. 4436: C.R. Stephens, M. Toussaint, L.D. Whitley, P.F. Stadler (Eds.), Foundations of Genetic Algorithms. IX, 213 pages. 2007.

Vol. 4433: E. Şahin, W.M. Spears, A.F.T. Winfield (Eds.), Swarm Robotics. XII, 221 pages. 2007.

Vol. 4432: B. Beliczynski, A. Dzielinski, M. Iwanowski, B. Ribeiro (Eds.), Adaptive and Natural Computing Algorithms, Part II. XXVI, 761 pages. 2007.